Thomas Jefferson and the
Fight against Slavery

AMERICAN POLITICAL THOUGHT

Jeremy D. Bailey and Susan McWilliams Barndt
Series Editors

Wilson Carey McWilliams and Lance Banning
Founding Editors

Thomas Jefferson and the Fight against Slavery

Cara Rogers Stevens

 University Press of Kansas

© 2024 by the University Press of Kansas

Published by the University Press of Kansas (Lawrence, Kansas 66045), which was organized by the Kansas Board of Regents and is operated and funded by Emporia State University, Fort Hays State University, Kansas State University, Pittsburg State University, the University of Kansas, and Wichita State University.

Library of Congress Cataloging-in-Publication Data

Names: Rogers Stevens, Cara, author.
Title: Thomas Jefferson and the Fight against Slavery / Cara Rogers Stevens.
Description: Lawrence, Kansas: University Press of Kansas, 2024. | Series: American
  political thought | Includes bibliographical references and index.
Identifiers: LCCN 2023008528 (print) | LCCN 2023008529 (ebook)
  ISBN 9780700635979 (cloth)
  ISBN 9780700635986 (ebook)
Subjects: LCSH: Jefferson, Thomas, 1743–1826. Notes on the state of Virginia. |
  Jefferson, Thomas, 1743–1826—Political and social views. | Antislavery movements—
  Virginia—History. | Slavery—Virginia—Public opinion—History. | Public opinion
  Virginia—History—19th century. | Public opinion—Virginia—History—18th century.
  | Virginia—History—19th century. | Virginia—History—18th century.
Classification: LCC F230 .J536 2024 (print) | LCC F230 (ebook) |
DDC 973.4/6092—dc23/eng/20230607
LC record available at https://lccn.loc.gov/2023008528.
LC ebook record available at https://lccn.loc.gov/2023008529.

British Library Cataloguing-in-Publication Data is available.

Printed in the United States of America

The paper used in this publication is acid free and meets the minimum requirements of the American National Standard for Permanence of Paper for Printed Library Materials Z39.48–1992.

To Jason
I cannot wait to start the next chapter with you.

Contents

Acknowledgments

I have much to be grateful for, starting with the generous research funding provided by Rice University and the Institute for Humane Studies at George Mason University, as well as by the International Center for Jefferson Studies in Charlottesville, Virginia, where I was a fellow in the summer of 2018. My thanks to the community of Jefferson scholars who commented on my work while I was at the ICJS, including Andrew Jackson O'Shaughnessy, John Ragosta, and J. Jefferson Looney. I am also grateful to the archivists and librarians of the ICJS, Library of Congress, University of Virginia, Rice University, College of William and Mary, University of North Carolina at Chapel Hill, Princeton University, and the American Philosophical Society, among others. Many thanks to the scholars who commented on versions of this work over the years, particularly to the attendees of the 2018 "Spirit of Inquiry in the Age of Jefferson" symposium at the American Philosophical Society; the attendees of the 2017 conference of the Association of British American Nineteenth Century Historians; Cynthia Kierner, James Marten, and the audience members at the Southern Historical Association's 2017 conference; and the Brooks Dissertation Forum attendees of the St. George Tucker Society in 2015.

Several scholars have gone out of their way to discuss my research or read drafts; my thanks to Jeremy Bailey, Christopher Curtis, Christa Dierksheide, Scot French, Kevin R. C. Gutzman, Caleb McDaniel, Robert M. S. McDonald, Terry L. Meyers, Peter Onuf, and my dissertation adviser, John B. Boles. Dr. Boles was looking forward to retiring from advising when I met him, but he graciously offered to take me on when he discovered my interest in Jefferson. His offer changed the trajectory of my life. Dr. Boles is not only a great teacher but also the best of mentors, and this book would not have been possible without his involvement and guidance.

My thanks to one of my own students, Carolina Amparo, for graciously stepping in at the last minute to help with copyediting. And my biggest thanks go to my parents, who sacrificed their homeland to give me a future as an American and then homeschooled me, cheered me on through all the years of graduate school, proofread multiple drafts of this book, helped me type when I could not, and now continue to support me in innumerable ways. No one could ask for better parents than them. Finally, in the last phase of writing this book, I got to marry an incredible man who will inspire me to grow as a teacher, scholar, and person for the rest of my life. I am so grateful.

Thomas Jefferson and the
Fight against Slavery

§ull. 13. The particular customs and manners that may happen to be received Manners.
in that state?

It is difficult to determine on the standard by which the manners of a nation
may be tried, whether Catholic or Particular. It is more difficult for a native to
bring to that standard the manners of his own nation, familiarized to him by
habit. There must doubtless be an unhappy influence on the manners of our people, produced by the existence of slavery among us. that tyranny, in the daily exercise
of which we are nursed & educated from our cradles cannot fail to stamp us with
odious peculiarities. the man must be a prodigy who can retain his manners
& morals undepraved by such circumstances. and with what execrations should
the statesman be loaded, who permitting one half the citizens thus to trample
on the rights of the other, transforms those into despots & these into enemies,
destroys the morals of the one part, & the amor patriae of the other. for if a
slave can have a country in this world, it must be any other in preference
to that in which he is born to live & labour for another: in which he must
lock up the faculties of his nature, contribute as far as depends on his
individual endeavors to the evanishment of the human race, or entail his
own miserable condition on the endless generations proceeding from him. with
the morals of the people, their industry also is destroyed. for in a warm climate, no man will labour for himself who can make another labour for him.
this is so true, that of the proprietors of slaves a very small proportion indeed are ever seen to labour. and can the liberties of a nation be thought secure
when we have removed their only firm basis, a conviction in the minds of the people that these liberties are of the gift of god. that they are not to be violated
but with his wrath? indeed I tremble for my country when I reflect that god is just: that his justice
cannot sleep for ever: that considering numbers, nature
and natural means only, a revolution of the wheel of fortune, an exchange of situation, is among possible events: that it may
become probable by supernatural interference! the almighty has no attribute which can take side with us in such a contest.
but it is impossible
to be temperate and to pursue this subject through the various considerations of policy, of morals, of history natural &
civil. we must be contented to hope they will force their way into every one's mind. I think a change already percep-
tible since the origin of the present revolution. the spirit of the master is abating, that of the slave rising
from the dust, his condition mollifying, the way I hope preparing, under the auspices of
heaven for a total emancipation, & that this is disposed, in the order of events, to be with
the consent of the masters, rather than by their extirpation.

Query XVIII, "Manners," from Thomas Jefferson's original manuscript of *Notes on the State of Virginia*. Jefferson's opposition to slavery is made explicit by his editing of this passage. Collection of the Massachusetts Historical Society.

Introduction

In the winter of 1831–1832, Virginia effectively held a referendum on Thomas Jefferson. Not for the last time, political leaders on either side of a momentous American debate invoked the third president and his opinions to justify their preferred policy. On one side, supporters of slavery in the Virginia General Assembly argued that Thomas Jefferson, who had died in 1826, might have spoken about wishing for slavery's end at one point or another, but those early musings were nothing more than the "day dream" of a "patriot and . . . philanthropist." Jefferson had never truly believed emancipation to be practical, they declared, for if he had been committed to the idea he would have freed his own slaves at the time of his death. Moreover, they claimed that the "fragments" of a great man's thoughts "are not only valueless but dangerous." Jefferson may have written against slavery, but now that he was gone it was even harder to imagine any way in which slavery could safely be ended; after all, "when Hercules died, there was no man left to lift his club."[1]

On the other side of the debate, the opponents of slavery had an ace up their sleeves: Jefferson's eldest and favorite grandson, Thomas Jefferson Randolph (known as "Jeff" to family), had recently been elected to the Assembly, and it was his emancipation proposal that had helped to stoke the fires of debate. Although he hated to speak in public almost as much as his grandfather had, Jeff Randolph rose on 20 January 1832 to counter the claims of the proslavery side. He felt compelled to speak up partly because his fellow delegates misunderstood his initial proposal as being that of "Mr. Jefferson" himself. Jeff reminded his colleagues that his grandfather's emancipation plan had long been before the public, since it was detailed in his 1787 book *Notes on the State of Virginia*.[2] Jeff's plan was inspired by his grandfather—not authored by him. Yet that did not mean, as some delegates implied, that Thomas Jefferson would not have approved of Jeff Randolph's ideas.

To rebut the claim that Jefferson's antislavery musings were nothing more than a "day dream" of long ago, Jeff Randolph produced a

1

letter that Jefferson had composed in 1814. A younger Virginian named Edward Coles had written to the recently retired president, asking him to take up a leading role in speaking out against slavery in Virginia. Jefferson had refused, citing his old age, but while doing so he had re-iterated his commitment to ending slavery. More important, Jefferson had urged Coles to take up leadership on the issue himself: "I have considered the silence which prevails on this subject, as indicating an apathy unfavorable to every hope. Yet the hour of emancipation is advancing in the march of time." Coles himself must "come forward in the public councils, become the missionary of this doctrine truly Christian ... [and] press the proposition perseveringly until its accomplishment." Referencing William Wilberforce's recent successes against the slave trade in England, Jefferson declared no good measure could fail if there existed people to fight for it. Eighteen years later, as Edward Coles watched approvingly from the gallery, Jefferson's grandson used this correspondence as proof that Jefferson may have only dreamed of abolition—but that dream had "lasted a long time—some sixty years." He had not freed most of his own slaves, but his public documents and private correspondence clearly showed that in "1770, 1814, 1824, he still deemed abolition indispensible." If Jefferson were alive in 1832, Thomas Jefferson Randolph said, he would have urged the delegates to vote for emancipation.[3]

Thomas Jefferson had no idea when he began composing *Notes on the State of Virginia* in 1780 that his work would still be a topic of debate in 1832, much less that its passages on race and slavery would remain at the center of our understanding of Jefferson today. He originally conceived of the project as a simple list of information about his home state, written in response to a questionnaire from the colonies' French allies. The first version covered topics such as flora and fauna, climate, and population size. But the project became Jefferson's favorite hobby over the ensuing years, which were some of the most challenging of his life. He continued to revise and expand his text while finishing his term as governor of Virginia in 1781, when the state was under British occupation and Jefferson himself was in hiding from enemy troops. The following summer, at the bedside of his dying wife, Jefferson continued working on *Notes*, by this time imagining a broader audience—and purpose—for what was turning into a full-length book. Specifically, Jefferson became aware that his statements on race and on slavery could have an outsize influence, both on America's international reputation and on local Virginia debates over the issue.

Notes on the State of Virginia ultimately became one of Jefferson's greatest contributions to the antislavery cause. Although it is today best known for its prejudiced sections on racial differences, an analysis of the original manuscript, only recently made available for detailed study, demonstrates that over a period of several years Jefferson became increasingly determined to clarify his views in order to strengthen his condemnation of slavery. In the process of revising the text, he also determined that the best way to influence debates over slavery was to direct copies of *Notes* to college students, young men studying to become future leaders of the state. Despite a fear that his controversial statements on emancipation would produce a backlash—against him personally and against the antislavery movement in Virginia more broadly—Jefferson eventually sent thirty-seven copies of his book to the College of William and Mary, then the premiere educational institution in Virginia. Knowing from personal experience that George Wythe, the esteemed professor of law at the college, had an antislavery influence on his students, Jefferson told several confidants that "it is to them I look, to the rising generation, and not to the one now in power for these great reformations." Jefferson believed his book, in the hands of the right educator, could help push Virginia's future leaders toward emancipation—and he was right.[4]

Over the ensuing years, students at the college learned that the third president believed that slavery was corrupting Virginia from the inside out, turning republicans into tyrants and every year increasing the threat that the state would be convulsed by a slave revolt. Several of these students subsequently became committed to emancipation, some freeing their own slaves in Virginia, others leaving the state in order to give their human property a better future. As the debates of 1831–1832 demonstrate, Jefferson's strategy was partly successful: men such as Thomas Jefferson Randolph became committed to ending slavery in Virginia, invoking Jefferson's own views and building upon his emancipation and colonization strategy with their own ideas. Ultimately, however, Jefferson's antislavery principles became more important *outside* his beloved home state than they were within it, as men like Edward Coles, eventually a governor of Illinois, took responsibility for shaping Jefferson's legacy into a useable antislavery nationalism. It was in this form that Jefferson's attempt to shape public opinion trickled down to the antebellum era's Republican Party.

Despite the lasting reputation of Jefferson's *Notes*, few historians have looked deeply at his composition, revision, and distribution process, which was protracted and complicated by everything from the price of printing to the unexpected death of a British spy (which resulted in a "mutilated" French edition being released to the public against Jefferson's wishes in 1785).[5] Moreover, because of the work's complex and unique construction—with Jefferson obscuring hundreds of words by pasting revised sections over original ones—no scholar thoroughly examined the original manuscript of the *Notes* until 1997. When the project of disassembling and studying all parts of the document was finally undertaken, Douglas L. Wilson was able for the first time to begin an analysis of the numerous ways in which Jefferson revised his work—revisions that speak to his concern over race and slavery but that no other historian has analyzed to date.[6] Also lacking are studies of Jefferson's intended audience and corresponding political strategy for his book, as these topics were also obscured by the extended revision process and by Jefferson's sometimes contradictory statements regarding his desires for the text and its audience.[7]

Much of the recent scholarship on the *Notes* and slavery is indebted to Winthrop Jordan's seminal 1968 tome *White Over Black*. Jefferson biographers such as Dumas Malone and Marie Kimball had written about *Notes* in some depth during the 1940s but passed over slavery as a separate issue—an institution that was entailed upon Jefferson and that he could not easily escape, though they believed he was sincerely opposed to it.[8] Jordan, however, applied a lengthy Freudian analysis to Jefferson's comments on race and slavery in the *Notes*, presenting Jefferson as a "sounding board for his culture"—a representation both of emerging scientific racism and of the white American psyche, a genuine opponent of slavery who was nonetheless profoundly hampered by his prejudice.[9] Subsequent scholarship produced critical examinations of Jefferson that—although not denying Jefferson's distaste for the institution of slavery—questioned his views on race and the depth of his antislavery commitment.[10] For a variety of reasons, many of these works mischaracterize the circumstances in which Jefferson published *Notes*; for example, William Cohen's influential 1969 article characterized Jefferson's reluctance to publish the *Notes* as evidence of the "ambiguity" of his position on slavery—without examining Jefferson's strategic targeting of young men at William and Mary as the best possible readers of his antislavery sentiments or discussing the proslavery climate in Virginia that made Jefferson's reluctance more understandable.[11]

In 1973 Jefferson's concerns about the proslavery climate of Virginia in the mid-1780s were given more weight when Fredrika Teute Schmidt and Barbara Ripel Wilhelm documented the discovery of previously unknown proslavery petitions from 1784 and 1785, signed by 1,244 individuals and receiving substantial support in the Assembly. This discovery contradicted Jordan, Cohen, and Robert McColley, who was the first to criticize Jefferson on the issue of slavery in general and who had argued that, at the time Jefferson was writing the *Notes*, Virginians were outwardly neutral on the issue of slavery. This study not only takes the proslavery petitions into account but also situates Jefferson's revision of the *Notes* within the context of his engagement with a debate occurring within the pages of *The Virginia Gazette, and Weekly Advertiser* in 1782 over the morality and usefulness of slavery in Virginian society. By more deeply contextualizing Jefferson's awareness of ongoing public opinion shifts regarding slavery within Virginia, it becomes possible to see his revisions to the *Notes* as an attempt to shape his rhetoric to appeal directly to the passions and prejudices of his prospective Virginian audience.[12]

Whereas scholars who tend to doubt Jefferson's sincerity on antislavery have been dubbed "revisionists" by Francis Cogliano, some Jefferson defenders—or "emancipationists," in Cogliano's historiography—built upon the early works of biographers like Dumas and Kimball to counter the revisionist arguments, shielding Jefferson's honor against what they perceived to be unfair, presentist attacks.[13]

The dispute between emancipationists and revisionists reached a peak in 1992, when Wilson and Paul Finkelman took up oppositional sides in what was becoming a national trial by jury of Jefferson's character. While Wilson spoke for the defense, Finkelman—perhaps the most severe of Jefferson's critics—prosecuted Jefferson as a "self-indulgent and negrophobic Virginia planter" whose antislavery reputation was entirely undeserved.[14] Cogliano notes that the debate between these two streams is "imbued with moral judgments," with Finkelman in particular adopting an "adversarial approach" and presenting history as "an ethical zero-sum game" in which Jefferson and any scholars who defend his record "lose."[15]

There is, however, a third interpretive route that scholars can take: following in the footsteps of William Freehling and Edmund S. Morgan, some—labeled "contextualizers" by Cogliano—synthesize elements from both prior traditions, accepting the sincerity of Jefferson's antislavery statements but also attempting to place the complexities of his thought, actions, and failures within a broader framework.[16] Cogliano argues that this third stream "offers the best way ahead for the study of Jefferson and slavery,"[17] and it provides the impetus for my own work, which falls in line with that of scholars such as Peter Onuf, Ari Helo, William Merkel, and John B. Boles.[18] Each scholar argues that Jefferson was a genuine and lifelong opponent of slavery but seeks to historicize his words, actions, and lack of action (particularly in his later years) through nuanced engagement with his moral philosophy, conceptions of race and nationhood, commitment to majority rule, financial entanglements, the existing laws, and more. When taking Jefferson's claims and actions seriously during the process of writing, revising, and publishing *Notes on the State of Virginia*, we find a revolutionary who was seeking to radically change his society: first through laws and then—honoring the democratic process—by influencing a new and enlightened generation of politicians with antislavery principles and strategies.

Jefferson's vision for a republican Virginia was inextricably linked to both his condemnation of slavery and his endorsement of education.

Slavery endangers the foundation of any republic, he explained in the *Notes*: children who grew up in slave-owning households were "nursed, educated, and daily exercised in tyranny"; masters inevitably became despots, "trampl[ing] on the rights" of enslaved citizens. In short, the only way Virginia could succeed as a republic would be if slavery were uprooted. Moreover, the only way that Jefferson believed slavery could be peacefully uprooted would be through the emerging democratic process. Jefferson was limited in his opposition to slavery not only by his stated belief that white and black people could not successfully live together as free citizens but also, as Onuf and Helo argue, by his consistent commitment to the principles of republicanism: "A democratic, majority decision was absolutely necessary before the existing legal order and the property rights in slaves that it secured were overturned."[19] Furthermore, Jefferson believed that "[a]ny premature effort to interfere with the institution would violate the fundamental rights of free citizens and jeopardize the progress of the community as a whole toward a more enlightened understanding of its true collective interests."[20] The only way to end slavery, in other words, was for the American public to become enlightened enough to *want* to end slavery through the democratic process—and the only way to accomplish that stage of enlightenment was through education. Thus, "Jefferson's advocacy of public education and the widening of the Virginia electorate to nonfreeholders reflect his hopes that the legislature would one day better reflect the sentiments of a more refined majority of free citizens."[21] I believe that Jefferson's educational intent for the *Notes* confirms this assessment.

As a young legislator, Jefferson made several efforts to ameliorate or end slavery in Virginia and in future states, as well as to ensure that Virginians would become better educated. Jefferson himself first became the owner of other humans at age fourteen, when his father died. At the time, it was illegal in Virginia to free slaves without receiving special permission from the governor. In 1769, at age twenty-six, Jefferson cosponsored a bill to permit individual slaveholders to manumit slaves, which the General Assembly harshly dismissed; as a young lawyer he took on several freedom suits pro bono, including one in 1770 on behalf of a young mulatto indentured servant. In that case, Jefferson argued that "under the law of nature, all men are born free, and every one comes into the world with a right to his own person."[22] The court in that case did not even wait to hear opposing counsel's argument before throwing out Jefferson's suit. In 1784 his draft of what later became the Northwest Ordinance failed in the United States Congress by one vote; it would have banned slavery in any new American state after the year 1800.[23] His 1776 draft constitution for Virginia would have ended slave importations—that is, had the Assembly adopted it. A few years later he also drafted a gradual emancipation amendment; however, he did not present it to the Assembly because "it was found that the public mind would not yet bear the proposition."[24] The "public mind" formed a primary consideration in all of Jefferson's reforms, for as much as he was committed to ending Virginia's "crime" against enslaved people, he was equally committed to the vision of self-government for which Americans were fighting.[25] Thus, in 1786 he wrote regarding his proposed laws for Virginia: "I think by far the most important bill in our whole code is that for the diffusion of knowledge among the people. No other sure foundation can be devised, for the preservation of freedom and happiness."[26] In targeting the students at William and Mary with his *Notes*, Jefferson was acting on long-held principles; while he doubted that his generation would embrace emancipation in Virginia, his actions preceding the release of the *Notes* demonstrate his commitment to ending slavery and his belief that the younger generation, if properly educated in the principles of liberty, would be able to see this through.

The years before the 1787 publication of the *Notes* in America were those in which Jefferson's antislavery actions and opinions can most easily be traced; after 1790 Jefferson was more heavily involved in national than in Virginian politics.[27] While devising his plan to distribute the *Notes*, Jefferson was optimistic that he would soon finally become free of his (largely inherited) debts. He began discussing schemes by which he could grant his slaves their freedom; shortly thereafter, however, Revolutionary War inflation and a series of economic developments and poor personal decisions rendered Jefferson's financial situation increasingly precarious. From 1792 until after Jefferson's death in 1826, enslaved people in Virginia could not be freed via indebted owners' wills; because he was over $100,000 in debt when he died, Jefferson could not have followed in George Washington's footsteps even had he wanted to.[28] Jefferson's failure to free most of his own slaves was further complicated by his belief that emancipation must be accompanied by colonization: after slaves were freed, they were to be sent out of the country. He gave two primary sets of reasons for this condition in the *Notes*: First, he stated that black people were (possibly) permanently inferior in many respects to white people, and therefore preventing racial amalgamation was imperative. Colonization would solve the problem of slavery while keeping the races separate. Jefferson's second line of reasoning was somewhat more commendable: he believed that African-descended peoples were members of a captive nation against whom America had committed the crime of enslavement. According to Onuf, "having conceptualized masters and slaves as two nations in a state of war, [Jefferson's] proposal for African expatriation and colonization" in the *Notes* "constituted a peace plan, the only way the two nations could recognize each other's equality and independence"—and the only way to avoid a catastrophic race war in which God himself would, and should, take the side of the black people. As the proslavery side of the debate in the House of Delegates in 1831–1832 correctly noted, Jefferson did not free most of his slaves, but his failure to do so does not reflect on his commitment to the principle, and practice, of emancipation.[29]

Chapter 1 of *Thomas Jefferson and the Fight against Slavery* introduces readers to Thomas Jefferson's antislavery thought by exploring its institutional and philosophical backgrounds: the College of William and Mary and the Scottish and English Enlightenment ideas that flourished there. After the teenaged Jefferson first arrived at William and Mary, he was invited to become part of a circle of political and intellectual elites who all happened to oppose slavery: Governor Francis Fauquier; the professor William Small, recently arrived from Scotland; the wealthy planter Robert Carter; and, most important, the law professor George Wythe. In classes with Small and Wythe, as well as during regular gatherings over meals and music at the Governor's Palace, young Jefferson developed the antislavery intellectual framework that can be recognized throughout his subsequent political career. In particular, I argue that Dr. William Small, a graduate of Marischal College, introduced Jefferson to the strains of antislavery thought then developing as part of the Scottish Enlightenment; Jefferson's school notebooks demonstrate his early embrace of this Moral Sense philosophy and its concomitant rejection of slavery as detrimental to any society. After documenting the evidence for the existence of this small circle of antislavery thinkers at William and Mary, and of their influence on Jefferson, I place them within the larger context of Virginia's historical engagements with slavery and racism; I conclude by arguing that, at the time of the American Revolution, Jefferson had every reason to believe that subsequent generations of students at the college could—if correctly educated—develop similarly enlightened views regarding the (im)morality of slavery.

Chapter 2 documents the composition and editorial process of Jefferson's *Notes on the State of Virginia*, from its inception in 1780 until Jefferson's departure for France in 1784. Because of his complex editing process—which included interlinear additions and entirely new sections of text pasted over old—Jefferson's book concealed its own revision process until the manuscript was disassembled in 1997. I offer a detailed analysis of his revisions, in addition to a discussion of the transatlantic scientific discourses with which Jefferson was consciously engaging. Thanks to the disassembled manuscript, it is now also possible to document the specific ways in which Jefferson began to engage with simultaneous newspaper debates in Virginia over race and emancipation, revising his text in significant ways to strengthen passages opposing slavery and dilute passages supporting an inherent and permanent racial hierarchy. In response to criticism from one Philadelphian friend and colleague in the American Philosophical Society, Charles Thomson, Jefferson changed the text to avoid providing any support to slaveholders—although, crucially, he failed to follow his friend's advice to completely excise his discourse on racial differences. Chapter 2 concludes with an examination of Jefferson's changing intended audience, from just a few French diplomats in 1780, to a transatlantic network of scholars in 1783, to a broader audience of

Virginians by 1784. As Jefferson's intended audience expanded, so did his intentions for the text—from the modest goal of providing statistics for a small French readership to a much more ambitious project encompassing local and international objectives. Most important, I demonstrate that, by the time he left for his diplomatic mission in France in 1784, Jefferson believed his book could have a significant influence on Virginians' debates over emancipation.

Chapter 3 deals with the period from 1784 to 1787, during which Jefferson completed and published his *Notes* in both French and English. The publication history of the *Notes* has been shrouded in confusion since the 1780s because Jefferson himself wrote misleadingly regarding the precise dates of revision and because the work had three separate releases—under very different circumstances—between 1785 and 1787 alone. After documenting those changing circumstances through careful analysis of the various editions and of Jefferson's correspondence, I argue that some of Jefferson's dissembling regarding his book's publication was a performance of authorial modesty that was typical for the time, while some of it was simply fear for his own reputation. However, Jefferson also wrote honestly regarding one of his primary goals for the text: to influence with antislavery principles the younger generation of Virginia leaders then studying at the College of William and Mary. He also had genuine reason to wish to control the timing of the book's publication and to be concerned over its reception in Virginia, not only because of his sentiments on slavery but also because of his criticisms of Virginia's constitution. In addition to Jefferson's own correspondence, I offer two main sources of evidence for these assertions: an analysis of Jefferson's close relationship with his private secretary, William Short, an antislavery lawyer and diplomat whom Jefferson considered his adoptive son, and an examination of the legislative debates over emancipation that occurred in Virginia as Jefferson considered sending private copies of his *Notes* to William and Mary.

Including Short in a discussion of the work's publication offers new insights, for not only did Short aid in the revision and publication process; there also exists strong evidence among his correspondence for the development of Short's antislavery views during this time, as well as for his own belief that Jefferson shared in his goals to end slavery in

Virginia. Both Jefferson and Short learned, with concern, of the controversy surrounding the anti- and proslavery petitions sent to the Assembly in 1785 and of the subsequent narrow defeat of a bill that would have
reinstituted prohibitions on individual manumissions. As James Madison reported from Virginia, there were proslavery elements, among
both the citizens and the legislature, who were deeply suspicious of any
manumission measures and who were ready to implement harsh proslavery laws, rolling back liberal revolutionary gains. But Madison also
informed Jefferson that, after consulting with a small group of confidants, he felt Jefferson should indeed send his *Notes* to the students at
William and Mary. Madison and his advisers believed that, because the
respected antislavery law professor George Wythe would oversee the
students' instruction, the *Notes* would be put into the hands of students
who were—as Jefferson and Short had been during their own time at
the college—willing to entertain antislavery arguments.

Chapter 4 discusses Jefferson's and Short's research into and experimentation with European forms of semi-free agricultural labor as a
transitional system for emancipated Virginian slaves. Building on recent research undertaken at the University of Virginia into a farm Jefferson managed on behalf of Short, I utilize Short's own papers from
the Library of Congress in order to demonstrate that during their time
together in Europe the two men began systematically researching *metayage*, an ancient European practice similar to sharecropping. This
research had the specific goal of developing a transitional labor system
that could help former slaves develop the skills necessary for independent life and attract German farmers to Virginia as tenants to replace
the soon-to-be-colonized black workforce.[30]

However, after Jefferson returned to America in 1789, Short remained
in Europe for several decades, serving as a diplomat in revolutionary
France, the Netherlands, and Spain. During this time, Jefferson began a
form of their planned metayage experiment on Short's behalf on a farm
near Monticello, while Short became increasingly convinced that the
Virginian economy would benefit from free labor and also that black
people were the equals of whites and should become full members of
society after emancipation, even advocating for racial intermarriage.
Short and Jefferson corresponded regularly from 1789 until a month

before Jefferson's death in 1826, discussing everything from the Haitian Revolution to Sierra Leone to serfdom. In chapter 4, I analyze the early years of their correspondence to illuminate new facets of Jefferson's research and experimentation into alternative forms of labor for his state and the unique circumstances (such as membership in France's antislavery La Société des Amis des Noirs, meaning "The Society of the Friends of the Blacks") that enabled Short to so completely outstrip his adoptive father in his expansive vision of a multiracial future for America.

Chapter 5 explores the influence of Jefferson's *Notes* at the College of William and Mary from 1787 through the first three decades of the nineteenth century. Although Jefferson's own antislavery mentor, George Wythe, retired from teaching not long after the arrival of the *Notes*, his successor was even more outspoken in his opposition to slavery. St. George Tucker published a lengthy essay proposing a gradual emancipation plan in 1796 and reprinted it as an appendix in his famous edition of *Blackstone's Commentaries* in 1803.[31] I argue that Tucker's essay is primarily in conversation with *Notes on the State of Virginia*: sometimes cited as an authoritative source, sometimes specifically countered, Tucker used the *Notes* as both a foundation and a foil for his own far more extensive and complex commentary on race, slavery, and emancipation in Virginia. Although the Virginia legislature ignored Tucker's essay when he sent it to them, students at William and Mary encountered its principles in his lectures and in his *Commentaries*, which was a popular legal text. One such student was George Tucker, younger cousin of St. George; he wrote his own antislavery pamphlet after a failed slave revolt in 1800, agreeing with many of the principles outlined in Jefferson's *Notes* and arguing that liberty for the slaves was inevitable.

Another student was Edward Coles, who became so convinced of slavery's immorality while studying at the college that he eventually left Virginia entirely, freeing his slaves en route to Illinois and becoming governor there after running on an antislavery platform. Coles became one of Jefferson's most eloquent spokesmen; although he was disappointed with Jefferson's 1814 refusal to publicly take up leadership of the antislavery cause, Coles always believed that Jefferson truly opposed slavery. For the rest of his life, Coles worked to persuade his fellow Americans that, in order to live up to the ideals of the Founding Fathers, they had to support emancipation. Coles has been of some interest to scholars of Illinois and of antislavery history; three books and several articles discuss various aspects of his life.[32] The excellent recent biography by Suzanne Cooper-Guasco places Coles, for the first time, as a link in the chain of antislavery ideas from the colonial period to the Civil War. I build upon her argument by more firmly contextualizing Coles's thought as the intentional product of Jefferson's own ideology and efforts to influence younger men. In short, where Cooper-Guasco points out the ways in which Coles independently invoked Jefferson's image to support his own antislavery nationalism, I argue that Jefferson was a willing and active participant in the crafting of that legacy.

Chapter 6 traces Thomas Jefferson's political legacy in Virginia during the antebellum period by following the careers of his son-in-law, Thomas Mann Randolph, and his grandson, Thomas Jefferson Randolph. Thomas Randolph was the first college student to receive a copy of Jefferson's *Notes*, having been a student at the University of Edinburgh in Scotland while Jefferson was publishing his book in France. Randolph is primarily known for his famous in-laws and for his mental health issues in later life, but prior to those events he served as Virginia's governor during the Missouri Crisis.[33] In response to the debates over slavery raised during that time, I demonstrate that Randolph crafted a critique of the ways in which he saw his fellow Southerners adapting themselves to slavery. Randolph also proposed an emancipation measure to the Virginia General Assembly—a proposal that hurt his political career but that made Jefferson proud.

Finally, I discuss the debates over slavery in the Assembly from 1831 to 1832, building upon the analytical and evidentiary work done by Eva Sheppard Wolf, Joseph C. Robert, William G. Shade, and Allison G. Freehling, as well as Erik S. Root's edited collection containing both the record of the debate and the petitions from around the state that motivated it.[34] As a leading figure in those debates, Thomas Jefferson Randolph has attracted surprisingly little attention from scholars.[35] Not a gifted politician or intellectual, the younger Randolph nonetheless felt that during these debates he was carrying out his duty; I place the younger man's efforts within the broader context of his actions as a slaveholder himself, his relationship with Jefferson, and his friendship with Edward Coles, who believed young Randolph had "inherited the feelings & principles of your illustrious Grand Father." No one else "of the young generation," wrote Coles, "could be more suitable to lead or could bring more moral & political weight of character to aid the good work" than could Thomas Jefferson's grandson. Paraphrasing Jefferson's own 1814 advice to him, Coles urged Jeff to fight the good fight "regardless of the scoffs & frowns of the perverse & short sighted," knowing that the reward would be "the happy consolation of doing a great good to your fellow man & to your Country." And although the Assembly ultimately did not choose to put young Jeff Randolph's plan into action, he won office again after running under a provocative slogan: "The 'avowed & unflinching advocate of abolition.'"[36]

In 1790 Jefferson encouraged another politician by saying "the ground of liberty is to be gained by inches. . . . It takes time to persuade men to do even what is for their own good."[37] I believe we can see, in the years surrounding the revision, publication, and early reception of the *Notes*, Jefferson supporting public education, calling for a constitutional convention to set Virginia's government on firmer republican ground, and advocating for universal white manhood suffrage—in short, doing all he could to ensure that Virginians *would* become more enlightened and therefore more committed to emancipating their slaves. This emancipation would not be immediate, but a plan of gradual emancipation and colonization, implemented by an enlightened majority of Virginians, would bring about a stable and peaceful transformation of the state's economy and its population. In his targeting of the students at the College of William and Mary as the primary audience for his *Notes* in 1785, Jefferson was expressing in a practical way the intellectual and moral commitment outlined by Onuf and Helo. And in the lives of men like William Short, St. George Tucker, Edward Coles, Thomas Jefferson Randolph, and others, we can see the results, and limits, of Jefferson's early efforts. The Jeffersonian heritage of *their* antislavery thought and political strategies, as well as their correspondence with the aging Sage of Monticello, has not yet been thoroughly contextualized: the intellectual web among these figures from the Revolutionary and Early Republic periods has yet to be connected. This book develops those connections, adding a new element to our understanding of the progress of antislavery thought in Virginia.

1. Antislavery at William and Mary

In 1785 Thomas Jefferson was alarmed to discover that one of the American Revolution's advocates in England, liberal minister Richard Price, was on the verge of abandoning all his hopes for the new republic—because of slavery. Price reported to Jefferson that the South Carolina legislature had attacked "my pamphlet on the American Revolution because it recommends measures . . . for gradually abolishing the Negro trade and Slavery." If all Americans indeed were as committed to slavery as the South Carolinians apparently were, Price told Jefferson, "I shall have reason to fear that I have made myself ridiculous by Speaking of the American Revolution in the manner I have done." Price was beginning to believe that "the people who have been Struggling so earnestly to save *themselves* from Slavery are very ready to enslave *others*." If this were true, then "the friends of liberty and humanity in Europe will be mortify'd, and an event which had raised their hopes will prove only an introduction to a new Scene of aristocratic tyranny."[1]

Jefferson hastened to assure his friend that, although those living "Southward of the Chesapeak" were indeed still attached to slavery, "the bulk of the people" who lived from "the mouth to the head of the Chesapeak" were theoretically opposed to the institution, and still further north there were already so few slaves that Jefferson expected slavery to have disappeared in a few years. But Jefferson's greatest hope was for the state of Virginia, the largest and wealthiest state, and "the next . . . to which we may turn our eyes for the interesting spectacle of justice in conflict with avarice and oppression." The "sacred side" of this conflict was "gaining daily recruits from the influx into office of young men grown and growing up." According to Jefferson, the younger generation of Virginians had "sucked in the principles of liberty as it were with their mother's milk, and it is to them I look with anxiety to turn the fate of this question." Knowing that Price was on the verge of washing his hands of the new republic, Jefferson urged him: "Be not therefore discouraged. What you have written will do a great deal of good." Even more poignantly, Jefferson asked the English minister for help, believing that "no man is more able to give aid to the labouring side." Specifically, Jefferson desired Price to target the College of William and Mary. At this one location, Jefferson wrote, were "collected together all the young men of Virginia under preparation for public life." Because they were being taught by Jefferson's own friend and mentor, George Wythe—"whose sentiments on the subject of slavery are unequivocal"—Jefferson was convinced that the students would be receptive to an antislavery appeal. If Price could write to them, his "influence on the future decision of this important question would be great, perhaps decisive."[2]

In principle, Price agreed with Jefferson: "Young men are the hope of every state; and nothing can be of so much consequence to a state as the principles they imbibe and the direction they are under." However, perhaps too stung by the criticism he was receiving, Price refused to give any further voice to antislavery ideas. "I cannot think of writing again on any political subject," Price informed Jefferson, and although he was still convinced of "the importance of the Sentiments I have address'd to the united States," Price was now resolved to "leave these Sentiments to make their way for themselves, and to be approved or rejected just as events and the judgments of those who may consider them shall determine."[3]

Price may have given up, but Jefferson did not. He remained convinced that younger generations, if properly educated, could turn the tide of antislavery thought in Virginia. Jefferson's confidence stemmed from his own experiences. When he arrived in Williamsburg as a fatherless teenager in 1760, Jefferson was taken under the wings of several older men who encouraged his intellectual pursuits, provided him with an outlet for his musical talents, and shaped his moral development. In later years, Jefferson often referred to these older gentlemen as the ones to whom he owed his success in life. And Jefferson's mentors in Williamsburg were—so far as we know from the available evidence—uniformly opposed to slavery.

Jefferson scholars have carefully documented his formative years at William and Mary, paying particular attention to the development of his unique religious beliefs and his engagement with the philosophies of natural rights. Until recently, however, little attention has been paid to the antislavery atmosphere at the college itself, and among several important members of its board of visitors, in the years surrounding the American Revolution.[4] I argue that not only was Jefferson himself a product of this climate of openness toward antislavery thought, but he was so confident that other young men could be similarly educated to love liberty that he also invested significant time and effort in attempting to ensure that antislavery arguments, like those of Price, would be readily available to future generations of William and Mary students. Examining Jefferson's intellectual roots at the college, in addition to the ways in which he acted upon his antislavery convictions as a young lawyer and politician, illustrates the depth of his commitment to liberty. It also sets the stage for understanding why he believed, in future years, that other college students could be the most important vehicles for cultural change in his beloved home state.

Before the American Revolution—with its ideologies of natural liberty and equality—began the process of remaking the world, most inhabitants of Virginia accepted slavery without question.[5] Indeed, in Virginia as in the rest of the New World, Native peoples had practiced their own forms of slavery long before the Jamestown colonists first purchased African slaves from a Dutch trading vessel in 1619.[6] Forms of unfree labor affected all ethnicities in the New World; a majority of European laborers in the American colonies first arrived as indentured servants, or "temporary slaves," entering into legal bondage for predetermined lengths of time in order to pay for their voyages across the Atlantic. Some indentured servants even came involuntarily, having been deemed pests on English society.[7] While unfree labor in Virginia was therefore not unique, for a variety of reasons it did develop—in common with other Atlantic colonies—an emphasis on race.

In Virginia's earliest days, black people were not always enslaved for life; some even owned other black slaves and had indentured white servants. However, as the supply of indentured servants from England dwindled over the course of the seventeenth century, the agriculturally based colony gradually shifted to a dependence on enslaved labor from imported Africans. By 1776 just over 40 percent of Virginia's total population consisted of enslaved black people (the number in northern states around the same time was typically 5 percent or less).[8] As Virginia's labor force changed from being one composed of white and black, of free and unfree individuals working side by side, to one in which the majority of agricultural laborers were "visually as well as culturally distinct"[9] slaves, abstract ideas about African racial inferiority—inherited from long-standing Middle Eastern and European prejudices—were gradually transformed into a concrete system of legalized racism. Slavery itself became associated with blackness even while white colonists began to experience greater freedom and equality.[10]

To justify keeping an entire segment of the population in perpetual bondage, rather than the "temporary slavery" Europeans utilized for one another, both theoretical and physical lines had to be drawn. Therefore, Virginia laws increasingly segregated African and African-descended people from the rest of the population and limited their rights, first prohibiting free black people from having indentured white servants in 1670, then banning people of color from traveling without documentation or from owning guns, and even criminalizing racial intermarriage and decreeing that every enslaved mother passed her unfree status on to her children.[11] From 1723 onward, manumission was illegal unless the legislature granted special permission; even if a master managed to free a slave in this manner, the law allowed only six months of liberty in Virginia before the freed person had to leave the colony forever—or else be re-enslaved.[12] Despite these policies, since at any given moment up to half of colonial society was legally unfree due to continuing practices of indentured servitude and apprenticeships, the hereditary slavery of African-descended peoples seemed to Virginians as the lowest among many different forms of legal dependencies.[13] For the hierarchical society in which Thomas Jefferson grew up, slavery was simply a fact of life.

But by the second half of the eighteenth century, the Western world was undergoing what David Brion Davis characterizes as a "fundamental change" in "moral perceptions of the institution" of slavery.[14] A primary driver of this change was Christianity: some of the first voices to question slavery's morality were Quakers, inspired by their religious conviction that all mankind is equal before God. Similarly, many (but not all) who came to embrace evangelical Protestantism during the Great Awakening also became fierce opponents of slavery.[15] A second path individuals could travel to antislavery convictions during the Age of Enlightenment was through an embrace of the natural rights philosophy encountered in texts by European luminaries such as John Locke and Baron de Montesquieu.[16] As we shall see, in Virginia even those advocates of emancipation who did not particularly embrace religion were usually educated in Enlightenment concepts by men with strong religious backgrounds; the combination often proved explosive. In 1740, when he was about fourteen years old, Jefferson's future mentor George Wythe left his antislavery Quaker family for the center of Enlightenment learning in Virginia: the College of William and Mary.[17]

The college was always intended to be a means of promoting morality in Virginia; its initial proponents envisioned it as a seminary, producing ministers who would help address such issues as gambling and drunkenness rather than human bondage. But the colonial authorities cared more about profits than anything.[18] According to legend, the first time the Reverend James Blair attempted to gain British governmental support for a seminary at Williamsburg, the response was "Souls! damn your souls! make tobacco."[19] This contest between morality and economics would come to define the American South. Fortunately, Blair was able to secure the college's charter from King William in 1693, the same year that George Keith wrote his groundbreaking antislavery pamphlet. A government-funded school, William and Mary originally comprised a president, six professors, and around a hundred students. And although its primary aim was to educate future ministers of the Church of England, it also offered a school for Native American boys and another for the sons of wealthy colonists. Eventually, the college began offering two levels of study for those sons: a preparatory grammar school with one master overseeing all the young students in their Latin and Greek, and a baccalaureate-level philosophy school with two dedicated professors, one for natural philosophy, the other for moral philosophy.[20]

Unlike a university today, it seems that until 1770 most students at William and Mary did not complete degrees, instead pursuing their studies only as far as they wished.[21] However, the seminary failed to attract many students; prospective clergymen still had to travel all the way to England in order to be ordained by a bishop, and wealthy Virginian parents did not embrace the grammar school for several decades, believing that their sons would get a better education in England or from private tutors. The school for Native American boys only ever had about ten students at a time. When Wythe is thought to have begun his studies at the grammar school in 1740, the entire institution had fewer than fifty students enrolled.[22]

As Jefferson later put it, "When [secondary] education is done with and a young man is to prepare himself for public life, he must cast his eyes (for America) either on Law or Physic"—and being a physician did not appeal to Wythe.[23] However, since no law degrees were yet offered in the colonies, the only way to qualify was by apprenticing with a local attorney or by journeying to London's Inns of Court. Wythe probably remained at William and Mary only for a short time before leaving to apprentice under his uncle Stephen Dewey, the King's Attorney in Charles City County. Wythe qualified as a colonial lawyer in 1746; over the ensuing decade he built a thriving legal practice, was elected to the House of Burgesses, was appointed attorney general, married, and moved into a beautiful house down the street from the Governor's Palace in Williamsburg.[24]

In 1758 a new phase began for Wythe, and for Virginia, when Lieutenant Governor Francis Fauquier[25] moved into that mansion. Born in 1704, Fauquier was the son of a French Huguenot refugee who had married an Englishwoman and become a director of the Bank of England. Fauquier himself achieved success in multiple fields: he became a director of the South Sea Company in 1748, and his accomplishments in science led to his being elected a Fellow of the Royal Society in 1753. A man of liberal Enlightenment ideals, Fauquier in 1760 declared "White, Red, or Black; polished or unpolished Men are Men."[26] Thomas Jefferson once referred to Fauquier as "the ablest man who ever filled the chair of government" in Virginia.[27] Fauquier replaced the unpopular Governor Dinwiddie, and Fauquier's gracious manners, cultured tastes, and support for the colonial legislature won him the hearts of many Virginians, including Wythe. In some ways, the two men were opposites: his students described Wythe as being of medium build, with a high forehead and "very bald"; he gave the impression of being constantly deep in thought by walking with his hands folded into one another behind his back, and he wore plain clothing cut in the "Quaker fashion."[28] Fauquier's portrait, by contrast, shows a fashionable man wearing a curled, powdered wig, and part of his popularity as governor stemmed from his prodigious gambling habits.[29] But the two quickly struck up an enduring friendship, with Wythe joining the acting governor at his mansion for dinners every week.

Their gatherings also included another recent arrival to the colony: a young William and Mary professor named William Small. The trio soon became "inseparable friends."[30] Small had been hired in the aftermath of skirmishes between the local elites and the religious establishment—particularly the clergymen teaching at the college, who tended to see themselves as intellectually superior to members of the colonial government. In 1757, after a series of disagreements, the college's board of visitors dismissed four of the faculty members, and a fifth quit.[31] Small, the son of a noted Scottish mathematician, was specifically recruited by the Virginians to fill one of those vacant spots because he was *not* an Anglican clergyman. Quite the contrary: as a man of science, Small would have been perceived as having no desire to promote the influence of the Church over the government.[32]

Twenty-four-year-old Small's education in Aberdeen, a center of the Scottish Enlightenment, had exposed him to the latest philosophical thought. At Marischal College, professors such as William Duncan, author of the popular textbook *Elements of Logic* (1748), utilized the same lecture notes year after year, sometimes sharing them with professors at nearby King's College, where other prominent philosophers—such as Thomas Reid, founder of the common sense school—taught. Small brought many of his own notes from those courses with him when he came to Virginia; thus "the basics of the Scottish Enlightenment . . . as they were delivered to Small, may have devolved undiluted" upon Small's students.[33] Soon after Small arrived, the other philosophy school professor was dismissed for his role in a rowdy brawl between the college students and the boys of Williamsburg. Originally, Small had been hired to be the professor of natural philosophy, and as such his classes included subjects like mathematics, physics, and metaphysics. But now

Small began teaching rhetoric, logic, and ethics in addition to all his other courses, and he became (according to Thomas Jefferson) the first professor in America to introduce the study of belles-lettres, or literature, and to replace rote memorization with the Socratic method.[34] (Jefferson would later duplicate Small's approach in his design for the University of Virginia.) Small also taught astronomy and meteorology and introduced scientific experimentation and observation into the curriculum, and soon some gentlemen in the colony also took up an interest in experimentation. All of this would have endeared Small to his new friend, Governor Fauquier, who was so intrigued by scientific inquiries that, when he observed a hailstorm in Williamsburg on 9 July 1758, he wrote a scientific paper about it and sent it off to London as an offering to the Royal Society. Most likely, Fauquier asked the meteorology expert, Small, to read over it first.[35]

Not long after professor Jacob Rowe was fired for brawling, the college president died of an alcohol-related illness.[36] Consequently, for many months Small was most likely left to supervise the curriculum and administration of the philosophy school entirely on his own. The future revolutionary leaders of Virginia who were beginning their studies at William and Mary—for many years exclusively the province of Anglican clergymen concerned with little more than maintaining their privileges in a hierarchical society of English tradition—were now quite literally in the hands of a vanguard of the Enlightenment.[37]

Thomas Jefferson was one of the fortunate students to arrive in 1760, just before Small took over all classes. The new pupil was sixteen years old, tall and lanky, with red hair and skin that freckled quickly, and had lived all his life in the rural countryside of Albemarle County. His father had died three years earlier, leaving his fourteen-year-old son an inheritance that included about forty enslaved human beings. Young Thomas worked hard to convince his guardians to allow him to travel to the capital city to continue his education, because, he said, "by going to the College I shall get a more universal Acquaintance, which may hereafter be serviceable to me; and I suppose I can pursue my Studies in the Greek and Latin as well there as here, and likewise learn something of the Mathematics."[38] Indeed, with William Small as his primary teacher from 1760 until 1762, Jefferson was able to learn much more than mathematics.[39] He later remembered that "it was my great good fortune, and what probably fixed the destinies of my life that Dr. Wm. Small," a man "profound in most of the useful branches of science," possessing "an enlarged and liberal mind," became "soon attached to me & made me his daily companion when not engaged in the school."[40] Jefferson did not retain a high opinion of William and Mary itself; in later years, he described living in the main building with all the other boys as akin to being in a "common den of noise" filled with "filth and fetid air" and posing a "danger of fire, infection and tumult."[41] Even the food was bad. But the men he met in Williamsburg, starting with Small, molded his mind and changed the trajectory of his life.[42]

Despite his rural upbringing, Jefferson arrived at William and Mary having already been exposed to fairly progressive ideas after spending the previous two years at the Reverend James Maury's school for boys. Like Fauquier, the Irish-born Maury's parents had been "deeply religious" French Huguenot refugees. Maury had been a student at William and Mary when George Wythe studied there in 1740, and the two probably met when Maury was appointed usher (assistant to the master) for the grammar school.[43] By the time Jefferson met him, Maury had made the journey to England to be officially ordained as an Anglican minister and was running "one of the finest private schools in the colonial South."[44] A "correct classical scholar," as Jefferson termed him, Maury emphasized reason and tolerance, rejecting the enthusiasm of the Great Awakening for more traditional religious forms.[45] However, like the Quakers, he believed in the fundamental equality of humans before God, as evidenced by an event that young Thomas probably observed in 1759. At a religious service, Maury attempted to simultaneously baptize white Virginians and enslaved black Virginians. Although a churchwarden prevented the mixed baptism from proceeding, Maury protested that ministers should baptize people of "all Nations . . . without any regards to their several Colors, Conditions, or Countries."[46] Although born and raised in a slave society, the teenaged Jefferson may have arrived in Williamsburg with the seeds of equality already in his mind.

Maury does get a one-sentence mention in Jefferson's autobiography, but it was William Small who did the most for the young man's "destinies." Only a few years older than the fatherless teenager, Small took Jefferson under his wing, spending hours together inside and outside of class and modeling the scholarly lifestyle for him. Jefferson recalled that Small was "to me as a father. [T]o his enlightened & affectionate guidance of my studies while at College I am indebted for every thing." Even better, Small invited Thomas into his circle of friendship with his own "bosom friend" Wythe and their mutual comrade Fauquier, who from 1761 to 1763 was also serving as rector of the board of visitors. The three intellectuals and the brilliant teenager formed a cozy "partie quarreé," Jefferson recalled, and the conversation he was exposed to during dinners at the Governor's Palace during this time offered "more good sense, more rational & philosophical conversations than in all my life besides."[47] When his own grandson went away to school for the first time many years later, Jefferson worried that the boy would fall into bad company. In a letter of advice, Jefferson remembered how alone he had felt when he first left home and arrived in "the society of horse racers, cardplayers, [and] foxhunters" in the big city of Williamsburg. In moments of moral temptation, he was saved by asking himself "what would Dr. Small, mr Wythe . . . do in this situation? what course in it will ensure me their approbation? . . . knowing the even & dignified line they pursued, I could never doubt for a moment which of two courses would be in character for them."[48]

The greatest moral challenge of Jefferson's generation, and for the succeeding generations, was slavery. And in the company of Wythe, Fauquier, and Small, Jefferson had stumbled into what can plausibly be characterized as an informal antislavery society, an association that no doubt did much to form his early antislavery convictions. Although we do not have specific records of their conversations over fine food and Baroque music in the Governor's Palace, their actions and writings in the surrounding years paint a clear picture of men morally opposed to one of the defining institutions of their time.

At the time that Fauquier governed and Small taught at the College of William and Mary, the school had itself developed something of a reputation for liberal views on race and education. Two years after

Small and Fauquier arrived in Williamsburg, a seminal moment in the history of black education in the American colonies occurred when the Bray School opened its doors to both free and enslaved black children of the Williamsburg community. Sponsored by a British religious group, the Bray School was placed on the campus of William and Mary at the recommendation of Benjamin Franklin. Franklin had apparently visited William and Mary in 1756 and found that the college president, the Reverend Thomas Dawson, and his brother William, who had served as president before him, had a history of encouraging equality in religious education. In the 1740s William Dawson had used college resources to buy books for religious instruction that he offered to mixed classes of white, Native, and black (free and enslaved) people; Thomas in 1754 urged the Bishop of London to support the creation of schools "for the educating of poor Children and negroes."[49] Franklin thus had ample reason to believe that the college would support the establishment of a school for black children in Williamsburg. College president Dawson became a trustee for the Bray School, and William and Mary "appears to be the first college or university in America to concern itself as an institution (through the support of its presidents and faculty and through expending its resources) with the education of blacks, free and enslaved."[50] The Bray School operated throughout the years that Jefferson lived in Williamsburg, and he was therefore most likely aware of its existence; it closed when its headmistress died in 1774.

A second trustee of the Bray School was another member of Fauquier, Wythe, and Small's inner circle: Robert Carter III, the grandson of the famed Virginia landowner Robert "King" Carter.[51] The younger Carter, two years Wythe's junior, gained a seat on the Governor's Council in 1758 at age thirty and was subsequently "adopted as a protégé" by Fauquier. Carter joined Small, Wythe, and Jefferson at the governor's house for dinner and to play harpsichord and flute in their musical ensembles.[52] According to John Page, another of Small's (antislavery) students, Carter "conversed a great deal with our highly enlightened Governor, Fauquier, and Mr. Wm. Small, the Professor of Mathematics at the College of Wm. and Mary, from whom he derived great advantage."[53] Although Carter never achieved fame or personal popularity like that of his fellow Virginians Wythe and Jefferson, leaving politics during the Revolution and eventually abandoning Virginia altogether, he did accomplish something quite remarkable for a man of his social stature: in 1791 he took advantage of a recent liberalization in Virginia's manumission laws to set in motion a gradual emancipation plan for more than 450 slaves, a private emancipation effort larger "than any individual in American history."[54]

His neighbors objected, his sons protested, and Carter died in obscurity; his decision to free so many slaves caused an uproar in Virginia and embroiled him in legal battles for years. A strict and somewhat eccentric father, Carter sent his children out of the state and refused to allow them to visit home, claiming that the atmosphere of slavery would corrupt them. What made Carter so committed to emancipation? His conversion to the evangelical Baptist faith during the revivals of the revolutionary period certainly played a part in his decision to free his slaves; after his personal awakening he began referring to the human property who had also converted as his "brothers" and "sisters." Moreover, Carter was never popular enough to win elections, so there was no danger that he would alienate his constituency by making such a controversial decision—and perhaps most important, he was so wealthy that he could pay considerable sums to fight the necessary court battles and to help ease his slaves' journeys to freedom. Whereas later slaveholders were stymied in their emancipation efforts by Virginian laws that re-enslaved people freed by masters who were themselves in debt, as we shall see, Carter had no such troubles. He was one of the few members of the Founding generation who had the motive, opportunity, and financial means to fully live out a commitment to the ideals of liberty and equality. His days in Williamsburg, overseeing the Bray School and conversing with Wythe, Small, and Fauquier at the Governor's Palace, surely laid the foundation for his later antislavery actions; he had a liberal fount of Enlightened ideas from which to draw. His subsequent religious convictions gave him the added push necessary to sacrifice so much of the family fortune by freeing his slaves. Carter finished his life in obscurity, residing in a small house in Maryland.[55]

The life of Carter's mentor, Fauquier, paralleled the younger man's in two important ways: Fauquier's will, written a year before he died of an unknown malady in 1768, expresses both his religious convictions and his hatred for slavery. Ever the scientist, Fauquier donated his body for autopsy so that he could "become more useful to my fellow Creatures by my Death than I have been in my life." His soul he believed was returning to "the Hands of a most Merciful and benevolent God." But Fauquier worried that his slaves would "rise up in Judgment against me" on Judgment Day, "when all my actions will be exposed to public view." Invoking James 2:13, Fauquier mused: "For with what face can I expect Mercy from an offended God, if I have not myself shewn mercy to those dependent on me." He claimed that he never desired to own slaves in the first place; they were "a part of my Estate in its nature disagreeable to me, but which my situation made necessary for me"—meaning his situation as a leading member of Virginian society, in which every elite family depended on slave labor to perform the necessary functions of life. But Fauquier felt guilty for holding this human property, whom he could not—according to the still-restrictive Virginian laws of the 1760s—set free, either while alive or in his will.[56] He hoped, therefore, to provide for them so that they would experience "as little misery during their Lives as their very unhappy and pitiable condition will allow."[57]

Accordingly, Fauquier desired his slaves to "have liberty to choose their own Master" and stipulated that "the Women and their children shall not be parted," apparently hoping that husbands and wives would at least be able to see each other on occasion if they found owners who lived near one another. The slaves would have six months to find suitable new owners, during which time the deceased man's estate would continue to provide for them. To sweeten the deal for any prospective purchasers and thereby enlarge the pool of potential owners for his slaves to choose from, Fauquier instructed his executors—including Wythe and Carter—to take 25 percent under market value in the sales. His distress at having to arrange such sales evident, Fauquier included a heartfelt plea "as my last Dying wish" that anyone "who shall retain a favorable opinion of me" would purchase those enslaved people who could not arrange their own sales and that they would treat the slaves well "for my sake." Of Fauquier's seventeen enslaved people, only three were apparently unable to find purchasers on their own, so most were able to remain close to one another in Williamsburg. Unfortunately, as Fauquier himself must have realized, the cruel reality of slavery dictated that even the best-intentioned master could not always prevent enslaved families from being split up. Within months one of the new owners sold several of Fauquier's former slaves out of the state. But the law prevented the governor from doing any better, despite his antipathy for the institution of slavery and his "Dying wish" for his human property to suffer as "little misery" as possible.[58]

Although proof of Small's antislavery convictions is less direct (and less poignant) than that of Fauquier due to the lack of surviving documentation, there is a good amount of circumstantial evidence to consider. To date, the only full-length study of Small is one unpublished dissertation; in it, Martin Clagett traces both the proto-antislavery Enlightenment influences on Small in Scotland and his emancipationist associations when he returned to England after teaching at William and Mary. The "Father of the Scottish Enlightenment," and therefore Small's intellectual progenitor, was the antislavery philosopher Francis Hutcheson (1694–1746), who along with other Scots thinkers created the philosophical underpinnings for a critique of slavery that is also prevalent in Jefferson's thought, as we shall see. After graduating from Marischal, Small spent his Virginia years in the company of Fauquier and Wythe, both of whom wrote eloquently of their opposition to slavery. Unfortunately, when he left Virginia in 1764 on a mission to procure scientific equipment for the college, it is possible that Small was already infected with malaria, from which he is believed to have died in 1775 at the age of forty-one.[59] But before his death in England, Small became a founding member of the Birmingham Lunar Society, an informal scientific club that included some of Britain's greatest intellectuals.[60] Small's friends in this circle included several strong advocates for abolition, such as Erasmus Darwin, Josiah Wedgewood, and Joseph Priestley, a Unitarian minister and scientist who went on to become a major influence on Jefferson's religious thought. Perhaps Small discussed his firsthand knowledge of slavery in Virginia with another emancipationist friend, Thomas Day, who in 1773 specifically critiqued the American South in one of the first British antislavery poems, "The Dying Negro."[61] Although Small did not produce any notable antislavery writings himself (that we know of), the list of his antislavery friends is long.[62]

Regardless of whether Small actually promoted antislavery thought to his young student, Jefferson certainly learned much about Scottish philosophy while studying with the Aberdeen immigrant, and Jefferson's embrace of the moral sense ideology in particular had deep implications for his future writings on slavery. In my discussion of moral sense ideology below, I do not attempt to draw straight lines between any particular philosopher and Jefferson. Perhaps more so than any other thinker of the Founding generation, Jefferson can best be characterized as *extremely* widely read, and as the biographer Dumas Malone sagely points out, the works that Jefferson cited in his college notebooks— our best sources for that period, since a 1770 fire destroyed most of his other early letters and writings—"cannot be assumed to have been the source of his ideas. These ideas he shared to greater or less degree with his contemporaries, and he could have plucked many of them from the air."[63] In other words, the very atmosphere of prerevolutionary America was charged with ideas drawn from a variety of European Enlightenments, as well as English political history.

It was also a society steeped in Christianity, but although Jefferson accepted Christian social values, participated in Christian churches throughout his life, and eventually became convinced that Jesus was the greatest of all moral teachers, during his years as a student in Williamsburg he seems to have questioned much of the Anglican orthodoxy of his youth. He investigated the skepticism of Bolingbroke and embraced ancient Greek and Roman philosophy as a way of coping with the sorrows of his life, and his idea of morality from this point on was less linked to the Ten Commandments than to his belief that God designed humans to receive internal and external benefits from acting virtuously.[64] In particular, Jefferson's moral philosophy drew upon specific elements of the Scots moral sense school. Because these elements are present consistently throughout his life, it is important to understand the background of the moral sense school as well as its major principles.

The Scottish Enlightenment in general emphasized morality: the school emerged during a time when a number of Scots Presbyterian clergymen were arguing that faith should be measured more by virtuous conduct than by strict adherence to a theological creed. Francis Hutcheson, the "Father of the Scottish Enlightenment," was a clergyman by training who became professor of moral philosophy at the prestigious University of Glasgow in 1730. He "presented conduct founded on charity rather than doctrinal orthodoxy as the essence of genuine religion and virtue alike."[65] Hutcheson felt he had to put the very concept of universal morality on firm footing again, because his fellow Scottish writer David Hume (1711–1776) was promoting an irreligious, skeptical philosophy with potentially drastic consequences for moral theory. This crisis first began when John Locke (1632–1704) persuasively argued that all humans were born as blank slates; all human ideas were formed as the senses interacted with the environment. Hume built upon Locke in ways indicating that morality itself "might be reducible to such nonmoral sources as habit, association, and self-interest." Morality, in other words, could be a social construct rather than a set of divinely instituted, universally applicable standards—and therefore one man's sin might be another man's pleasure. To argue against Hume's moral relativism, Hutcheson aimed to "derive from self-evident intuitions principles which would preserve faith in individual responsibility and in the moral order of the world."[66]

Hutcheson deduced from his own observations that God implanted in all people a moral sense, an instinct that guided people toward virtuous behavior and rewarded them with "a pleasant Sensation of Joy"[67] whenever they conducted themselves well, so that "by the moral sense . . . actions become of the greatest [import] to our happiness or misery."[68] Hutcheson argued that the moral sense made humans fit for society, for every person's innate moral sense took pleasure in benevolence, causing him or her to naturally seek out policies that promoted "the greatest happiness of the greatest number of people."[69] It was innate, not produced by education, because even little children and women felt sympathy on behalf of others' pain and desired to relieve it, without requiring anything in return.[70]

Since every person—regardless of race or social status—possessed the same moral sense and the same desire for liberty, happiness, and property, all people therefore had the natural right to defend themselves, to have freedom of conscience, and to pursue their own happiness. These constitute "unalienable" rights, Hutcheson argued, existing despite differences in talent or wealth; therefore, making some men slaves of others would never serve the public good.[71] In making these claims, according to David Brion Davis, Hutcheson became the first intellectual "to give antislavery a basis in moral philosophy."[72] Hutcheson's follower James Beattie, who was at Marischal College with William Small and later became a professor there, took Hutcheson's arguments even further, writing and lecturing that it was impossible to speak of morality without condemning slavery, for if slavery "be equitable, or excusable, or pardonable, it is vain to talk any longer of the eternal distinctions of right and wrong, truth and falsehood, good and evil."[73]

Much debate among historians of Thomas Jefferson has occurred regarding whether he was primarily influenced by the members of the Scottish Enlightenment or by the liberal, individual rights–oriented thought of John Locke. In point of fact, since the Scots thinkers generally took Locke as the starting point for their own philosophy, many of these arguments are moot: as Daniel Walker Howe puts it, "the Scots always honored Locke and considered themselves to be working within his tradition."[74] For example, Hutcheson accepted Locke's general conception of the role of government: not to make people virtuous or religious, but rather to protect the conditions needed for individual liberty. Thus Hutcheson had a Lockean liberal, rather than civic republican, political stance. But for Hutcheson, as Samuel Fleischacker has pointed out, it was also important to recognize that communities had to be based in the "natural human inclination to care for other people"; communities could not be imposed, for their true purpose was to provide a space for the development of virtue and for "the happiness of individuals" to be developed through the exercise of empathy—not just to ensure that individual rights were protected.[75]

Line-by-line comparisons of Hutcheson, Jefferson's Declaration of Independence, and Locke's *Second Treatise* reveal that Jefferson needed Lockean thought in order to build his case against King George, and in this instance he is rightly described as a Lockean liberal. However, whenever Jefferson wrote about the fundamentals of morality, he conversed in terms of an innate moral sense, a notion more Hutchesonian and Kamesian than Lockean. And when Jefferson imaged an empire of liberty spreading across North America, he was concerned not only with the natural rights of future citizens but also with ensuring that all citizens could be bonded by cords of natural affection for one another, in order to create communities in which individual happiness could be pursued. As we shall see, this particular Hutchesonian concern had drastic implications for Jefferson's philosophy regarding the presence of freed slaves in America.

The crucial distinction between Locke and Hutcheson with regard to morality and slavery is that Locke theorized that war could result in a legitimate cause for enslavement. His premise was that in cases in which a man attacked another without cause, thereby "wantonly violating [his] natural rights"—as Peter Onuf and Ari Helo put it—the attacker became a criminal.[76] In the event that the attacker was defeated, the injured party had the right to execute him. But if the injured party decided *not* to execute the attacker but rather to hold him perpetually as a servant, this is what Locke defined as "the perfect condition of Slavery, which is nothing else but the State of War continued, between a lawful Conqueror, and a Captive. . . . [And] having, by his own fault, forfeited his own Life, by some Act that deserves Death; he, to whom he has forfeited it, may . . . delay to take it, and make use of him to his own Service, and he does him no injury by it." Indeed, the slave may actually desire his own death and could seek death for himself if at any time he found the burdens of slavery to "out-weigh the value of his life"; the master was under no obligation to preserve the slave's life, since the slave deserved death for his actions and was, in a sense, morally dead.[77]

Locke did not argue for hereditary slavery: only the criminal himself, not his children, could possibly be enslaved as an alternative to instant death. Some scholars have accused Locke of supporting the African slave trade in his personal life, because he drafted the plan of government for the Carolina colonies in 1669—a plan that supported an aristocratic, slaveholding society. However, as Holly Brewer has pointed out, Locke only did so in his capacity as a lawyer to the Carolina proprietors, not because he personally supported slavery. But other Europeans used a similar "just war theory" (in which slaves were supposedly the attackers/losers in an unfair war and therefore justifiably enslaved) to excuse their participation in the African slave trade.[78]

While he was studying in Williamsburg, Jefferson came to disagree with the just war theory on this point and to believe that those who established slavery in the American colonies were mistaken. Instead, Jefferson concurred with Henry Home, Lord Kames (1696–1782), that the universal and innate moral sense gave even "savage" peoples some minimum standards for justice and that—even better—it was possible for a society's moral sense to be refined over time.[79] In his copy of Kames's 1751 *Essays on the Principles of Morality and Natural Religion*, on the page discussing humane treatment for prisoners of war, a young Jefferson commented in the margin on one way in which he saw "a remarkeable instance of improvement in the moral sense":

> the putting to death captives in war was a general practice among savage nations. when men became more humanized the captive was indulged with life on condition of holding it in perpetual slavery; a condition exacted on this supposition, that the victor had right to take his life, and consequently to commute it for his services. at this state of refinement were the Greeks about the time of the Trojan war. at this day it is perceived we have no right to take the life of an enemy unless where our own preservation renders it necessary. but the ceding his life in commutation for service admits there was no necessity to take it, because you have not done it. and if there was neither necessity nor right to take his life then is there no right to his service in commutation for it. this doctrine is acknoledged by later writers, Montesquieu, Burlamaqui &c. who yet suppose it just to require a ransom from the captive. one advance further in refinement will relinquish this also. if we have no right to the life of a captive, we have no right to his labor; if none to his labor we have none to his absent property which is but the fruit of that labor. in fact, ransom is but commutation in another form.[80]

Clearly, Jefferson put Locke's philosophy of slavery into the category of an outmoded idea, one superseded by the more morally sophisticated philosophies of the Baron de Montesquieu (1689–1755) and Jean-Jacques Burlamaqui (1694–1748). And young Jefferson optimistically looked forward to the day when "one advance further" in the moral sense of Western societies would cause slaveholders to admit that they had "no right" to the labor of people who never should have been enslaved to begin with.

How would this refinement in the moral sense occur? Like many other thinkers of his age, Jefferson came to believe that education was the key: indeed, the essence of the Enlightenment was the notion that man was emerging from the darkness of ignorance and superstition into the light of reason, through rational inquiry. The perfectibility of man was likewise a key doctrine of the age, and Jefferson was one of its disciples. Civic republicanism also taught that virtue was a vital ingredient in the success of a republic, and virtue was understood to be tied to knowledge.[81] Perhaps he also based his morality-through-education theory on the evidence of his own life, for as we have seen, Jefferson credited the Williamsburg circle—Small, Fauquier, and especially Wythe—for forming both his mind and his character.

After two years studying with Small, Jefferson became Wythe's first private law student (Wythe's next known students are Bishop James Madison and St. George Tucker, both of whom studied law in the mid-1770s and became leading antislavery figures).[82] In his many years as a lawyer, private tutor, professor of law at the College of William and Mary, judge, legislator, and scholar, George Wythe (pronounced "with") acted as teacher, mentor, and sometimes father figure to several generations of Virginian leaders. Among his two hundred or so intellectual descendants were diplomats, US Supreme Court justices, secretaries of state, attorneys general, state legislators and federal congressmen, governors, and at least one American president.[83] Wythe is significant not only for the disproportionate number of high-profile students he taught; he was also one of the very few Virginia revolutionaries who managed to combine an intellectual commitment to the rights of men with practical efforts to end slavery. He employed multiple tactics, both public and private, and attempted to change the law through both legislative and judicial means. He started by cowriting a gradual emancipation amendment for Virginia and petitioning the legislature to pass another emancipation bill, then moved to freeing his own slaves, even providing them with education and leaving them much of his property. Toward the end of his life, he decreed from the bench that Virginia's Declaration of Rights applied to black as well as white Americans—a decision that was overturned a year after his death.[84]

Perhaps the most meaningful of Wythe's antislavery actions, however, was less obvious: the unique influence he held over his students, in part because he was the best (and, for a time, the only) law professor in Virginia, and in part because his gentle personality, generosity, and reputation for integrity led his students to hold him in universally high esteem. Most of Wythe's papers have been lost to history, making any study of his life difficult. He left deep impressions on his many students and colleagues, however. From their accounts, we learn that to know Wythe was to love him: Spencer Roane, a judge, politician, and writer, always spoke of his former teacher "with a veneration that was almost a religion on his lips."[85] Another student rejoiced at being taken in by Wythe, for "nothing would advance me faster in the world, than the reputation of having been educated by Mr. Wythe, for such a man as he, casts a light upon all around him"; Wythe "certainly approaches nearer to perfection than any man I ever saw."[86] Young Richard Randolph enthusiastically informed his mother that Wythe was the "best of men!" When Randolph died at age twenty-six in 1796, he freed 150 slaves in his will, begging their forgiveness and bequeathing each of them 400 acres. He also mentioned Wythe, from whom he had learned that all men are equal, describing him as the "brightest ornament of human nature."[87]

Jefferson later recalled that Wythe was "my antient master, my earliest & best friend; and to him I am indebted for first impressions which have had the most salutary influence on the course of my life." Wythe "directed my studies in the law, led me into business, and continued until [his] death my most affectionate friend." Indeed, if Wythe had not been murdered in 1806, Jefferson had hoped to persuade him to retire to Monticello, "inducing him to spend much of his time with me." (His murder was due in part to his decision to free his slaves and leave them substantial portions of his estate in his will.) Wythe had been, Jefferson told a fellow former student, "my second father." And on the question of slavery, as Jefferson put it, Wythe was "unequivocal." If Jefferson had not already become convinced of the immorality of slavery while conversing with Governor Fauquier or studying with Dr. Small, Wythe's influence was certainly decisive.[88]

Wythe had Jefferson begin his legal studies by reading foundational English legal texts; he was particularly influenced by the freedom-loving Whig Sir Edward Coke. Jefferson also meticulously summarized, or "commonplaced," decisions by English judges. In the process of these studies, according to the legal scholar David Konig, Jefferson concluded that slavery had no legitimate basis in either common law or statutory law. After he was admitted to the Virginia bar in 1765, Jefferson built a respectable practice as "essentially a land patent lawyer"; however, he also "became known as an advocate for those whose enslavement he could challenge in novel ways based on precedent and statutory interpretation," particularly those whose mixed racial ancestry exposed the weak areas of the legal code. (When Jefferson was practicing, Virginia law dictated that the children of enslaved women would also be slaves for life, but with qualifications when it came to Native Americans.) At his own expense, Jefferson took on six freedom suits during his seven years of legal practice. The fact that these cases were undertaken pro bono (without charging a fee) seems to indicate a level of emotional commitment on Jefferson's part.[89]

The record survives for only one of Jefferson's freedom suits, *Howell v. Netherland*, in which a mixed-race indentured servant named Samuel Howell was attempting to gain his freedom from a three-decade term of service. Howell based his claim to freedom on the fact that, though he had African blood, his great-grandmother had been white. Importantly, the twenty-seven-year-old Jefferson did not argue that Howell should be granted liberty because he *looked* white; indeed, it is likely that Howell's skin was not light, because a lower court had not granted him freedom based on that fact (as often happened).[90] Instead, Jefferson methodically built a case based on the legal ramifications of his client's "white ancestry, but [then] proceed[ed] to build on that fact in a manner that call[ed] into question the moral legitimacy of slaveholding irrespective of the color of the bondmen."[91] In no uncertain terms, Jefferson appealed to natural rights:

[U]nder the law of nature, all men are born free, and every one comes into the world with a right to his own person. This is what is called personal liberty, and [it] is given him by the author of nature, because necessary for his own sustenance. The reducing the mother to servitude was a violation of the law of nature: surely then the same law cannot prescribe a continuance of the violation to her issue, and that too without end.[92]

Jefferson then invoked the German legal theorist Samuel von Pufendorf to support his natural law doctrine. Pufendorf was not opposed to slavery in all cases but contended that, because slavery went against natural law, the legislature had to "rediscover, reinvent, and reassert positive proslavery law over the years" in order to justify holding some people in perpetual slavery.[93] Obviously unwilling to open a Pandora's box by discussing the various laws that enforced slavery in Virginia in contradiction to natural rights, the court, composed of men Jefferson liked and looked up to, did not even wait to hear the opposing counsel's argument before throwing out Jefferson's case. This might have been quite humiliating for the young lawyer. Although a few years later in the momentous *Somerset* case an English jurist would rely on similar reasoning to declare slavery illegal in England, the Virginia court seems to have decided that God himself decreed "some Nations should serve others; and that all Nations have not been [born] equally free."[94]

Ironically, opposing counsel in the *Howell* case was none other than Jefferson's mentor, George Wythe. Because the court summarily ruled against Jefferson, there is no record of Wythe's prepared response to Jefferson's eloquent natural rights argument. Some scholars speculate that, because Wythe was opposing counsel in a freedom suit, he might have been proslavery at this point in his life and even perhaps have been influenced to become antislavery by Jefferson's stirring argument.[95] However, given his membership in the Williamsburg circle, as well as his consistent record of antislavery actions, it seems more likely that Wythe was, as lawyers often must, acting on behalf of a client rather than on his personal beliefs in this instance. During the ensuing decades, his true opinions were much better reflected when he presided as judge (on Virginia's High Court of Chancery) over even more consequential cases. In 1798 he upheld the will of a deceased antislavery Quaker, John Pleasants, that freed hundreds of slaves—and then decreed that Pleasants's recalcitrant children owed the slaves sixteen years' worth of back pay![96] In the landmark 1806 case *Hudgins v. Wright*, a Native American family sued for their freedom from slavery. Wythe ruled in the family's favor on two grounds: first, because the family appeared to be either Native or white, not African American. The family was therefore presumptively free, and the burden of proof (of slavery) rested on their owner. Second, Wythe ruled that, because the Virginia Declaration of Rights (1776) held that all men "are by nature equally free and independent," the family deserved their liberty.

In making this claim, Wythe was following in the footsteps of several northern states that also had "free and equal" clauses in their founding documents; because these clauses were written when slavery was still almost universally legal, judges had been called upon to rule on their implications. In places like Massachusetts, where public opinion was mainly against slavery, judges were able to rule on behalf of slaves. In Virginia, though, Wythe's attempt to invoke the "free and equal" clause for the enslaved family suffered two fatal flaws: first, the men who voted for the Virginia Declaration of Rights had absolutely no intention of ending slavery, and everybody knew it. The Declaration's carefully worded first section states that rights are guaranteed only when men "enter into a state of Society," leaving a loophole that could be (and was) construed to exclude enslaved Africans from equality. Since they had not entered into Virginian society as free and equal individuals, the reasoning goes, Africans "did not fall under this declaration."[97]

Second, Wythe's attempt to invoke the "free and equal" clause failed because public opinion in the state was turning even more drastically against emancipation in the wake of Gabriel's Rebellion (1800). In the same year that Wythe heard the *Hudgins* case, the legislature made emancipations infinitely more difficult by passing a bill requiring any freed slaves to leave the state within one year or else be re-enslaved. Perhaps as a desperate attempt to hold back this rising proslavery tide, Wythe tried to invoke the most expansive meaning of the words in the Declaration of Rights, rather than the intentions of the authors, to free a family. He died believing that he had been successful.[98]

Wythe therefore most likely supported Jefferson in his attempt to free Mr. Howell in 1770, and he certainly supported Jefferson in the antislavery actions he took in the legislature during this revolutionary period—indeed, he joined in some of them. Jefferson later recalled that his first attempt to attack slavery occurred in 1769, just after he was elected to the House of Burgesses. The session began in May; that same month, a Quaker named Edward Stabler traveled to Williamsburg to see if the Burgesses would pass a law allowing individual Quakers to manumit their slaves. The Quakers of Virginia had recently decided that purchasing slaves would not be permitted among their membership, but since the law of the colony prohibited masters from liberating their property except under the tightest of provisions, the Quakers who already owned slaves were stuck. Perhaps Stabler found a willing ally in young Jefferson, for the newly minted burgess persuaded his cousin, a respected older gentleman named Richard Bland, to propose a bill that would have returned the right of individual owners to manumit their slaves, just as the Quakers wished to do.[99] But the legislature rejected the bill unequivocally. The twenty-six-year-old Jefferson was "more spared in the debate," but the "most respected" member Bland was "denounced as an enemy to his country, & was treated with the grossest indecorum."[100]

In his autobiography, Jefferson blamed this moral failure on the "regal government": first, because living under colonial rule had "circumscribed" the minds of the legislators "within narrow limits by an habitual belief that it was our duty to be subordinate to the mother country in all matters of government." The burgesses refused to liberalize their laws not from "reflections & conviction" but from "habit and despair." Second, the "mother country" had made her will clear on this matter; the "Royal negative [the King's veto] closed the last door to every hope of amelioration," meaning progress, on the issue of slavery.[101] In his revolutionary 1774 pamphlet *A Summary View of the Rights of British America*, Jefferson similarly claimed that "[t]he abolition of domestic slavery is the great object of desire in those colonies where it was unhappily introduced in their infant state." Before abolishing slavery, however, it would be necessary to end the importation of slaves from Africa, and this would harm the Royal African Company's profits. Thus each time the Virginia legislature attempted to place prohibitory duties on the importation of slaves, whether for economic reasons or because, as Jefferson claimed, they truly wished to end slavery, the king had essentially vetoed their bills.[102] Jefferson argued that the king, in doing so, preferred "the immediate advantages of a few British corsairs to the lasting interests of the American states, and to the rights of human nature deeply wounded by this infamous practice."[103]

Jefferson's draft of the Declaration of Independence condemned the king in even stronger terms:

> He [George III] has waged cruel war against human nature itself, violating it's most sacred rights of life & liberty in the persons of a distant people who never offended him, captivating & carrying them into slavery in another hemisphere. . . . Determined to keep open a market where MEN should be bought & sold, he has prostituted his negative for suppressing every legislative attempt to prohibit or to restrain this execrable commerce.[104]

The other delegates edited out this paragraph from the final version. Historians offer varying explanation as to why,[105] but Jefferson himself explained it in his autobiography by pointing to two groups: Deep South slaveholders who did not wish to condemn slavery in such terms, and northerners who were financially embedded in the slave trade.[106] Regardless, the removal of this paragraph from the final version of the Declaration had the unfortunate effect of obscuring two important facts about Jefferson's political philosophy: first, that Jefferson saw enslaved Americans as a distinct "people," having "sacred rights of life & liberty," a "captive nation" (as he would later call them) who were unjustly held in bondage in a foreign land and who must be given justice all at once. And second, he referred to the slaves bought and sold in markets as "MEN"; by this he clearly meant *people*, male and female, young and old. Thus, when we read "all men are created equal" in the opening lines of the Declaration, what we should see is "all *people* are created equal, that they are endowed by their Creator with certain unalienable rights."[107] While some are tempted to believe that the Declaration intended to declare the equality of white men exclusively, Jefferson had a much broader meaning in mind: despite differences in gender, race, talent, beauty, intelligence, or other respects, all people nonetheless are equal in their possession of certain basic, God-given rights.

Certainly, in the context of listing reasons for breaking with the English monarch, Jefferson may have exaggerated the colonists' commitment to emancipation, and he may have felt inspired to blame George III alone for Americans' sins—sins that he would himself profit from for the rest of his life. However, when Jefferson's 1769 attempt to change Virginia law and his six pro bono freedom suits are viewed as precursors to this expansive antislavery language, it suggests a consistency in his intellectual development. Another private piece of evidence regarding Jefferson's view of slavery at this point in his life comes from an antislavery poem by William Shenstone that he copied into his Memorandum Book in 1771. Titling it "Inscription for An African Slave," Jefferson chose lines that described how Africans were "unjustly ripped from their homeland and made to toil for others in a foreign land." As Annette Gordon-Reed notes, the passage demonstrates that "the slave trade as a focus of evil was very much on Jefferson's mind early on."[108]

By 1778 the revolutionary Virginian General Assembly was finally ready to end the importation of slaves. Some historians have questioned whether or not Jefferson authored the antitrade bill, as he claimed, but the confusion is more likely due to the bill's complicated legislative history and Jefferson's forgetfulness than to outright deceit. In his 1821 autobiography, Jefferson recalled that "this subject was not acted on finally until the year 78. when I brought in a bill to prevent their further importation. This passed without opposition, and stopped the increase of the evil [slavery] by importation, leaving to future efforts its final eradication."[109] In fact, such a bill was first introduced in 1777, there *was* some opposition, and Jefferson was not present when a modified version of the bill did pass in 1778. However, Jefferson's memory in 1821 was faulty on a number of topics (for example, he misremembered both the date that Small returned to England and the date that he passed his own bar exam). As the editorial note in Jefferson's *Papers* points out, Jefferson is the most likely author of the 1777 bill, which was then altered and resubmitted in 1778; and Jefferson frequently authored bills that were then taken up by other people—particularly James Madison—in Jefferson's absence. Jefferson was also careful not to take credit for other people's work, and his outspoken opposition to the slave trade (see the *Summary View* and his draft of the Declaration of Independence) makes it likely that he would also have authored the anti-importation bill, then given it to Madison to push forward, and that he simply forgot this detail when writing his autobiography four decades later.[110]

The Assembly delegates may have dithered for a time before passing this legislation, but the bill itself stands as a testament to Virginians' desire to limit the growth of their enslaved population: Both the foreign and domestic trade were outlawed; the ban went into immediate effect; the penalty for violation was very high; and slaves brought in illegally were to be given their freedom.[111] Again, historians differ over whether Virginians desired to limit their enslaved population because they simply wanted to inflate the prices of Virginia-born slaves or because they truly desired to set slavery on the path to extinction. Throughout the northern states, Quakers had called for banning the importation of slaves as an antislavery measure since 1711, and ending the trade was proving to be a natural precursor to passing gradual emancipation bills. According to Matthew Mason, "most Northerners trusted that slavery would effortlessly disappear once they abolished the slave trade and hoped it would keep to itself in the meantime." In southern states this step was also viewed as a safety measure—keeping down the numbers of a potentially homicidal population.[112] But the salient point for Virginia in 1778 is that the slave trade itself was generally regarded as "a 'wicked' commerce."[113] A ban on slave importations passed because there was popular support for such a bill; whether or not popular support existed for ending slavery itself was another matter entirely. Jefferson happily noted that the law "will in some measure stop the increase of this great political and moral evil, while the minds of our citizens may be ripening for a complete emancipation of human nature."[114]

For Jefferson, the massive social upheavals that began with the Revolutionary War served to crystalize theories that he had begun considering as a student. We have seen that Jefferson's "moral sense" philosophy promoted a progressive vision of humanity: an educated and virtuous populace, living together in bonds of voluntary community, would naturally desire to do good for one another. And as Peter Onuf puts it, America's revolutionary "'experiment' in republican government constituted an epochal moment in the history of mankind precisely because it enabled subjects to become citizens who recognized in themselves and each other a capacity for moral improvement."[115] Jefferson seized this epochal moment with both hands, promoting policies that would transform what was in many ways a feudal society into a community of equals, each free to pursue happiness—and that meant slavery had to end.[116]

And after slavery ended—what then? In considering Jefferson's recommendations on what should be done with freed slaves, it is important to remember that there was no example for the American revolutionaries of a free, multiracial republic. Indeed, there were very few examples of *republics*, period. The ancient Greeks and Romans were considered, and the Dutch and the Swiss and—briefly—the English had experimented with forms of republicanism. But in general, the Americans felt themselves to be beginning something totally new in world history, and for Jefferson—a southerner living in a racially divided society that was part slave, part free—it was difficult to imagine how the equality and communal affection necessary for a republic to succeed could be achieved.[117] His concern was not new; in 1755 Benjamin Franklin was already worrying that growth in both the German and African populations would hinder the abilities of the colonies to succeed. Franklin did not object to Africans merely because of racism but rather because the enslaved immigrants were understandably resentful toward the white population.[118]

During the revolutionary period, northern legislatures were willing to consider gradual emancipation for all their slaves because the proportion of slave-to-free among the population was very low; the freed people could be assimilated with relative ease. As Robert McDonald puts it, however, "[s]upport for emancipation . . . did not equal approval of miscegenation."[119] Even the pro-emancipation Massachusetts governor James Sullivan said in 1795 that his objection to abolition, which "embraces all my feelings," was that "it will tend to a mixture of blood, which I now abhor." But this abhorrence was fortunately outweighed by the belief that, as Jonathan Edwards wrote, "[black people] are so small a portion of the inhabitants [that], when mixed with the rest, they will not produce any very sensible diversity of colour."[120] In the South, where slaves sometimes made up a majority of the inhabitants, racial and cultural integration would be a much larger undertaking. In both regions, colonization, or the resettlement of former slaves in territory separate from white populations (either in the American West, Africa, or the Caribbean), was early on considered as a possible solution to the dilemma of slavery. African colonization was proposed in April 1773 by four slaves in Massachusetts: they asked the colonial assembly to allow them to work one day a week for wages in order to save and buy their own freedom. Then they would "transport ourselves to some part of the coast of *Africa*." Their petition was printed by a sympathetic Boston newspaper. Similar plans were conceived in the pre-Revolution period by the Quaker abolitionist Anthony Benezet and the Rhode Island minister Samuel Hopkins. Jefferson came to support colonization, too.[121]

Colonization was not simply a means of separating races for Jefferson; it also stemmed from his notion of national identity. As he warned regarding the immigration of large numbers of white, non-English Europeans to America, "it is for the happiness of those united in society to harmonize as much as possible in matters which they must of necessity transact together. civil government being the sole object of forming societies, its administration must be conducted by common consent." If immigrants from European "absolute monarchies" came, they would either bring those principles of monarchy with them or, "if able to throw them off, it will be in exchange for an unbounded licentiousness, passing, as is usual, from one extreme to another. It would be a miracle were they to stop precisely at the point of temperate liberty." Their children would inherit the parents' ideas, and their votes would change the shape of the American government: "[I]n proportion to their numbers, they will share with us the legislation. They will infuse into it their spirit, warp and bias its direction, and render it a heterogeneous, incoherent, distracted mass."[122]

Although Jefferson did not oppose all immigration, and indeed strongly disagreed with Federalist policies of targeting foreigners who had seemingly dangerous ideas, he did believe that, for the American experiment in republicanism to succeed, the nation had to be relatively homogenous. Small numbers of immigrants could easily integrate themselves into society, but not large masses of foreigners. This was not just a uniquely American problem: It would also be highly unstable if "20 millions of republican Americans [were] thrown all of a sudden into France"; that country would be "more turbulent, less happy, less strong." Peoples who were attached by shared history and custom could, Jefferson believed, develop the governments best suited to their particular needs. Republicanism was ideal, of course, but as we shall see, Jefferson always thought that Americans were exceptionally suited for self-government—and he guarded their experiment in liberty jealously. In addition to his racial prejudice—prejudice that was widely shared by almost all white people of his day—Jefferson believed that African-descended peoples were culturally distinct from Americans. Moreover, because they had every right to hate the people who held them in unjust bondage, Jefferson claimed to be unable to foresee a peaceful, republican future in which white and free black people lived together as fellow citizens.[123]

Virginia's future was very much on Jefferson's mind in 1776. As soon as he had returned from Congress to meet with his state legislature, he "moved and presented a bill" calling for the laws of Virginia to be "reviewed, adapted to our republican form of government, and, now that we had no negatives [vetoes] of Councils, Governors & Kings to restrain us from doing right, that it should be corrected, in all it's parts, with a single eye to reason."[124] Since Jefferson had publicly argued, twice, that the "king's negative" had played a role in limiting Virginians' ability to end the slave trade, it stands to reason that he was here thinking of slavery as well as such fundamental issues as voting rights, inheritance laws, and public education. Jefferson was appointed head of a committee for revising the laws, and he was joined by Wythe and three others. When one committee member died, and another quit, Jefferson took up their portions of the work, rendering the final product very much a creature of his and Wythe's philosophies; he relied on Wythe's judgment and knowledge and sent drafts of his revised laws to his old teacher, asking Wythe "scrupulously to examine and correct" them.[125]

When Jefferson and Wythe wrote Bill no. 51—the bill concerning slave laws—they also drew up an amendment, "to be offered to the legislature whenever the bill should be taken up," that provided for the gradual emancipation, education, and colonization of Virginia's enslaved population. It would have freed all slaves born after the act passed, and it proposed using public funds to first educate them, and then assist them with tools and supplies in a colony, located in "such [a] place as the circumstances of the time should render most proper." The ultimate goal, as Jefferson later expressed it, was to declare that Virginia's slaves, whom Jefferson saw as a "captive nation" that had been unjustly kidnapped from their homelands, were now "a free and independent people." The Virginians should give this people their own land "and extend to them our alliance and protection, till they shall have acquired strength" to exist as an independent black republic.[126]

However, when the committee presented its report to the Assembly, this amendment was held back, as Jefferson later related, because "it was found that the public mind would not yet bear the proposition."[127] The "public mind" formed a primary consideration in all of Jefferson's reforms, for as much as he was committed to ending Virginia's "crime" against enslaved people, he was equally committed to the ideal of self-government for which American colonists were fighting a revolution. As Onuf puts it, "[t]he people could not be forced to embrace progressive policy prescriptions, for then they would cease to govern themselves, and their capacity for moral improvement would diminish accordingly." Jefferson's commitment to democracy was therefore also a commitment to reliance upon public opinion for legislative changes, and even then only after public opinion "had advanced sufficiently to see and act on the injustice of slavery was there any hope for Jefferson's emancipation scheme."[128] As we shall see, although some citizens of Virginia were eager to free their slaves, most others—including many in the legislature—absolutely refused to consider doing so. Finding the best way to influence these slaveholders became one of Jefferson's primary concerns over the next decade.

Wythe and Jefferson continued to discuss their revisal of the laws for years, pleased that its liberality—particularly in promoting freedom of religion—served to convince the European powers that the Americans were successfully able to govern themselves (and were not, as the British press liked to report, mired in anarchy). After observing Europeans' "ignorance, superstition, poverty and oppression of body and mind in every form" that were "so firmly settled on the mass of the people, that their redemption from them can never be hoped," Jefferson still wondered if "[o]ur act for freedom of religion" might "produce considerable good" after being printed in numerous European books and circulated among ambassadors and courts.[129] If the Europeans could be free to follow their own consciences in matters of faith, perhaps they could follow in Americans' footsteps in other areas as well?

But even more than the law guaranteeing Virginians' religious freedom, Jefferson told Wythe that "by far the most important bill in our whole code is that for the diffusion of knowledge among the people. No other sure foundation can be devised, for the preservation of freedom and happiness."[130] The bill to which he was referring, the 1778 Bill for the More General Diffusion of Knowledge, was far more than simply an education proposal. Because of its sweeping vision, it was designed to take the first steps needed to reorder Virginian political structure from an aristocracy to a meritocracy. The bill provided for broad, publicly financed education of "the people at large," and it ensured that Virginia's future leaders would be drawn from all ranks of society, according to their individual "genius and virtue." Jefferson argued that nature endowed individuals "with genius and virtue," regardless of their wealth or parentage. Equality of opportunity must therefore be guaranteed through the provision of free public education. Leaders "should be rendered by liberal education worthy to receive, and able to guard the sacred deposit of the rights and liberties of their fellow citizens"; "they should be called to that charge without regard to wealth, birth or other accidental condition or circumstance." All free Virginian children should therefore receive a basic education—which for Jefferson and Wythe constituted moral principles, along with reading, writing, and arithmetic—and scholarships should exist so that many could attend higher grammar schools.[131] The best and brightest of the state's young men could then be selected from the grammar schools to attend the College of William and Mary on scholarship. The Assembly did nothing with this bill upon receiving it in 1779, but Jefferson never gave up on his dream of public education for Virginians. He told James

Madison in 1787 that he hoped "[a]bove all things" that "the education of the common people will be attended to; convinced that on their good sense we may rely with the most security for the preservation of a due degree of liberty."[132]

His bill might have failed, but when Jefferson was appointed governor of Virginia and elected to the College of William and Mary's board of visitors in 1779, he was able to begin changing Virginia's educational establishment in one vitally important way: by creating a new professorship at William and Mary and giving it to Wythe. Jefferson first proposed changes for the college in Bill no. 80 of the revisal; it would have reorganized the college, transforming it into a modern, secular university with an updated curriculum and more professors. The college had been founded as an Anglican stronghold in a time when the Anglican Church was the official church of the state and professor-clergymen had an outsized influence on political matters. Jefferson opposed this religious monopoly at the school, having seen firsthand the numerous ways in which the clergymen who taught there interfered with Virginia's government, and believing that education should emphasize moral principles over doctrinal particulars. Ironically, religious dissenters misunderstood Jefferson's intentions, and as a result the bill did not pass the Assembly; however, as governor Jefferson was able to abolish the professorship of divinity and substitute the country's first professorship of "Law & Police," meaning law and political science. Finally, the future leaders of Virginia could be formally trained by fellow Virginians in the art of politics and the science of republicanism.[133]

By 1780 Wythe's presence had already had a massive impact on education and politics in the state. As Jefferson informed Madison:

> Our new Institution at the College has had a success which has gained it universal applause. Wythe's school is numerous, they hold weekly Courts & Assemblies in the Capitol. The professors join in it, and the young men dispute with elegance, method & learning. This single school by throwing from time to time new hands well principled, & well informed into the legislature, will be of indefinite value.[134]

Wythe, who "seem[ed] to enjoy himself no where, so much as with his pupils," was not only holding traditional classes; he also set up a moot court and a mock legislative assembly in the Capitol Building for his students in order to give them experience in the roles for which many of them were destined.[135]

As Speaker of the House, Wythe was easily able to instruct his students in parliamentary procedure; and he used his and Jefferson's pet project—revising the laws—as an exercise for the students in constitutional theory. Every Saturday, his students would gather in the Capitol Building and "take under our consideration those Bills drawn up by the Comtee appointed to revise the laws, then we debate & alter (I will not say amend) with the greatest freedom." By participating, one shy young student hoped "to rub off that natural Bashfulness which at present is extremely prejudicial to me"; but at least he felt that "[t]hese Exercises, serve not only as the best amusement after severer studies, but are very usefull & attend with many important advantages."[136] Just as he had so successfully done with young Jefferson, Wythe was training the future leaders of Virginia. And though Wythe and Jefferson's efforts to curtail slavery had failed while they were legislators, when a discouraged Richard Price wrote to him in 1785 Jefferson was optimistic that those future leaders could still become convinced, as Jefferson himself had been, that slavery was immoral and a violation of natural law.

2. Writing *Notes on the State of Virginia*

From 1779 to 1783, the final four years of the Revolutionary War, Thomas Jefferson made two decisions that would eventually have outsized effects on antislavery thought in Virginia and beyond. Creating the Chair of Law and Police at William and Mary was the first; the antislavery professor George Wythe would train the future leaders of Virginia and of the nation, and several of his students—from Jefferson to St. George Tucker, William Short, and Richard Randolph—subsequently contributed in various ways to the antislavery movement. Jefferson's second decision seemed, at the time, far less consequential. In 1780 a Virginia congressman forwarded Jefferson a survey of sorts, originally sent out by the secretary of the French delegation in Philadelphia: a man named François, marquis de Barbé-Marbois. The French had at that point been aiding the Americans in their revolution for two years, but accurate information about the defiant former colonies was still relatively scarce in the Old World. Even in America, basic statistics on demographics, geography, and commerce were sparse. Marbois therefore sent a list of twenty-two queries to each congressional delegation; only two states responded.[1] Luckily for Marbois, one of those replies came from Jefferson, an avid naturalist and obsessive keeper of records. Luckily for the world, Jefferson was not content even with writing a detailed reply for Marbois; he decided to keep working on his answer for the next several years, and the resulting book is unique among early American literature. But what Jefferson could not have imagined when he first received the questionnaire in the winter of 1780 was that his reply would eventually become one of America's most significant works on race and slavery and that Virginia's legislators would still be referencing his words in their most important debate on that issue over fifty years later.

The history of this book—its composition, publication, and particularly its extensive revision—has only recently begun to be fully understood by historians, due in part to the way Jefferson himself misreported this process.[2] When he officially published it in English as

Notes on the State of Virginia in 1787, he added an explanatory notation after the title page: "The following Notes were written in Virginia in the year 1781, somewhat corrected and enlarged in the winter of 1782, for the use of a Foreigner of distinction." (In fact, in his first draft of this preface Jefferson stated that he wrote in 1781 and "corrected and enlarged in the winter of 1782–1783"—but he ultimately deleted "1783.") The reader should not expect too much from the *Notes*, the preface continues, for the "subjects are all treated imperfectly." This imperfect scholarship was due to the "circumstances of the time and place of their composition"—meaning an occupied state during a revolutionary war.[3] But almost every element of this preface is misleading.

Jefferson did indeed write in war-torn Virginia, among other places; and although he began to work on the project in 1780, he did write around forty pages in 1781. But the process of correcting and enlarging the *Notes* took place over the subsequent *four* years, in several locations; resulted in a project three times the size of the 1781 version; and was primarily motivated by an entirely different "Foreigner of distinction" than had prompted the project in the first place. So why did Jefferson write such a misleading preface? Perhaps he wished to minimize his labors as a way to preemptively discourage criticism of his book; he may have been acting in accordance with the convention of exaggerated authorial humility common at that time; or perhaps he simply placed more importance on the period of initial composition than on the period of revision. In any event, the ways in which Jefferson referred to his composition and revision process obscured the true intensity of his labors. Not until very recently has investigation into Jefferson's surviving manuscript enabled scholars to compile a fairly exact timeline for his revision process and therefore place the different sections of the *Notes* within the context of specific events and communications that inspired Jefferson to think differently about his topics.[4]

The "circumstances of the time and place" of composition and revision—from 1780 through 1785 in Virginia, Maryland, Pennsylvania, and Paris—included the darkest period of Jefferson's personal life, in addition to one of the worst moments of his political career. It was also a time of great upheaval in relationships between Virginians and their slaves. The Revolution created opportunities for enslaved people and indentured servants to run away from their masters to fight with the British. Some Virginians also chose to legally free their own slaves, after increasing pressure from Quaker emancipationists and willingness on the part of revolutionary legislators resulted in the passage of a private manumission law in 1782. Jefferson wrote about race and slavery during this time of immense upheaval, public debates over the humanity of black people and the morality of slavery, and growing fears of the possibility of former slaves rising up against their former masters. But this was also the period during which Jefferson felt the most hope regarding the future of freedom in Virginia: thanks to Jefferson's actions as governor, the liberal law professor George Wythe was in charge at the college in Williamsburg; more and more slaveholders were showing willingness to free their slaves; and a "ball of liberty" seemed ready to "roll round the globe."[5] Situating the *Notes* in the contexts of Jefferson's personal and professional dilemmas, his changing society, and his engagement with the wider Atlantic world serves to shed new light on the harshest criticism of slavery published by any of the Founders—as well as on one of the most deeply disturbing passages of racism.

In the eighteenth century, leading European scientists believed that the New World had an inferior climate (cold, damp) and that this moldy atmosphere rendered every bit of flora and fauna—including the American colonists themselves—inferior to their Old World counterparts.[6] The French were therefore understandably curious about their new allies. Marbois's twenty-two queries covered a wide variety of topics: colonial history; past and current political organization; a precise account of borders and cities; an estimate of the inhabitants, along with accounts of their religion, customs, and manners; the laws, currency, mineral riches, and geographical features; and many others.[7] When Jefferson received the list of questions in September or October 1780, he was delighted to answer them, being a compulsive observer of natural phenomena and a maker of lists who "always made it a practice whenever an opportunity occurred of obtaining any information of our country, which might be of use to me in any station public or private, to commit it to writing." Instead of merely answering the queries as Marbois listed them, Jefferson eventually rearranged and reworded the questions, making them both more logical and more comprehensive. He had already amassed a collection of state papers and histories of Virginia, and he had personally composed a variety of "memoranda" on the state, though they were disorganized and stored far from the capital, at Jefferson's mountaintop home.[8]

In November 1780, Jefferson told a friend that he was "busily employed for Monsr. Marbois . . . and have to acknolege to him the mysterious obligation for making me much better acquainted with my own country than I ever was before." Jefferson took "every occasion which presents itself of procuring answers" to Marbois's queries, but the reply could not be sent until he found "leisure" to travel to Monticello from the capital, where he was busily engaged in all the mundane and time-consuming details that came with being the state's governor.[9] Unfortunately for Jefferson, around the same time that Marbois had been composing his list of queries, General Benedict Arnold had also been planning his treason. Just after Christmas, Arnold invaded Virginia at the head of an army of Loyalists, Hessian mercenaries, and British regulars. He burned the state's capital city on 5 January 1781. Richmond fell with hardly a shot fired in its defense, a humiliation rendered even worse by the fact that the invasion was led by a traitor. The fallout from Arnold's campaign would change the course of Jefferson's political and scientific careers.

As governor, Jefferson's defense of his embattled state was complicated by the disadvantages of his position. In this newly formed republic, the executive branch was purposefully designed to be weak: the governor could not act without the consent of an eight-man council. The young Marquis de La Fayette (known as Lafayette in America) informed General Washington after observing the workings of the Virginian government: "The governor [Jefferson] does what he can. The wheels of his government are so very rusty that no governor whatever will be able to set them free."[10] Moreover, in 1781 Virginia was heavily indebted and constantly short on militia and supplies and was therefore ill-prepared for an invasion. Intelligence from the front lines was so spotty and slow to reach the capital that Jefferson recalled that Arnold's invading fleet "almost brought the first news themselves of their movements."[11] Fleeing as the sound of cannon fire reached his residence, Jefferson spent several days on horseback, first seeing his family to safety, then attempting to secure records and arms and to communicate with the scattered Virginian militia. Arnold's occupation of Richmond lasted only a few days before his forces withdrew to occupied Portsmouth, but it inflicted maximum damage to supplies and morale.[12]

Nonetheless, in March 1781, Jefferson informed Marbois that he intended to undertake a reply to the "sundry enquiries into the present state of Virginia" that had been passed on to him. Although "present occupations disable me from compleating" this research, Jefferson intended to retire from the governorship as soon as his second term ended, which would give him the necessary "leisure to take [it] up."[13] A peaceful transition to retired life was not to be, however. On 3 June Jefferson's term as governor officially ended; on 4 June the British invaded his hometown, aiming to capture Jefferson and several prominent members of the General Assembly who had retreated there.[14] After capturing seven legislators, British troops arrived at Monticello "about five minutes" after Jefferson made his escape through the woods.[15] Although the dragoons spared his residence, shortly afterward Lord Cornwallis made Jefferson's nearby Elkhill plantation his headquarters and destroyed Jefferson's crops, barns, livestock, and fences in what Jefferson bitterly described as a "spirit of total extermination."[16] Though Jefferson was a comparatively wealthy man, the extent of the devastation was no small matter, and he had trouble even paying his taxes the following year.[17]

Part of having an enslaved workforce was always being on the lookout for a rebellion, a fact that became all too clear when British leaders implemented a strategy of promising freedom to any enslaved people who fought against their Patriot masters. Two years before the Boston Tea Party the royal governor, Lord Dunmore, informed London that Virginians "with great reason . . . trembled" at the idea that slaves were "ready to join the first that would encourage them to revenge themselves, by which means a conquest of this Country would inevitably be effected in a very Short time." In 1775 Dunmore's Proclamation had put this strategy into effect. British officials were not motivated by antislavery sentiments; they desired to keep the colonial economy profitable, and slavery was necessary if that was to be. Offering emancipation was, for the British, a temporary, wartime necessity. But for white Virginians, who were already terrified of being murdered in their beds by their slaves, Dunmore's Proclamation had a unifying effect, providing yet another reason to support independence from Great Britain.[18]

Enslaved Virginians, by contrast, took advantage of this opportunity, many believing that the king truly wished to free them and care for them. The majority were disappointed, for Dunmore did not inoculate or properly provide for the hundreds of runaways who made it to his camps and ships. When Dunmore withdrew to New York in 1776, he took 500 formerly enslaved Virginians but left behind 1,000 who were dead or dying of smallpox. During the invasion of the summer of 1781, during which Jefferson had to flee from Monticello, 4,500 slaves ran from plantations—including some of Jefferson's. He later indignantly remembered that Cornwallis "carried off also about 30. slaves: had this been to give them freedom he would have done right, but it was to consign them to inevitable death from the small pox and putrid fever then raging in his camp. This I knew afterwards to have been the fate of 27. of them." Jefferson's personal records from the period, however, indicate that many of these slaves left with Cornwallis of their own free will, rather than being violently "carried off"; Jefferson's later description of the incident was filtered through his own perception of himself as a benevolent patriarch, deserving of loyalty even from unjustly enslaved people.[19]

In total, 6,000 Virginian slaves joined the British, and about a third of these were abandoned by the British to die of sickness or hunger. After the war, another third were taken to New York City, then evacuated to Nova Scotia and other locations within the British Empire, while the remaining third were returned to their masters. Another 500 enslaved Americans fought for the Patriot side, receiving their freedom as a reward.[20] The Revolutionary War taught Virginians two lessons: that their slaves' loyalty could not be counted on, and that African Americans could fight well. For many, including Jefferson, the experience also brought into sharp relief the paradoxes inherent in claiming to be fighting for liberty while "trampl[ing] on the rights" of half the state's inhabitants.[21]

Losing slaves to the British and to disease turned out to be the least of Jefferson's problems during that summer of 1781. The expiration of his term in June came at the worst possible time for the state, which was reeling from the invasion. In the panicked House of Delegates, Jefferson's political enemies almost succeeded in passing a measure calling for a military dictator to be installed in Jefferson's place—an antidemocratic scheme that Jefferson would heartily denounce in *Notes on the State of Virginia*.[22] Worse still, they opened an official inquiry into the conduct of the Executive (technically referring to the entire Executive Council but in practice directed at Jefferson alone) at the time of Arnold's invasion. Offended and humiliated by this unfair and public disapprobation, Jefferson would spend the summer of 1781 drafting an impassioned defense of his actions.[23]

While in refuge with his family at his Poplar Forest plantation in June, yet another hardship befell Jefferson: he was injured by a fall from his horse and was confined to bed from the end of June throughout much of July.[24] During his recuperation, Jefferson received startling news, forwarded to him by his new friend General Lafayette: not knowing about his trouble with the Virginia legislature, Congress had secretly appointed Jefferson to the five-man team that was to travel to Europe and negotiate with Great Britain.[25] Lafayette's correspondence arrived on 9 July, and Jefferson apparently agonized over his response for a month. In a letter to Congress begun on 10 July at Poplar Forest but not completed until 4 August at Monticello, Jefferson apologized for the delay in answering, blaming his injury and explaining that he was obliged to remain in the state "till a later season of the present year than the duties of this appointment would admit."[26] In a private letter to Lafayette, Jefferson explained more bluntly: his best efforts in aid of the revolutionary cause had "not been such as to give satisfaction to some of my countrymen and [it] has become necessary for me to remain in the state till a later period in the present [year]." The delay caused by the impending General Assembly inquiry into his conduct as governor would make it impossible for Jefferson to journey to Europe in time for the negotiations. Retirement was now all he had to look forward to.[27]

While he was in hiding from the invading forces at Poplar Forest in June and July 1781, "confined to his room by an accidental decrepitude," contemplating his coming trial in the General Assembly and agonizing over Congress's offer, Jefferson also began in earnest to write his response to Marbois's queries—or at least that is how he remembered it in a letter to Giovanni Fabbroni four years later.[28] To Marbois, Jefferson wrote that his response to the queries was delayed still further, until he was finally able to return to Monticello in August, at which point he "immediately engaged in the work of digesting the materials I had collected in answer to your quries, and supplying their defects." This process of sorting through his research notes and writings took only a "short time"—Jefferson initially wrote "a few days"—except for several sections that required information from "very distant parts of the country." Jefferson planned to delay finishing his manuscript until October, "when I hoped to get the information I wanted" while attending the General Assembly's next session. Presumably, this was information that representatives from those districts could give him or that was stored in the capital city.[29]

Marbois had to wait a bit longer, however, as Jefferson's ordeal with the General Assembly dragged on into the winter months. Not until December—after the British surrender at Yorktown—was he given the opportunity to defend himself to the House of Delegates. But by that point, his fellow assemblymen's desire to find a scapegoat for the disaster of Arnold's invasion had cooled; no one was willing to read the charges against Jefferson aloud. Jefferson therefore read them himself, and rebutted each point. On 19 December the House and Senate unanimously passed a resolution thanking Jefferson for his wartime service and declaring their high opinion of him.[30] Though exonerated and praised in the end, the whole incident deeply wounded Jefferson, who later described slander as "worse than assassination, theft, suicide or robbery." "I do not love difficulties," he told his friend Abigail Adams; "I am fond of quiet, willing to do my duty, but irritable by slander and apt to be forced by it to abandon my post."[31]

And that is exactly what Jefferson did in 1781: first turning down Congress's appointment to the European peace commission in August, and then—on the same December day that he was exonerated in the General Assembly—resigning his recent appointment to represent Virginia in Congress.[32] A few months later, Jefferson declined his election to the General Assembly, to which the state Speaker of the House responded by threatening to bring Jefferson to Richmond by force.[33] Jefferson wrote an impassioned letter responding to this situation. In addition to defending his right to choose to remain a private citizen for his family's sake, Jefferson explained that the several months' period between Nicholas's accusations being made and the General Assembly's exoneration of Jefferson's actions had been torture, for "I had been suspected and suspended in the eyes of the world without the least hint then or afterwards made public which might restrain them from supposing I stood arraigned for treasons of the heart and not mere weaknesses of the head." After serving his country for thirteen years, "so totally abandon[ing] all attention to my private affairs as to permit them to run into great disorder and ruin," he felt that the "only reward I ever asked or could have felt"—the "affection of my countrymen"—had been taken from him. The fact that members of the legislature, who should have known better, were the ones accusing Jefferson "inflicted a wound on my spirit which will only be cured by the all-healing grave."[34] The opinion of his colleagues in the General Assembly, and of the public in general, mattered greatly to Jefferson. He was willing to do his duty—but only when his doing so earned him the esteem of his fellows. Criticism was his weak spot.

Retirement from public life did finally afford Jefferson the leisure to focus on something else that brought him only satisfaction: his research into matters philosophical and scientific. As if to mark his transition from the life of a public statesman to that of a private philosopher, on 20 December 1781, more than one year after first receiving the queries—and exactly one day after being exonerated by the General Assembly—Jefferson finally mailed his answers to Marbois. No copy of this original text is extant, but since a later iteration had "swelled nearly to treble bulk" compared to the original, and that later iteration was 104 pages long, the document that Marbois received may have been around thirty-five to forty pages in length.[35] Jefferson self-effacingly described it in his cover letter as "very imperfect and not worth offering but as a proof of my respect for your wishes."[36] And Jefferson was truly dissatisfied with his work, knowing that he had not been able to collect all the information that was available due to the dislocations of war.[37]

It took many more weeks for this manuscript to actually reach Marbois, but on 22 April 1782 Marbois ebulliently informed Jefferson that it had arrived. "I cannot express to you how grateful I am," he wrote, "for the trouble you have taken to draft detailed responses to the questions I had taken the liberty of addressing to you. The Philosophy which has inspired them, the understanding they give me . . . created the most valuable work that I could take from this country."[38] Marbois also complimented Jefferson for his "candidness and Frankness" in discussing political matters, attributes that seemed to Marbois to be those of a "true statesman" who saw that a republican society's defects should not remain hidden. Unfortunately, since no copy of this original manuscript survives, we can only speculate as to which matters Jefferson discussed so frankly in this first iteration of the *Notes*. Jefferson would continue his frankness in the revised version, to the extent that he would attempt to keep its contents hidden from the general public until forced—by the untimely death of a British spy, of all things—to authorize its publication.

Although the *Notes* had begun as Jefferson's attempt to satisfy the French delegation's curiosity, not long after he commenced his research he realized that the document he was crafting could have value for fellow Americans as well. In February 1781—a month before Jefferson informed Marbois that he was working on a response to the queries— the secretary of the prestigious American Philosophical Society (APS) wrote to inform Jefferson that he had been elected to a two-year term in that body. Originally founded by Benjamin Franklin in 1743 and similar to the Royal Society of London, the APS was revised in 1769 for the purpose of "Promoting Useful Knowledge," encompassing both technological and scientific investigations. Its membership grew to include leading American statesmen and European scholars, including eminent French naturalists such as the Comte de Buffon, the Abbé Raynal, and Condorcet.[39] The turmoil caused by the invasion, the fall from his horse, and the impending trial at the General Assembly all distracted Jefferson from his APS appointment over the ensuing months. But being vindicated in December allowed Jefferson to contemplate new pursuits: on the same date that he sent off his manuscript to Marbois, Jefferson also wrote a letter to Charles Thomson, the longtime congressional secretary and a man of science who had also recently been elected to the APS. Although Jefferson was still "quite a stranger" to the duties of APS members, "in framing answers to some queries which Monsr. de Marbois sent me, it occurred to me that some of the subjects which I had then occasion to take up, might, if more fully handled, be a proper tribute to the Philosophical society." Since Marbois and Thomson both lived in Philadelphia, Jefferson asked Thomson if—as "my antient friend"—he would be willing to "take some spare half hour" and examine Jefferson's answers to Marbois. Perhaps Thomson could "take the trouble of communicating to me your opinion whether any and which of the subjects there treated would come within the scope of that learned institution, and to what degree of minuteness one should descend in treating it."[40]

Even before reading the manuscript, Thomson sent an encouraging reply to Jefferson: not only did he believe that "your answers to Mr. Marbois queries will be an acceptable present" for the APS, but Thomson also thought Jefferson should broaden his scope of investigation. The whole of the country presented a naturalist's dream, "an extensive, rich[,] and unexplored field" positively ripe for inquiry and experimentation by people like Jefferson. Unlike Europeans who held that the New World's climate rendered it inhospitable to life, Thomson was optimistic that agriculture's potential was untapped, and even the "human mind" itself seemed to be "just awakening from a long stupor of many ages to the discovery of useful Arts and inventions." Little was known about the Native peoples; the state governments were "yet unformed and capable of great improvements." Someone like Jefferson, "of a contemplative and philosophical turn," would have an "inexhaustible" source of subjects to investigate. Future generations were fortunate that Jefferson was "retiring from the busy anxious scenes of politics" and could therefore devote himself to the research and writing that would benefit them.[41] Since Jefferson felt that his political career had just come to an abrupt and humiliating end, this letter must have provided him with a much-needed source of inspiration; the world of science encouraged Jefferson to step away from politics and toward the other great love of his intellectual life, expressed so well in the nascent *Notes on the State of Virginia*.[42] All subjects, Thomson wrote, should be considered within Jefferson's scope.

Another encouragement arrived in the person of François-Jean de Beauvoir, chevalier de Chastellux (soon to become the Marquis de Chastellux). Serving in America as a major general in Rochambeau's army, Chastellux was a member of the French Academy (a small, eminent body established in the seventeenth century for the regulation of the French language) and a noted author of such works as the 1772 social history *De la Félicité Publique* (An essay on public happiness). In recognition of Chastellux's achievements, the College of William and Mary bestowed on him an honorary doctorate of "civil Laws" in March 1782.[43] In April, Chastellux continued his journey across Virginia, making observations for his forthcoming work *Travels in North America* (1786). For three days he stayed with Jefferson at Monticello, and the men became close friends. Although Chastellux initially found Jefferson's manner to be "grave and even cold," after two hours Chastellux felt as though "we had spent our whole lives together."[44] Jefferson—"not yet forty, tall, and with a mild and pleasing countenance . . . a philosopher, in voluntary retirement from the world"—had withdrawn to "the arts and sciences" and to his "mild and amiable wife," then heavily pregnant with their fifth daughter.[45] He and Chastellux passed several happy hours playing chess and discussing a variety of subjects, including Jefferson's project for Marbois.[46] They likely also discussed the theories of climate degeneration propagated by Buffon and other European scientists, for as Chastellux's account of his North American travels indicates, he was keenly interested in the relative sizes of Old and New World animals.[47]

Jefferson would later inform his former guardian and longtime friend, the explorer and physician Dr. Thomas Walker, that he began writing the *Notes* "in answer to certain queries sent me by Monsr. de Marbois in 1781" but continued to work on them because "another foreigner of my acquaintance"—meaning Chastellux—"having asked a copy of them, I undertook to revise and correct them in some degree."[48] Jefferson therefore specifically identified two reasons for his continued work on his answers to Marbois's queries. As a result of his correspondence with Charles Thomson, Jefferson realized that further research would expand scientific knowledge of the New World in a manner befitting a member of the American Philosophical Society. And in response to the curiosity of his new friend Chastellux—a prominent European scholar, after all—who wanted to read his work and who perhaps drew Jefferson's attention in particular to the intriguing matter of refuting Buffon's and other's scurrilous theories about American degeneracy, Jefferson was further inspired to extend his work.[49] He was excited at the prospect of increasing knowledge of Virginia for the APS, an organization whose membership included leading European scientists as well as the greatest minds in America. And the chance to represent his "country" in Europe was significant, for without European support the newly independent republic could not endure. Chastellux has not received sufficient credit for his role in motivating Jefferson to revise and expand his earlier project. No sooner had Chastellux left Monticello than he began reminding Jefferson that he owed Chastellux: he had promised Chastellux that he would allow him to read his completed observations on Virginia, and Chastellux was determined to collect on that debt.[50]

Jefferson would need his friend's encouragement more than he realized: shortly after the French party departed, Jefferson's wife, Martha, fell seriously ill following the difficult birth of their daughter Lucy Elizabeth on 8 May.[51] Jefferson spent the summer either by Martha's side or writing at a small table nearby; since he corresponded very little during this period, it seems likely that he distracted himself from his wife's suffering by focusing on elaborating his answers to Marbois. On 6 September Martha passed away, and Jefferson entered a deep depression.[52] He was still an elected member of the General Assembly, and the impatient delegates finally sent the sergeant-at-arms to escort him to their session on 8 November. But the grieving husband's condition was apparently so pitiable that he was released from further duty on the same day.[53]

Jefferson's salvation arrived in the form of a new appointment from Congress: correctly guessing that "the death of Mrs. Jefferson had probably changed the sentiments of Mr. Jefferson with regard to public life," Congress unanimously reappointed Jefferson "minister plenipotentiary for negotiating peace," giving him back the opportunity that his troubles with the General Assembly had stolen the previous fall.[54] Even better, Jefferson heard that Chastellux would be leaving for France around the same time as his own scheduled departure, and thus in November Jefferson informed his new friend that "my only object now is . . . to be ready to join you in your voiage, fondly measuring your affections by my own and presuming your consent." Receiving Chastellux's letters after his beloved wife's death had helped to pull Jefferson from a "stupor of mind" that had rendered him "dead to the world"; now he looked forward to a long, companionable transatlantic voyage that would give him "full Leisure . . . to communicate to you my answers to the queries of Monsr. de Marbois."[55] The *Notes* were once again on Jefferson's mind, and the prospect of sharing his research with other inquiring minds gave him something (besides his daughters) to live for.

Jefferson spent the winter of 1782–1783 in Philadelphia and Baltimore, waiting for the ice to thaw and enjoying some time with Chastellux before their anticipated departure.[56] But when word arrived that peace had already been finalized in Europe and his mission was therefore no longer necessary, Jefferson returned to Virginia; Chastellux departed for France without him. Back at Monticello for the summer of 1783, the widowed Jefferson threw himself into reorganizing his massive library—and into finishing what was swiftly becoming his own respectably sized book. By the time he departed for Philadelphia on 16 October to once again represent Virginia in Congress, Jefferson had written out a 104-page "fair copy"—a version of the manuscript that incorporated all the changes up to that point and to whose pages Jefferson added all additional sections from then on.[57] It is this fair copy manuscript that survives today at the Massachusetts Historical Society, and it is invaluable to scholars because every change Jefferson made between October 1783 and the time of its printing in 1785 is visible in the pasted-on and interlinear additions and the crossed-out deletions. By the time Jefferson was done revising, it had grown to 116 full pages of text, plus numerous tabs of paper affixed to the preexisting pages with sealing wax, as well as several appendices—140 full pages in total.[58] When disassembled, the entire manuscript comprises 133 individual leaves and tabs.[59]

Over the course of that summer of 1783, Jefferson had sent pages of text to several friends, asking for their expertise on a variety of topics; he incorporated their replies as additions to the "fair copy" manuscript, and when he departed to join the Congress in Annapolis on 16 October, he took a circuitous route so as to conduct further research on several natural features, documenting them on additional tabs.[60] Since this method of pasting tabs onto tabs every time he wrote an addition was rendering the manuscript rather unwieldy, and since it had drastically increased in size since 1781, Jefferson decided that a printed copy would be the best way to share his work with the American Philosophical Society and with his interested friends, especially Chastellux. While passing through Philadelphia that November, he showed the book to the printer and bookbinder Robert Aitken, who gave him an estimate of "£4. a sheet."[61] Despite being quoted this reasonable price, Jefferson left Philadelphia with only the handwritten manuscript in hand. He was not finished revising it yet.

Jefferson resided in Annapolis for five and a half months, through the winter of 1783 and the spring of 1784, and when not in congressional meetings he continued to paste new sections onto his manuscript, crossing out and covering up old ones as he went along. In January he informed Chastellux that the version he had seen—probably the previous year, in December 1782 when they spent a few days in Philadelphia together—should no longer be trusted. Using a "little leisure" time in order to revise his "answers to Mons. de Marbois' queries," Jefferson had found "some things should be omitted, many corrected, and more supplied and enlarged. They are swelled to nearly treble bulk." Because this new size was "now too much for M.S. copies," meaning copies written out by hand, Jefferson planned in the spring "to print a dozen or 20 copies to be given to my friends, not suffering another [manuscript copy?] to go out."[62]

He also continued to gather information from his network of scientifically minded friends, although their slow responses to his requests sometimes caused Jefferson not a little consternation. One correspondent, Isaac Zane, delayed for nine months in sending Jefferson the temperature readings of the cave Jefferson needed to complete Query V (the chapter about Virginia's "Cascades and Caverns"). By May 1784 Jefferson must have been in a frenzy, since he had not heard from Zane and was so near completing all other aspects of his book that he was negotiating with the printer in Philadelphia again. Fortunately for Zane, Aitken had not only raised his price since Jefferson's last enquiry; he also could not print it for three weeks, which was longer than Jefferson could afford to wait.[63] On 7 May he had been appointed minister plenipotentiary to France by Congress. Writing home to Virginia, Jefferson asked Madison to give Zane a message in person: "[T]ell him I have written three letters to him and find him unpunctual." If Zane did ever take the needed measurements, he should send them "to Paris. I could not get my notes printed here and therefore refer it till I shall cross the water where I will have a few copies struck off and send you one."[64] Zane's information finally reached Jefferson, and a darker shade of ink clearly distinguishes his temperature readings from what Jefferson had previously written in the manuscript.[65]

At least one other European had the opportunity to view the manuscript during the period of revision in Annapolis: a brilliant and effusive young Dutchman named G. K. van Hogendorp, whom Jefferson befriended during the cold Maryland winter.[66] Hogendorp's reflections on Jefferson's character and conduct were published by the Dutchman's descendants. From them we learn that during this time Jefferson was still deep in the grieving process for his wife; that he spent his free moments shut up in his room, reading and writing; and that "the gradual emancipation of the Negroes is one of his favorite projects."[67] Hogendorp and Jefferson may have been discussing the plan for emancipation that Jefferson included in Query XIV ("Laws"), since Hogendorp recalled that he read Jefferson's manuscript while walking in the woods behind Jefferson's residence. After the book was printed, Jefferson reminded Hogendorp that, at the time he first viewed the manuscript, its condition proved "how hastily [it] had been originally written"; the document contained "numerous insertions I had made in them from time to time, when I could find a moment for turning to them from other occupations."[68]

Charles Thomson, Jefferson's friend and fellow American Philosophical Society member, was also in Annapolis during the winter and spring of 1783–1784. Since Thomson had been one of the first people to encourage Jefferson in his quest to write a philosophical treatise, it must have given the Irish-born American great satisfaction to read an almost-completed manuscript. Sometime after 26 March, and before Jefferson left Annapolis on 11 May, Thomson wrote a thirty-three-page commentary for Jefferson, offering numerous suggestions for alterations and additions.[69] Jefferson ignored some of his friend's ideas, but he also altered his manuscript drastically in response to parts of Thomson's critique. He even added several pages from the commentary—mostly those parts pertaining to Native cultures—as the first appendix to the *Notes*. The most significant part of Thomson's commentary for this discussion, however, consists of the very last few sentences. If Jefferson had taken the advice Thomson gave him in those sentences, modern readers would look much more kindly upon him.

Thomson's advice concerned Query XIV ("Laws"), in which Jefferson discussed the "remarkable alterations proposed" to the legal code by the committee on which he and Wythe had served from 1777 to 1779.[70] Jefferson devoted particular attention to the bill concerning slaves, revising this section of the *Notes* several times.[71] These revisions perhaps indicate that Jefferson and Wythe, when they first worked on the bill, had difficulty deciding how best to present it to the General Assembly. Jefferson initially wrote that their final committee report included a straightforward gradual emancipation bill and that although "the bill . . . does not proceed to say what shall be done with them [the freed slaves] after their birth . . . an amendment was prepared" containing a plan for colonization. However—perhaps after checking his records to see exactly what the bill contained?—Jefferson realized that the proposal to "emancipate all slaves born after passing the act" was not actually included in the bill itself but was rather also written in an amendment. He therefore scratched out the middle part of that sentence, changing it to "the bill . . . does not itself contain this [emancipation] proposition; but an amendment containing it was prepared." As we have seen, Jefferson and Wythe eventually decided not to present the amendment to the General Assembly with the rest of their report, apparently feeling that public opinion—or what Jefferson referred to in the *Notes* as "the public mind"—was not yet willing to "bear the proposition" of ending slavery.[72]

Jefferson's alterations to the manuscript raise an interesting question: Did he and Wythe initially intend to include a wholesale gradual emancipation bill in the report to the General Assembly, later decide to place the measure in an amendment, and finally choose to hold that amendment back until a more propitious time? Because the antislavery amendment is one of several of the revision committee's bills that is no longer extant (and no complete report was ever published), some scholars have speculated that Jefferson was being less than truthful in his *Notes* about the existence of an antislavery amendment.[73] But given that he was collaborating with his old law professor and lifelong antislavery advocate Wythe, this seems unlikely; proposing emancipation would have been one of Wythe's priorities too. Moreover, since both Wythe and the other committee member, Edmund Pendleton, were still alive when Jefferson wrote the *Notes*, he must have known that they could have contradicted his account had he embellished it in any way.

Not satisfied with simply mentioning the existence of an emancipation amendment, Jefferson proceeded to list, in detail, all the elements of the plan that he and Wythe had devised. For the rest of his life Jefferson referred to the three main elements of their plan, elements that aligned with his philosophy of natural rights and of the capacity of man for improvement, as the best possible way forward for Virginia's enslaved population: *emancipation*, *education*, and *expatriation*. Freedom should come, he proposed, to the entire generation of slaves born once the act passed. The state should provide funds to train the freed children "according to their geniusses," giving education in agriculture, arts, or science according to the talent of the individual. As Arthur Scherr notes, this educational plan "was perhaps the most startling

proposal for black education until . . . the late 1960s, theoretically providing the emancipated black [people] with greater access to schooling
than most Southern whites of [Jefferson's] time."[74] Finally, when the
freed children reached adulthood, the state was to equip them with
everything needed to begin a successful colony of their own and then
send them to "such place as the circumstances of the time should render most proper." Virginia should continue to support the colony until
it became self-sufficient.[75]

Expatriating former slaves—sending them to a colony outside the
United States—was not a new idea; northern emancipationists and
even some enslaved people were promoting this idea before the Revolutionary War.[76] But Jefferson's *Notes* was the first American publication
to carefully outline a rationale for colonization that appealed to notions
of national identity, to the concept of restitution for the sin of slavery,
and to the need for racial separation—which can be identified as one
early form of the infamous "separate but equal" argument.[77] As Peter
Onuf has argued convincingly, colonization was a necessary part of Jefferson's emancipation bill because he conceived of African-descended
slaves as "a distinct nation," made one people through their experience
of "captivity, transportation[,] and amalgamation" in the New World.
Therefore, "crimes against slaves"—for Jefferson did view enslaving Africans as a crime—"had to be understood in national terms." Changing
the laws to allow individual owners to free their slaves (something that
had only just occurred, in 1782) was not good enough; freeing slaves
and allowing them to remain in the country that had oppressed them
would also not suffice, for, "[d]efining slavery as a state of war, Jefferson
could only conceive of its abolition in terms of a peace that would secure the independence and integrity of two distinct nations, each with
its own 'country.'"[78]

To the obvious objection—why not simply incorporate the freed
slaves into the republic?—Jefferson gave several answers in his *Notes*:
"Deep rooted prejudices entertained by the whites; ten thousand recollections, by the blacks, of the injuries which they have sustained; new
provocations; the real distinctions which nature has made; and many
other circumstances." All of these issues, Jefferson believed, "will divide
us into parties, and produce convulsions which will probably never

end but in the extermination of one or the other race." Because black and white composed two distinct nations, the sins of the one could not be overlooked by the other. Restitution must be made by helping the "captive nation" become prosperous and independent, otherwise race war was inevitable.[79]

The most troubling portion of the *Notes*, to some readers of his day and most of our own, was next: rather than simply outlining the political reasons why the two races could not peacefully coexist, Jefferson proceeded to give an extremely derogatory summary of ways in which he believed black people to be inferior to whites—differences in color, in beauty, in hair texture, in the amount of sleep needed, in the ability to love and to grieve. The two races were equal in their capacity for memory, he believed, but not in imagination or reason.[80] Acknowledging that the causes of racial difference were still undergoing scientific inquiry, and therefore "many observations" were still required to "justify a general conclusion," Jefferson nonetheless expressed a belief that racial differences were so numerous and significant that the white and black races should be kept "as distinct as nature has formed them."[81]

Because of Jefferson's stature in the American mind, and because of his work's place in the American canon, his discourse on race has attracted much scrutiny from scholars who have traced subsequent strains of proslavery discourse back to this source, positing that Jefferson was creating a new, virulent form of distinctly American racism. It would be difficult, however, to show that this was his intent. As we have seen, Jefferson initially revised the *Notes* because he wished to offer it as a contribution to a network of scientists and intellectuals, including members of the relatively new American Philosophical Society and the long-established Académie Française. As a scholarly text, the *Notes* had to engage with other significant works of scholarship, including a large body of French work on racial differences. Moreover, when this text is considered in the context of the political and social climate of 1780s Virginia, and of Jefferson's extensive revision process, it becomes apparent that he included a discussion of race in part to justify his plan for spending large amounts of tax revenue on freeing, providing for, educating, equipping, transporting, and supporting Virginia's labor force as they created their own country somewhere else—"free and independent"—and on importing white laborers to replace them. Incredible as it seems today, Jefferson did *not* include several pages of racist observations in his *Notes* simply because he was prejudiced against African Americans; he also included them because he was antislavery.

There is, of course, a major paradox in writing about the inferiority of African people in order to justify freeing them from slavery—and Charles Thomson had the foresight to point this out to Jefferson. In the last suggestion he offered in his commentary, Thomson began by criticizing a short reference Jefferson had made to a Roman leader's unscrupulous treatment of his female slaves. He continued by suggesting Jefferson remove not only his comparative history of Roman slavery and Virginian slavery but also all of what he had written about race:

> The reflections on Cato's conduct are not worthy a place here and wd. therefore propose to expunge them, & a great deal of p 70—because many people encourage & comfort themselves in keeping slaves because they do not treat them as bad as others have done. And though I am much pleased with the dissertation on the difference between the Whites & blacks & am inclined to think the latter a race lower in the scale of being yet for that very reason & *because such an opinion might seem to justify slavery* I should be inclined to leave it out.[82]

It is a stunning suggestion, both praising the hard intellectual work Jefferson had put into crafting his dissertation on racial difference—a dissertation that, as we shall see, drew upon both ongoing regional debates and the most advanced scientific thought of the day—and arguing that Jefferson's racial speculation could have an (unintended) proslavery implication. Although it seems obvious to modern readers that what we now understand to be racist descriptions of African people served to justify their enslavement, some of the brightest minds of the eighteenth century failed to comprehend their complicity in perpetuating the slave trade by preserving negative stereotypes of Africans. In order to fully understand Jefferson's discourse on race, it is first necessary to consider those Enlightenment sources from which he drew, for Jefferson did not invent a new strand of racist physiology for modern

Americans to find in his *Notes*. And in order to understand the ways in which Jefferson revised his *Notes* after receiving Thomson's critique, it is first necessary to see this text as part of an emerging public debate about the nature of slavery in the Virginian republic.

In 1782, the year that Jefferson began revising his answers to Marbois, most people of African descent in Virginia were living as the property of about half the white citizens.[83] Many of those same white citizens also happened to be the only people who met the requirements for voting, since the reigning political wisdom held that none but substantial landholders had enough of a stake in the community to be responsible participants in its government. At the same time, as we have seen, seminal anti- and proslavery arguments were beginning to be articulated publicly. Antislavery sentiment had begun to percolate through the state during the 1760s, partly as a result of rising religious conviction and partly as a result of Enlightenment philosophies being imported along with European professors like William Small.

The first elite Virginian to publish an antislavery argument was Arthur Lee, whose 1767 newspaper essay "Address on Slavery" drew upon natural rights theorists and the Bible to demonstrate that slavery was "a violation both of justice and religion." And though slaves from Africa were obtained "by violence, artifice[,] and treachery" on the part of "British merchants," supported by the British parliament—not by the American colonists—that was no excuse for Virginians to keep their slaves. On Judgment Day, God would still hold them accountable for "breaking a law too plain to be misunderstood"—"do unto others as you would they should do unto you." In case the philosophical and theological rationale for the immorality of slavery was not convincing enough, Lee issued a severe warning: a slave uprising, falling upon "us, or on our posterity," would "inevitably" occur. Lee cited horrific examples, from ancient Rome to contemporary Jamaica, to scare Virginians into action.[84]

It must be noted, however, that Lee was not motivated to emancipate slaves by an unequivocal belief in the natural equality of man. He considered Africans to be an "abject, coward race," and "as cowards are invariably cruel," white people could expect no mercy in case of a slave uprising. In response to Adam Smith's heated critique of slaveholding colonists in North America, Lee defensively referred to Africans as "a race the most vile and detestable that ever the earth has produced." In a moment of supreme irony, Lee continued his attack on Smith: "Prejudice is indeed a stain that will fasten on the best minds." This maxim would prove true for Lee and almost every other enlightened and liberal Virginian of that period who fought to end slavery.[85]

Lee's antislavery "Address" was considered so controversial that *The Virginia Gazette, and Weekly Advertiser* printer William Rind refused to publish the second part of it. However, other newspapers did publish letters by proslavery individuals whose antiblack prejudice lined up perfectly with their support for enslaved labor. One such 1773 essay was written by an anonymous author who claimed that African peoples were not "the same Species of Man with the White People" but rather were "formed in common with Horses, Oxen, Dogs &c, for the Benefit of the white People alone, to be used [by] them either for Pleasure, or to labour with their *other* Beasts."[86] Even before the concentrated antislavery movements of the nineteenth century developed to challenge them, southern slaveholders were utilizing dehumanizing rhetoric to defend their peculiar institution.

As Jefferson was beginning to expand his *Notes* at his wife's bedside in the summer of 1782, the controversy over slavery heated up again. In May the *The Virginia Gazette, and Weekly Advertiser* became the site of a public debate over the implication of revolutionary principles for slaveholders.[87] The first entrant to the debate was a (probably Quaker) writer calling himself "A Friend to Liberty"; he argued that practicing slavery while fighting for liberty was inconsistent. Since God was just, and slavery was unjust, Americans should ask themselves "how can we expect he will decide [the Revolutionary War] in our favor?" Echoing many similar Revolution-era warnings, particularly in northern states, "A Friend to Liberty" wrote that in order to avoid "divine retribution," Virginians should "release our slaves from bondage" immediately.[88]

Perhaps "A Friend to Liberty" was part of a contingent of Quakers who were in the midst of a renewed antislavery lobbying effort at the General Assembly. Shortly after his essay was published a manumission measure finally passed, due largely to the Quakers' persistence and the fortuitous presence in the legislature of "a set of liberal-spirited

members," as one of the Quakers put it. The manumission bill, probably similar to the one Jefferson first advocated in 1769, allowed private
individuals to free their slaves—albeit under a strict set of conditions,
of course.[89] Its passage marked the start of a very short period during which (typically religious) individuals freed slaves for antislavery
reasons (by the mid-1790s, the promise of emancipation was unfortunately being used by many as a tool to manipulate slaves to work
harder).[90]

In August and September, two rebuttals to "A Friend to Liberty" were
published in the same newspaper, listing a range of reasons why slavery should continue. One writer, styling himself "A Holder of Slaves,"
pointed out that "thousands of our best citizens" held property in slaves;
and even if reasons could be found to take that property away from
them, what then should happen to the freed slaves? If allowed to live
nearby, they might wage "war [against] their former masters," something that Dunmore's Proclamation had just made a terrifying reality
to Virginians; or if allowed to remain in the same neighborhoods, they
would be "ravishing and cohabitating with our white women, and in a
century or less, our offspring would be a mixed mongrel of mulattoes,
of whites and blacks, bays, chestnuts, sorrels, and skewbalds"—terms
normally reserved for horses and implying that mixed-race children
would be less than human. Slaves should also be kept, "A Holder of
Slaves" went on, because their labor freed white men to cultivate their
minds. Half a century before John C. Calhoun set forth his "positive
good" argument, Virginians were already arguing that civilization depended on slavery.[91]

A second rebuttal to the antislavery essay by "A Friend to Liberty,"
attributed in the *Gazette* to "A Scribbler," contended that slavery was
not even wrong in the first place; it was actually "sanctioned by the
concurrence of all nations, even those we enslave." And Africans, more
than anyone else, deserved to be enslaved. In a diatribe on racial difference, the proslavery "A Scribbler" disagreed with natural scientists like
Buffon, who held that racial differences were caused by environmental
factors. For "A Scribbler," race was obviously biological and immutable.
The "organs, passions, and appetites" all marked people of African descent as savage, they could never change, and they therefore were fit

for nothing more than "the state of slavery in which they have for a great length of time been held by us, with as much general happiness to themselves, as they seem susceptible of."[92] Interestingly, according to Eva Sheppard Wolf, neither "A Holder of Slaves" nor "A Scribbler" evinced any sense of alarm in their rebuttals; the two anonymous writers "did not perceive A Friend to Liberty's words to be a grave threat." Instead, "Virginia slaveholders saw the antislavery writers of the 1770s and early 1780s more as noisome mosquitoes to be shooed away than as menacing foes to be engaged in battle."[93] That would change a few short years later when Jefferson's *Notes* was officially published.

Jefferson spent a fortnight catching up on all the political news in Richmond in April and May 1783, shortly after the debate took place. While he was there, he would almost certainly have stopped by the *Gazette* office to get copies of the recent editions, as was his long-standing habit.[94] He was just about to spend the summer writing at Monticello. And as we shall see, several parts of his writings clearly reflect the language and topics of this publicly printed conversation. Unlike the anonymous Quaker, however, Jefferson was working on a document that, if published, would forever be attributed to him. Engaging in a printed war of words with proslavery Virginians was not his goal; his intended audience at this point was merely a small circle of transatlantic intellectuals. Always sensitive to personal criticism—and particularly so after his recent humiliation in the General Assembly—even when he became the leader of America's first opposition party, Jefferson hardly ever engaged his opponents head-on. He always encouraged other like-minded men to do the writing for him, or he communicated his sentiments in privately written letters to carefully chosen individuals. On the volatile issue of slavery, Jefferson never claimed to have a desire to lead the charge for reform. But receiving Thomson's commentary in 1784 apparently caused Jefferson to reconsider how men like "A Holder of Slaves" and "A Scribbler" would interpret his *Notes*. Thomson made an appeal to Jefferson's sense of responsibility to his audience, and Jefferson responded by making his comments even more unmistakably antislavery.

Thomson's major critique of Jefferson was that his "dissertation on the difference between the Whites and blacks" could "seem to justify slavery." Why had Jefferson written such a long "dissertation" in the first place rather than simply referencing common racial attitudes as a reason for colonization and then moving on? In his *Notes*, Jefferson deliberately presented himself as a participant in an ongoing transatlantic scientific discourse. When he discussed the "real distinctions which nature has made" between white and black people—mentioning as possible causes "the reticular membrane between the skin and scarfskin," the "colour of the blood, the colour of the bile," or "some other secretion"—Jefferson was referencing debates dating to 1618, when the Parisian anatomist Jean Riolan the Younger performed the first dissection of black skin.[95] From that time onward, European intellectuals had been seeking the precise reasons for racial difference, disagreeing on whether humans descended from a single set of parents (monogenesis) or were the product of multiple creations (polygenesis), but in general concurring that blackness was inferior to—possibly a degenerated form of—whiteness.

The most comprehensive scientific publication of its day was the *Encyclopédie*, edited primarily by Denis Diderot (1713–1784) and published in a series of volumes from 1751 to 1772.[96] In November 1780, as Jefferson began his work for Marbois, he wrote that he was "exceedingly anxious to get a copy of Le grande Encyclopedie," though he worried about its high cost and the difficulty of obtaining it.[97] The war apparently made delivery of packages in and out of Virginia rather challenging. But happily, the December issue of *The Virginia Gazette* advertised that "the Encyclopedy or Dictionary of Arts and Sciences, printed in *French*," was available for sale in Alexandria. Acting in his official capacity as governor, Jefferson promptly asked his Executive Council to approve the purchase of the *Encyclopédie* for the state of Virginia, and upon gaining their consent he sent off instructions to buy the work for 15,068 pounds of tobacco.[98]

Jefferson may have purchased the *Encyclopédie* for the state, but he borrowed it for himself right away—on 5 July 1782, the Executive Council issued a resolution asking for Jefferson to return it. Perhaps distracted by his wife's illness or by his ongoing work on the *Notes*, Jefferson must not have returned it at that point, for when the president of the College of William and Mary, the Reverend James Madison, asked to borrow it the following year, Governor Benjamin Harrison had to send for it from Monticello.[99] The *Encyclopédie* was a multivolume compendium of tens of thousands of articles; its broad coverage of topics proved informative but was also somewhat contradictory, since it reflected the work of many authors over a period of twenty-one years. Several of those authors dealt with the topic of race, which in the eighteenth century was a term that "connoted roughly geographic groups of people marked by supposedly common physical characteristics" or was used to distinguish all members of the "human race" from the other species—but was also increasingly employed to differentiate between superior (white) and inferior (usually everyone else) humans.[100]

Several scholars have argued that Jefferson's racial discourse was new, or particularly vile for its day, but a comparison of his work with the sources he was familiar with and referenced in the *Notes*—the writers of the *Encyclopédie* and other European treatises, primarily published *before* 1785—demonstrates that, as Bruce Dain puts it, Jefferson's "understanding of natural science . . . was not prescient. It was in fact based on what were becoming, by the 1780s, rather old-fashioned Enlightenment concepts" rooted in what someone could perceive through the senses (and particularly in the aesthetic sense) rather than in questions of anatomical structure or causes of difference.[101] Jefferson certainly could—and should—have updated his views on race over ensuing years, when writers such as Condorcet began to point out that naturalists' speculations regarding black peoples' origins and supposed inferiority were helping to strengthen the proslavery cause. But his *Notes* was a product of the early 1780s, relying on texts that were already published; it must be understood in the context of what Jefferson had experienced and read at that time.

Europeans had been struggling to categorize people with dark skin for centuries: the historian James Sweet points out that European notions of African inferiority did not originate with the Atlantic slave trade but rather can be traced to Islamic conceptions of Africans as far back as the eighth century. From Iberia to North Africa to Persia, "blackness equaled slavery . . . and the degradation that slavery implied," and in places where people of all races were enslaved, harsher forms of treatment for dark-skinned people were justified using environmental, cultural, and theological rationales that would be familiar to scholars of eighteenth- and nineteenth-century America.[102] Just as Jefferson would later do in *Notes on the State of Virginia*, slaveholding intellectuals described differences between themselves and their dark-skinned slaves in terms of smell as well as appearance, mental capability, and character.[103] As in some Enlightenment scientific thought, in the medieval world climactic factors were blamed for Africans having hot tempers: "[T]heir humors fiery, their color black and their hair woolly . . . they lack self-control and steadiness of mind and are overcome by fickleness, foolishness, and ignorance."[104] Islamic readings of the story of Noah and Ham contributed to notions of black peoples as divinely cursed, as would Christian interpretations in the antebellum South and elsewhere.[105] And although the Enlightenment thinkers who contributed to Diderot's *Encyclopédie* may have fancied themselves to be objective observers of natural difference, they were in fact as influenced by a prejudice against enslaved people that also marked the Islamic writers of earlier centuries. The *Encyclopédie*'s contributors used remarkably similar language to disparage the dark-skinned people they described—most of whom they encountered only in the context of enslaved plantation labor or read about in fantastical travel narratives.

As Andrew Curran demonstrates in his excellent study of Enlightenment racial thought, race-based slavery could flourish during this supposedly enlightened age of progressive and liberal intellectuals because these men had "a general tendency to unbundle the moral status of enslavement from the physical status of those people being enslaved," writing disparagingly about race while demonstrating a "general blindness to the biopolitics of representation."[106] (This was the blind spot Charles Thomson attempted to point out to Jefferson in his commentary: "[I] am inclined to think [black people] a race lower in the scale of being yet for that very reason & because such an opinion might seem to justify slavery I should be inclined to leave it out.") Their blindness was in part the result of the era's emphasis and reliance on natural history; the most prominent anatomical thinkers focused on their research into the source of blackness and ignored the connections between their work and African chattel slavery. In fact, antislavery naturalists like Buffon actually "put forward an understanding of blackness that was both derived from and compatible with the context of slavery."[107] Slaveholders had both cultural and financial reasons to see and discuss their enslaved workers only as inferior beings suited for labor and nothing else. Naturalists who accepted slaveholders' depictions at face value unwittingly reified the stereotypes that benefited the trade, and the cycle continued.

By the 1760s a developing consensus among progressive European thinkers deemed African slavery to be immoral and brutal, but this consensus did not result in the end of derogatory depictions of Africans.[108] Curran presents Voltaire (1694–1778) as one example: "[D]uring his entire career, Voltaire never understood the link between his sneering representations of Africans and the justifications of human bondage espoused by pro-slavery thinkers." In the 1750s Voltaire both wrote a heart-wrenching indictment of slavery on French sugar plantations *and* claimed that black people's "round eyes, their flat noses, their invariably fat lips, the wool on their head, even the extent of their intelligence reflects prodigious divergences between them and other species of men"; he retained similar views for the rest of his life.[109] Contributors to the *Encyclopédie* were much the same: starting with the 1755 volume, articles began to emphasize natural equality and liberty, with one in particular—"Esclavage," or "Slavery," by Louis de Jaucourt—uniquely providing a strong and emotionally moving condemnation of slavery.[110] Jaucourt's other entries, however, described Africans as "a credulous, dirty lot with an animalist sexuality who 'know neither modesty nor restraint in the pleasures of love'" and who were themselves responsible for the slave trade's continuation. Diderot's entry on natural history likewise exhibits both a strong religious and philosophical condemnation of slavery and also a declaration of black people's inferior intelligence.[111] Late eighteenth-century thinkers very often were blatantly inconsistent on the subjects of race and slavery—whether or not they themselves owned slaves. Searching for consistency, even by attempting to break down thinkers into categories such as polygenist/pro-slavery and monogenist/antislavery, is a futile exercise; Voltaire was a polygenist who believed black people were of an entirely different species, while Cornelius de Pauw was a monogenist who held that Africans had gravely degenerated from white ancestors—and yet both thinkers were opposed to slavery.[112]

In addition to the *Encyclopédie*'s articles on race, Jefferson was familiar with many other major European works on the topic, including those of fellow APS members Abbé Raynal (1713–1796) and of course Buffon (1707–1788), both of whom he mentions in the *Notes*.[113] Raynal's *Histoire des deux Indes* (1770) argued that Africans had been "mistreated" by nature; refuting Buffon and de Pauw's climatic explanations for darkening, Raynal asserted that Africans were black not only on the level of skin but also in their bodily fluids, from blood to brain matter, which resulted in inferior mental capacity, in addition to being "more effeminate, lazier, weaker, and unfortunately more suitable to become slaves." "Furthermore," Raynal continued, "since their intellectual faculties have been nearly exhausted by their overindulgence in physical love, they have neither the memory nor the intelligence to compensate (by cleverness) for the force that they lack." Unwittingly combining derogatory reports from Caribbean slaveholders with the latest in anatomical research, Raynal attempted to demonstrate scientifically that Africans were "a different species of men" who were inferior to white people—and yet he was also antislavery. By the publication of the 1780 edition of the *Histoire*, Diderot (acting as editor) painstakingly altered the text to emphasize anatomical sameness on every level except for blood and skin, but even then he left many of Raynal's negative conclusions in place.[114]

In his discussion of race in *Notes on the State of Virginia*, Jefferson summarized European debates over the cause of blackness before dismissing them: he did not know whether "the black of the negro resides in the reticular membrane between the skin and scarf-skin, or in the scarf-skin itself" (whether the sun darkened the outer layer of skin or whether a distinctly African layer of material underneath the top layer, *reticulum mucosum*, caused the darkness). Or perhaps "it proceeds from the colour of the blood, the colour of the bile, or from that of some other secretion"; for their part, Buffon and Diderot held that dark bile colored the skin and blood of Africans, while de Pauw and Raynal held that the fundamental cause of blackness resided in the "spermatic fluid."[115] The seat of blackness was significant, to these philosophers, since it would indicate whether black people were different in fundamental ways (transmitted from father to child through the sperm, indicating a difference in species) or simply because of climatic circumstances. After acknowledging all these possible explanations for different skin colors, Jefferson brushed them aside: "[T]he difference is fixed in nature, and is as real as if its seat and cause were better known to us." No matter what the scientific cause for blackness turned out to be, Jefferson held, the white and black races were different and should be kept separate for the sake of maintaining the "superior beauty" of the white race. While disgusting to the modern reader, Jefferson's opinion that white people were the most attractive was commonly held by European peoples (Buffon, for instance, believed that European women's features were more attractive than Native Americans' because Europeans had a better climate).[116] Whereas de Pauw held that blackness should be eradicated through a long period of deliberate race mixing, Jefferson took the position that "those in the department of man"—for black or white, all were men—should be kept "distinct as nature has formed them."[117] Thus, Jefferson simultaneously affirmed the basic sameness of mankind and reified "natural" racial boundaries, and these two positions justified his insistence on both emancipation *and* colonization.

In writing about race in the *Notes*, Jefferson explained why colonization was a necessary corollary to statewide emancipation, a view he—along with most of his Virginia antislavery contemporaries—held to for the rest of his life (with one possible exception, as we shall see). But his racial comments were also part of *two* conversations being held simultaneously on both sides of the Atlantic. In Virginia, as the newspaper essays of *The Virginia Gazette, and Weekly Advertiser* indicate, antislavery arguments were being refuted by claims that Africans were less than human and that slavery was their natural state. In Europe, the Enlightenment's emphasis on the collection and categorization of knowledge made the differences in appearance among regional groups of people (such as between Europeans and Africans) a major topic of study. Jefferson's detailed explanation of the differences between races was prompted partly by his engagement with Virginia's prejudiced society and partly by his desire to participate in a European discourse that had been combining natural history with racist ethnographies for centuries.[118] For him, there was no inconsistency between enumerating the supposed inferiorities of the African race and still holding to a belief in the natural equality of all humans—and of the right of all people to be free.

His Declaration of Independence argued for the equality of all men, and his original draft of that document made clear that by "men" he meant "people," explicitly including enslaved Africans.[119] In 1809 he reiterated his position: "[W]hatever be [black people's] degree of talent it is no measure of their rights. Because Sir Isaac Newton was superior to others in understanding, he was not therefore lord of the person or property of others."[120] Parts of Jefferson's discourse on race in the *Notes* can today be rightly categorized as despicable, but it was neither new nor particularly remarkable, except insofar as it was written by an American slaveholder and attached to a proposal for emancipation— and this is the point that Charles Thomson felt Jefferson needed to emphasize.

In the unfinished manuscript that Thomson originally read, Jefferson had stated his observations on race, without equivocation, across five pages. His antislavery section was far shorter, taking up only one paragraph in a separate query. After receiving Thomson's critique, however, Jefferson apparently reconsidered both the tone and length of these sections. In a passage that seems partly designed to praise Virginia slaveholders as superior to the Romans, and partly to denigrate the African slave as compared to white slaves of antiquity, Jefferson had cited the historian Plutarch to comment on Cato's "deplorable" practice of "stooping to receive from his female slaves the little earnings of those [sexual] favours" which they sold to male slaves.[121] Thomson felt that these "reflections on Cato's conduct are not worthy a place here"; Jefferson duly crossed out that particular sentence, instead inserting a direct quotation from Plutarch—in Greek—as a footnote. Thomson next suggested that "a great part of p. 70," the rest of Jefferson's description of how terrible slavery was under the Romans, should also be "expunge[d]." This was because "many people encourage & comfort themselves in keeping slaves because they do not treat them as bad as others have done," an insightful observation that Jefferson chose to address not by removing the section but rather by adding a long tab with around 300 new words.

This addition addresses a common charge against black people:

"[T]hat disposition to theft with which they have been branded." Directly following a sentence arguing that nature, not slavery, corrupted the intellectual abilities of black people, Jefferson added that he desired to wait for "further observation" to "verify the conjecture, that nature has been less bountiful to them [than to white people] in the endowments of the head." Wanting to make clear that even hazarding the opinion that black people were "inferior in the faculties of Reason and Imagination" must be done "with great diffidence," or hesitancy, he declared himself certain that "in those [faculties] of the heart" nature "will be found to have done them justice." Jefferson believed that his slaves' moral sense was the same as his own. The situation of slavery, and not natural inferiority, was to blame for any thefts committed by black people, for "the man, in whose favor no laws of property exist, probably feels himself less bound to respect those made in favor of others." Moreover, Jefferson turned to accuse his fellow slaveholders: "[I]t is a problem which I give to the master to solve [a phrase that replaced his original wording, "a problem yet to be solved"], whether the religious precepts against the violation of property were not framed for him as well as his slave?" Going even further in his classification of slavery itself as a theft that nullified normal property law, Jefferson asked whether "the slave may not justifiably take a little from one, who has taken all from him, as he may slay one who would slay him?"[122]

Jefferson's next addition further undermined his previously certain racial hierarchy while simultaneously addressing the competing European theories regarding the origins of blackness: "I advance it *as a suspicion only*, that the blacks, whether originally a distinct race, or made distinct by time and circumstance, are inferior to the whites in the endowments both of body and mind" (emphasis added). And later on the same page, another tab contains a prolonged explanation of the ways in which white prejudice prevented emancipation: "This unfortunate difference of colour, and perhaps of faculty, is a powerful obstacle to the emancipation of these people," because some antislavery advocates (including Jefferson himself), while wishing to "vindicate the liberty of human nature," were also "anxious" to preserve racial boundaries. These nervous libertarians who were "embarrassed by the question 'What further is to be done with them?' join themselves in opposition with those who are actuated by sordid avarice only." Jefferson and Wythe's emancipation and colonization plan would solve this uniquely America dilemma by removing the freed slaves from the country and thus putting the former slave "beyond the reach of mixture."[123]

Although Jefferson was not the first American to suggest colonization as a solution to slavery, his reasoning in the *Notes* was perhaps the first to address white people's prejudices and fears directly, turning colonization into a way of removing any excuses for not doing what they knew to be right. Both before and after receiving Thomson's critique, Jefferson specifically countered objections to emancipation raised by the proslavery essayists who published in *The Virginia Gazette, and Weekly Advertiser* during the summer of 1782. Whereas "A Holder of Slaves" contended that emancipation would place the white population at risk of attack by their former slaves, Jefferson offered his colonization plan as a way to make both white and black populations safe from each other. "A Holder of Slaves" argued further that slaves could not be freed because then widespread miscegenation would contaminate the white race; Jefferson agreed that "[d]eep rooted prejudices entertained by the whites" and "the real distinctions which nature has made" would prevent black people from being fully integrated into the state. But colonization would solve that problem too.[124] The "unfortunate difference of colour" no longer had to be an obstacle to doing what was right.

The proslavery citizens of Virginia would also have found much to think about in Jefferson's revised Query XVIII ("Manners")—a query devoted entirely to the consequences of slavery. Originally, this paragraph took up a single manuscript page; after revision, it doubled in length via interlineal additions and a double-sided tab that has to be unfolded in order to be read. The section originally focused on ways in which slavery was a violation of the principles of nations. "A Scribbler" had argued that slavery was right because it was "sanctioned by the concurrence of all nations, even those we enslave," and because it was "generally usefull" and "general utility is the basis of all law and justice, and on this principle, is the right of slavery founded." But Jefferson undercut the idea that utility could be the foundation of slavery in a republic: he argued instead that the statesmen of a slaveholding nation were fundamentally corrupt, because rather than protecting the rights of all citizens they permitted "one half the citizens . . . to trample on the rights of the other," and in doing so they "transformed those [slavehold-ers] into despots, & these [slaves] into enemies, destroy[ing] the mor-als of the one part, & the amor patriae [love of country] of the other." Patriotism was an essential ingredient of citizenship in a republic, but enslaved people could not be patriotic, Jefferson argued, because they had no connection either to the land or to their descendants. A slave was forced "to live & labour for another" and must choose either to refuse to have children or to "entail his own miserable condition on the endless generations proceeding from him."[125]

In his expansion of this section, Jefferson continued the theme of subsequent generations, but this time he focused on the children of the corrupted class—the masters. Perhaps thinking of the Virginians like "A Holder of Slaves" who held that civilization itself depended on having slaves to perform the labor, Jefferson argued that the relation-ship between master and slave was in fact "a perpetual exercise of the most boisterous passions, the most unremitting despotism on the one part, and degrading submissions on the other. Our children see this, & learn to imitate it; for man is an imitative animal." Drawing from John Locke's principle that man is born a blank slate, Jefferson contin-ued: "[F]rom his cradle to his grave he is learning to do what he sees others do"; thus the parent was responsible for the sins of the child. "[I]f a parent could find no motive either in his philanthropy or his self-love" for exercising restraint in his actions toward a slave, then his child's presence should suffice—but because slavery brought out the worst in slaveholders, their children were "nursed, educated, and daily exercised in tyranny."[126]

In a moment of irony that Jefferson must have been aware of, given that he was himself a parent who owned slaves, he commented that "the man must be a prodigy who can retain his manners and morals undepraved by such circumstances." This statement has earned Jeffer-son criticism from modern scholars: it seems incredibly self-centered to focus on how much *white people* suffered under African chattel slavery. However, if one considers that Jefferson was addressing him-self to fellow (white) Virginians, refuting their argument that slavery benefited them, then his remarks seem more calculated than selfish.

Persuade Virginians that slavery threatened the virtuous liberty they just fought a revolution for, and perhaps public opinion could shift toward emancipation.[127]

Finally, Jefferson added what is perhaps his most famous condemnation of slavery, the one that sounds drastic coming from a man who prided himself on his rationalist religious outlook: "I tremble for my country when I reflect that God is just: that his justice cannot sleep forever: that considering numbers, nature and natural means only, a revolution of the wheel of fortune, an exchange of situation, is among possible events: that it may become probable by supernatural interference! The Almighty has no attribute which can take side with us in such a contest." Far from believing, as "A Scribbler" did, that African-descended people were fit for nothing more than "the state of slavery in which they have for a great length of time been held by us, with as much general happiness to themselves, as they seem susceptible of," Jefferson here was arguing that Virginia's sin against Africans was so great that God himself might overthrow the white people and place them under the feet of their former slaves. Jefferson may have been imitating the dire warning of the Quaker who had warned of "divine retribution" in the 1782 *Gazette* article, but he was not being totally disingenuous.[128] Perhaps precisely because it sounded so drastic, and evoked such fear, he reiterated versions of this prophecy numerous times over the ensuing years.[129]

Thomson was likely disappointed when Jefferson did not fully take his advice; Jefferson did not "expunge" the section on slavery in ancient Rome that Thomson worried would "comfort" American slaveholders "because they do not treat [slaves] as bad as others have done," and he did not remove everything that supported white supremacy even though "such . . . opinion[s] might seem to justify slavery." However, he did modify his conclusions in ways that seem designed to remove any doubt about his own antislavery views: he added "suspicion[s]" to replace white supremacist certainty; praised Africans' morality; condemned slaveholders as thieves; and offered a sweeping critique of states that imagined they could remain both slaveholding and republican. By turning his attention to the ways slavery corrupted masters, turned innocent children into tyrants, and inevitably brought divine retribution, Jefferson rebuffed the claims of Virginians who believed slavery to be beneficial to both slaves and masters. He concurred with the critique of the Quaker "A Friend to Liberty," utilizing similar religious arguments, but he also addressed the foundational issue that prevented many white Virginians from imagining emancipation: their racist abhorrence of amalgamation. Colonization would solve all of Virginia's problems, Jefferson said: It would serve as political restitution for the sins of slavery by forming a "free and independent" nation of former slaves; and it would preserve the "natural" division of the races.

It seems that by 1784 Jefferson was no longer writing his *Notes* solely with the highbrow, transatlantic members of the American Philosophical Society in mind. Particularly after receiving Thomson's critique, Jefferson was engaging with Virginian worries, and addressing Virginian excuses, in addition to offering a Virginian solution to the dilemmas of slavery and race. But the only Virginians who knew about his project were close confidants, and Jefferson meant to keep it that way: as he told Thomson in 1785, "I am desirous of preventing the reprinting this, should any book merchant think it worth it, till I hear from my friends whether the terms in which I have spoken of slavery . . . will not, by producing an irritation, retard that reformation which I wish instead of promoting it."[130] In Virginia the public argument over slavery was gaining intensity: an antislavery petition had "irritated" slaveholders across the state into a petitioning campaign, and the legislature responded by proposing to rescind the recently passed individual manumission legislation. Cautious of provoking a legislative backlash that would erase the gains antislavery activists had only recently made, and still hesitant to expose himself to criticism, Jefferson nonetheless began to wonder if there was a way for him to influence the lawmakers of his state—by targeting them while they were still young and impressionable at the College of William and Mary.

3. Authors in Paris
Printing the *Notes*

Charles Thomson's comments on the original manuscript of *Notes on the State of Virginia* in 1784 had helped Thomas Jefferson revise his book with an audience of Virginian slaveholders in mind, but for the first five years of its existence Jefferson never spoke of allowing anyone to read the *Notes* other than a small circle of friends and fellow cosmopolitan intellectuals. In fact, like many authors at the time, Jefferson took up a position of modesty when speaking of his work to anyone outside his intimate circle, even insisting in 1786 that "had I, at the time of writing them, had any thing more in view than the satisfying a single individual, [the *Notes*] should have been more attended to both in form and matter"—when in fact he had certainly had more than just Marbois in mind when he began his major revisions in 1782. To modern readers this dissembling seems dishonest, but it was customary in the eighteenth century for authors to seek anonymity and even to apologize for publishing. For several years after he authored the Declaration of Independence Jefferson did not publicly admit to that either.[1]

Jefferson later claimed that his hesitation to publicize the *Notes* stemmed from his fear that peers in the Virginia legislature might be so offended by his forthrightness that both his own career and future antislavery and prodemocracy legislation would be hindered. He vividly remembered the public humiliation that had been heaped upon his older cousin, Richard Bland, when Bland took the lead in cosponsoring his and Jefferson's pro-manumission bill in 1769. Even more fresh in his mind was the embarrassment of having his defense of Richmond called into question by political opponents in 1781, when he was governor. Jefferson was determined to avoid controversy for the sake of his own feelings and career—but also for the sake of the issues he cared about deeply, such as a constitutional convention in Virginia and, even more vitally, ending slavery. That changed on 11 May 1785. "I wish to put [the *Notes*] into the hands of the young men at the college," he wrote in confidence to James Madison. At some point in the process of revision, Jefferson had hit upon a new reform strategy: "[S]et our young students into a useful train of thought," then sit back and watch *them* change the laws.[2]

Why was the reluctant author now considering a wider readership for his *Notes*? It is significant that Jefferson's decision to send his book to Virginia students occurred while Jefferson himself was out of the country during his tenure as a diplomat in France. For the five years that Jefferson lived in Paris, his closest working companion was a young William and Mary graduate, and fellow student of George Wythe's, named William Short. Over the course of his life, Jefferson would mentor dozens of young men, but Short was the only one he called his "adoptive son."[3] Short gave up a promising political career to serve as Jefferson's private secretary from 1784 to 1789. He also served as a researcher and editor for Jefferson's *Notes*, and their friendship lasted until Jefferson's death almost five decades later. Most important, Short had emerged from William and Mary vehemently opposed to slavery. During their time in France, the two men debated slavery and abolition in Virginia with an openness that would have been difficult to achieve while surrounded by slavery's supporters back home. Beyond theoretical opposition, their conversations entailed detailed plans for helping black people transition from slavery to freedom and practical research into alternative forms of labor in Virginia.[4]

Jefferson was also no doubt inspired by the other company he kept while living in Paris. He and Short befriended many of the leading members of the Enlightenment in Europe, and in these rarified circles topics such as the abolition of slavery were openly discussed. Several of their acquaintances published works dealing with America in general and slavery in particular, often not very well. Short and Jefferson tried their best to counter false reports, and Jefferson became willing to consider distributing his *Notes* more widely as he became aware of the misleading and defamatory arguments about America then in circulation. Concerned with presenting the very best possible image of America to liberal European allies, Jefferson spoke optimistically about the potential for ending slavery in Virginia—more optimistically and openly than he ever would again. And during the early 1780s, his optimism did not seem misplaced. Back in Virginia, many hundreds of

Methodists and Baptists actually were inspired following a period of religious revival to free their own slaves and to petition the legislature for a general emancipation bill.[5]

Jefferson viewed this rising tide in Virginia as part of the larger wave of emancipation sentiment sweeping southward across the former colonies, beginning with Vermont in 1777 and reaching Pennsylvania, New Hampshire, Massachusetts, New Hampshire, Connecticut, and Rhode Island by 1786. Virginia was, he believed, "the next state to which we may turn our eyes for the interesting spectacle of justice in conflict with avarice and oppression." The "sacred side" of this conflict was "gaining daily recruits from the influx into office of young men grown and growing up." Although he had been bitterly disappointed by his own colleagues' reactions to antislavery legislation, Jefferson observed that the younger generation of Virginians had "sucked in the principles of liberty as it were with their mother's milk, and it is to them I look with anxiety to turn the fate of this question."[6] In young William Short, who in many ways must have reminded Jefferson of a shorter, blonder version of himself, he saw the embodiment of the best revolutionary ideals and the possibility of change.[7]

Jefferson was not, as some historians have suggested, merely promoting hype about Virginia antislavery sentiment to his European friends for the sake of appearances. During this brief window of time, it did seem as though the tide was truly turning, that enough people in Virginia could be persuaded, that the next generation of legislators— men like Short—might actually vote to institute sweeping reforms. It was during this hopeful period that Jefferson decided the best place for his *Notes* was in the hands not only of his few elite liberal friends but also in those of the William and Mary students—so long as James Madison and other Virginian confidants could assure Jefferson that sending the *Notes* to the college students would not result in a political and personal backlash, a backlash against Jefferson and against supporters of antislavery policies in general. But before he could carry out his careful plan, events would carry Jefferson's *Notes* out of his control.

In 1818 a report of the board of commissioners for Jefferson's proposed University of Virginia contained a line that was almost certainly from

Jefferson's pen: "The affectionate deportment between father & son offers, in truth, the best example for that of tutor & pupil."[8] This sums up
Jefferson's own views about education. Particularly because his father
died when Jefferson was fourteen years old, young Thomas's relationships with his teachers were, as we have seen, important influences on
both his ideas and his moral standards. Jefferson took seriously his
own responsibility to act with similar filial concern for numerous other
young men, beginning with educational advice for his cousin Philip
Turpin in 1769. Some young men (like Short) came to Monticello and
studied law with Jefferson for extended periods of time; others (like
Turpin and Jefferson's nephew Peter Carr) received letters giving detailed catalogs of books to read, as well as guidance regarding how they
should spend their time. The list of men who studied law with Jefferson
includes Short, John Banister Jr., John Wayles Eppes, James Madison,
James Monroe, Jefferson's own future son-in-law Thomas Mann Randolph Jr., his future grandson-in-law Nicholas P. Trist, Robert Skipwith,
and Archibald Stuart.[9] Given the importance of education in Jefferson's
moral philosophy and theory of republicanism, it is safe to say that he
viewed his contributions to these young men's lives as more than good
deeds or favors to their parents, or even as the continuation of the traditional reciprocal relationships among members of the gentry. He was
performing a vital duty, helping to ensure the progression of morals
and the continuation of republican values in Virginia.[10]

   For William Short, whose relationship with Jefferson was the closest
of his mentees, the connection came at a particularly important moment: in 1782 the twenty-four-year-old Short lost his father around the
same time that Jefferson lost his wife, and the two men would provide
significant emotional and intellectual support to one another over the
coming years.[11] Even before then, the trajectory of Short's life was indirectly shaped by Jefferson. When Short was a teenaged student at William and Mary, Governor Jefferson reorganized the departments and
curriculum of the college, emphasizing modern languages and sciences
and creating the first law professorship in the country. Short excelled
under this system, and his biographer speculates that his enjoyment of
the modern languages, in particular, accounts for the unusual length
of his stay at the college. Moreover, Jefferson was instrumental in the
hiring of Bishop James Madison as professor of natural philosophy and

mathematics in 1777. Madison (cousin to the future president) would, like Dr. Small and George Wythe, be a strong antislavery influence on the students at William and Mary. And just as Jefferson had visited the Governor's Palace in Williamsburg when he was a student, enjoying lively conversation with Governor Fauquier and the law professor Wythe, so, too, it is possible that history repeated itself with young Short—although William did not play the violin as his predecessor had.[12]

Short's acquaintance with Jefferson deepened until he was practically a member of the Jefferson family during the crucial years that the older man composed, revised, and printed *Notes on the State of Virginia*. Short was studying law under George Wythe in 1780, the year Jefferson first began composing his reply to Marbois's queries, but he was with Jefferson in June 1781 when the family had to flee Monticello before invading British dragoons, and he remained with them that summer at their Poplar Forest residence while Jefferson completed the first draft.[13] In September and October, Short and the Jefferson family were back at Monticello, and while they were there Jefferson supervised Short's bar exam (he passed). Before Chastellux journeyed to Monticello and began his momentous friendship with Jefferson in the spring of 1782, Short had already befriended him in Williamsburg, where the French army had taken over the college for their wounded troops.[14] The three men would later enjoy one another's company together in France. During the summer of 1782, while Jefferson composed the first set of major revisions to the *Notes* at his dying wife's side, Short was again staying at Monticello, and Jefferson began encouraging the younger man to purchase land nearby so that they could be neighbors (he made a similar request of James Monroe, who also studied under Jefferson around this time, and of James Madison, and for years Jefferson maintained the hope that they would form their own version of his cherished Williamsburg "partie quarreé").[15]

By the time Martha passed away in September, Jefferson's trust in Short was so deep that he asked the younger man to handle the complicated legal claims by various extended family members against her sizable estate. Jefferson's trust proved to be well-founded, as Short managed—after months of labor—to settle most of the claims in Jefferson's favor.[16] Jefferson reposed even more trust in Short the following year by asking him to assume the guardianship of his ward and favorite nephew, Peter Carr, after Jefferson had to leave to serve in Congress.[17]

Although Short was successful in handling Jefferson's wife's affairs, he did not feel himself to be a great lawyer, and he had abandoned the legal profession by 1783. Jefferson joined Short's best friend and fellow William and Mary graduate, William Nelson, in urging Short to return to the law, but Short demurred. Like Jefferson, he did not enjoy public speaking, and although Jefferson felt Short could have a successful legal career, Short told Nelson that this was only due to Jefferson's fatherly "partiality."[18] Not long after his father's death in the spring of 1783, Short decided to enter politics instead. He was elected to the Executive Council, the advisory body that shared authority with the governor of Virginia. It was a prestigious post, and Short later encouraged his younger brother, Peyton, to pursue a similar position, remarking: "The affection of the People is the most honorary Mark of Distinction a Young Man can have—it is worthy of cultivating with assiduity."[19] In his free time, Short did research for Jefferson's *Notes*: while Jefferson was revising from Annapolis in the winter of 1783, he asked Short to look into the vocabulary of the Nottaway Indians.[20]

Had Short continued in state-level politics he might have been elected governor.[21] Instead, only a year and a half after his election to the Executive Council, he chose to follow his mentor across the Atlantic in the position of private secretary. Short's tasks in Paris would be much less glamorous than they had been in the capital of Virginia, and he was warned before leaving that the hierarchy-conscious French would consider him, as secretary, to be merely "one of the higher Order of [Mr. Jefferson's] Domestics" if he did not have some officious-sounding title from Congress (which he ultimately did not receive).[22] For instance, while a member of the Executive Council he had helped to write a bill commissioning a statue of George Washington by the French sculptor Jean-Antoine Houdon. Later, as Jefferson's secretary, Short found himself acting as errand boy while helping Jefferson fulfill this commission.[23] But Short was willing to give up any official title for the opportunity to continue his mentoring relationship with Jefferson in Paris (and the fact that he had just had a disappointing romantic entanglement with a young lady in Richmond certainly did not hurt).[24]

When he was delayed from reaching the ship that was to carry Jefferson across the ocean, Short wrote to his mentor in desperation:

> And I insist on it with the more sollicitude, that no Body may be allowed to supplant me either in your Partiality or your Confidence. I do not discover from the Journals of Congress that the Commissioners are to be allowed a private Secretary. Whether they are or not, will not influence my Determination. I shall be perfectly happy to be with you, and although to have some Employment under you would be very agreeable, yet it will be enough for me to enjoy the Advantage of your friendly Instructions. I shall hope you will command my Services on every Occasion where they can save you any Trouble.[25]

Jefferson's own road to Paris was long and complicated. After much deliberation he had turned down an appointment to the peace commission in 1781 in order to remain near his sickly wife and defend his reputation in the General Assembly; but after his wife died in 1782 he welcomed the opportunity to leave the country. He spent February 1783 in Maryland waiting to sail on the same ship as his good friend Chastellux—only to be disappointed again when the diplomatic team that was already in Paris signed the treaty that ended the war, and Congress accordingly cancelled his commission. By spring 1784 Congress was asking him to accept the role of minister plenipotentiary to France, needing him to augment the "ambassadorial team of Franklin and John Adams" in order to promote commerce between the two nations.[26] Between his disappointment in 1783 and the appointment of 1784, Jefferson had not only composed the "fair copy" manuscript of his *Notes* but also written another document of enormous importance for our understanding of his thoughts on slavery and republicanism during this period: a replacement constitution for Virginia.

Because Virginia's 1776 constitution had been adopted in some haste, Jefferson expected that the coming of peace would prompt the General Assembly to call a formal constitutional convention, and his journey home through Virginia's capital city of Richmond in May 1783 led him to believe that the time was ripe. In *Notes*, he argued that the current Virginia constitution was "formed when we were new and unexperienced in the science of government. . . . No wonder then that time and trial have discovered very capital defects in it." Among those defects were unequal representation, too much power in the hands of the legislature, and the fact that the constitution was placed on the same level as an ordinary bill, rather than "an act transcendent to the powers of other legislatures," because it had not been properly adopted by a specially called constitutional convention.[27]

Therefore, in preparation for an expected constitutional convention, and on the same batch of paper that he used for the first twenty-two pages of the "fair copy" *Notes* manuscript, Jefferson wrote "Draught of a Fundamental Constitution for the Commonwealth in Virginia."[28] In a move that was certain to generate controversy, he included the following stipulation: "The general assembly shall not have power . . . to permit the introduction of any more slaves to reside in this state, or the continuance of slavery beyond the generation which shall be living on the thirty-first day of December, one thousand eight hundred: all persons born after that day being hereby declared free." This clause is similar to the gradual emancipation measures adopted by northern states; however, unlike Pennsylvania's law (which applied only after slaves born in 1780 reached twenty-eight years of age), or that of New York (where all slaves born after 4 July 1799 were freed, but only after male children reached age twenty-eight and females age twenty-five), Jefferson proposed that Virginia unconditionally emancipate *all* slaves born after 31 December 1800. Interestingly, he made no mention of colonization in his proposed constitution.[29]

Jefferson sent the "Draught" document to James Madison for feedback in June 1783, optimistic that it could soon be put into effect.[30] But the General Assembly failed to call a convention. Bitterly disappointed, Jefferson added an extended critique of this failure to his *Notes*, warning of the tyranny waiting for Virginia if a new constitution was not properly ratified clearly delineating the government's authority. No matter how concerned he was, he did not make his sentiments widely known, fearing that he could now be censured not only for attacking slavery but also for criticizing the existing constitution. As he later confided to John Adams, a dark "foreknowlege" of how his countrymen would likely respond to his *Notes* had "retarded my communicating them to my friends [for] two years," from the period he completed most of the revisions in 1783 until he finally printed 200 copies in 1785 for distribution among those "friends" only.[31] Once the *Notes* was printed, however, Jefferson decided to include his draft constitution as an appendix. Now, in addition to becoming familiar with his personal views on the corrupting nature of slavery for a republic, his readers would also discover that Jefferson's legislative vision for Virginia would have ended slavery even more rapidly than the northern state of New York had done.

The inclusion of the "Draught" constitution as an appendix in the *Notes* is significant: some scholars have erroneously argued that Jefferson never offered more than "an occasional private thought on the subject" of emancipation.[32] But as we have seen, Jefferson in fact not only described his plan for gradual emancipation and colonization in the body of the *Notes*; he also included the "Draught" in that earliest printed edition of 1785—and it has been included in editions of the *Notes* ever since. Any person who read his book 200 years ago, and any person who picks up a copy today, can see that Jefferson publicly advocated ending slave importations into Virginia and enacting gradual emancipation for slaves already living in the state. It is true that after returning to America and becoming secretary of state in 1790 Jefferson spoke less often on the topic, but as he noted in 1814 this was partly because "the public" had by then already been made aware of his sentiments, which had not changed.[33]

Jefferson was not just writing legislation to end slavery in Virginia during this interim period before his departure for France. One of his last efforts before leaving the Confederation Congress in spring 1784, if his proposal had passed, would have stopped the spread of slavery within the new United States entirely. Jefferson had been placed on a committee tasked with developing a plan "to organize and administer the newly created National Domain, the western reserve of territory stretching from the Atlantic seaboard states to the Mississippi river, forged from the cessions (and to be supplemented by anticipated future cessions) of the Atlantic states' western claims."[34] But he took the opportunity (he almost certainly wrote the committee's report) to craft a sweeping proposal dealing with all territory *ever to be ceded* to the federal government. This became, in truncated form, the Northwest

Ordinance of 1784.[35] In this road map from territory to statehood, Jefferson demonstrated his commitment to a more democratic form of government than any yet in existence: Universal male suffrage was guaranteed, the central government's control was strictly limited, and "after the year 1800 of the Christian era, there shall be neither slavery nor involuntary servitude in any" new state.[36] This prohibition on slavery failed to pass Congress by a single vote—a defeat that Jefferson characterized by remarking, "Thus we see the fate of millions unborn hanging on the tongue of one man, and heaven was silent in that awful moment! But it is to be hoped it will not always be silent and that the friends to the rights of human nature will in the end prevail."[37] And eventually, some "friends" in the Reconstruction Congress of 1865 resurrected Jefferson's antislavery clause, quoting it almost verbatim in section 1 of the Thirteenth Amendment.[38]

In April 1784 it finally seemed certain that Jefferson would replace John Jay in Europe as a member of the commission that by then included Benjamin Franklin (minister to France), John Adams (about to be named minister to England), and their secretaries, and he sent word to Short to be ready to leave at a moment's notice.[39] The commission was very much a family affair: Franklin's secretary was his grandson, William Temple Franklin, while Adams's was his son, John Quincy.[40] Jefferson explained his own secretarial choice of his "adoptive son" to James Madison: "You know my high opinion of his abilities and merits. I will therefore only add that a peculiar talent for prying into facts seems to mark his character as proper for such a business. He is young and little experienced in business tho well prepared for it. These defects will lessen daily."[41] When Congress, still debating how the nascent republic should structure its diplomatic delegations, refused to pay for Jefferson to have a private secretary, Jefferson paid Short out of his own pocket, in addition to giving him free room and board in his residence in Paris.[42]

Short was in need of as much financial assistance as Jefferson could offer, for although he did inherit a fair amount of property from his father—including slaves—in 1784, he did not have access to much cash at all. As he told Jefferson prior to their departure, he was "at a Loss" as to how he would secure "Funds for my Support whilst in Europe," "although I have been devising Ways & Means for some Time."[43] He and his younger brother, Peyton, were waiting to divide their father's estate between themselves and their sisters until the economy improved sufficiently for them to settle his debts and obligations without incurring heavy losses.[44] The subsequent legal maneuvering would take years. When he left America, Short did have one personal slave, but he instructed his family to let this man be in charge of his own time and keep his own income. It would be the last time he ever had such an intimate connection to slavery.[45]

Between Short's money troubles, the slow communication by mail, and kinks in their method of encoding letters, Jefferson and his new secretary were unable to sail together for Europe.[46] By the time Short reached Paris in late October 1784, Jefferson had set up housekeeping in a Paris house named the Hôtel Landron. Rather than joining Jefferson's household immediately, Short moved in with a French family in the Paris suburb of Saint-Germain in order to immerse himself in the language, visiting Jefferson and the other members of the delegation more to socialize than to work.[47] In May 1785 Jefferson officially succeeded Franklin as America's minister (ambassador) to France, and his need for a private secretary of his own greatly increased. The bond between the two men is evident in the nature of a letter Jefferson sent requesting his young assistant to end his language lessons. Short had apparently become involved with a local girl referred to in letters only as "The Belle of St. Germaine" and was therefore reluctant to assume his duties in the city, leading Jefferson to take a fatherly, though humorous, tone with him. "Come home like a good boy," Jefferson chided in a letter, and continue studying French "at your leisure."[48] Short dutifully took up his work. He spent the summer helping negotiate a treaty with Prussia, and a year after Short's arrival in France, he and Jefferson both moved into new quarters in a townhouse named the Hôtel de Langeac, which served as their home base in Europe for the ensuing four years.[49]

Jefferson and Short had already befriended several Frenchmen before leaving America, and these compatriots quickly facilitated their

entrance into Parisian society. One such contact was St. John de Crèvecoeur, a Frenchman who settled in New York after the French and Indian War, married an American, and then published a book explaining
American culture, *Letters from an American Farmer* (1782), that became quite popular in Europe. Upon hearing that Jefferson was de-
parting for France, Crèvecoeur wrote to Jefferson to urge him to "put
Mr. Franklin in Mind of Introducing you To the Good duke of La ro-
chefoucaud." This duke was a leading figure in French political and
intellectual society; Crèvecoeur described him as the "pearl of all the
Dukes a Good Man and an most able Chemyst." And it was important
that Jefferson meet the Duke de La Rochefoucauld, according to Crèvecoeur, because "His House is the Cente[r] of [meeting] where Men of
Genius and abilities Often Meet. You have therefore a great Right To
Share his Friendship."[50]

Benjamin Franklin, who was then so popular in France that his face
was "as well-known as that of the moon,"[51] seems indeed to have introduced Jefferson to the "pearl of all the Dukes," and Mr. Short also
befriended the duke and his wife; within a few years Short and Rosalie,
who was many years younger than her husband, were conducting a
secret love affair.[52] A few months after Jefferson and Short had settled
in Paris, Crèvecoeur joined them in his native country. His presence
perhaps helped make up for the loss of Franklin and Adams, who both
departed in 1785—Franklin for America, Adams and his family for
London. Jefferson and Short were now the highest-ranking American
diplomats in France.

Their circle of friendship expanded to include many of the greatest minds in science and politics and literature, people who would
also soon form the leadership of the moderate French Revolution. In
addition to the amiable Duke de La Rochefoucauld, they befriended
his cousin the Duke de La Rochefoucauld-Liancourt, the Marquis de
Condorcet, the Abbé Morellet, and the Marquis de La Fayette, along
with many others. George Washington's young protégé was particularly taken with Jefferson: "Words cannot express . . . how much I am
pleased with Jefferson's conduct," La Fayette wrote. "[Jefferson] unites
every ability that can recommend him with [government] ministers
and at the same time possesses accomplishments of the mind and of

the heart which cannot but give him many friends."[53] La Fayette was only two years older than Short, and they soon became friends as well; in 1786 Short described La Fayette as "an incomparable man" who would "go a great way" if not thwarted by political intrigues.[54]

Paris in those final days before the outbreak of the French Revolution was the cultural capital of the Age of Enlightenment.[55] It was also the center of pro-American sentiment in Europe. More than 9,000 young Frenchmen, including several aristocrats, had volunteered to join the American revolt against the British, and they were now returning with enthusiastic endorsements of American ideals. Many members of Jefferson and Short's circle were so enthralled with the possibilities they saw embodied in the American Revolution that they playfully referred to themselves as "*les Américains.*"[56] In 1787 several of *les Américains*, including Crèvecoeur and Warville de Brissot, formally founded the Gallo-American Society. Its mission was to strengthen Franco-American commerce through friendship by "fix[ing] a point, a center, in which all the good things in each nation are deposited. Our Society will form this center."[57] Members of the society met, often with Jefferson or Short in attendance, to discuss the American republic and the ways in which its ideals could be transported across the Atlantic.

For the two Virginians, completing diplomatic tasks was no less important than the informal work of representing the United States, including the ideas of the American Revolution itself, to their cosmopolitan audience. As George Washington put it in his widely published "Circular to the States" at the end of the war, "the eyes of the whole World are turned upon" the United States: "The Citizens of America are, from this period, to be considered as the Actors on a most conspicuous Theatre, which seems to be peculiarly designated by Providence for the display of human greatness and felicity."[58] The Americans had accomplished what seemed, at that point in history, to be impossible: they had thrown off the chains of their Old World rulers and established a functioning democracy, as if the pages of Enlightenment philosophy had sprung to life and manifested themselves in the persons of simple colonists from the wilderness. Jefferson and Short—who had never even experienced a symphony orchestra before arriving in Paris—were now conscious that they had a vitally important role to play on the stage of diplomacy in France, and they were constantly searching for ways to demonstrate the accomplishments and positive attributes of Americans.

The New World was still very new at that time in the eyes of Europeans, whose primary scientific understanding of America came from the French naturalist George-Louis Leclerc, Comte de Buffon, especially his 1761 theory of climatic degeneration. Buffon believed that the American continents had only recently arisen from underneath the floodwaters and that they were therefore younger, more humid, and less beneficial to human society. These arguments were augmented by international scholars, from Cornelius de Pauw to the Abbé Morellet to the University of Edinburgh principal William Robertson. The Abbé Raynal, among the worst offenders, claimed that when Europeans migrated to America they aged more quickly and were smaller and weaker, as well as less intelligent, failing to produce "any man of genius in a single art or science."[59] Benjamin Franklin—a genius who was slightly taller than average and who was venerated by the French for his charm and scientific accomplishments—did much to combat these misconceptions during his Paris tenure, perhaps most humorously during a dinner party at which Buffon became a topic of conversation. Upon being asked about the degenerate nature of America, Franklin merely looked pointedly around the dinner table at the (tall) American guests and the (short) Europeans and asked all to stand. As one eyewitness recounted it to Jefferson: "In fact there was not one American present who could not have tost out of the Windows any one or perhaps two of the rest of the Company, if this Effort depended merely on muscular force"![60] Nonetheless, misconceptions about the United States prevailed.

Europeans were also being consistently told by the prejudiced British press that the American revolutionaries were ill-equipped to govern a new nation, that their economy was collapsing, and that the republic would fail at any moment. Without support, both diplomatic and financial, from other European nations, the republic would indeed fail; Jefferson and Short therefore picked up where Franklin had left off as the faces of their nation (it probably helped that Jefferson was over six-feet-two). Short made a particularly good impression on the ladies: Abigail Adams described him as having a "good figure . . . , looks and manners."[61] He soon had a reputation for knowing the most—and the "most agreeable"—French ladies of any American (including, fatefully, the beautiful, then–twenty-three-year-old Duchess de la Rochefoucauld).[62] Jefferson and Short's relationships with this cosmopolitan circle of intellectual elites in France were key, for these were the authors whose publications shaped academic discourse around the world.

Jefferson did not yet think of himself as an author, despite his years of work on *Notes on the State of Virginia*. He even said as much to James Madison on 11 May 1785: "[D]o not view me as an author, and attached to what he has written. I am neither. . . . [I]n no event do I propose to admit them [the *Notes*] to go to the public at large."[63] Although Jefferson's authorial humility was no doubt partly in deference to the cultural norms of the time, which dictated that writers should always downplay their efforts and even remain anonymous much of the time, the *Notes* truly underwent a change in audience over the seven years between Jefferson receiving Marbois's questionnaire and its official London publication.[64] Beginning in 1781 Jefferson wrote first for the French government, and later he imagined that his research would benefit a small, select group of fellow intellectuals. In doing so, he was following the long-standing tradition among elite thinkers of circulating manuscripts within their own networks rather than putting ideas before the masses in print. This tradition may seem odd to modern readers. But becoming a member of the larger circle of philosophers and scientists in Paris from 1784 onward opened Jefferson's eyes to the role his book could play in influencing transatlantic discourses and correcting misconceptions about America—if it were printed and distributed more broadly.[65]

Correcting representations of America was an early topic of discussion for the Virginia transplants and their French allies. At one memorable 1785 house party attended by *les Américains*, as well as Jefferson, Short, and their friend the Italian-American physician/spy/historian Philip Mazzei, the conversation turned to a recent, flagrantly inaccurate book written by the Abbé Mably, *Observations sur le gouvernement et les Lois aux États-Unis d'Amérique* (Observations on Government and Laws in the United States of America [1784]), in which he prophesied the downfall of the American republic.[66] Knowing that uncertainty regarding the stability of America jeopardized its credit in Europe, the group debated the best way to counter Mably. William Short persuaded Mazzei to compose a book that would upend Mably's arguments, and Mazzei subsequently produced the four-volume *Recherches Historiques et Politiques sur les États-Unis de l'Amérique Septentrionale* (Historical and Political Studies on the United States of North America). Privately, Short felt that Mazzei's attempts to defend America went overboard, "not sticking close enough to the point," but at least Mably had been refuted.[67] Their mutual friend Crèvecoeur had written a more skillful and persuasive explication of American culture in his 1782 book *Letters from an American Farmer*, which was published in London toward the end of the American Revolution. It introduced Europeans to the idea of the self-made American, celebrating the characteristics that made individuals successful in the New World, and had been highly influential in converting future French Revolution leaders such as Brissot Warville to American principles. Now back in Paris after his American sojourn, Crèvecoeur and the other members of the Gallo-American Society soon joined Mazzei in taking up their pens on behalf of America, publishing "a number of books and pamphlets between 1786 and 1788," including a French edition of the still-popular *Letters*.[68]

Another of Jefferson and Short's good friends, the Marquis de Chastellux, had begun work on his own book about America in 1780, not long before Jefferson received Marbois's questionnaire that prompted him to work on the *Notes*. Chastellux had been second-in-command to French General Rochambeau, who utilized George Wythe's Williamsburg home as his headquarters during their Virginia campaign. Chastellux wrote portions of his manuscript in May 1782 while living in Williamsburg, having completed a tour of Virginia in April. During his travels he had stayed with Jefferson at Monticello, where they developed the friendship that would be so instrumental in encouraging Jefferson to keep revising his *Notes*.[69] But Jefferson was not the only one to receive inspiration from that visit; Chastellux also seems to have based some of Part Two of his *Travels in North America* on his discussions with Jefferson.

As with Jefferson's *Notes*, Chastellux's three-part *Travels* had a complicated journey toward publication. Chastellux printed a few dozen copies of Part One in early 1781, and these copies were passed around—Marbois had one, and Jefferson could conceivably have seen it—before Chastellux even began drafting the second and third parts. After he returned to Paris in early 1783, Chastellux circulated a few manuscript copies of the completed book "among his closest friends." Portions of the work were soon published (without Chastellux's permission) in French-language periodicals and then collected by publishers into unauthorized editions, beginning in Germany in 1785. Chastellux eventually agreed to publish the entire work himself in order to prevent these truncated versions from multiplying; the first complete authorized version was published in early 1786 in Paris.[70]

While preparing for publication in 1785, Chastellux specifically sought Jefferson's advice regarding the section on Virginia. He asked for feedback within a "fortnight," but Jefferson reported that he had been so engrossed upon reading it that he "devoured it at a single meal."[71] The antislavery Chastellux had tempered his criticism of that institution by remarking that, although he had seen many slaves "ill lodged, ill clothed, and often oppressed with labor,"[72] "in general they [white Virginians] seem afflicted to have any slavery, and are constantly talking of abolishing it, and of contriving some other means of cultivating their estates." Different parts of the population had different motivations for this, he observed: although some had purely economic interests at heart, the philosophers and "young men, who are almost all educated in the principles of a sound philosophy, regard nothing but justice, and the rights of humanity." This observation echoes and perhaps confirms Jefferson's own faith in the younger generation. Chastellux also concurred with Jefferson's suspicion that people of African descent might be "not people entirely of the same species [as white people]; for the more we regard the negroes, the more must we be persuaded that the difference between them and us, consists in something more than complexion." In one particular, however, the two philosophers differed:

whereas Jefferson advocated emancipation and wholesale colonization of the freed people to their own nation, Chastellux argued that "[t]he best expedient would be to export a great number of males, and to encourage the marriage of white men with the females."[73] In this way, the more threatening part of the enslaved population—the men—would be removed, while the race itself could be integrated into white American society by intermarriage between white men and black women. Jefferson had no comment on this section.

Chastellux's book was not well received, either in France or Virginia. In a 1786 letter to his best friend in Virginia, the twenty-seven-year-old William Short bemoaned that "General Chastellux has published his work in two volumes. . . . Would you suppose that a Philosopher could have written such a thing"? Although Short did not comment specifically on Chastellux's recommendation that white men marry freed black women, he did note that the work was quite controversial among the "literary parties" in France, which Short reported "are as violent as those of politics in other countries." Chastellux's "real friends," "of which I profess myself one, are very sorry that he has published his voyages—he has been attacked most furiously."[74] A few months later, Bishop James Madison wrote from Virginia: "I have just been honoured by Genl. Chastellux with a Copy of his Travels thro N. America. I find It is but little relished by most here."[75]

Short was also disappointed with the intellectuals responsible for articles in France's vaunted *Encyclopédie*.[76] This massive series was primarily edited by the Enlightenment philosopher Denis Diderot and included articles by leading experts on a variety of topics, and provincial Americans went to great lengths to read its fountains of knowledge. Jefferson secured a copy for the state of Virginia while he was governor in 1781, and when he heard that a new publication—the *Encyclopédie methodique*—was underway in 1782, he advised Bishop Madison to buy it for the College of William and Mary. Once in Paris, Jefferson was able to help many of his American friends secure subscriptions to the *Encyclopédie*, from Franklin to Charles Thomson to Madison and Monroe. In January 1786 the Duke de La Rochefoucauld connected Jefferson to the young philosopher responsible for the sections of the new *Encyclopédie* dealing with the United States, Jean-Nicolas Démeunier, and Jefferson subsequently served as consultant for this part of the project.[77]

Démeunier had been heavily influenced by the Abbé Raynal's environmental theories, and although he incorporated many of Jefferson's corrections and suggestions, resulting in an article of eighty-nine pages (by comparison, France received only forty), Jefferson was ultimately unsatisfied with many of Démeunier's representations of America.[78] Short wrote openly about the situation in his letter to his friend William Nelson in Virginia: "[W]hat [Démeunier] had said of the *Etats Uni* was as erroneous & false as might be expected from a man who has made the Abbe Raynal's model & his own lively imagination his guide —fortunately he has candor & after putting this article under Mr. Jefferson's inspection, he readily struck out & altered the most flagrant errors." Still, Short added, "the article is very imperfect." From this experience behind the scenes of the magnificent and respected *Encyclopédie*, Short had been made quite cynical: "[I]s it not a melancholy reflexion my dear Nelson . . . that books which we are taught to worship from our infancy, should be merely the works of legend & uncertainty." The young Virginian concluded that, although authors were often venerated "like the oracles of the ancients," once they are "seen naked & unclothed but in the simple garb of truth, they are no longer regarded but as men & frequently as very little men. Whoever intends to derive much amusement from reading must not penetrate this veil." If a man lifted the veil, Short concluded, "he there meets his own punishment—or rather his own reward—for truth should be pursued at whatever expense it may cost, & the more truths with which the mind is stored the better." For Short, amassing truth, not "the number of leaves [pages] that a man has turned over," was now "the standard of learning." This emphasis on pursuing truth, even when it was unpopular, characterized Short's life from that point on.[79]

Despite the increasing number of French authors inking their quills to write about America, Jefferson and Short wrestled with the high number of falsehoods about their country that remained engrained in the popular European imagination. The work of scientists like Buffon and Raynal remained accepted uncritically by most, and the Europeans who wrote from their experiences in America—like Chastellux and Mazzei—proved disappointing to Short and perhaps to Jefferson as well. There was clearly a need for an *American* natural historian to refute the climate degeneracy theories and illustrate that a former colonist was the intellectual equal of his Old World counterparts—and this need no doubt pushed Jefferson to think again about more widely distributing his *Notes*.

But the most important push came in the form of gentle encouragement from Charles Thomson, Jefferson's friend and fellow American Philosophical Society member. It was Thomson's advice about how Jefferson's words on race might be misconstrued to support slavery that had prompted Jefferson to reframe his argument in significant, albeit insufficient, ways. Thomson had also been one of the first to encourage Jefferson to print enough copies for his friends in the intellectual community. Before Jefferson left America, in May 1784, he let Thomson know that "[m]y matter in the printing way is dropped" due to his chosen Philadelphia printer almost doubling his rates at the last minute. "Perhaps I may have a few copies struck off in Paris," Jefferson added, "if there be an English printer there. If I do you shall assuredly have one."[80] By spring 1785 Thomson was getting impatient: "I long to see your answer to Mr. M[arbois]'s queries. I hope by this time you have found leisure to revise and compleat that work and have it committed to the press or at least struck off some copies for the satisfaction of your friends, among whom I hope to be ranked." Ever the encourager, Thomson not only urged Jefferson to submit the manuscript to a publisher; he also argued that Jefferson "owe[d] it to your reputation to publish your work under a more dignified title" than merely the understated "Notes on the State of Virginia." The version that he had seen, incomplete as it was, he believed to be "a most excellent Natural history not merely of Virginia but of No. America and possibly equal if not superior to that of any Country yet published."[81]

Eight days after receiving Thomson's letter, Jefferson privately printed his *Notes* (although without changing the title).[82] He was able to find a Parisian printer who gave him a much better rate than the one in Philadelphia and had 200 copies made for himself. The next day he sent an encoded letter to his good friend James Madison, informing him that "they yesterday finished printing my notes" and explaining his new purpose for the book: although he had first written "only for Marbois," and then revised the *Notes* for "three or four friends" (probably meaning Chastellux and Thomson, though obscuring the fact that he had also considered offering the *Notes* to the other members of the small but international membership of the American Philosophical Society), Jefferson now wondered if it "might set our young students into a useful train of thought." "I beg you to peruse [the *Notes*] carefully," he wrote to Madison, "because I ask your advice on it and ask nobody's else." Although Jefferson did not mention the issue of slavery yet, he made it plain to Madison that he was concerned about the controversy his words could generate: "I wish to put it into the hands of the young men at the college [of William and Mary]," partly because of the scientific information it contained but particularly because of its "political" arguments. However, he added vaguely, "there are sentiments on some subjects which I apprehend might be displeasing to the country [Virginia] perhaps to the assembly or to some who lead it."

Displeasing leading Virginians would have two consequences: "I do not wish to be exposed to their censure, nor do I know how far their influence, if exerted, might effect a misapplication of law to such a publication were it made." Madison was to "communicate it . . . in confidence" to a select few like-minded Virginians, meaning men such as James Monroe and George Wythe. If they concurred that its political "sentiments" would not result in Jefferson's being attacked (as Bland had been in 1769, the first time Jefferson attempted to cosponsor a manumission bill), or produce a proslavery legislative backlash, then Jefferson was determined to "send a copy to each of the students" at the College of William and Mary. But if Madison and the other Virginian confidants replied in the negative, Jefferson would send a "very few copies to particular friends in confidence and burn the rest."[83] Until he knew better how his book would be received, Jefferson tightly restricted the number of copies sent to Virginia. Not even his old mentor, Professor Wythe, received his own copy until two years later.[84]

Indeed, in 1785 Jefferson distributed fewer than thirty copies of his *Notes*; all of the recipients were members of the Republic of Letters— leading scientists, politicians, and intellectuals from France, Italy, the Netherlands, England, and a few fellow Americans. Although he was concerned about the effect it would have on Virginia politics, these concerns were irrelevant when it came to representing America in Europe and among politicians from northern states. The earliest copies went to such luminaries as Benjamin Franklin, John Adams, La Fayette, Giovanni Fabbroni, G. K. van Hogendorp, David Rittenhouse, Francis Hopkinson, the Count de Rochambeau, the Abbé Morellet, Chastellux, and Jefferson's intellectual nemesis on the issues of climactic degeneration, Buffon. (Franklin and Rittenhouse were both cited in the *Notes* as examples of American genius to counter claims that people born in the colonies were inferior to Europeans.) In each copy, Jefferson handwrote a message informing the recipient that he was "unwilling to expose [the *Notes*] to the public eye" and asking the recipient to "put [it] into the hands of no person on whose care and fidelity he cannot rely to guard them against publication."[85] Although Jefferson was pleased enough with his work to circulate it among this small circle of thinkers, and understood that they would lend it to others, he was still determined to control the extent of its readership.

Some historians speculate that this reluctance for publicity stemmed from Jefferson's belief that the book itself was flawed, as he repeatedly said to friends such as George Wythe. And indeed, since Jefferson kept editing and updating the work—even if only in the margins of his own personal copy—for the rest of his life, it does seem plausible that Jefferson was reluctant to have the book widely read because, like most authors, he viewed it as perpetually in need of further revision. But I do not believe that this was the primary reason Jefferson did not publish the work right away, and there is ample evidence that the amount of time Jefferson dedicated to revising his work to show that it was far from the hastily assembled, poorly researched text he often said it was.[86] A much more plausible explanation for the timing of official publication and distribution, in my view, rests in Jefferson's—and others' —oft-repeated concerns regarding the ways in which the book would be received in Virginia, specifically how the sections on slavery (and the Virginia constitution) would provoke the opposite responses to those that Jefferson desired.

As the few private copies made their way to their intended audience, Jefferson began receiving enthusiastic feedback. John Adams, who was still in Europe and therefore one of the first to read the book, told Jefferson on 22 May that the "Passages upon Slavery, are worth Diamonds. They will have more effect than Volumes written by mere Philosophers."[87] Encouraged, Jefferson in June sent out several more copies, including one to James Monroe in Virginia. In language even more precise than his letter to Madison had been, Jefferson told his former student that he had "taken measures to prevent it's publication" because he feared that "the terms in which I speak of slavery and of our constitution may produce an irritation which will revolt the minds of our countrymen against reformation in these two articles, and thus do more harm than good."[88] Similarly, in a 21 June letter to Charles Thomson, Jefferson responded to his friend's enthusiasm for the book's official publication by telling Thomson he was "desirous of preventing the reprinting this, should any book merchant think it worth it, till I hear from my friends whether the terms in which I have spoken of slavery and of the constitution of our state will not, by producing an irritation, retard that reformation which I wish instead of promoting it."[89]

And when Chastellux asked Jefferson's permission to reprint portions of the *Notes* in the French *Journal de physique*, Jefferson elaborated on his concern. Chastellux was welcome to reprint extracts from the *Notes*, but "the strictures on slavery and on the constitution of Virginia . . . are the parts which I do not wish to have made public, at least till I know whether their publication would do most harm or good." This was because "it is possible that in my own country [meaning Virginia] these strictures might produce an irritation which would indispose the people towards the two great objects I have in view, that is the emancipation of their slaves, and the settlement of their constitution on a firmer and more permanent basis." If Jefferson learned from Madison that "they will not produce that effect," he told Chastellux, then he had printed enough copies for every young student at the College of William and Mary, because "it is to them I look, to the rising generation, and not to the one now in power for these great reformations."[90]

We have now seen that Jefferson gave the same reasoning to several different correspondents, both Virginians and Frenchmen, regarding why he did not wish for the *Notes* to be made widely available in his home state. Several historians have questioned whether Jefferson was genuinely concerned about a legislative backlash that would worsen conditions for slaves in Virginia or if he was just using that as an excuse to cover his true concern—namely, becoming the target of criticism again.[91] Did Jefferson have genuine reason to believe that a legislative backlash was possible? The answer to that question is found in a series of events then occurring an ocean away—in the religious communities and legislative halls of Virginia.

Beginning in 1723, Virginia law stated that slaves could be freed only for "meritorious service," and even then only by the special approval of the governor and his council. Jefferson and his cousin Richard Bland unsuccessfully attempted to lessen these restrictions in 1769. In 1778 the issue was properly debated for the first time when an enslaved man named George petitioned for his freedom. George based his case on having "received repeated assurances from his late master that he would set him free at his [the master's] death" as a reward for being a loyal servant. The General Assembly actually considered broadening George's case into a general manumission law, perhaps spurred by revolutionary era liberality, though their liberality did not extend so far as to state that slaves had a natural right to freedom; they instead emphasized the right of a master to free a slave for good behavior, so long as the freed slaves left Virginia and so long as other members of the white community were not financially affected.[92] Though the 1778 bill did not pass, public sentiment regarding the issue shifted over the ensuing years due in large measure to the efforts of Quakers, Methodists, and Baptists.

Quakers had been among the earliest abolitionists, believing that Jesus's command—do unto others as you want others to do unto you—applied to Africans as well as to Europeans. In an effort to fully live out their faith, many Quakers in Virginia attempted to free their slaves but were prevented from doing so by the law. In 1780 they petitioned the legislature to authorize private emancipations for members of their society, appealing to the principles of the Declaration of Independence that all men are naturally born free. And in 1782 they tried again, this time successfully. According to the Quaker abolitionist Warner Mifflin, the General Assembly members that year were "liberal-spirited" and therefore more open to the petition than previous legislators had been.[93] The resulting law finally permitted owners to manumit their slaves, though with several restrictions. Crucially, however, the law did not require that newly freed slaves leave the state. For a short window of time, until that cruel provision was voted into place in 1806, it was possible to free slaves for genuinely antislavery reasons, since kind-hearted owners could be sure that they were not tearing families apart by freeing someone whose spouse or parents or children were retained in slavery by another master. Thus the 1782 manumission bill resulted in a growing free black community.[94]

For several reasons—racism and the recent memory of armed run-away slaves joining the British army during the American Revolution not least of these—many white Virginians were none too happy about the growing number of free black people living among them. Only two years after the law passed, petitions began arriving in the General Assembly, protesting the legislation and forecasting dire consequences for the state if the free black population was allowed to increase. These petitions unfortunately demonstrate that, contrary to the assertions of important works like Winthrop Jordan's *White Over Black*, proslavery arguments were alive and well in Virginia even during the revolutionary period. The petitioners asserted that enslaved laborers were more likely to steal from their masters or even rebel due to the ever-present example of these free persons before their eyes. Proslavery delegates in the legislature responded to the petitions by drawing up a bill to repeal the 1782 manumission law; fortunately, this was defeated by a vote of fifty-two to thirty-five.[95] At the same time, the Quakers were joined in their institutional support for emancipation by growing numbers of Methodists. Unlike the dissenting Quakers, Methodists arose from within the established Anglican Church—the Episcopal denomination, as it was known in Virginia after the Revolutionary War. The year 1784 was the Methodists' first as a separate denomination in Virginia, and it was a great one for opponents of slavery.[96]

The Methodists had recently experienced rapid growth in the region; although there were only about 200 Methodists in southern Virginia and North Carolina in 1774, by 1779 their numbers approached 5,000.

In 1784, frustrated by the Anglican Church's restrictive and hierarchical means of governing, Methodism founder John Wesley effectively allowed the American churches to separate from the Anglican fold in England.[97] He appointed two superintendents to serve the American Methodists exclusively; and like Wesley these men, Francis Asbury and Thomas Coke, were ardently opposed to slavery. Asbury wrote in 1779 that "I am strongly persuaded, that if the Methodists will not . . . emancipate their slaves, God will depart from them."[98] The Methodists joined the Quakers in believing that every human will stand before God to answer for his or her actions; no church or priest can interfere. The Methodists were particularly focused on personal holiness, and for a time this facilitated their willingness to make sacrifices in order to end what they saw as a grave moral injustice. As historian Eva Shepherd Wolf puts it: "Especially because manumitters who emancipated all their slaves were giving up so much—valuable property and the status that accompanied that wealth—community pressure, cajoling, and example were often necessary to help slaveholders translate antislavery ideals into the act of manumission."[99]

The denomination banned slavery in 1784, and in 1785 Bishop Coke rode his horse through Virginia preaching the necessity of emancipation—even though as a direct result he was threatened with whipping, indicted twice, almost clubbed on another occasion, and stalked by a would-be assassin. Even many faithful Methodists rejected the new official position on slavery. Nonetheless, in May twenty Virginia preachers meeting with Coke and Asbury had a change of heart and agreed to circulate a petition asking the General Assembly to emancipate all slaves.[100] Antislavery sentiment was at a new high in Virginia during this time. As Wolf has documented by looking at eight representative counties, although at other periods proslavery owners used manumission as a carrot—a tool to reward loyal slaves for good behavior (and thereby actually *strengthen* the system of slavery)—legitimate antislavery deeds "made up about half of all deeds of manumission from 1782 to 1793."[101]

The Methodists' petitions arrived at the General Assembly in October 1785, but they were met by counterpetitions from several proslavery counties. In the *Notes* (still unpublished at this moment), Jefferson argued that African peoples had a national right to self-government; one of these counterpetitions expressed precisely the opposite view, arguing that "it was ordained by the Great and wise Disposer of all Things, That some Nations should serve others; and that all Nations have not been equally free."[102] Perhaps word of Jefferson's antislavery *Notes* or the emancipation measure in his draft constitution had spread in Virginia despite his best efforts, because several petitions also spoke ominously of a "subtle and daring Attempt" being made to "dispossess us of a very important Part of our Property" by the "Enemies of our Country, Tools of the British Administration, and supported by certain Men among us of considerable Weight." These leading citizens, the petitioners suspected, were trying "To WREST FROM US OUR SLAVES, by an Act of the Legislature for a general Emancipation of them."[103]

Madison described the atmosphere in the Assembly for Jefferson: "Several petitions (from Methodists cheifly) appeared in favor of a gradual abolition of slavery, and several from another quarter for a repeal of law which licenses private manumissions." The antislavery petitions were not discarded, or "thrown under the table," although they were "treated with all the indignity short of it." Support for the proslavery petitions, by contrast, was high enough for a bill to be drawn up, once again repealing the law allowing individual manumissions, but fortunately the repeal bill was defeated "by a considerable majority."[104] This battle of the petitions occurred on 10 November; five days later Madison wrote to Jefferson to tell him to send the *Notes* to the students at William and Mary.[105] Clearly, although the current members of the General Assembly were unwilling to even debate a bill manumitting the slaves, Madison felt there was enough support for emancipation among evangelical and liberal-minded Virginians that the younger generation of leaders might be able to pass such a bill—if they could be converted to the cause. Jefferson's *Notes* was one such tool for educating the next generation and turning the tide of public opinion against slavery. But obviously Jefferson was correct to think that caution must be exercised, lest the proslavery forces around the state use the *Notes* to stoke proslavery fears, rendering it ammunition in another legislative battle and potentially even ending an individual owner's ability to independently manumit slaves. And tragically, official Methodist sentiment was short-lived: within six months of the denomination banning slavery among its membership in Virginia, lay resistance was so great that the leadership withdrew the ban. Individual Methodists continued to emancipate their slaves, but organized emancipation in the state had suffered another blow.

In the months before Jefferson received news of the battle of petitions, he was feeling optimistic regarding the rising tide of antislavery sentiment in America, and in July 1785 he began corresponding with the British minister and emancipationist Richard Price about the prospects for ending slavery in several parts of the South. Price, one of the first to receive a private copy of Jefferson's *Notes*, had recently published his own pamphlet in support of the American Revolution and opposing slavery. On 2 July he wrote to inform Jefferson that he had read the *Notes* "with Singular pleasure" and remarked that "happy would the united States be were all of them under the direction of Such wisdom and liberality as yours." Price was not so sanguine about the wisdom and liberality of *other* Americans, however. "I have lately been discouraged," wrote Price, "by an account which I have received from Mr. Laurens in South-Carolina." Henry Laurens, a fellow member of the American Philosophical Society, had just returned to his home state after being imprisoned in the Tower of London during the Revolution, and he wrote to their mutual friend Price with disappointing news about South Carolina's sensitivity on the issue of slavery.[106]

Although both Henry Laurens and his son, George Washington's aide-de-camp John Laurens, opposed slavery, they were just about the only prominent South Carolinians to do so.[107] When Henry Laurens distributed a political pamphlet written by Price among the South Carolina legislature, he ruffled several feathers: two prominent statesmen, Price reported to Jefferson, had "agree'd in reprobating my pamphlet on the American Revolution because it recommends measures . . . for gradually abolishing the Negro trade and Slavery." The state Speaker of the House, John Grimké, had written to Laurens to inform him that those measures would "never find encouragement in that State." Worse yet, an offense against southern honor had taken place: "Mr. Grimkey thought himself almost affronted" merely "by having the pamphlet presented to him by Mr. Laurens." Price was extremely disillusioned by the manner in which South Carolinians had received his pamphlet, as he told Jefferson: "Should Such a disposition prevail in the other United States, I shall have reason to fear that I have made myself ridiculous by Speaking of the American Revolution in the manner I have done."[108]

Jefferson immediately replied to Price, attempting to reassure him that not *all* Americans believed as Grimké did. Although it was true that those living "Southward of the Chesapeak" would indeed oppose Price's pamphlet, "the bulk of the people" who lived from "the mouth to the head of the Chesapeak" would "approve it in theory, and it will find a respectable minority ready to adopt it in practice." And north of the Chesapeake, since there were "but few slaves, they can easily disencumber themselves of them, and emancipation is put into such a train that in a few years there will be no slaves Northward of Maryland."[109]

Furthermore, Jefferson believed that in Virginia—the largest and wealthiest of the states and with an outsized influence on the politics of the entire country—the "sacred side" of the slavery debate was "gaining daily recruits from the influx into office of young men grown and growing up." Raised in the revolutionary climate of liberty, the younger generations were receptive to emancipationist arguments; they were the ones who would decide "the fate of this question."[110] Speaking to Price almost the same words he would soon hear from his own friends in Virginia, Jefferson wrote: "Be not therefore discouraged. What you have written will do a great deal of good." Not only would the pamphlet be beneficial, Jefferson believed, but Price had yet more to offer: "[N]o man is more able to give aid to the labouring side." Price should write another antislavery tract, this one specifically for the College of William and Mary. All the future leaders of Virginia were there, Jefferson said, being taught by Mr. Wythe—"whose sentiments on the subject of slavery are unequivocal"; such a pamphlet would thus have a "great, perhaps decisive" affect on the "future of this important decision."[111]

When Price replied to this appeal, he agreed with Jefferson in one important respect: "Young men are the hope of every state; and nothing can be of so much consequence to a state as the principles they

imbibe and the direction they are under." But the South Carolina de-
bacle had soured Price on pamphlets. "I cannot think of writing again
on any political subject," he told Jefferson. Though still opposed to
slavery, Price was determined that what he had already said on the
topic was sufficient. It should "be approved or rejected just as events
and the judgments of those who may consider them shall determine."[112]
Thus we see that, in the summer of 1785, Jefferson was not only hoping
to influence the College's students with his own *Notes*; he was also attempting to recruit other leading antislavery individuals to join in the
battle—albeit unsuccessfully.

Jefferson was not the only Virginian living in Paris to be optimistic
about the prospects for ending slavery at home that summer of 1785.
On 25 July Short wrote a letter to a mutual friend of theirs in America
in which he discussed the "Spirit of Exertion" that "seems to be gaining ground in Virginia . . . taking Measures for a gradual Abolition of
Slavery." Just as Jefferson focused on the need for a new constitution
alongside the need for an emancipation of Virginia slaves, so Short also
coupled his optimism about abolition with a call for a constitutional
convention. This would set the government on the "broad Basis of the
Authority of the People & universal Consent," and then the state would
become "the most desirable Spot on Earth." Apparently Jefferson's vision of the bliss to be found amid Virginia's agricultural society had
also taken hold of his young friend: "The Scope of Imagination cannot
carry my Idea of human Happiness," Short rhapsodized, "beyond that
of a free Citizen living in such a Country upon his own Farm & with
his own Wife & Family independent of all the World." A Virginia free
of slavery, and with a democratic constitution that provided a more
level playing field for all citizens, was what both Jefferson and Short
dreamed of from Europe that year.[113]

Finally, in December 1785 Jefferson received the response he had
been waiting for from Charles Thomson, who had received "a copy
of your Notes" and wrote once more to encourage Jefferson. Thomson began by affirming Jefferson's fears: "It grieves me to the soul that
there should be such just grounds for your apprehensions respecting
the irritation that will be produced in the southern states by what you

have said of slavery." All was not lost, however—"I would not have you discouraged. This is a cancer that we must get rid of. It is a blot in our character that must be wiped out." And once again Thomson proved himself to have particular insight into the future, remarking that, if slavery could not be "wiped out" through "religion, reason and philosophy, confident I am that it will one day be by blood." Thomson was more afraid of a war caused by slavery than of any European invasion; but he also reported that he had the "satisfaction to find that philosophy is gaining ground of selfishness," and if slavery could be "rooted out, and our land filled with freemen," this would go a long way toward preserving union in the republic and making America strong among nations.[114]

A few weeks later, James Madison's reply also finally arrived. Written partly in code, as had been Jefferson's to him, the letter is almost totally devoted to Madison's research into the potential fallout of distributing the *Notes* at the College of William and Mary. "I have looked [the book] over carefully myself," wrote Madison, "and consulted several judicious friends in confidence." These readers all agreed that the "*freedom of your strictures* on some *particular measures* and *opinions* will displease *their respective abettors*"—in other words, Jefferson's opposition to slavery and endorsement of a constitutional convention would indeed provoke some forms of backlash. However, Madison continued, "we equally concur in thinking that this consideration ought not to be weighed against the *utility of your plan*. We think both the facts and remarks which you have assembled too *valuable* not to be made known, at least to those for whom *you destine* them" (referring to the college students). Jefferson's like-minded Virginia friends did have one change to suggest for his plan: Professor Wythe believed it would be better to put the copies of the *Notes* into the library, instead of handing them out to students individually, both in order to make sure future students would have access to the copies of the *Notes* and to avoid offending any "narrow minded parents."[115] Monroe's reply arrived a few months later, and it was even more optimistic. Monroe told Jefferson that he would keep the book confidential, but he also hoped that Jefferson would soon consent to publish it, believing that "the observations you have made on the subjects you allude to would have a very favorable effect since no considerations would induce them but a love for the rights of man and for your country."[116]

Sooner than Jefferson expected, that decision—to publish or not to publish—was taken out of his hands in a most unexpected way. One of his closest friends while living in Paris that first year was a Swiss-born man named Charles Williamos, who began his career in America fighting for the British during the French and Indian War. He remained in the service of the British government, perhaps until the end of his life—although he seems to have concealed that rather important fact from his American friends during and after the Revolution. When Williamos arrived in Paris in 1785, he quickly ingratiated himself with Jefferson and is mentioned in Jefferson's account book even more than Short (who was often away courting the lovely "Belle of St. Germaine" that summer). By May Abigail Adams was noting in her journal that Williamos "always dines with Mr. Jefferson."[117] A stunning letter from Jefferson to his erstwhile friend of 7 July, however, hints that Jefferson had received information from a French politician about Williamos being a British spy and that something more had gone wrong between Jefferson and Williamos—but the details are lost to history. Although unfailingly polite, as always, Jefferson's indignation regarding the mysterious affront is apparent in every line: "Did the humiliating light in which you have represented me concern me as an individual only, I should be disposed to neglect it, and to spare myself the pain of the present letter. But in my present situation my conduct and character is interesting to the nation whose servant I am." Jefferson was apparently so upset by what he had learned about his supposed friend that he closed the letter by requesting they never have communications again. Soon afterward Williamos fell gravely ill, and his financial situation became so bad that Jefferson forwarded him money—anonymously, through their mutual friend Philip Mazzei.[118]

The worst was yet to come, however. In November Williamos died, and among his possessions was one of the original, privately printed copies of the *Notes*. Although Jefferson had carefully written "in every copy a restraint against it's publication," a Parisian bookseller named Louis François Barrois somehow got hold of Williamos's copy; as Jefferson related the tale to Madison, Barrois promptly "employed a hireling translator and was about publishing it in the most injurious form possible." Fortunately for Jefferson, another early recipient, the Abbé Morellet, caught wind of the scheme. Morellet, a respected scholar in his own right, had been confined to bed in November and December 1785, and around the time that Barrois obtained Williamos's copy, Morellet reported to Jefferson that reading (and beginning to translate) his personal copy of the privately printed edition of the *Notes* was a great comfort to him in his illness. Furthermore, Morellet had discussed the work with its early cheerleader, Chastellux, as well as their mutual friend the Marquis de St. Lambert, and they had together determined to persuade Jefferson that he should publish the book. Calling it "one of the most interesting works I have ever read," Morellet assured Jefferson that Morellet could not make better use of his time than by paying "homage" to the Virginian by translating his work into French.[119]

The details are lost to us today, but it seems that Morellet persuaded the unscrupulous bookseller Barrois to allow him to serve as his translator, since Barrois was anyway determined to release an unauthorized French edition. Upset that he had no say over the timing and language of publication, Jefferson reported: "I found it necessary to [agree to] this, and it will be published in French, still mutilated however in it's freest parts." It seems that the "mutilation" consisted of changes to Jefferson's structure and style, from rearranging the chapters to taking out whole phrases and rewording several sections.[120] Worse yet, once books were published in France, English printers inevitably reprinted them, for everything, "good or bad, is thought worth publishing there." The book would therefore have been translated twice—from English into French and back again—without Jefferson's having total control over it, and as a perfectionist this drove him crazy.[121]

As soon as it became apparent that his book was being published, whether he liked it or not, Jefferson threw himself into fixing errors and adding additional elements, such as an updated map of Virginia.[122] In 1750 his father, Peter Jefferson, had been commissioned to create what his son described as the "1st map of Virginia which had ever been made"; this project was completed when young Thomas was eight years old.[123] Now, Jefferson worked with the London engraver Samuel Neele to update his father's work and create a new map of Virginia and the surrounding states in time for the release of the French "abominable translation," as Jefferson called it. Since it would replace his father's earlier work as the most accurate existing representation of Virginia and the surrounding areas, Jefferson planned to offer separate copies of the map for sale in Virginia, where it would be invaluable to landowners and explorers alike; and while he was at it, he planned "to have as many maps struck off as might be necessary for the original [privately printed] edition in English, and even for a new edition in English, should one be ever printed."[124] However, just as he was reluctant to broadcast his authorship of the *Notes*, he specifically did not want his name to appear on the updated map, telling a friend that "I do not propose that my name shall appear . . . because it [should] belong to it's original authors, and because I do not wish to place myself at the bar of the public" to have his skills as a mapmaker put under the microscope.[125]

The *Notes* was published under a pseudonym as *Observations sur la Virginie* in late 1786; it was 390 pages long, although the last twelve pages were all misnumbered. Unlike the privately printed copies that Jefferson had distributed to fewer than thirty individuals in 1785, the 1786 French edition did not include appended material, such as the draft constitution for Virginia, but it did at least include a version of Jefferson's map.[126] Although Short's official duties consisted of negotiating a treaty in the Netherlands for much of the summer and fall of 1785, on 24 September Jefferson officially requested that he take up his post as private secretary in Paris. Short's assistance became even more vital the following summer, when Jefferson dislocated his right wrist. The injury was severe enough that two surgeons had to be called in to set the bones, but unfortunately they did a poor job; the wrist was painful for the rest of his life. Short had to write Jefferson's letters for him for at least a month, leading their mutual friend William Smith to joke that Short had truly become "Mr. Jefferson's right *hand man*" (with the emphasis appearing in the original).[127]

In addition to being Jefferson's right-hand man, Short also unofficially became his assistant editor as work on the *Notes* continued. By November 1786 Jefferson's prophecy about English publishers immediately reprinting French books came true: he was contacted from London by the prominent political publisher John Stockdale. "Some time past two French Gentlemen call'd upon me," wrote Stockdale, "with a Copy of your Minutes of Virginia, with a View to have it Printed." Fortunately, Stockdale contacted Jefferson first, rather than immediately reprinting this version, having heard rumors that a "New Edition was coming out with corrections by the Author." The rumors were true; Jefferson was indeed planning an English version that would correct the mutilations of the French 1786 edition, and eventually he did settle on Stockdale as his printer. Stockdale used Jefferson's personal "fair copy" manuscript—including the crossed-out sections and pasted-on tabs—for this first official English edition.[128]

As word spread about the existence of the *Notes*, Jefferson and Short began fielding requests for copies. On 12 May 1786, for instance, Short's relative Fulwar Skipwith, who was visiting England at the time, asked Short to "intercede with Mr. Jefferson for his Notes on Virginia & favor me with a sight of them."[129] By 6 June he had received a copy, and he gratefully wrote to say he was "much indebted" to Short.[130] Unfortunately for Skipwith, however, he only had the *Notes* for three months before he was "so unfortunat[e] as to leave them in the Chaise," and this horse-drawn carriage had apparently then carried away the book. About to board a ship back to Virginia, Skipwith wrote again, begging Short for another copy to be sent to him there. This time, Jefferson must have instructed Short to find a tactful way to turn down his forgetful relation Skipwith, and in December Short replied, somewhat misleadingly, "I am extremely sorry not to be able to furnish you with the Copy of Mr. Jefferson's notes. He has given away all those which he had printed." (This was not strictly accurate, since Jefferson would be distributing books from his batch of privately printed copies until 1787. Perhaps Jefferson had already decided who the recipients of those precious last copies would be and did not wish to spare a copy for a man who had already lost one.) Short had some comforting news, however: "As it is probable . . . that there will be a new impression made, I will take the first opportunity of procuring you one." Once the Stockdale version was available in England, it would be easier to distribute copies to acquaintances like Skipwith. Short continued by sharing his own impression of his mentor's writings, utilizing the criteria he had developed after being disappointed by some of the other authors he knew in France: "I am glad you were pleased with them, and wish they may be often read and studied by our countrymen. They contain many valuable truths that I should be happy to see disseminated: being persuaded that whatever is true is good to be known, and that the more truths, either in government or religion with which the world is enlightened, the better for mankind."[131]

Another reason for Jefferson's reluctance to distribute copies in 1786 may be gleaned from a letter he wrote explaining to his William and Mary mentor, George Wythe, why he had been slow to send even him a copy of the *Notes*: "Madison, no doubt, informed you of the reason why I had sent only a single copy to Virginia. Being assured by him that they will not do the harm I had apprehended, but on the contrary may do some good, I propose to send thither the copies remaining on hand, which are fewer than I had intended." By this point, however, Jefferson had discovered several areas of the *Notes* that he wanted to correct by printing out "a few new leaves and substituting them for the old." He intended to have his trusted Paris printer do this work while the map was being engraved and then to amend the remaining privately printed copies with these corrections and the new map.[132] Having correct information in circulation was so important to Jefferson that, once the corrected pages were printed, he gave new copies of the *Notes* to several of its first recipients. And he also promised to send Wythe one of these revised copies, although he declared humbly it was only because Wythe had asked for one: "Otherwise I should as soon have thought of sending you a horn-book," referring to a children's schoolbook, "for there is no truth there that is not familiar to you, and it's errors I should hardly have proposed to treat you with." Wythe firmly replied that Jefferson's "notes on Virginia" were "eagerly sought after; and this not by youth alone," no matter what Jefferson himself "writes, says, or thinks."[133]

In the same letter, Jefferson addressed the Virginia legislature's recent votes on the revisal of the legal code that he and Wythe had worked on in the late 1770s. "I think by far the most important bill in the whole code," he wrote, "is that for the diffusion of knowledge among the people. No other sure foundation can be devised for the preservation of freedom, and happiness." Jefferson had always been proud of their bill to make publicly funded education available to children in Virginia, but his time living in Europe had made him even more convinced that such measures to undergird republicanism were vitally important: "If any body thinks that kings, nobles, or priests are good conservators of the public happiness, send them here. It is the best school in the universe to cure them of that folly." France was a particularly effective teacher, he continued, "where notwithstanding the finest soil upon earth, the finest climate under heaven, and a people of the most benevolent, the most gay, and amiable character of which the human form is susceptible . . . surrounded by so many blessings from nature, are yet loaded with misery by kings, nobles and priests, and by them alone." Wythe had a vital role to play in saving Virginia from a descent into similar misery: "Preach, my dear Sir, a crusade against ignorance; establish and improve the law for educating the common people. Let our countrymen know that the people alone can protect us against these evils."[134]

As we have seen, Jefferson also believed that Wythe, as an educator, had a vital role to play in ending slavery in Virginia—after all, he had charge of future leaders of the state at the College of William and Mary, and he was "one of the most virtuous of characters, and whose sentiments on the subject of slavery are unequivocal." And Jefferson had not given up on his plan to add his own antislavery sentiments to Wythe's by sending copies of the *Notes* to William and Mary, especially after Wythe's assurance that the *Notes* was a sought-after book arrived in Wythe's letter of April 1787.[135] But work on the map took much longer than Jefferson had anticipated, and a series of misunderstandings further delayed the book's passage back across the ocean. A metal plate engraved with the map was finally sent from London by Neele the engraver on 21 December 1786, but when Jefferson examined it he found 172 errors. He handed the plate over to Short when Jefferson journeyed to the south of France to seek a cure for his injured wrist, and Short found an additional sixty-three mistakes, which he worked with a Paris engraver to fix before the plate was used for printing. The corrections were complete by the end of March; Short delivered the plate to Barrois, the French publisher who was printing the "mutilated" edition. The nefarious Barrois proceeded to wear down the plate so that it was much less readable, and then he refused to release it to Stockdale in London for months.[136]

Poor Stockdale resorted to writing frantic letters to Short, begging him to send the completed plate as soon as possible, since by May he had all the other sections of the *Notes* "printed & waiting for Publishing some time," and furthermore he was losing money because "the Season for Sale of Books in London, is now far advanced."[137] Jefferson had seemingly been more confident in the map than in any other part of his labors: "The map will be worth more than the book," he informed his publisher, "because it is very particular, made on the best materials which exist, and is of a very convenient size, bringing the states of Virginia, Maryland, Delaware and Pennsylvania into a single sheet. It will make the book sell."[138] But Barrois ignored Short's repeated requests to release the plate so it could be sent to London, and in the end Jefferson had to threaten him with the police.[139]

Finally, on 10 July 1787, Stockdale notified Jefferson that he had completed printing 1,000 copies of the first official English version of *Notes on the State of Virginia*. The work that had begun seven years earlier as a short answer to a Frenchman's questionnaire was, perhaps somewhat to Jefferson's chagrin, at last publicly available (in nonmutilated form) for critique. Jefferson wanted Stockdale to send 400 copies to America—200 for Philadelphia and 200 for Virginia. He also made a special request that two copies be sent to a young Virginian then studying at the University of Edinburgh: Thomas Mann Randolph Jr., a distant relation (and Jefferson's future son-in-law) whom Jefferson was mentoring long-distance.[140] Stockdale happily complied with this second request and reported that the book was being "well spoke of in London," but he had heard rumors that pirated copies of the book were already circulating in the United States and, therefore, was reluctant to send 400 precious copies to be sold there.

Stockdale was wrong; the *Notes* was not yet being circulated in America in its entirety, although it was being printed piecemeal in newspapers.[141] From Connecticut, a fellow author named Joel Barlow wrote to

Jefferson in June 1787 to inform him that "Your Notes on Virginia are getting into the Gazetts in different States, notwithstanding your request that they should not be published here." Despite this bad news, Jefferson must have been happy to hear from Barlow that other American authors were pleased with his work, particularly its defenses of American natural and political accomplishments: "We are flattered," Barlow wrote, "with the idea of seeing ourselves vindicated from those despicable aspersions which have long been thrown upon us and echoed from one ignorant Scribbler to another in all the languages in Europe."[142]

Still, Stockdale refused to send more than a few copies to be sold in Charleston and New York. As Jefferson told him the following year, this was a mistake that cost them dearly, both in profit and in the reputation of the book, for "as the work could not be bought there, the periodical papers retailed it out to the public by piecemeal till at length (as I am informed) a bad edition is printed, either without a map or with a slight sketch of one."[143] (And in reply, Stockdale sheepishly admitted that "[f]rom Letters which I have received from different Gentlemen in America I am convinced that the whole of the Impression of your Book would have been sold immediately had they been sent there."[144]) Fortunately, Jefferson did not let Stockdale's recalcitrance prevent copies from landing in the hands of the students at William and Mary; in September 1787 he took matters into his own hands, packing up the remaining copies from his private edition of 1785 (now edited and with copies of the map) to be shipped across the Atlantic as he had promised Professor Wythe he would do.[145] He included a note giving instructions as to how the books should be distributed: "10. copies of the Notes on Virginia for Mr. Wythe, P. Carr, Mr. Madison, Mr. Page, Mr. Bellini, Genl. Nelson, Mr. D. Jamieson, Colo. Innes, Colo. Richd. Cary of Warwick, and Colo. Wilson Miles Cary," in addition to "37. copies for such young gentlemen of the college as Mr. Wythe from time to time shall think proper, taking one or more for the college library." He also allotted copies for sale in Richmond and in New York, but Jefferson's contact in Richmond was not optimistic that even forty copies there would sell, since "you [Jefferson] may remember that your countrymen in general are not much given to books." Fortunately, the book was enthusiastically received at William and Mary.[146]

Bishop James Madison—the second professor of chemistry in America, Jefferson's fellow member of the American Philosophical Society, and president of the College of William and Mary from when Governor Jefferson appointed him in 1777 until his death in 1812—was an ardent and early supporter of Jefferson's *Notes*.[147] Bishop Madison's (younger) second cousin, the future president, had shown him one of the two tightly guarded copies of the *Notes* that Jefferson sent to Virginia after the first printing, and in 1786 the older Madison wrote to persuade Jefferson that "[s]uch a Work should not be kept in private. Let it have the broad Light of an American Sun. It will assist greatly in dispelling some Misty Fogs, which still hover about us."[148] A second letter that year demonstrates that Bishop Madison shared Jefferson's optimism for the young students at the college and their potential to ensure the continuation of the republican experiment: "I hope the best supporters to our Republic will go forth from our University," he told Jefferson, "and that with the Assistance of Science, Time will only serve to give [America] more and more Stability. Sure I am, and I believe you will rejoice to hear it, that the Spirit of Republicanism is infinitely more pure as well as more ardent in the rising Generation than among any other Class of Citizens." Since this was Jefferson's own belief, Madison's words must have reassured him that sending the *Notes* to the college was the right thing to do.

And to bolster that very decision, Madison added as a postscript: "Your Book is read here, by every one who can get a View of it, with the greatest Avidity.—I flatter myself you would favour our University with some Copies, and I have not yet relinquished the Hope."[149] Although the various misadventures Jefferson endured with the map slowed down the process, and the journey from Paris to Williamsburg lasted months, those copies finally arrived at the college in July 1788. In early 1789 an appreciative Bishop Madison gave Jefferson a more thorough review: "Your Notes on Virginia I shall always highly esteem not only on Account of their intrinsic worth, but also, the Hand from which they came." Perhaps referring to the issue of slavery, Madison added that "I know not how your Confutation of a certain opinion so derogatory to America, may be received in Europe, but, to my Mind, it is compleat." He concluded with his hope that "your Notes judiciously distributed among our young Men here, will tend to excite the spirit of philosophical observation amongst us."[150] The *Notes* was placed in the library, and as we shall see, it did prove instrumental in shaping the opinions of several generations of young leaders regarding slavery.

In France, the Barrois edition—*Observations sur la Virginie*—was well received by the literary elites. Although it had been published without Jefferson's name on it, the esteemed French literary journal *Mercure de France* declared that the work itself put its anonymous author into the same category as Benjamin Franklin, who enjoyed celebrity status in France as a scientist and philosopher.[151] The sympathetic reviewer furthermore asserted that the author of *Observations* skillfully challenged Buffon and Raynal, and he seemed to hint at Jefferson's identity as the author by stating that Franklin, George Washington, the Adams family, and Jefferson himself proved that the degeneration theory was flawed when it came to the new leaders of the American republic. And the reviewer praised the French edition's treatment of slavery, which the reviewer described as a "horrible practice, the shame of humanity." Jefferson's colonization plan received particular approval from the reviewer, who noted that the *Observations* promoted emancipation despite its author's obvious belief in the inferiority of black people. To the reviewer, this demonstration of humanity trumping prejudice showed that the author was a truly wise *philosophe*.[152]

The publication in France came at a particularly opportune time, not only because of the rising surge of liberal ideas that would lead to the Revolution in 1789 but also because the ardent abolitionism that had been percolating across the English Channel was making its way over to Paris. Along with Portugal and Britain, France was among the primary slave-trading and -owning European nations, having transported close to a million Africans to plantations in the French Caribbean during the Age of Enlightenment. The French economy was heavily dependent on these islands, and despite the successful slave rebellion on the island of Saint-Domingue (Haiti), slavery was not permanently abolished by France until 1848.[153] But when Jefferson and Short lived in Paris, French abolitionism was gaining ground, due in part to the aid of British leaders such as Thomas Clarkson. In 1787 Clarkson drew together a (mainly Quaker) group of experienced antislavery activists to form the London Society for the Abolition of the Slave Trade. Although their goal was the eventual abolition of slavery itself, these English activists believed—as did their French and American allies—that ending their country's participation in the slave trade was the best first step toward that larger goal. In 1788 Clarkson encouraged a friend, the French journalist, politician, and emancipationist Jacques-Pierre Brissot de Warville, to found the French equivalent of Clarkson's London society: La Société des Amis des Noirs (The Society of the Friends of the Blacks).[154]

Its core membership was drawn from the same group of Frenchmen that made up the Gallo-American Society, or *les Américains*, those elite thinkers and friends of Jefferson and Short—Brissot, Mirabeau, Condorcet, La Fayette, Rochefoucauld—who loved to debate the ideas embodied in the American republic. The Gallo-American Society's concern with "illegitimate political institutions" led naturally to a concern with slavery's illegitimate constraints on natural liberty; however, because actual French slaves toiled on islands far removed from France, this problem was generally superseded by more pressing domestic matters.[155] Those members of the Gallo-American Society who became "Friends of the Blacks" were willing to devote time and political capital to ending the slave trade, but the Société was essentially an elite Parisian organization, made up only of those who could afford a hefty membership fee, and the members were primarily affiliated with the Girondin political faction—which meant, unfortunately, that in only a few short years their ranks would be decimated during the purgings of the Terror.

The Société would also be far less effective than its British and American allies, in part because of its narrow membership base, in part because it was secular (and therefore lacking in the religious motivations that served the American and British abolitionists so well), in part because it failed to perform the kinds of persuasive, in-depth research that its British allies conducted into the economic and human realities of the trade, and in part because its first president, Brissot, was frequently absent in America. When Clarkson visited in 1789, he complained that meetings were infrequent and poorly attended.[156] Instead of cultivating grassroots support, the Société relied on its printed works: pamphlets and newspaper articles, which Brissot incorrectly believed would prove tremendously powerful. He also cultivated international support, traveling to meet with the antislavery society in Philadelphia and even taking his antislavery pamphlet to George Washington at Mount Vernon; tragically he met his end under the guillotine only a few years later.[157]

On 10 February 1788, Brissot invited Jefferson to the inaugural meeting of the Société (stating that, if Jefferson were not available, "[w]e hope that Mr. Short, whom we invite to come, will replace you").[158] Brissot and Jefferson were frequent correspondents in those years; Jefferson aided Brissot in writing about America, and Brissot gave Jefferson wine recommendations. Brissot was also an early and enthusiastic recipient of the *Notes*, and he knew from it and personal conversation that Jefferson opposed both the slave trade and slavery itself.[159] The following day, Jefferson responded, and his answer is worth quoting at length:

> [N]obody wishes more ardently to see an abolition not only of the trade but of the condition of slavery [than I do]: and certainly nobody will be more willing to encounter every sacrifice for that object. But the influence and information of the friends to this proposition in France will be far above the need of my association. I am here as a public servant; and those whom I serve having never yet been able to give their voice against this practice, it is decent for me to avoid too public a demonstration of my wishes to see it abolished. Without serving the cause here, it might render me less able to serve it beyond the water.[160]

Although he asserted support for the Société, Jefferson held that it would be wrong for him to join an antislavery organization in another nation when his own constituents were still deeply divided over the issue. As a private citizen, he could publish a book attacking slavery; as a public figure on a diplomatic mission, he claimed that he could not join the Société. Brissot immediately replied that he and the other founding members "applaud the motives which prevent you from surrendering to Our invitation, and our regret diminishes a little by thinking that your opinion is the same as Our own, and that You second it by means which will not compromise Your public character and what You owe to the respectable body of which you are the [mouthpiece]."[161]

But William Short was under no such compunction; he no longer had any constituents in America and was paid privately by Jefferson to serve as his secretary. So Short joined his friends at the Société, keeping Jefferson apprised of its activities. As we shall see in the ensuing chapters, Short also became a lifelong advocate for emancipation, as well as a key member of transatlantic networks of abolitionists that stretched from Europe to Philadelphia and beyond.

Scholars frequently speculate as to Jefferson's motives for arguing against slavery in the *Notes*. Defending America's reputation in Europe was one of his primary goals as minister to France, and taking up an antislavery pose was often favorably received among enlightened audiences. Therefore, it seems plausible that "[e]ven Thomas Jefferson," with his less-than-sterling antislavery reputation among many modern historians, "recognized how slavery could stain the nation's reputation in the eyes of French liberals," as François Furstenberg puts it.[162] It is possible that Jefferson was a public-relations expert who chose to bolster his antislavery credentials while living abroad in order to appear like an enlightened and humane *philosophe*. But it is important to recall that Jefferson wrote the antislavery passages in the *Notes* long before he was sent to Europe. Moreover, he proposed gradual emancipation in his constitution for Virginia while fully expecting that the General Assembly would see and vote on this plan: he did not devise it after the fact to impress European liberals.

Jefferson began the book with a French audience in mind, but as he revised it during the final stages of the Revolutionary War, he became increasingly aware of the way it would be read by his fellow Virginians. After Charles Thomson's prescient advice about the way in which his dissertation on race could embolden slaveholders, Jefferson penned the most stirring condemnation of slavery to come from any Founder. He also refused to delete the passages speculating on racial inferiority, in part because these passages reflected the latest in (primarily French) anatomical and philosophical scholarship. His double audience—Virginian and French, slaveholding provincials and cosmopolitan elites—shaped the composition of the text in seemingly contradictory ways. Likewise, Jefferson's desire to achieve respect and recognition for his country and himself via the *Notes* was at war with his fear that his countrymen would reject both him and the prospect of emancipation for Virginia.

At this moment the British, just as they had been in 1776, were indirectly responsible for pushing Jefferson's words onto the international stage. The death of the British spy Williamos in Paris, and the subsequent "mutilated" French edition of 1786, forced Jefferson's hand. But by now, surrounded by other elite intellectuals whose printed words were guiding world opinion on the new United States, he embraced publication and pressed his printer, Stockdale, to send copies to America as well as to London and other parts of Europe. Even before the Stockdale edition made its way to Richmond and Philadelphia, the *Notes* was already becoming well known in America. It was reprinted in the United States at least thirteen more times before Jefferson's death in 1826, and it has never been out of print since.[163]

As we have seen, early readers including John Adams, the emancipationist Richard Price, James Madison, and James Monroe, in addition to many of Jefferson's French compatriots, praised the book for its antislavery passages. From deeper in the American South, other early readers reacted somewhat differently: one leading South Carolina politician, Francis Kinloch, wrote in 1789 to warn Jefferson that the *Notes* was not having Jefferson's desired antislavery effect in that state. Kinloch ominously described "the general alarm which [a] passage in your Notes occasioned amongst us," evidently meaning one of the antislavery passages, and remarked: "It is not easy to get rid of old prejudices, and the word 'emancipation' operates like an apparition upon a South Carolina planter."[164] Another anonymous southern reader later wrote angrily in the margin of an early copy: "This kind of morbid sensibility in our great men is the salient down from which abolitionism of the North took life and motion."[165] For proslavery southerners, the most significant—and dangerous—part of Jefferson's work was his strong attack on slavery.

For some antislavery readers, however, Jefferson's attack on slavery was weakened by his speculations on race. The historian and fellow American Philosophical Society member David Ramsay warned Jefferson that, though the *Notes* was an impressive achievement, "You have depressed the Negroes too low." Ramsay seems to have discussed Jefferson's work with a fellow Princeton graduate, Samuel Stanhope Smith, who was then working on a monogenist essay on race. Ramsay was so impressed with Smith's ideas that he arranged for Smith to speak at the American Philosophical Society in early 1787; the APS requested that Smith's speeches be published in a book titled *Essay on the Causes of the Variety of Complexion and Figure in the Human Species.* In addition to Jefferson's *Notes,* Smith's 1787 *Essay* was one of the only American publications to be reprinted in London and Edinburgh and positively received throughout Europe. It was also one of the first published attacks on Thomas Jefferson's racial theories.[166]

In part, Smith argued that Jefferson's insistence on examining black people in the context of slavery was unfair: Jefferson and other slaveholders were incapable of seeing their slaves' true potential because they despised enslaved people and kept them in ignorance. But even Smith retained the ubiquitous belief that whiteness was the pinnacle of the human species, speculating that black and Native peoples could improve and lighten their color in the right environment, arguing as evidence for this that black slaves who lived close to white people (house slaves, for example) grew to have features similar to those of white people. That Jefferson failed to notice such changes in his own slaves when they lived in close proximity to himself perhaps meant, speculated Smith, that Jefferson and his fellow Virginians were actually the deficient ones! Smith, like Jefferson, was a slave owner who publicly opposed slavery and emphasized the need for educating enslaved people before freeing them. Unlike Jefferson, Smith tentatively advocated emancipation facilitated by both colonization *and* racial intermarriage as a way to rid the nation of both slavery and blackness. A colony in the western region of America could be settled by freed people, and white people could be paid to join and marry them, eventually "obliterat[ing] those wide distinctions which are now created by diversity of complexion." Although Smith (correctly) doubted that public enthusiasm for his plan would be sufficient to spur the necessary state and federal government funding, he still predicted that, without *something* being done, slavery would produce "many moral and political evils." Jefferson agreed with this, and his own emancipation plan was similar to Smith's in its insistence on education and colonization. But Smith's support for interracial marriage within a colony (albeit one that had to be encouraged by government payments to the white colonists) marks him as a thinker ahead of his time.[167] Smith himself became the president of Princeton University in 1802, confident that slavery was "not nearly so awful as most of its critics claimed, and [that] in any case eventually it would end."[168]

At least one part of Smith's critique was correct, of course: Jefferson's attempt at a scientific categorization of race was hopelessly flawed by prejudice—as were the attempts of the European scholars Jefferson was attempting to engage. If Jefferson had heeded Charles Thomson's advice and deleted his entire discourse on race, Jefferson's work would seem more consistent, and perhaps his criticism of slavery and plan for emancipation and colonization would also have received more unvarnished recognition, in his own day and in ours.

Despite Ramsay's and Smith's criticisms, the *Notes* was still read by many as an antislavery text. In 1791, for example, a black astronomer named Benjamin Banneker wrote Jefferson a letter in which he referred to the then–secretary of state as having a reputation for being "measurably friendly and well disposed toward [black people] . . . willing and ready to Lend your aid and assistance to our relief from those many distresses and numerous calamities to which we are reduced." Although Banneker had battled race prejudice all his life, he believed that Jefferson was "a man far less inflexible in Sentiments of this nature, than many others." After all, Jefferson's *Notes* did leave open the possibility that "further observation" of the race would prove his suspicion of black mental inferiority to be incorrect. Banneker therefore enclosed "a copy of an Almanack which I have calculated for the Succeeding year . . . the production of my arduous Study."[169]

Jefferson replied to Banneker's letter immediately. "No body wishes more than I do," said Jefferson, "to see such proofs as you exhibit, that nature has given to our black brethren, talents equal to those of the other colours of men, and that the appearance of a [lack] of them is owing merely to the degraded condition of their existence both in Africa and America." At first, Jefferson seems to have been willing to accept Banneker's almanac as evidence that black men could have innate mental capabilities equal to those of white people and that, given the right environment, those capabilities might be realized. Jefferson promptly forwarded the almanac to the Marquis de Condorcet, an antislavery French politician (and member of the APS), informing him that "we have now in the United States a negro ... who is a very respectable Mathematician." Not only had Banneker compiled an almanac—"which he sent me in his own handwriting"—he had also completed "very elegant solutions of Geometrical problems," and he was a "very worthy and respectable member of society." In fact, Jefferson had himself previously recommended Banneker for work on a federal surveying project. It appears that, for Jefferson, Banneker was one of the first signs that "the want of talents observed in [Africans] is merely the effect of their degraded condition, and not proceeding from any difference in the structure of the parts on which intellect depends."[170]

Banneker and his antislavery patrons soon printed the Jefferson correspondence. Other antislavery advocates also cited Jefferson and his *Notes* to bolster their arguments. Some edited out his speculations on race, while others were more inventive. Thomas Branagan, for instance, referred to Jefferson as the "greatest statesman and philosopher in America," whose antislavery passages in the *Notes* were strengthened because they were pronounced by someone "who cannot be supposed to be prejudiced in favor of the African race." The fact that Jefferson could advocate for emancipation *in spite of his racism* served to demonstrate to Branagan the authenticity of his words—or at least that is how Branagan chose to interpret Jefferson for the purposes of furthering the antislavery cause in his 1804 essay.[171]

Jefferson's political opponents had less favorable interpretations of both the *Notes* and his letter to Banneker. In the heightened atmosphere of the election of 1796, a South Carolina Federalist congressman, William Loughton Smith—who only six years earlier had selectively quoted from the *Notes* to support the slave trade—now argued both that Jefferson's section on race was confusing and contradictory and that his "fraternizing epistle" to Banneker was an attempt to "acquire a little popularity with the free negroes." Jefferson, argued Congressman Smith, must be a secret abolitionist! Since Jefferson wrote to Banneker shortly after returning from five years as minister to France, Smith speculated that his Virginian common sense had deserted Jefferson, making him even more radical in his commitment to emancipation because he had imbibed too many French "delusive and visionary principles." All southern slaveholders should thus see Jefferson as a poor philosopher and as a threat to their constitutionally guaranteed property rights. In 1804 another Federalist, Thomas Green Fessenden of New Hampshire, similarly mocked Jefferson for abandoning the speculative racial hierarchy of the *Notes* after naively being taken in by the "wonderful phenomenon of a Negro Almanac, (probably enough made by a white man)." A black man, in other words, surely could not have completed a sophisticated mathematical work without help.[172]

Eventually, Jefferson himself began to state that Banneker had likely written with assistance from white patrons. However, Jefferson never recanted his conviction that all men (and women) were naturally entitled to liberty, no matter their color or intellectual ability. As he said regarding darker members of the "human family" in 1809, "whatever be their degree of talent it is no measure of their rights. Because Sir Isaac Newton was superior to others in understanding, he was not therefore lord of the person or property of others."[173]

Most important to the future of his state, by the late 1780s Jefferson's book was in the hands of the students at the College of William and Mary, and two copies were in the possession of future governor Thomas Mann Randolph, then a student at the University of Edinburgh. As Jefferson had hoped, his words on slavery would become part of the curriculum for future leaders at William and Mary. Under the guidance of George Wythe and the professors Wythe trained, the *Notes* became an important element in convincing several of those future leaders to oppose slavery. By 1832 versions of Jefferson's emancipation and colonization plan had been proposed by three generations of Virginians, including his own son-in-law and his grandson.

4. Alternatives to Slavery, 1785–1798

On 22 June 1798 Thomas Jefferson received a letter that was rather remarkable for its day. It was written by William Short, the orphan who had been mentored by Jefferson since he was nineteen years old. He called Jefferson his "father," and Jefferson referred to Short as his "adoptive son." Short, who was negotiating a treaty in Spain at the time, began his letter with an inquiry about the farm that Jefferson was managing for him in Virginia. The two men had decided to utilize this property as a kind of emancipation experiment, renting out sections of land to poor white farmers for the explicit purpose of proving that free labor was more efficient and profitable than slave labor.

Jefferson's long-term goal for this experiment was to secure emancipation for all slaves in Virginia and then to export those freed people to a colony. But Short was becoming increasingly convinced that exporting former slaves would hurt the state economically and that therefore they should be allowed to remain in Virginia as citizens. Furthermore, Short now thought that black and white people were equals and that therefore the best solution to the problem of race would be for citizens of all races to simply marry one another. He acknowledged that mixing the two races might be considered evil by some people but asked Jefferson: "If this be an evil, is it not the least that can take place under present circumstances? It is certainly less" than having "free people living in the same country & separated from the rest of the community by a marked & impassable line." And anyway, Short added, was racial mixture really so bad? He gave Jefferson the example of an elite Virginian lady they both knew, a Mrs. Tucker, and argued that her darker-than-usual complexion was the perfect blend of the lily and the rose. What nation, Short asked his mentor, could possibly object to having all its ladies looking like that?[1]

Jefferson did not specifically answer Short's question for another twenty-eight years, even though Short raised it again several times. In fact, Jefferson did not reply at all until 1800. By that time he was embroiled in one of the most contentious presidential elections in American history, and he warned Short that a "campaign of slander" against him had begun. Although Jefferson did not specify *what* that slander consisted of, rumors about a relationship between Jefferson and his enslaved worker, Sally Hemings, would soon become part of Federalist attacks against him. Though there is, so far as we know, no evidence to show exactly *what* Short knew about the relationship, or *when* he knew it, we do know that, because of the tense political environment and the tendency of private mail to be opened and published without the correspondents' consent, Jefferson probably felt he could not openly address Short's radical ideas about racial equality, even if he wanted to. But Jefferson could not have been surprised by the content of Short's letter. Short had, like Jefferson, emerged from his training at the College of William and Mary and his legal studies with George Wythe inculcated with a firm opposition to the institution of slavery. More important, while they were in Europe between 1785 and 1789, it was Jefferson who had encouraged Short to begin pursuing the issue of how best to end slavery; it was Jefferson who enlisted Short's help in researching the ancient practice of *metayage*, or tenant farming; and together they developed a plan to utilize metayage in Virginia as a transitional form of labor for freed slaves. When their relationship became strained by personal and professional disagreements in the wake of the French Revolution and Jefferson's return to America, it was this conversation about free labor in Virginia that brought them back together again in the late 1790s. By that time, William Short's many years away from Virginia's slave society, his allegiances to liberal French abolitionists and reformers, and his experiences as a diplomat had led him to more radical conclusions than Jefferson could accept.

Even before Jefferson and Short began their dialogue about slavery, another intergenerational pair had a similar discussion. In 1783, the year before Jefferson arrived in Paris, the Marquis de La Fayette wrote a momentous letter to the man he frequently referred to as his "father," George Washington.[2] The victorious general was looking forward to retirement at his farm, Mount Vernon, when young Lafayette (the common spelling in America) proposed, in his characteristically enthusiastic style, a daring idea:

> Let us Unite in Purchasing a small Estate Where We May try the Experiment to free the Negroes, and Use them only as tenants—Such an Example as Yours Might Render it a General Practice, and if We succeed in America, I Will chearfully devote a part of My time to Render the Method fascionable in the West indias—if it Be a Wild scheme, I Had Rather Be Mad that Way, than to Be thought Wise on the other tack.[3]

Washington responded favorably but deferred further discussion until Lafayette arrived for his next visit at Mount Vernon in the summer of 1784. Another houseguest, the Reverend William Gordon, witnessed this meeting and later summarized it thusly to Washington: "You wished to get rid of all your Negroes, & the Marquis wisht that an end might be put to the slavery of all of them. I should rejoice beyond measure could your joint counsels & influence produce it, & thereby give the finishing stroke & the last polish to your political characters." Gordon concurred with Lafayette's idea, adding that, if the most "industrious among" the slaves produced a greater profit from the farmland while working as tenants than they had as slaves, it could "excite the lazy [slaves] to exertions [tha]t might prove highly beneficial." Gordon hastened to reassure the general that "I am not for letting them all loose upon the public; but am for gradually releasing them & their posterity from bonds, & incorporating them so in the states, that they may be a defence & not a danger upon any extraordinary occurrence."[4]

Gordon's letter to Washington reveals two of the major concerns Virginian slaveholders had on the topic of emancipating their slaves: profit and stability. As an agricultural-based economy heavily dependent on its enslaved workforce, Virginia did not seem likely to thrive if all the slaves were freed at once. Most antislavery proposals of this period therefore contained references to gradual emancipation, rather than immediate, and were often also concerned with compensation for the slaveholders. But if, as Gordon suggested, slaves were given both freedom and a financial incentive to work diligently on their former masters' land, resulting in higher profits for the master-turned-landlord, emancipation would be recognized as economically *and* morally beneficial.

Gordon also referred to a second major concern of white southerners, of "letting [slaves] all loose on the public." Even antislavery advocates in the North, where the ratio of slave to free was very small, were concerned with how well slaves—largely illiterate, landless, and impoverished—would integrate into free society. Colonization was therefore routinely linked to emancipation from the late eighteenth century until well into the Civil War.[5] In Virginia, where black people made up at least 40 percent of the population in 1800, white citizens were particularly concerned about what could happen after widespread emancipation. As Alan Taylor has extensively documented, the experience of having slaves run away to fight for the British during the American Revolution increased Virginians' paranoia about potential slave uprisings, even the possibility of seeing freed slaves side with invading armies.[6] Many now feared that a large population of free black people living among them could tip the scales toward destruction in the event of another war. Jefferson addressed this concern in his *Notes*, albeit with an emphasis on the righteousness of slaves' anger: freeing the slaves without subsequently removing them to another location would, he speculated, "produce convulsions which will probably never end but in the extermination of the one or the other race" due to whites' prejudice and to the "ten thousand recollections, by the blacks, of the injuries they have sustained" under slavery.[7] But Gordon, inspired by Lafayette's plan, felt sure that gradual emancipation coupled with a system of tenant farming on their former owners' land would result in a contented and loyal population of free and productive laborers who could even aid in America's defense, if necessary.

Although Gordon did not possess the insight or vocabulary to describe the psychological and social processes by which enslaved people might transition to freedom and membership in the broader community, this is a vital part of what "incorporating" slaves gradually into "the states" would mean. Often legally prohibited from learning to read, and constrained in the skills they could learn, enslaved people lived extremely limited lives, and these limitations made transitioning to life in freedom extremely challenging. Moreover, even the kindest of masters in eighteenth-century Virginia held the power of violence over their slaves, and more significant, slaves were by definition alienated from vital social institutions—denied basic legal rights, the most important being marriage and custody of children. At any moment, a slave could be torn away from husband, wife, children, parents, and friends, then sold to another master in another state. Enslaved people built their communities and maintained their traditions in the face of terrible suffering and despite constant uncertainty. The transition from slavery to freedom therefore required far more than a simple legal transaction: it also entailed massive shifts in a freed person's self-conception.

Moreover, slaves in the American South typically did not receive wages, and they were often housed in sparse quarters and fed basic rations doled out in regular installments. These items were not given in payment for labor; they were "by no means the reward of superior service, for all received the same allotment. The slave's inducement to work was the negative one of evading the 'driver's lash.'" Emancipation thus generally entailed a transition from a fear- and force-based economy into a free market economy, motivated by profit and reward. White Virginians, by contrast, would have to adjust to an entirely different societal structure, one in which being white would not necessarily automatically confer a higher rung on the social ladder. Men like Washington and Gordon were only just beginning to fathom the depth of cultural and economic upheavals that emancipation would bring to a state as dependent on slavery as was Virginia.[8]

For Lafayette, however, the economic and cultural entanglements of slavery were less of a challenge: his life and fortune were securely centered in France, and France's slavery existed only in its far-off colonies. A few months after his momentous meeting with Washington and Gordon, Lafayette wrote from Paris to tell his mentor that he did not want to wait any longer. He had decided to begin the experiment on his own: in June 1785 he secretly instructed his attorney to purchase a plantation and slaves for him in the French colony of Cayenne (present-day French Guiana, on the coast of South America). He told Washington that he was "going to free my Negroes in order to Make that Experiment which you know is my Hobby."[9] Although he did not formally free them, almost seventy slaves were paid to work on

Lafayette's far-off clove and cinnamon plantation, La Belle Gabrielle, and they were provided with schooling and religious instruction.[10] The overseers reported some success in encouraging labor without recourse to corporal punishment but were frustrated by what they believed to be innate characteristics that made the race unsuitable for equality with whites. Unfortunately, this experiment with semi-free labor was short-lived; when Lafayette fell out of favor during the French Revolution, all his property was confiscated and the laborers were sold.[11]

When Washington first heard of Lafayette's generosity, he could only reply that he wished "to God a like spirit would diffuse itself generally into the minds of the people of this country, but I despair of seeing it." Washington's despair was due to a circumstance discussed in chapter 3: in 1785, as Washington received Lafayette's good news, he was also hearing about the Methodist petitions that were "presented to the Assembly at its last Session, for the abolition of slavery." Echoing James Madison's report to Jefferson, Washington ruefully told his "adoptive son" that these petitions were looked at with disgust by many legislators and "could scarcely obtain a reading."[12] But Washington had not given up all hope. Although he never spoke out publicly against slavery and believed that immediate emancipation would "be productive of much inconvenience & mischief," he also held that if it were accomplished "by degrees" then "it certainly might, & assuredly ought to be effected & that too by Legislative authority."[13] Like Jefferson, Washington believed that public opinion in Virginia could still turn in favor of emancipation, and when that occurred, then the legislature should enact appropriate measures. Lafayette remained, for the time being, full of optimism regarding the possibilities of transforming slaves into freedmen while still maintaining profitability on plantations.[14]

The same summer that Lafayette began his momentous experiment at La Belle Gabrielle, Jefferson began discussing a similar plan while dining at the French country estate of a former minister to America, the Chevalier de la Luzerne. Also present were the anti-Buffon botanist (and leading French politician) Guillaume-Chrétien de Lamoignon de Malesherbes and Dr. Edward Bancroft, known to Jefferson as a physician, author, and prominent chemist (but also secretly working as a double agent for the British).[15] At some point during the visit, the conversation turned to emancipation—specifically the practical question of how well former slaves handled their newfound independence. As Dr. Bancroft later remembered it, Jefferson "mentioned the Case of a Gentleman in Virginia, who had benevolently liberated all his Negroe Slaves and endeavoured to employ them on Wages to Cultivate his Plantation," a plan much like that of Lafayette. Unfortunately, according to Jefferson's sources, the "Gentleman in Virginia" had found after some time that "Slavery had rendered them incapable of Self Government, or at least that no regard for futurity could operate on their minds with sufficient Force to engage them to any thing like constant industry or even so much of it as would provide them with food and Cloathing." Jefferson had further heard that the "most sensible" among the freed slaves "desired to return to their former state" of slavery.[16]

These dismal reports from Virginia perhaps reinforced Jefferson's existing prejudice, developed over a lifetime of interacting with black people almost exclusively in the context of slavery. As he wrote in his *Notes*, he suspected that "the blacks, whether originally a distinct race, or made distinct by time and circumstances, are inferior to the whites in the endowments both of body and mind." Like the medieval Islamic intellectual Sāʾid al-Andalusi in Spain, who knew Africans primarily in the context of slavery and therefore believed that Africans "lack self-control and steadiness of mind and are overcome by fickleness, foolishness, and ignorance," Jefferson ascribed a series of negative traits to people of African descent.[17] For example, although he thought that black people needed less sleep than did whites, he also observed that, when they had time off from their labors on his plantation, they often used it to catch up on sleep. From this, rather than coming to the rather obvious conclusion that his hardworking slaves were tired, or that their recreational options were limited by their financial and educational hindrances, he decided that they were simply more lazy than white people.

He also doubted that black people possessed the mental capacity to govern their actions as well as did whites. Even in the midst of praising the writings of the former slave Charles Ignatius Sancho, Jefferson argued that his race caused Sancho to indulge in "wild and extravagant" flights of imagination, rendering him "incoherent and eccentric" and lacking "sober reasoning."[18] It makes sense, then, that Jefferson would not have expected black people to handle the responsibilities of independence in the same manner as the yeoman farmers he was familiar with, and in this letter he made no allowances for the psychological and cultural transitions that would have to occur before former slaves could be expected to flourish as independent farmers. Still, despite his prejudices, Jefferson did not dismiss the possibility that, given the right circumstances, a similar experiment with freedom could produce better results than the Virginian experiment he recounted at the French dinner party.

In late 1788 Dr. Bancroft brought up their conversation again. Having witnessed slavery as a physician on a plantation in Dutch Guiana, Bancroft was now keenly interested in the rising antislavery movement in France. Members of the antislavery Société des Amis des Noirs, hearing about the discussion that had taken place three years earlier, had asked Bancroft to solicit from Jefferson a fuller accounting of the Virginia "Experiment" of making slaves into tenants.[19] In his remarkable reply, Jefferson not only detailed what he believed to be the challenges facing owners who attempted to implement a tenancy model but also demonstrated that his years in Europe had caused him to become committed to trying that experiment himself.

He began his reply to Bancroft with a strong word of caution tinged with paternalism: "[A]s I can judge from the experiments which have been made, to give liberty to, or rather, to abandon persons whose habits have been formed in slavery is like abandoning children." These "experiments" to which he referred had been undertaken by those earliest proponents of abolition, the Quakers: Jefferson recalled hearing that many members of the sect had "seated their slaves on their lands as tenants," although whether those tenants paid "rent in money, or a share of the produce," Jefferson could not say. He had lived some distance away, and therefore could not describe the situation firsthand, but recalled hearing that the benevolent Quakers had to expend far too much effort to ensure the success of their crops. Jefferson reported to Bancroft that one landlord was "obliged to plan [the workers'] crops for them, to direct all their operations during every season and according to the weather, but, what is more afflicting, he was obliged to watch them daily and almost constantly to make them work, and even to whip them."[20]

Worse, the former slaves resorted to stealing from their neighbors, a situation that Jefferson excused, as he had in the *Notes*. In that book, he argued that the "disposition to theft with which they have been branded, must be ascribed to their situation, and not to any depravity of the moral sense." Because a slave's own right to property had been unjustly stripped from him, Jefferson believed a slave could "justifiably take a little from one, who has taken all from him." (Frederick Douglass would agree, remarking that for a slave to steal a chicken was simply "taking [the master's] meat out of one tub and putting it in another."[21]) Jefferson conceded that the propensity for theft was a product of the environment in which a slave lived rather than an intrinsic moral failing. This was proven by the fact that not all slaves succumbed to temptation: "[W]e find among them numerous instances of the most rigid integrity."[22] To Bancroft, Jefferson repeated a similar refrain: "A man's moral sense must be unusually strong, if slavery does not make him a thief. He who is permitted by law to have no property of his own, can with difficulty conceive that property is founded in any thing but force." The Quakers' semi-free tenants unfortunately "chose to steal from their neighbors rather than work. They became public nuisances, and in most instances were reduced to slavery again."[23]

However, rather than concluding from these dismal stories that African Americans were simply unfit for freedom, Jefferson warned Bancroft that his information was "imperfect," so Bancroft should not make it public. Instead, Jefferson asked the doctor to wait until Jefferson had made his planned visit to America in the spring of 1789. "During my stay in Virginia," he wrote, "I shall be in the neighborhood where many of these trials were made. I will inform myself very particularly of them, and communicate the information to you." Jefferson had also heard rumors about Joseph Mayo, a young Virginian who had died in 1785 and granted his approximately 200 slaves their freedom in his will. Jefferson proposed to also find out what had happened to those people in the intervening years.[24]

In what is perhaps one of the most startling pronouncements in all of Jefferson's correspondence, however, he concluded by informing Bancroft that the "discouraging results" of the Quakers' experiments had not deterred him from making his own emancipation plan. After he moved back to America permanently, Jefferson had decided that he would "import as many Germans as I have grown slaves. I will settle them and my slaves, on farms of 50. acres each, intermingled, and place all on the footing of the Metayers (Medietarii) of Europe." Jefferson was here referring to the ancient agricultural system, similar to sharecropping, that was practiced throughout France and parts of Italy. "Their children shall be brought up," he continued, "as others are, in habits of property and foresight, and I have no doubt but that they will be good citizens." As we have seen, Jefferson subscribed to the belief that education was vital in the construction of character and the inculcation of virtue.[25] This principle applied to the children of slaves just as much as to the children of white Virginians, and Jefferson therefore fully expected that being brought up with the responsibilities of property would produce a generation capable of independent life. However, Jefferson expected only a portion of the older generation of slaves to thrive independently, while "others I suppose will need government." Those of the "fathers" who did not fare well with freedom would be obliged by Jefferson "to labour as the labouring poor of Europe do, and to apply to their comfortable subsistence the produce of their labour, retaining such a moderate portion of it as may be a just equivalent for the use of the lands they labour and the stocks and other necessary advances."[26]

In many respects, Jefferson's emancipation strategy of January 1789 was just a repetition of the emancipation amendment he had earlier described in Query XIV of his *Notes*—but with one very important change.[27] That amendment, originally coauthored by Jefferson and George Wythe in 1779, provided for emancipation of all slaves born after a certain date, education of these newly freed slaves, and importation of white agricultural laborers from "other parts of the world."[28] The white laborers were to be a *replacement* workforce, because the entire generation of freed slaves was to be colonized—shipped to some other place, wherever was "most proper" at the time, and supported with supplies, weapons, and livestock so that they could form "a free and independent" nation of their own.[29] It was a vision of a more racially homogenous Virginia, freed from the metaphorical stain of slavery through the financial and bureaucratic oversight of the state government. This plan was calculated to appeal to both the best and worst parts of white Virginian consciences: they could end the sin of slavery without having to deal with their own prejudices. "White inhabitants" from other parts of the world would ostensibly be more suitable workers than the people of African descent who had been farming Virginia soil for generations.[30]

But as described in his 1789 letter to Bancroft, Jefferson's plan to import white immigrants had an entirely different purpose. Between his arrival in France in 1784 and this astonishing missive less than six years later, Jefferson had come to the conclusion that the Old World held the solution to the problem of New World slavery—which was itself a "vestige of the Old World."[31] Laborers from Germany should be the ones to live side by side with emancipated slaves in Virginia, apparently possessing qualities that would enable them to succeed both at producing crops and at living in an interracial setting. All would be employed as *metayers*, or sharecroppers, utilizing the tenant farming system that dated back to Roman times. In Jefferson's time, metayage was still predominant in much of France and Italy; the workers were referred to as "metayers" or "metairies." Although metayage and sharecropping as practiced in the American South after the Civil War share several common traits—such as a landowner providing land and often tools in exchange for tenants' labor and a share of the harvest—metayers in Europe generally had greater liberty to choose the location and terms of their tenancy. Moreover, because European metayers were less likely to become trapped in a cycle of debt to local businesses and landlords, metayage was closer to renting land than to slavery.[32]

Jefferson believed that the experience of working with and learning from willing European immigrants would transform the children of ignorant and oppressed slaves into "good citizens." But for those former slaves who were too old or otherwise unable to adapt to freedom, Jefferson proposed a semi-free working situation similar to that of the European "labouring poor" who had less control over their circumstances than did metayers but who were nonetheless provided for by the master/landlord. Colonization was not even mentioned; the racially homogenous vision of Virginia described in that 1779 amendment was replaced by the idea of a Virginia in which Germans and African Americans apparently labored side by side.

Interestingly, Jefferson's new plan also mirrored a much earlier one designed by the Quaker abolitionist Anthony Benezet: as Benezet described it in a 1773 letter to a fellow antislavery activist named John Fothergill, freed slaves and white people should be given plots of land to farm in the region between the Allegheny Mountains and the Mississippi River. By settling former slaves "amongst the whites, and by giving them a property amongst us," they would succeed in making a formerly hostile captive nation into people "interested in our welfare and security." Rather than colonizing black people to an independent settlement, as he had earlier proposed, Benezet now suggested settling new territory with a mixture of white and black pioneers. They could, as Nicholas Guyatt puts it, "perfect the alchemy of integration without [the] pressures of the heavily settled seaboard."[33]

No evidence exists, so far as I am aware, that Jefferson discussed the idea of emancipation and integration with Benezet or Fothergill, although he could perhaps have heard of Benezet's plan from a mutual friend such as Benjamin Rush. Nonetheless, the similarity in their thinking is striking; the only difference is that Jefferson proposed to attempt the mixed-race farming in Virginia, on his plantations, rather than as part of an internal colonization strategy. It is possible that when Jefferson told Bancroft that black children raised in this mixed-race environment at Monticello would become "good citizens," he meant they would become qualified for citizenship of some other country. But for some reason Jefferson did not make that distinction in this letter. Was he actually considering a free and multiracial future for Virginia?

Between his arrival in Europe and his astounding letter to Bancroft in 1789, Jefferson spent many hours considering the differences between the working populations of Europe and Virginia. One of the first evidences we have of this dates to the fall of 1785, just over a year after his arrival in France and a few months after his momentous conversation about emancipation with Bancroft at Vincennes. Jefferson had followed the royal court to Fontainebleau, where the king hunted every year. During his visit, Jefferson explored the mountainous region on foot, and on 27 October he met an impoverished woman who was walking the same direction as he. The encounter affected him so deeply that he wrote about it the next day to James Madison. "Wishing to know the condition of the labouring poor," Jefferson recounted, "I entered into conversation with her." The woman was a "day labourer," often unemployed or earning less than she needed to pay rent for herself and her two children, and on the day he met her she had no money even to buy bread. Moved by her distress, when they parted company Jefferson gave her a sum equivalent to three day's wages; the woman "burst into tears of gratitude."[34]

Jefferson was struck by the desperation of her situation, which he blamed on "that unequal division of property which occasions the numberless instances of wretchedness which I had observed in this country and is to be observed all over Europe." A small number of French nobility and clergy owned most of the land in France, and large portions of it were purposely left uncultivated to create hunting paradises like the one the king and his court were enjoying at Fontainebleau. Although these elites employed a fair number of the population, the most numerous class in France consisted of "the poor who cannot find work" and who had no land of their own from which to grow food. Jefferson asked himself why it was that "so many should be permitted to beg who are willing to work, in a country where there is a very considerable proportion of uncultivated lands." Equal division of the land was, he conceded, impossible; however, because "the consequences of this enormous inequality [result in] so much misery to the bulk of mankind, legislators cannot invent too many devices for subdividing property."[35] Short agreed, believing wider distribution of the land would "best insure the protection of personal liberties and private property by cultivating submission to, instead of independence of, the law."[36]

Jefferson's concerns about land ownership in France were an extension of his long-standing work to ensure a more equitable division of land among white people in his home state. As a legislator during the Revolutionary War, he played a decisive role in ending the feudal legal doctrines of primogeniture and entail, practices that had kept approximately two-thirds of all land in the hands of a small number of elite families. Under his leadership, the General Assembly passed laws ensuring that, when a deceased person did not leave a will, all children—including girls—would inherit equally. And since Virginia law required that citizens own fifty acres of land before they were allowed to vote, Jefferson also advocated that any (white) "person" (without specifying men) not meeting that land requirement should receive the appropriate amount out of publicly held lands.[37] Now, horrified by the needless landlessness and resultant poverty that confronted him in France, he expounded on what would become one of his most famous political philosophies: "The earth is given as a common stock for man to labour and live on. . . . It is too soon yet in our country to say that every man who cannot find employment but who can find uncultivated land, shall be at liberty to cultivate it, paying a moderate rent. But it is not too soon to provide by every possible means that as few as possible shall be without a little portion of land. The small landholders are the most precious part of a state."[38] Enslaved people in Virginia, who labored on the earth without ever owning it, did not fit into this eloquent vision for the state's future.

Jefferson likely felt, as did several of his European contemporaries who had observed slavery at Monticello firsthand, that his own enslaved workers were better off than people like the desperately impoverished woman he encountered at Fontainebleau. *At least*, he may have thought to himself, *my slaves are always fed and clothed.* But Jefferson's slaves also served as ever-present reminders that the republican principles he loved were not being fully implemented in Virginia. So, it seems, Jefferson began to imagine an alternative option, one that would culminate in a plan to change himself from a master to a landlord and his own slaves into tenant sharecroppers.[39]

Jefferson began to document France's sharecropping system while traveling through its southern region in the spring of 1787, leaving William Short to oversee the final stages of publishing his *Notes*.[40] The ancient, feudal agricultural system of metayage had come under scrutiny by forward-thinking French *philosophes* in the decades prior; the Marquis de Mirabeau referred to it as the "mother of misery" in his popular 1756 economic treatise *L'ami des hommes, ou traité de la population* (The friend of man, or treatise on population).[41] Jefferson found plenty of misery in his travels: as he described it in letters to his fellow revolutionary reformer, Lafayette, the peasants were generally "over worked, the excess of the rent required by the landlord, obliging them to too many hours of labor, in order to produce [the rent], and wherewith to feed and clothe themselves." An even bigger hindrance to the happiness of the laborers and the prosperity of the French economy, Jefferson believed, was the length of metayers' leases. For example, he had found "the soil of Champagne and Burgundy" to be "more universally good than I had expected," and yet the region failed to reach its potential for one reason: the manure. Or, rather, the lack thereof, which in turn was the product of bad laws that prevented long leases.[42]

In England, Jefferson explained, tenant farmers' leases generally lasted "for twenty-one years, or three lives, to wit, that of the farmer, his wife, and son, renewed by the son as soon as he comes to the possession, for his own life, his wife's and eldest child's, and so on." The ability of a son to renew his father's lease rendered farms in England "almost hereditary." And since a single family of tenants farmed the same land for generations, it was worth their while to put in the effort required to "manure the lands highly," resulting in improved soil quality and therefore better harvests. This situation also benefited landlords, who could occasionally raise the rent to "keep pace with the improved state of the lands." But as practiced in the French metayage system, leases were given "either during pleasure, or for three, six, or nine years, which does not give the farmer time to repay himself for the expensive operation of well manuring, and therefore, he manures ill, or not at all."[43] French peasants had no job security, so to speak, and therefore little incentive to put in the extra work to ensure the soil's long-term productivity.

If France's "unwise and unjust" lease laws were changed—perhaps by Lafayette and his fellows in the Assembly of Notables, which was meeting for the first time in more than a century—and if the duration of leases extended to allow several generations to farm the same land, then Jefferson predicted that within Lafayette's lifetime he would see agricultural productions increased by 50 percent. Likewise, Jefferson estimated that landowners could expect a 50 percent increase in rent over twenty-five years.[44] In general, Jefferson disapproved of what he saw when he traveled in southern France, since peasants—even when "well clothed, and hav[ing] the appearance of being well fed"—still experienced "all the oppressions which result from the nature of the general government, and from that of their particular tenures, and of the Seignorial government to which they are subject."[45] He recognized all the flaws of the feudal nature of French society, but this did not prevent him from continuing to imagine ways in which a version of their metayage system could be implemented in Virginia.

Returning to Paris in the summer of 1787, Jefferson began to think seriously about the future of his own plantations. His deceased wife's brother-in-law, Francis Eppes, and his friend and neighbor Nicholas Lewis were looking after Jefferson's affairs while he was on his diplomatic mission, which he expected to last for several years. Jefferson hoped that by the time he returned they would have been able to use the profits from his harvests to pay off his substantial debts, primarily inherited from his wife's estate and made far worse by the economic ravages of the Revolutionary War.[46] But in May 1787 Eppes wrote with bad news: the outstanding balance still far outweighed the profits from the previous harvests.[47] Jefferson's debts weighed heavily on him: he told Lewis that "the torment of mind I endure till the moment shall arrive when I shall not owe a shilling on earth is such really as to render life of little value." He was determined to find a solution, one that did not include selling off portions of land, since "I have sold too much of them already, and they are the only sure provision for my children." Selling slaves was an option, but Jefferson hated to think about it. As he told Lewis, he would not "willingly sell the slaves as long as there remains any prospect of paying my debts with their labour." Jefferson believed himself to be "governed solely by views to their happiness" in this decision, hoping that if he did become free of debt he would be able "put them ultimately on an easier footing," whereas if he sold them he would have no ability to protect them from abusive masters or over-seers.[48] He gave similar reasoning to Eppes: "This unwillingness [to sell slaves] is for their sake, not my own; because my debts once cleared off, I shall try some plan of making their situation happier, determined to content myself with a small portion of their labour."[49]

In order to free himself of debt and enable himself to put his slaves "on an easier footing," Jefferson had determined to rent out his "whole estate; not to any one person, but in different parts to different persons, as experience proves that it is only small concerns that are gainful, and it would be my interest that the tenants should make a reason-able gain." In keeping with his overarching philosophy regarding the advantages of small-scale farming, Jefferson proposed finding multiple tenants—"tenants known to be kind and careful in their natures"—to rent parcels of his lands, and groups of his enslaved workers to farm those parcels, for a period of three to five years. This was not a long-term arrangement, like the one he advocated in France; this was a temporary measure designed to free Jefferson and his children from debt. It would, he hoped, conclude around the time that he returned to America from his European mission. Of course, the plan was not without its dangers: "I feel all the weight of the objection that we can-not guard the negroes perfectly against ill usage. But in a question be-tween hiring and selling them (one of which is necessary) the hiring will be temporary only, and will end in their happiness; whereas if we sell them, they will be subject to equal ill usage, without a prospect of change." Having thus reasoned, Jefferson concluded that being rented to strangers was "for their good therefore ultimately" and worth the risk. Once he was debt-free, Jefferson would have much greater flex-ibility in managing his properties.[50]

The next part of Jefferson's plan for his slaves' future might have become clear to him in the spring of 1788, while he was traveling in the Netherlands and the northern Rhineland region (in what is now Germany). William Short was once again temporarily in charge of diplomatic affairs in Paris. Jefferson wrote from Frankfurt on 9 April to tell Short that he felt as if he were back in America, because to an American in the late eighteenth century that particular part of Ger-many was like a "second mother country." From the Palatinate region had emigrated "those swarms of Germans" who now lived in Maryland and Pennsylvania, forming "the greatest body of our people" (meaning white Americans) apart from the descendants of English immigrants. Jefferson ended his missive on a mysterious note: "I have taken some measures too for realizing a project which I have wished to execute for 20 years past without knowing how to go about it. I am not sure but that you will enter into similar views when I can have the pleasure of explaining them to you at Paris."[51]

We get some idea regarding Jefferson's "project" from his personal notes about his trip through the area. On 3 March he documented a conversation he had with a "Mr. Hermen Hend Damen, merchant-broker of Amsterdam," about increasing the number of German migrants to the American states. The merchant described the route such people took: "[T]he emigrants to America come from the Palatinate down the Rhine and take shipping from Amsterdam," paying ten guineas for the voyage across the Atlantic. When Jefferson inquired about the possibility of increasing the rates of migration, Damen was optimistic, telling Jefferson that German families "might be had in any number to go to America and settle lands as tenants on half stocks or metairies." Jefferson and Damen were apparently discussing an immigration plan that was one part a vestige of colonial-era indentured servitude—the immigrants could "serve their employer one year as an indemnification for the passage"—and one part European metayage, or tenancy system.[52]

Jefferson had already devoted a great deal of thought to the issue of immigration, which he initially regarded with skepticism. Query VIII of his *Notes* (on the number of inhabitants) catalogued the population of Virginia, which he estimated in 1782 to consist of 567,614 "inhabitants of every age, sex, and condition."[53] However, as he put it, "the present desire of America is to produce rapid population by as great importations of foreigners as possible." Jefferson predicted that, relying on natural reproduction alone, it would only take "81¾ years" to reach Virginia's goal of 4.5 million inhabitants, a number many believed to be "a competent population for the state."[54] If the government utilized immigration to speed up this process, it would distort the culture and laws of the state irreparably. He believed that "it is for the happiness of those united in society to harmonize as much as possible in matters which they must of necessity transact together"—in other words, republican government works best when the governed already agree on as many principles as possible.

The citizens of Virginia had governing principles "more peculiar than those of any other in the universe"—a combination of English constitutionalism and philosophies "derived from natural right and natural reason." If large numbers of immigrants from "absolute monarchies" came to Virginia, they would be unable to adapt to the "temperate liberty" of Virginia; they would teach their monarchical values to their children—or else descend into anarchy. As a result, the legislature would turn into a "heterogeneous, incoherent, distracted mass." It would be much safer for the state to rely on natural population growth, resulting in a government "more homogenous, more peaceable, more durable."[55] Jefferson did not object to *all* immigration and supported granting the rights of citizenship to those who did arrive; in the 1780s, he just did not wish to attract mass immigration "by extraordinary encouragements."[56]

But there was one major problem with relying exclusively on natural reproduction in Virginia: slavery. According to Jefferson's 1782 calculations, slaves already made up almost half the population of the state—and their rate of natural reproduction was "faster . . . than the whites," a situation Jefferson attributed to their "mild treatment" and "wholesome, though coarse, food."[57] Left unchecked, the enslaved population of his state would soon outnumber the free, a situation that was both immoral and (considering the possibility of uprising) extremely dangerous. So when he considered encouraging large amounts of German settlers from the Palatinate region to come to Virginia, Jefferson was compromising his desire for a relatively homogenous citizenry, although for good reason. His first inducement in making this compromise was his apparently growing conviction that slaves would become better equipped for independence if they worked side by side with European agricultural laborers; his second was most likely his experiences with this particular group of Europeans. Traveling along this portion of the Rhine reminded him that the Germans who settled in Maryland and Pennsylvania before the Revolutionary War had already proven both their agricultural prowess and their ability to adapt to

American cultural norms and political principles. Therefore, Jefferson felt secure in encouraging immigration from the Palatinate to Virginia as a way of gradually phasing out slavery, without recruiting a foreign population that would irremediably alter the sociopolitical makeup of the citizenry.[58]

When Jefferson returned from the Dutch and German provinces, he shared his insights regarding metayage in Virginia with William Short, and they began making plans for Short to look more closely at variations of the system in both France and Italy.[59] The twenty-nine-year-old Virginian had been eagerly awaiting his own opportunity to travel in the Old World, and he had befriended two young Americans— Thomas Lee Shippen of Philadelphia and John Rutledge Jr. of South Carolina—who were embarking on an adventure across the western half of the continent. They invited Short to join them; Jefferson helped them plan their trip and gave them a nickname: "the triumvirate."[60] Although Rutledge and Shippen left Paris without Short in the spring of 1788, he planned to catch up to them in time to see Italy, the country he most wished to explore.[61] In the meantime, Short was regaled by letters relating his fellow Americans' adventures. Lafayette had advised the young pair to travel in fictitious military uniforms, so that they would be mistaken for high-ranking officials and treated with deference. Unfortunately, the plan backfired spectacularly in Rotterdam, and Rutledge and Shippen were almost arrested as spies.[62]

After that near-miss, the two tourists made their way to present-day Belgium. In the town of Spa they were surprised to meet a group of former slaves from South Carolina. These dozen or so men were probably the surviving members of the "black Hessians"—slaves who had volunteered to join the Hessian mercenaries after South Carolina was invaded during the Revolutionary War, either to escape slavery or to gain employment after being separated from their former masters. Approximately thirty of these former slaves went to Europe with their units after the war, but many died soon afterward of diseases such as tuberculosis. One deceased man was dissected at the Collegium Carolinum in Cassel, where bewildered scientists discovered that the color of his skin was the only way in which he was different from white corpses.[63]

When Rutledge and Shippen met them in the early summer of 1788, the surviving black Hessians were apparently regretting their decision to journey across the Atlantic. Upon receiving Shippen's report about the encounter, Short mused that the men's "repentance of their change" from slavery to soldiering—which he considered to be "so honorable a service," even if in the cause of the British—caused him "a mixture of pleasure & pain." He received pleasure because the fact that the former slaves wanted to return to South Carolina was proof that "the situation of our poor slaves in America [is] not the most wretched in the world." But was the honorable career of serving in the Hessian military *really* "worse than being in slavery in So. Carolina"? If this unit was representative of a typical experience, then Short concluded "there must be thousands & ten thousands of poor mortals in the world, more unhappy & more wretched than even our slaves themselves"—a sad commentary on European life indeed.[64] Like Jefferson, Short was led by his time in Europe to the conclusion that, although American slavery was evil, there were worse existences. His search for a way to end slavery was therefore broadened to include options, such as forms of indentured servitude, that would be unacceptable to us now.

In the fall of 1788 Short had his chance to view European poverty firsthand when he left Paris to join Rutledge and Shippen on their tour, stopping along the way to conduct research into metayage in both France and Italy. (He also performed a great national service by tracking down a "Maccaroni machine" that Jefferson subsequently used in the White House, introducing an entirely new comfort food to the country.[65]) Jefferson had previously spent time at the Château de Laye in the Beaujolais region; Short returned in October 1788 and diligently spent eight days "in constant walking over the estate of M. de Laye, in constant examination and constant enquiry." Jefferson had been primarily struck by the inefficiency of the judiciary in the feudal system, since Monsieur de Laye was both landowner and judge over his tenants and was disposed to ignore crimes merely because prosecuting them was so expensive. Short devoted his visit to looking deeper into the tenancy system itself, with an eye to implementing it in Virginia. Adoptive father and son must have felt, based on Jefferson's first impression, that metayage as practiced in the region of Laye could be easily modified for use as part of a gradual emancipation program in Virginia. But after spending more than a week observing the system, Short reported to Jefferson: "I fear we shall find a greater difficulty than I had expected in the article of Metairie." In the first place, the cultivators at de Laye's estate were farming grain in teams, since "that kind of husbandry could not be carried on by one person alone," and therefore each metayer had "a certain number of hands employed by him." Short was concerned that becoming accustomed to being both free and a supervisor would be too much for people long accustomed to taking orders: "[I]t will be a long time before our slaves become sufficiently intelligent and provident to direct the work of others, viz. to employ themselves and others under them."[66]

Moreover, Short discovered that metayage as practiced in the Beaujolais region involved the proprietor, or landlord, providing land, houses, and cattle to the tenants. On their end, the tenants were expected to provide a "considerable" amount—not only "the instruments of husbandry" but also laborers to care for the cattle and, presumably, the grain itself. This would constitute a considerable outlay of capital upfront, which, of course, a newly emancipated slave would not have.[67]

Short did not give up, however. A few weeks later he wrote to his mentor from Milan to let him know that he had made it safely over the Alps and rendezvoused with Rutledge (Shippen had been called home to America by his parents). They were visiting with Count Luigi Castiglioni, a young Italian nobleman who had recently returned from a two-year visit to the United States. Like so many other elite European tourists in America, Castiglioni was now engaged in writing a book about his travels; and, like Chastellux, he cited passages from Jefferson's *Notes* to refute Buffon's degeneracy theory. Castiglioni also opposed slavery, quoting a Philadelphia antislavery magazine to condemn the practice but specifically praising Washington, Jefferson, and Madison for the way they treated their slaves. He had visited Monticello on his trip, although without meeting its master, since Jefferson had already departed for his diplomatic mission. Short no doubt enjoyed the opportunity to talk about his home state with a recent appreciative visitor.

Castiglioni now played host and introduced Short to the farming systems in his region.[68]

After Milan, Short was planning to visit the country estate of Count Antonio Barziza at Alzano, in the province of Bergano. Count Barziza had eloped with the young Lucy Paradise, daughter of an American couple Jefferson and Short befriended in Paris. Now, Short looked forward to visiting the lovebirds at their estate, hoping "to find at Count Barziza's some new information respecting the Metairie." Metayage was used in this region of Italy as well as in France, but Short believed the Italian version was "less complicated in one respect than in France, and of course better for the genius [intelligence level] of the negroes."[69] Unfortunately, while staying with the count and countess, Short was stricken with influenza, and his next letters to Jefferson do not contain further details.[70] As he traveled on toward Rome, he became increasingly distracted by the sights. As he put it: "I find myself so fully possessed by the objects which surround me, and so stunned as it were by the pleasure of considering myself on that classical ground which I have so long been accustomed to admire, that I cannot call my attention to any particular object."[71] He did not mention metayage again for some time.

Short returned to a Paris "run politically mad" in May 1789—the French Revolution was in its opening days.[72] By September the Bastille had fallen, the "Great Fear" had begun to spread throughout the countryside, and the Declaration of the Rights of Man and of the Citizen (principally authored by Lafayette, with Jefferson's help) had been approved by the National Assembly. Although their own revolution had been bloody, the Americans in Paris now believed themselves to be observing a peaceful French political reform movement, and it seemed likely to produce enough moderate changes to set the people on better footing—even without becoming a fully fledged republic. When he sent his last update to Thomas Paine before leaving France in September, Jefferson explained that moderate forces should be able to achieve the "final establishment of a good constitution, which will in it's principles and merit be about a middle term between that of England and the

United States."[73] Short agreed with Jefferson's assessment, believing that once "the thousand intermediary tyrants" were removed from power—referring to the nobility and clergy who paid no taxes yet benefited from a feudal social hierarchy—Louis XVI would be better able to govern the "enslaved" French people. With highly respected liberals like Lafayette leading the reforms, it seemed France would soon become a stable constitutional monarchy.[74]

However, almost immediately after Jefferson departed in September 1789 for what he believed would be a brief visit to America, everything changed. On 8 October Short wrote his mentor a breathless account of how a large mob had just stormed the palace at Versailles. Mobs would become increasingly powerful in France over the ensuing years, something Short witnessed with increasing alarm. But for Jefferson, who never witnessed any violence firsthand, the French Revolution remained a moderate and promising one. When he sailed for home, he carried with him the hope that the whole world could change if France—an ancient, wealthy, and populous nation—could throw off the chains of superstition and tyranny that had bound her for so long.[75]

Short's experience with the French Revolution was almost the opposite of Jefferson's; he became increasingly distraught at the corruption, political infighting, and mob mayhem he saw spreading across the country.[76] Tragically, many of Short's closest French friends and colleagues died in the various purges; Lafayette survived but was imprisoned for five years, and Short was powerless to render aid to his good friend.[77] Unfortunately—in part because of the difficulties in communication between France and America (from Virginia to Paris took an average of sixty days in peacetime) and in part because of their diverging perspectives on a number of issues, including the French Revolution—Jefferson and Short's relationship suffered from miscommunication, misunderstanding, and hurt feelings (on Short's end, at least) for several years.[78]

Jefferson had been counseling Short to return to America for some months prior to Jefferson's own departure. It would be painful for Jefferson to lose him: "[A]ffection and the long habit of your society have rendered [your presence] necessary to me. And how much more so will it be when I shall have parted with my daughters? But I am to say what is for your interest, not what is for my own."[79] Although Jefferson worried that Short had spent the crucial postrevolutionary years far away from the exciting world of American politics and had "perhaps . . . already let pass the most favorable opportunity of putting himself in the way of preferment," Jefferson felt sure that "these opportunities will recur" if Short returned from Europe. And Jefferson wished above all that Short would succeed in life: "He is to me . . . as an adoptive son, and nothing is more interesting to me than that he should do what is best for himself."[80]

Short ignored his adoptive father's career advice and worked to remain in Europe, in large measure because of his growing attachment to a married French noblewoman, the Duke de la Rochefoucauld's wife, Rosalie.[81] Without saying so in as many words, Jefferson expressed his disapproval of the clandestine affair.[82] "A young man indeed may do without marriage in a great city," Jefferson counseled. "In the beginning it is pleasant enough; but take what course he will whether that of rambling, or of a fixed attachment, he will become miserable as he advances in years." Jefferson firmly believed that true domestic happiness could be found only in marriage and children, and the best marriage for an American man would be to an American woman: "The only resource then for a durable happiness is to return to America." Jefferson's disapproval may have been complicated and his authority undermined, however, by the possibility that by this point he had begun an extramarital relationship of his own with his slave, Sally Hemings.

Hemings had arrived in Paris in 1787 as a companion to Jefferson's younger daughter, Maria; at that time, Hemings was fourteen years old. According to Annette Gordon-Reed, the leading expert on the Hemings–Jefferson relationship, Hemings likely lived at the Hôtel de Langeac with Jefferson, Short, her brother James Hemings, and several other male servants, although it is possible that Hemings spent much of her time living at the same convent where Martha and Maria Jefferson resided. According to Hemings's son Madison, at some point before their return to America in 1789 Hemings and Jefferson began a relationship, and Hemings family tradition holds that she gave birth to a child in 1790.[83] Madison Hemings later recounted that his mother could have remained in France as a free woman had she so chosen, but instead she and Jefferson came to a mutual understanding, and she chose to return with him to her family and friends in Virginia, assured that she would have a comfortable life and that her children would be freed. During the time that Hemings may have lived at the Hôtel de Langeac, Short was often traveling: she arrived in 1787, but he was away for eight months on his tour of Europe in 1788, and he also often traveled to Saint-Germaine and other rural locations. If Jefferson and Hemings became romantically involved in Paris, Short might have been unaware. Or if he did know about their relationship, Short might have begun to think differently about the future of race relations in America—after all, if Thomas Jefferson could put aside his stated objections to race mixing, and act in ways that belied his insistence on the aesthetic inferiority of black women, perhaps other Virginians could also come to view black people as potential romantic partners. In any event, as we shall see, one letter Short wrote in 1798 would take on great significance if he did, in fact, have knowledge of such a relationship.[84]

Jefferson initially intended to return to Paris after a brief sojourn in Virginia to settle his affairs. But Short heard the rumors even before Jefferson finished his voyage across the Atlantic: George Washington wanted Jefferson as the nation's first secretary of state, and he would therefore not be returning to France. Short's friends in France—including Lafayette and the Rochefoucaulds—immediately began assuring him that he would be allowed to stay in France, perhaps even promoted to Jefferson's role as minister plenipotentiary.[85] After nine long months of waiting in suspense, Short received word that President Washington had decided that some other "veteran" politician would actually be given the ministerial role in France. Short was deeply wounded by the news, having believed Jefferson would easily secure the promotion on his behalf. He referred to Jefferson as the "*dimidium animae meae*" ("half of my life" or "partner of my soul") and mourned that the loss of that friendship was "embittered by finding in a moment those hopes blasted, which I had cherished for a long time."[86] Even though Jefferson had warned him that Jefferson's own recommendation would not be enough to guarantee Short's promotion, Short was for some time seemingly unable to shake the nagging fear that his "father" had rejected him. His failure to secure a permanent diplomatic position in France would have tragic repercussions, for both his career and his personal life.

Jefferson and Short's correspondence during the 1790s must be read in light of this tension in their once-close relationship, a tension that unfortunately only increased as the French Revolution entered ever-more precarious stages and American domestic politics became increasingly polarized. [87] From Europe, Short could not understand the rising tension between the emerging parties of the Democratic–Republicans, led by Jefferson, and the Federalists, led by Alexander Hamilton.[88] Short criticized the French government freely in his letters, only to earn a rebuke from President Washington himself, and eventually Short's correspondence was published by Hamilton in what Jefferson and Short believed was an attempt to deflect criticism away from Hamilton himself. Short's career never recovered.[89] After all his years in Europe, Short was so out of touch with the political climate in America that he was simply unable to understand how his honest concerns about the anarchy and violence in France were being perceived at home.

Jefferson resigned his post as secretary of state and went home to Monticello at the end of 1793, in part because of his disagreement with President Washington's increasingly cautious opinion of the French Revolution. After a brief term as minister to the Netherlands, Short was sent to Spain to negotiate Spanish-American boundaries, navigation rights for the Mississippi, and several other contentious issues. His Spanish appointment was a mark of President Washington's continued confidence in him, and approval of his previous work as fiscal agent in the Netherlands, despite the damage done to his reputation by the publication of his antirevolutionary letters.[90] But a month after Short arrived in Madrid, Spain and France went to war.[91] The next two years were some of the worst of Short's life. He was again separated from the newly widowed Rosalie—after a reunion that had lasted just long enough for her to refuse his marriage proposal—and he found himself trapped in a country he disliked, suffering in the hot climate while attempting to negotiate with status-conscious Spanish diplomats who disdained him because his title ("chargé d'affaires") was too lowly.[92] To add insult to injury, after months upon months of hard diplomatic work, he was unceremoniously replaced as treaty commissioner by

Thomas Pinckney—just before the treaty was signed.[93] During this dismal period, Short suffered from terrible headaches and wrote long, melancholy letters detailing all his troubles to Jefferson.[94] From Spain, he finally decided that Jefferson had been right after all: Short should have gone back to America when he had the chance. His numerous diplomatic misfortunes had been due to "the principle of the destiny which has constantly pursued me since I have had the now irremediable misfortune not to have followed your friendly advice of abandoning this infernal and for me pernicious and humiliating career. It will embitter the rest of my days."[95] Although replies often took months to arrive, Short's relationship with Jefferson seems to have improved to some extent, particularly once Jefferson was no longer secretary of state and could correspond as friend and father rather than as a supervisor. The two men once again turned their thoughts toward Virginia, slavery, and their planned experiments in freedom and metayage.

By the time Short finally brought up the topic of metayage again in 1793, his views on race and slavery had undergone a transition. For the rest of his life Short would advocate and pursue more radical solutions than Jefferson, including racial intermarriage. But what had caused this shift in the younger man's perspective after so many years of emulating Jefferson and seeming to agree with the views expressed in the *Notes*? The answer seems to begin not in 1793, when Short arrived in Spain, but much earlier: in 1788, the year he joined the antislavery Société des Amis des Noirs.[96] Many of the founding members of this group— including Condorcet, Rochefoucauld, and Lafayette—were Jefferson's friends, too, but Jefferson himself had declined membership because he believed that, as a representative of the US government, he could not advocate for causes when not officially directed to do so.[97] Short, however, was under no such compunction; after Jefferson left France in 1789 Short became even more closely identified with the membership and goals of the Société . In many respects, his philosophies on racial equality came to line up more closely with those of French antislavery politicians than of Jefferson.

The French experience with slavery was quite different from the

American, which helps explain the different ways in which French and American antislavery politicians spoke of racial equality. For example, when Americans spoke of emancipating their slaves, they also had to think about whether the freed population could integrate into American society at large. For the French, however, slavery was primarily something that existed in far-off colonies. (Short could identify with the French mindset, since he lived in Europe and was no longer directly in control of any slaves.) In three small French Caribbean colonies—Saint-Domingue (soon to be known as Haiti), Guadeloupe, and Martinique—lived almost as many slaves as in all the American states combined, some 700,000 people. Saint-Domingue was the most important French colony, producing half the world's coffee and more sugar than Brazil, Cuba, and Jamaica put together.[98] French attitudes on interracial relationships were more liberal than most Americans: in Saint-Domingue many slave masters freed their mixed-race children, creating a separate class of free "colored" people, or *gens de couleur libres*. These children were often sent to France to be educated, and when they returned to Saint-Domingue some grew to be prosperous slaveholders in their own right, although they were still discriminated against by the white planters.[99] By 1789 the population in Saint-Domingue consisted of 30,000 white people, 465,000 slaves, and 28,000 free colored people—and although *gens de couleur libres* could not legally vote, they owned about one-third of the slaves.[100] Racial prejudice, as well as jealousy over their superior social status, helps explain the white ruling class's oppression of the *gens de couleur libres*.

But in the French metropole, liberal thinkers embraced the revolutionary language of natural rights and began attacking both slavery and racial inequality. The stakes were perhaps less high for these egalitarians than for Americans: Their wealth was not always directly dependent on slavery, and they did not have to wrestle with the social and cultural consequences of emancipation, since France's slaves didn't actually live in France. But opposition was nonetheless fierce, and in 1788, as the Société des Amis des Noirs was being established, the debate over race and slavery in France began in earnest with the republication of Condorcet's antislavery work *Réflexions sur l'esclavage des nègres* ("Reflections on the Slavery of the Negroes") and a subsequent rebuttal by the Saint-Domingue administrator and planter Pierre-Victor Malouet.[101]

Jefferson was particularly close to Condorcet, and he spent time that summer of 1788 working on an English translation of *Réflexions*.[102] In it, Condorcet attacked the slave trade and slavery, criticized slave owners, held that it was a crime to reduce another person to slavery, and argued that black people were the equals of whites. Although in agreement with many of Condorcet's views, Jefferson was less sure of this final proposition. Still, he continued to correspond with Condorcet regarding slavery and race after returning to America.[103] He might also have been intrigued by Condorcet's proposal to divide plantations in the Caribbean into smaller plots so that the former slaves would become self-sufficient small farmers.[104] But the French planter class was much less intrigued; Condorcet's work, along with the political advocacy of other Société members in the National Assembly, prompted heated attacks from proslavery groups such as the Club Massiac.

Short was also an early admirer of Condorcet, but it took him somewhat longer to appreciate one of France's other leading emancipationists, Jacques-Pierre Brissot de Warville, the lawyer, journalist, and principal founder of the Société des Amis des Noirs. Back in 1786, when Jefferson and Short's mutual friend the Marquis de Chastellux published his *Travels in North America*, Short had been agitated by "a young man here who has some merit as a standing author" but who had attacked Chastellux "most furiously—not to say in a blackguard manner." The young man was none other than Brissot, who at that time was most famous for writing a political pamphlet about Great Britain. Short dismissed Brissot as an author, believing his pamphlet was merely "written to make money," although he conceded such a motive was common—"the end of nine tenths of those who write at present."[105]

By 1788, however, Brissot was no longer known merely for his pamphlet. After becoming an honorary member of Thomas Clarkson and William Wilberforce's British Society for the Abolition of the Slave Trade, Brissot determined to establish a similar organization in France. He traveled to America soon after establishing the Société in

1788, and by this time Short thought so highly of Brissot that he wrote the Frenchman letters of introduction, ensuring his access to leading Americans. Brissot joyfully met his counterparts among Philadelphia's antislavery society, observing their efforts to help the free black population of that city, and was able to give his own antislavery pamphlet (coauthored by Clarkson) to George Washington at Mount Vernon. He soon published a book, *New Travels in the United States of America, 1788*, documenting his travels.[106]

In some ways, the disagreements between Chastellux and Brissot—who was twenty years younger—prefigured the ones that would develop between Jefferson and Short.[107] In Chastellux's *Travels*, which Brissot had attacked so harshly, Chastellux expressed opinions similar to Jefferson's own—perhaps even opinions that he formed after spending time with Jefferson at Monticello in 1782, when the Virginian statesman was deeply engaged in writing his *Notes*. Chastellux went so far as to assert that black people were perhaps of a different species than whites: "[T]he more we regard the negroes," he wrote, "the more must we be persuaded that the difference between them and us, consists in something more than complexion."[108] Chastellux also held that the large number of black people in Virginia—a "distinct people" because of their "color" and innate inferiority—made emancipation more difficult than it had been for ancient societies, in which slaves were of the same race. Only in his solution did he deviate from Jefferson's *Notes*: he recommended colonization just for the *male* slaves. The females should be freed, and then marriage should be promoted between them and white Virginia males. In that way, slavery and blackness would both be removed from the state.[109] But because interracial marriage was illegal in Virginia (and many other states) until the United States Supreme Court finally ruled otherwise in 1967, Chastellux's plan was totally impracticable. As George Washington's neighbor and friend, Ferdinando Fairfax, put it in a 1790 essay promoting colonization: "Where is the man of all those who have liberated their slaves who would marry a son or daughter to one of them?" At this time, not even staunch northern emancipationists would go that far.[110]

Whereas Chastellux mentioned slavery in passing, Brissot devoted large portions of his *Travels* to analyzing the different states' approaches to emancipation and to praising various antislavery activists he had met or heard about. Chastellux followed Jefferson's suspicions of black inferiority, but Brissot wrote eloquently about the potential he saw in black people. When he visited a school for free black children in Philadelphia, he found "proof" that their memories were equal to those of whites. And while traveling in Maryland Brissot claimed he could tell the difference between a field planted by enslaved laborers and those planted by free laborers, as free labor was "much superior."[111]

Sadly, whereas Chastellux believed the revolutionary Virginians he met were moving toward the abolition of slavery, Brissot—traveling the same areas fourteen years later—found the opposite to be true: "They speak not here of projects for freeing the negroes; they praise not the [antislavery] societies of London and America; they read not the works of Clarkson." The true obstacle to emancipation in Virginia was the "character, the manners[,] and habits of the Virginians." Jefferson had criticized slavery's ability to turn republicans into tyrants; Brissot wrote scathingly that Virginians "seem to enjoy the sweat of slaves"; they wanted to hunt and display luxury and hated the idea of actually working.[112]

Americans might treat their slaves mildly, comparatively speaking, because the "general extension of the ideas of liberty" made them less harsh than owners in the Caribbean. However, because slaves were "naked, ill fed, lodged in miserable huts on straw," in addition to being completely uneducated, even in religious principles, they became "lazy, without ideas, and without energy." Their greatest happiness was found in being inactive; therefore they were completely unmotivated to work to improve their situations. Likewise, Brissot believed that freed black people living in northern states were not reaching their full potential, partly because of the habits engrained in them by their previous enslavement and partly because of white prejudice. "Deprived of the hope of electing or being elected representatives, or of rising to any places of honor and trust, the Negroes seem condemned to drag out their days in a state of servility." And when the white people accused them of being lazy and dirty, Brissot complained, "how can they be industrious and active, while an insurmountable barrier separates them from other citizens?"[113]

Although he believed free black people in the North were as yet unable to reach their full potential, Brissot had met a black physician in Philadelphia who was as capable as a white, and he heard stories of other such examples of mental acuity. Without mentioning him by name, Brissot later implied that, when Jefferson speculated in the *Notes* that black people were inferior to white people in their mental capacity, it was because Jefferson simply did not have enough experience with free black people living in the North.[114]

While in America, Brissot embraced the colonization model he heard about from William Thornton, a physician from the Caribbean who spent the winter of 1786–1787 speaking to both white and black audiences on behalf of a plan of colonization like the one that was about to begin in Sierra Leone: free black people voluntarily moving to a colony in Africa, where their labor would "generate profits that could be used to liberate caravans of captured Africans before they were shipped from the West African coast."[115] Brissot had already become convinced of the necessity of colonization by his observation that even in places like Massachusetts, where slavery was abolished, black people were not allowed to fully participate in the rights of citizenship. Even if that situation changed, Brissot observed that "we are so strongly inclined to love our likeness, that there would be unceasing suspicions, jealousies, and partialities, between the Whites and Blacks."[116] Like so many other "enlightened" thinkers of the time, even Brissot could not imagine a successful biracial republic, and so he encouraged consideration of Thornton's colonization project.[117]

Supporters of African colonization saw many benefits not only for Africa but also for Europe and America. They believed that African Americans would happily consent to travel back to their continent of origin and that they would there "gradually civilize" other Africans, teaching them the Christian religion as well as other habits learned during their time in America. The newly civilized Africans would then want to buy European manufactures and would provide "at a cheap rate" goods that the Europeans currently obtained through slavery. Most significant, Brissot asserted that Thornton's African colonization project would be "a solution to the problem of Mr. Jefferson. See Notes on Virginia."[118]

The Marquis de Chastellux grew ill and passed away suddenly in April 1788, so he did not join other antislavery French writers and politicians during the ensuing revolutionary years. The antislavery charge in France was spearheaded by the members of the Société, including men such as Condorcet and Brissot—joined enthusiastically by Short. The young Virginian answered Brissot's call for Americans to actively seek solutions to the problem of slavery rather than waiting passively for public opinion to shift. And Short seems to have been convinced by Brissot's experiences with free black people living in the North, adopting Brissot's opinion that southern slaveholders were so prejudiced by their own interests and lack of interactions with free black people that they were incapable of judging the true capabilities of that race. But Short would go even further, refusing to believe with Brissot and Jefferson that colonization was the only "solution."

In December 1789 Short wrote to Jefferson about the persecution that he and other members of the Société faced. Having decided to petition the National Assembly for an end to the slave trade, the Société had asked British friends for strategic help, and Thomas Clarkson journeyed to Paris to provide advice. Proslavery French planters claimed that he was a British spy, part of a conspiracy to "ruin French colonies by cutting off their labor supply." Lafayette moved Clarkson to a hotel close to his home so that he could protect him in case a mob formed.[119] A few weeks later, a pamphlet titled "Decouverte d'une conspiration contre la France" (Discovery of a conspiracy against France) was circulated in Paris. As Short recounted to Jefferson: "The conspiracy is the society Des amis des noirs. . . . It is said there, [that] under the vain pretence of being useful to the slaves of the Islands, the society is formed by the court of London and that all its members are a sect of illuminés, paid by England." The pamphlet specifically named Brissot, claiming he was a criminal and British spy. "This and a thousand other absurdities fill the work." In what Short considered a ridiculous tactic, "all the names of the members are subjoined"—including his own—as part of a ploy to "defeat any attempts the society may make towards the abolition of the slave trade." Publishing the society members' names might not have been effective, but Short *was* concerned with another of the proslavery groups' tactics: threatening to "assassinate the first member who should make the motion [to abolish the slave trade]. Mirabeau has been frightened by them and it is said others also."[120] Mirabeau, a leading antislavery voice in the National Assembly, and the other members of the Société subsequently changed their focus from ending the slave trade to pursuing rights for the *gens de couleur libres*.[121]

This strategic shift had drastic ramifications that would send shock waves throughout the Atlantic world. As David Brion Davis puts it, when a decree of 15 May 1791 gave the rights of citizenship to some free people of color, "it represented a break in the color wall" that had held together colonial slavery. The unintended consequences of the decree were many, starting with a revolt from the outraged white planters on the island of Saint-Domingue; then turning into a complicated and terribly bloody war involving white, free mixed-race, and enslaved populations fighting against one another or, in various combinations, against French, British, and Spanish troops; and culminating in a successful slave uprising, the brutal massacre of almost every remaining white person, and the declaration of Haitian independence in 1804.[122] The Haitian Revolution would completely change the ways in which American planters, such as Thomas Jefferson, thought about gradual emancipation and colonization; it would alter the rhetoric of American politics; it would inspire some African Americans to rise up and fight for their own freedom; and it even led, indirectly, to the Louisiana Purchase. In later years the Haitian Revolution would become a topic of conversation between Short and Jefferson as they reconsidered the best place for colonies of freed American slaves, but during the 1780s and 1790s their conversation on this topic was typically brief.

When Jefferson replied to Short's letter about the proslavery planters' assassination threats, he did not comment on the goals of the Société des Amis des Noirs, but his letters soon began to address another important topic: Short's property in America.[123] When Short left for Paris in 1785 he left behind a complicated tangle of affairs due to his father's recent death. Although he had all but freed his only personal slave, a man named Stephen, Short—along with his brother, Peyton, and their sisters—had inherited additional land and slaves from their father.[124]

Rather than settle the estate's debts and divide their inheritance immediately, the brothers chose to wait for a more promising economic climate. In Short's absence, however, neither his brother nor the other financial managers he appointed did a good job of either managing or communicating to Short, who grew increasingly desperate for news. Peyton Short seems to have absorbed much of his brother's inheritance into his own personal funds. Much to William's distress, Peyton also sold the family's slaves to strangers without even telling his brother; he then took their sisters and moved the whole family to Kentucky.[125] Short felt abandoned, a Virginian with very few reasons to care about Virginia anymore—except for Thomas Jefferson.

By 1792 Jefferson had discovered how badly Short's inheritance was being mismanaged, and he began looking for ways to help.[126] Jefferson had already decided to resign from his post as secretary of state, and now he cast his eye back toward life as a farmer in Virginia. It had long been a dream of Jefferson's to surround himself with family in his retirement, and with the young men who were like family to him—Madison, Monroe, and Short. When both paper money and property values fell drastically in America, Jefferson worried about Short's investments: "I wish to god you had some person who could dispose of your paper [money] at a judicious moment for you, and invest it in good lands." But the falling land values could be a blessing in disguise: "E. Carter's lands in Albemarle are for sale, and probably can be bought for 30/ the acre." The land that Jefferson seems to be referring to in this letter was the 1,334-acre Indian Camp property, so named because of its history as a sojourning spot for the Monacan tribe. In 1730 it had been part of a land grant by the English king to the Carter family, and Jefferson now had his eye on it partly because of its low price and partly because of its proximity to Monticello.[127] A month later, in April 1792, Jefferson again wrote regarding the financial crisis that he had "been unable to refrain from interposing for you on the present occasion" and had moved to ensure that Short's stock was not tampered with. But Jefferson would feel much better if Short would send him authority to secure Short's money by investing it in "Ned Carter's lands at 5. dollars the acre."[128]

Around this time, Short was feeling deeply wounded by the lack of communication he was receiving from America, and from Jefferson in particular, about whether or not he would be permitted to remain a diplomat in France. Jefferson earnestly defended himself: "Had you been here, there should have been no silence or reserve, and I long for the moment when I can unbosom to you all that past on that occasion [when the diplomatic posts were decided]. But to have trusted such communications to writing and across the Atlantic would have been an indiscretion which nothing could have excused."[129] Although their relationship would remain strained for several years, Short must have accepted that Jefferson was still interested in his life and affairs.[130] But although he was very grateful for Jefferson's quick actions on his behalf, and officially asked Jefferson to take over managing his American finances, he did not immediately jump at the chance to buy Carter's land. Short still wanted to live near his brother and sisters once he finally returned to America, even if he hated the idea of leaving the glamor and culture of Europe for the relative wilderness of Kentucky.[131]

Then, in July 1793, Jefferson wrote to tell Short that, once he retired from the state department, he was considering a drastic change to his system of farming: dividing it into sections and hiring it out to tenants, as he had observed in Europe. "I believe it will be practicable," Jefferson wrote, "at a rent of 5. per cent on the value. It will still however be a troublesome revenue, but an increasing capital."[132] Rather than receiving payment in the form of a percentage of the harvest, he would rent land for 5 percent of its value yearly. Short received this news with great enthusiasm; to him, Jefferson considering tenancy was "proof of the increasing prosperity of my country, and of the practicability of placing one's fortune, in that solid, substantial and patriotic way" (i.e., landholding). If the plan worked, then Short wanted to invest all his money—or "at least the greater part"—the same way. He was also considering buying shares in canal companies and becoming a landlord for small properties in established cities, but "[c]ould lands be tenanted in Virginia it would certainly be to me the most agreeable of all kinds of property."[133]

In a lengthy letter on 7 October 1793, Short continued to outline all his hopes for tenancy in Virginia. He believed the practice would "unquestionably be adopted in time" across the entire state, though he felt land values would have to increase first, since poor farmers could easily obtain cheap land of their own rather than having to rent it from a large landholder. But what if Jefferson were actually referring to metayage— "that humane and philanthropic system of letting them [plots of land] to the slaves, in the way of metairies"? If that is what Jefferson meant by "tenanting," then Short believed "it would not answer my present purpose," not because he did not support the idea but because "the capital to be laid out in the purchase of slaves would be too considerable to admit of any reasonably adequate revenue." With his finances so recently in dire straits, Short hesitated to pay the considerable amount it would cost first to purchase slaves *and* land, then to free the slaves and train them to be metayers. "Still," he continued, "I think those who have the misfortune to own slaves [already], should for the sake of humanity make the experiment. When I shall return to America it is my intention to preach this not only by precept but by example."[134]

From his frustrating post in Spain, Short dreamed about implementing metayage on his Virginian property: "[I]t is a subject my mind goes much on." He would first purchase a "small number" of slaves and was already developing a strategy to try "exciting in these people the idea of property and the desire to acquire it, which I think would be easily done, and which when done, I think would insure the success of the experiment." Transitioning from *being* property to *owning* property would take time, he expected, and he therefore planned a gradual program of education for some of the former slaves combined with a backup plan for "such as were found unworthy of being employed in another way." Echoing his report on metayage in the French town of Laye, back in 1788, Short still felt that some of the older slaves would find freedom too much to handle, and those individuals would have to labor on Short's own land under more direct supervision. But Short, as Jefferson first told Bancroft in his own letter of 1788, expected that "all their children grown up and formed in a different way would be capable of being at least metayers," and others would become so capable that they should become independent "farmers." Short here introduced a new step to the gradual emancipation plan he and Jefferson had discussed previously: "It seems to me therefore that there should be those three gradations of *slaves—metayers* and *farmers—*to secure the business." Short's plan was based on his observations in Europe; he argued that both metayers and farmers "exist in France and indeed all the civilized part of Europe almost may be divided into them," and "[i]n many parts there exist also what may be compared to our slaves." In Poland and Russia, for example, serfs were comparable to American slaves (although serfs were not sold away from the land they farmed), and comparing those countries to France or England would show "any person . . . what our southern states would be could our slaves be made free tenants, compared with what they are now." America should therefore combine all three forms of European agricultural labor—serfs, metayers, and farmers—using those degrees of semi-free to free labor as a long-term system for transitioning African slaves into citizens.[135]

Although both his personal and professional lives were in tatters, thinking about emancipation in the American South was "one of the most pleasing reveries in which I indulge myself," Short told Jefferson. It must have been a pleasant distraction from his frantic worries about his lost love, the recently widowed Rosalie. Because she was a member of the nobility, she and her grandmother were called before France's Committee for Public Safety and imprisoned in 1793, and Short was unable to help in any way or even to receive news of them for months at a time.[136] Isolated in Spain, he blamed himself for her imprisonment, thinking if he had turned down the Spanish appointment she might not have been arrested. He dreamed about the future: if she survived, they could marry and either live in Paris or move to Virginia.[137] If the latter, and if his metayage plan could be implemented, it would unite "the purest principles of humanity with the prosperity of one's country." In the meantime, he wanted Jefferson to invest in land for him, and if it could be tenanted to free (white) farmers at a yearly profit of 5 percent of its value, as Jefferson hoped to accomplish with his own farms, so much the better. Although Short had doubts that Carter's land, Indian Camp, was the best site for his permanent home—"the soil and position of any estate immediately round Monticello, do not seem to me to admit of such a grazing, meadowy farming establishment as I should like"—he left the current decision in Jefferson's hands. His only concern was that Jefferson choose a location, and set the terms of tenants' leases, in such a way that Short could easily sell the property when he returned to America in order to reinvest the money in purchasing the perfect land for his own home. If Short could also purchase a property near Monticello as a summer house, so much the better—but in 1793 "such things are beyond my capital I fear, and to be indulged only in idea." He had, Short felt, "lost the best part of my life" and now had nothing to look forward to but "to live retired and forgotten" once his superiors in the government finally cast him aside.[138]

Jefferson followed Short's wishes, investing his money in canal shares and farmland, but he disagreed vehemently with Short's critique of soil in Albemarle.[139] In 1795 he wrote to Short that he had purchased the 1,334-acre Indian Camp property after all. Although Jefferson was obviously excited at the prospect of Short owning land only "2 ¾ [miles?] from me" and "¾ from Monroe," he carefully explained why he had bought land in an area Short had objected to: "I bought the Indian camp for you because you have expressed some partiality for our neighborhood and climate, because there are no lands in this state of equal fertility and equal advantages as cheap as ours, and you can always get them off your hands for the same money and it's interest, should you not like the purchase." Jefferson was enthusiastic about farming in this particular area for another reason: since his retirement he had begun implementing a new crop rotation program with great success. Instead of relying on tobacco, which depleted the soil and was most cheaply produced by enslaved labor, Jefferson had switched to a rotation system involving wheat, corn and potatoes, rye, and red clover, and this combination of crops showed great promise. If Short wished him to sell the land, Jefferson assured him he would—but there were already four tenants farming it, two on short "at will" leases, one with a three-year term and one for life.[140]

Short was pleasantly surprised at this news, especially because the rents the tenants paid, if a few more could be found, would bring in the same amount—6 percent—as he had received in interest from his stocks during the best of times. Short concluded that Indian Camp's tenancy system was "much better than having slaves or any thing else."[141] Since Short was at this time finding out that he was being replaced as treaty negotiator by Pinckney and was feeling utterly "disgraced and dishonored," discussing the Indian Camp tenancy plan was a welcome respite.[142] He longed to be "again settled in my own country with the person [Rosalie] who will share all the blessings & misfortunes of the rest of my life and who, alas!, would have been there perhaps at the present if my ill-fated stars had not conducted me here [to Spain]."[143]

Jefferson did not attempt to contact Short again for two years, having heard that Short was released from his Spanish mission and therefore expecting that Short would arrive back in Virginia at any moment. When Short failed to appear, or to write, Jefferson must have begun to suspect that the younger man had returned to France to seek out Rosalie again, and in March 1797 he finally wrote Short a letter that included assurances of his good wishes and "my heartfelt sympathies in all [Rosalie's] sufferings." [144] In fact, Short had left Spain at the first possible moment, in November 1795, and traveled with all haste back to Rosalie, who was by this time under house arrest at her deceased husband's country estate.[145] Short had "aged . . . twenty years" since he had last seen her, developing gray hair and "sunken cheeks" due to the inhospitable Spanish climate, illness, and the years of enforced separation, and he felt that he had been abominably treated by America, the country he sacrificed so much to serve.[146] But the reunion was sweet. Short spent the next several years living with Rosalie in France, hoping that, if he waited until her grandmother died, she would marry him and come to live with him in Virginia.[147]

Short was so distracted by the reunion that he neglected his correspondence with Jefferson, to whom he had written dozens of detailed letters since their time together in Paris ended in 1789. Only one of his letters to Jefferson from 1797, when Short resumed communication, survives; in it he informed Jefferson—who was by this point the vice president—that when Short returned to America he would invest "every thing I have in lands rented out at a sure and annual interest." Both James Monroe and one of Short's cousins had offered to buy Indian Camp from him, but Short refused their offers and asked Jefferson to continue the search for more tenants.[148] He apparently also had decided *not* to acquire any slaves.[149]

But in February 1798 William Short more than made up for the many months of silence by sending Jefferson the letter of a lifetime, one that would explicitly reference Jefferson's claims regarding race and slavery in *Notes on the State of Virginia*—before demolishing several of them with a rhetorical sledgehammer.[150] In reopening the conversation that Jefferson had begun so many years ago, Short updated and strengthened Jefferson's moral condemnation of slavery by sharing the latest evidence that the "black race" was, in fact, capable of equality with the white. But if the two races were equally capable, what possible reason could there be for attempting to keep them separate, as Jefferson had argued for in the *Notes*? Emancipation did not have to be coupled with colonization; black people could receive the full rights of citizenship due them in America; and marriage between the races would soon erase the "marked & impassable" color barrier between the two peoples.[151] In making these claims, Short was pushing even beyond what his revolutionary friend and co-emancipationist in the Société, Brissot, had argued for. But Brissot—and many other members of the Société, including Condorcet—was by this time a victim of the Terror. Short was one of the lucky young men who had experienced the most idealistic time in French history--and survived to continue dreaming of a better world.[152]

Ironically, as Short wrote down his revolutionary ideas regarding racial intermarriage, he was preparing to leave France after once again being disappointed in his own marital hopes. The Duchess d' Enville, Rosalie's grandmother, had passed away, and even though Rosalie now had no relatives to tie her to France, she still had not consented to marry Short. He was therefore planning a trip to America "in the spring or early summer" of 1798, at which time he would see now–Vice President Jefferson for the first time in almost a decade. In the meantime, he hoped that Jefferson was still tenanting Indian Camp, even though Short remained worried that low land values would preclude free farmers from seeking tenancies. After all, if "they are able to purchase lands of their own" and "they are accustomed to see only slaves, working such lands," why choose the humiliation of manual labor without the honor of property ownership? But Short also mused that farmers from England might be migrating to America because of the effects of the Napoleonic Wars on the English economy and that the appearance of these immigrants would "in time facilitate the letting out lands at rent." In fact, it seems the reason Short was now hesitating about whether white farmers were the best tenants for large Virginia plantations was that one of his true purposes for this letter was to convince Jefferson to put into operation the plan they had discussed in France in 1788–1789: freeing slaves and putting them on the footing of metayers.[153]

Short began his lengthy epistle with some observations on Sierra Leone, the colony of former slaves being established by philanthropic antislavery British leaders on the western coast of Africa. He assumed that Jefferson was already familiar with the project, and he recommended a recent book on the topic: the Swedish explorer and antislavery activist C. B. Wadstrom's *Essay on Colonization . . . of Sierra Leone*.[154] Although Short had low expectations for Sierra Leone, believing the colony itself was destined to turn into merely another British colonial commercial enterprise, its very existence had already "done infinite good, by turning the researches of Philanthropes & of Philosophers, towards the black inhabitants of Africa." In his *Notes*, Jefferson insisted on examining black people as they lived under slavery in Virginia: "It would be unfair to follow them to Africa for this investigation. We will consider them here, on the same stage as the whites, and where the facts are not apocryphal on which a judgment is to be formed."[155] But the research undertaken by these scholars, several of whom had traveled into Africa on fact-finding missions, gave Short "very encouraging hopes with respect to the perfectibility of the black race." One such explorer claimed to have "discovered a city larger than London"—possibly a reference to the rumored city of Housa (Hausa), which was believed to be in the Niger River watershed, in the same region as Timbuktu (in today's country of Mali).[156] Even if the city's size *was* exaggerated, Short argued, there now existed enough evidence to offer "sanguine hopes that our posterity at least will see improved, populous & extensive nations of the black color, formed into powerful societies who will par in every respect with whites under the same circumstances." Although Short did not mention the successful slave revolt then underway in Saint-Domingue, it must surely have been on his mind (and Jefferson's).[157]

The reason Short was willing to consider evidence from Africa, rather than only from observing black people enslaved in America, was that he now believed there was always a level of prejudice among white people who had been raised in slave states. Even those who were "least subjected to prejudice" could not help this, since they had only known black people "in the state of degradation inseparable from the most mitigated [least severe] degree of slavery." For a slaveholder like Jefferson to study a slave, in other words, would produce skewed results: black people had to be considered in the context of freedom, otherwise the observer—himself a product of slavery just as much as the slave—would be unable to observe without bias. The bias might even continue when the slaveholder observed free black people in America. Moreover, Short continued, white Americans raised in such uneven societies naturally developed an "aversion . . . to the mixture of the two colors." But now, with such clear evidence of the equality of the races emerging from scientific voyages of discovery into Africa's interior, and the future evidence that Short expected to see from "improved, populous & extensive nations of the black color," Americans would surely have to offer "the rights of citizenship of those blacks who inhabit" the United States.[158]

Once their citizenship had been granted, Short believed, the black population would soon be viewed by white people as potential marriage partners. When writing his *Notes*, Jefferson believed the possibility of intermarriage would *prevent* white people from freeing their slaves; he addressed white fears by advocating a two-step emancipation program: "[W]hen freed, he is to be removed beyond the reach of mixture." Now, Short put a new question to his mentor: "As to the evils to be apprehended from the mixture of the two colors (& I know that the most enlightened & virtuous minds do apprehend such) the subject is certainly worthy of serious attention." And yet:

> If this [amalgamation] be an evil, is it not the least that can take place under present circumstances? It is certainly less than keeping 700,000 people & their descendants in perpetual slavery even if it were possible—Is it not less also than having that number of free people living in the same country & separated from the rest of the community by a marked & impassable line?—Is it not less even than the expopulation of the U.S. of so great a number of their inhabitants by any possible means?

Short's time in Spain had taught him valuable lessons, including about the "deep . . . wounds" that still had not healed in that country after the "Moors" (Muslims) were expelled more than a century earlier. He

noted that Spain's expelled population consisted of the "most industrious artisans & manufacturers of the country," and if the South were to
lose the black "tillers of the land" it would be "a greater evil." Colonization was not worth it, Short now believed: it would cause irreparable
harm to the American economy.[159]

Spain had also taught Short an even more important lesson: brown
is beautiful! If prejudiced slaveholders' worst fears were realized—they
freed their slaves, but the gradual influence of the climate did not
change the skin color of the freedman from dark to light over time, as
many still believed could occur—then intermarriage would mean that
"all of our Southern inhabitants should advance to the middle ground
between their present color & the black." That "middle" complexion
would be the same as that of the "inhabitants of some of the provinces
of Spain—& I do not see that these provinces labour under any inconvenience greater than the rest of the Spaniards . . . merely on account
of their color." If that generalization was not comforting enough for
Jefferson, Short had a more personal example in mind: "I don't know
if you ever saw, a Mrs. Randolph afterwards Mrs. Tucker." The Mrs.
Tucker mentioned here was Frances Bland Randolph Tucker, wife of
St. George Tucker, who was George Wythe's successor at the College
of William and Mary. Although there exists no evidence at this time
that Mrs. Tucker was of mixed race, she apparently had a darker complexion than most and was quite beautiful; Short argued that she was
"the perfect mixture of the rose & the lilly." "There is no country," Short
concluded, that would "not be content to have its women like her."[160]

It is possible that Short, in making an example of Mrs. Tucker, was
tactfully avoiding one that would have struck even closer to home for
Jefferson: Sally Hemings, the mixed-race half-sister of Jefferson's own
wife, Martha.[161] Sally was described by those who knew her as "mighty
near white . . . very handsome, [with] long straight hair down her
back."[162] If Jefferson began a romantic relationship of some sort with
her while they all lived together in Paris, Short could have been one
of the few people in the world to know that Jefferson himself found
darker-skinned women to be beautiful.[163] But Short, knowing that their
correspondence could easily be lost or even published, would never
have stated such a thing openly. Thus his reference to Mrs. Tucker is

the closest we will get to an acknowledgment by Short that interracial relationships could easily occur in Jefferson's world.

After making his remarkable case for interracial marriage, Short moved onto safer ground, asking "how is to be effected this great & momentous object, the transformation of 700,000 slaves into free citizens"? Short humbly acknowledged that his musings on the topic were hindered by his great distance from America, and how many more "difficulties" could be seen by "a penetrating genius" (meaning Jefferson?) "capable of diving into the bosom of futurity, & who examines the subject on the spot"? Nonetheless, Short did have several suggestions for achieving their "momentous object." First, "such geniuses should turn their attention towards the examination of this subject," and they should do so "ne soyez pas jaloux du tems" (a French idiom meaning to act quickly, but not so quickly as to make careless errors). Emancipation must be enacted, but Short still believed it should be enacted *gradually*, and he pointed to "what has taken place there within these last seven years" as proof that freed people who were not carefully prepared for that freedom "cannot fail to become beasts of prey if their numbers surpass at once the means of subsistence." (Short here refers to "Hispaniola," the Spanish word for the island containing the French colony of Saint-Domingue—modern Haiti—from which thousands of white people had either fled or been killed during the ongoing slave rebellion.) Short's experiences with the French and Haitian revolutions had both jaded him, for he now expressed the "melancholy consideration . . . that the only way to bring men in general to desire an event is to shew that they have an interest in it—if they see their interest on one side & humanity on the other, never count on the majority for the last." Even men who called themselves Christians were, after all, able to "go to Africa, wrest the mother from the infant—the husband from the wife—chain them to the whip & lash, they & their posterity for ever," without once realizing that they were "violating the whole doctrine of the author of their religion."[164]

To get slaveholders to free their slaves, therefore, "the enlightened & virtuous citizens, who toil for public instruction" (again referring to Jefferson?) must "turn the public mind towards this subject," persuading the public that emancipation *was* actually in their best interests.

Short wanted "the slave holders to be attacked by proofs that their interest would not suffer" if their slaves were freed. That proof could be provided by men like Jefferson: if he would lease equal quantities of land to free tenants (white or black) as was cultivated by slaves, carefully document the results, and then publish them in the newspapers, then "time & repetition will I think infallibly shew the advantage of free, above forced, labor."

In addition to his suggestions regarding proving the advantages of free labor, Short included a long list of ideas for ameliorating slaves' conditions while waiting for the public mind to embrace emancipation: In October 1793 Short had first brought up the topic of serfdom; he now elaborated on a plan to convince southern legislatures to convert slaves into serfs. The advantage would be that a serf, unlike a slave, could not be sold away from the land on which he or she toiled—and "slaves would thus gain an exemption from the cruel separations of father, mother, husband, wife, so often seen." Americans could also follow Spain's example in having every slave's value assessed by a neutral third party so that slaves could more easily purchase their own freedom from their masters. Finally, Short suggested the formation of "humane societies" whose goal it should be to raise funds to buy what slaves "appear most worthy, preferring always the females, because each individual thus manumitted stops one continual source of slavery." Free a woman, Short argued, and you will free "all future generations," since the status of the mother legally became the status of the child.[165]

It is clear that Short wrote this letter with the hope that the "enlightened & virtuous" "genius" to whom it was addressed would begin to set in motion some of the more daring plans the two men had discussed before the French Revolution, when they researched metayage across Europe and discussed the ways in which slaves could be transitioned to free labor. Since their relationship had subsequently come under severe strain, and for the previous two years only a handful of letters had crossed the Atlantic between them, this missive is remarkable for its open and bold tone. Despite Short's obvious concerns regarding the limitations of human generosity—after all, he believed that men could turn into beasts and monsters—his time away from America had strengthened his antislavery convictions and his belief not only that emancipation was necessary but also that there were many ways in which wise men in Virginia could encourage its adoption. Short pinned his hopes on Jefferson—but Jefferson did not reply.

William Short felt free to write about emancipation, black citizenship, and racial intermarriage because of his long and intimate relationship with Thomas Jefferson and because he expected that Jefferson would be receptive to his radical ideas. This expectation was founded in their shared history—both having studied with George Wythe and having experienced the revolutionary wave of antislavery thought at the College of William and Mary—as well as in the hours of conversation they shared in Paris. Short knew better than anyone that Jefferson, as early as 1785, was discussing Virginian emancipation efforts with his European friends; by 1787 he was planning to import German farmers and place them and his slaves on equal footing as metayers. Having never managed a property himself, Short learned from Jefferson's experiences as a Virginia planter, and after discussing Jefferson's observations of European labor practices Short became a willing coresearcher during his 1788–1789 travels. Revisiting the same locations and traveling to new regions, Short reported back to his mentor on the suitability of metayage in Italy versus in France and began formulating his own ideas about how to help slaves transition to lives as free people. When Jefferson left France in 1789, the two men seem to have been in perfect agreement about almost everything. Only a few storm clouds hovered on the horizon of their friendship, as Short struggled to leave his *amour* in France and return to a family and career in America.

But the French Revolution changed everything. Within a few months Jefferson and Short were viewing the world from fundamentally different perspectives. Jefferson's determined positivity about the innate perfectibility of man led him to embrace the French Revolution, despite tales of its violent excesses, for several years. Short's traumatic experiences in the same event led him to view humanity with more distrust—but, ironically, until moving back to America in 1810 he also held a more idealistic vision of an interracial America than most of his contemporaries dreamed possible. Short's emphasis on racial equality seems to have developed during his membership in the Société des Amis des Noirs, the French emancipationist society that took inspiration from similar organizations in London and Philadelphia but also went a step further by calling for equal rights for free people of color. Within a few years, the Haitian Revolution would forever change Americans' perspectives on their slaves, for better and for worse. Enslaved people now appeared somehow more capable *and* more dangerous.

Despite their disagreements over the French Revolution, and Short's hurt feelings over perceived neglect and betrayal from his beloved adoptive father, the two men reconnected over their Indian Camp experiment starting in 1793. From his diplomatic post in Spain, Short imagined that Indian Camp could serve as the first step in a three-step plan toward complete emancipation and equality for Virginia's black population by proving that tenancy on smaller plots of land was more profitable than larger-scale plantations utilizing enslaved workers. Once that point had been made, freed slaves could be employed as metayers and then finally achieve the status of free farmers. Although he was reluctant to settle in Albemarle County, Short allowed Jefferson to pursue tenancy on his behalf, and by 1798 he felt free to push Jefferson to consider implementing step two: placing slaves on the footing of metayers, as they had previously discussed.

What Short did not know when he wrote his remarkable 1798 letter was that Jefferson *was* pursuing a step in his own metayage plan, albeit at a slower pace than Short would have liked. Back in 1788 Jefferson had decided that German workers were best suited for the task of working alongside black people on his plantations, since the German-descended populations in Maryland and Pennsylvania had adapted so well to republicanism. In 1798, perhaps in advance of encouraging immigration from Germany itself, Jefferson began attempting to recruit tenants from Maryland, and in anticipation of their arrival he set aside 480 acres of his land, broken into several plots. In a letter explaining his tenancy plans, Jefferson wrote "I find I am not fit to be a farmer with the kind of labour we have" (referring to slaves). Unfortunately, an economic downturn in northern US regions prevented many farmers from journeying to Virginia, and Jefferson soon became distracted from the project by his political career.[166]

The other thing that Short could not have known when he wrote in 1798 was that Sally Hemings had given birth to a son, Beverly Hemings, in April. We can only imagine what Jefferson thought when he received this letter from Short, his "adoptive son," only two months after the birth of this child. When Short spoke of marriage between the races as a natural way for America to move forward, when he praised the beauty of mixed-race or darker-skinned women, was he thinking of Sally Hemings in particular? Did Jefferson feel that Short was directing these questions to him as a subtle way of exposing the older man's hypocrisy, since the staunch advocate of racial separation and harborer of "suspicions" regarding black inferiority in the *Notes* may have been living a completely different life behind closed doors? No matter how Jefferson felt about Short's subtext, he could not have openly discussed the issue in writing. His letters were frequently opened and read by persons other than the intended recipients, and while gossip about Hemings was likely still local in 1798, by 1800 it would be the talk of the entire country. Jefferson's political enemies joked about "Dusky Sally" and "Black Sal" throughout his presidency; John Quincy Adams—who would later argue before the Supreme Court on behalf of rebels from the slave vessel *Amistad*—gleefully published long, racist poems about the president and his black "mistress." Jefferson's white children and grandchildren were mortified and worked long after Jefferson's death to move suspicion regarding the crime of miscegenation away from their illustrious ancestor and onto another family member, such as Jefferson's nephew Peter Carr. For Jefferson to have commented on the suitability of race mixing in a letter to Short, either in 1798 or in later years, would have potentially given ammunition to his enemies.[167]

Finally, six months before his death in 1826, the enfeebled Sage of Monticello commented on this issue in his reply to yet another letter from Short that had repeated questions about slavery, amelioration, and racial mixing:

On the subject of emancipation I have ceased to think because not to be a work of my day. The plan of converting the blacks into Serfs would certainly be better than keeping them in their present condition, but I consider that of expatriation to the governments of the [West Indies] of their own colour as entirely practicable, and greatly preferable to the mixture of colour here, to this I have great aversion; but I repeat my abandonment of the subject.[168]

Up until the end, Jefferson held to the same plan he had set forth in *Notes on the State of Virginia*: emancipation and colonization. He also still claimed to have an "aversion" to racial mixing. But it seems that in this case future generations of Americans should pay more attention to what Jefferson *did* rather than to what he *said*. He may have remained outwardly committed to racial separation, but in his practice Jefferson followed through on the commitment described by Sally Heming's son Madison in his account of their time together in Paris. After she returned with Jefferson to Virginia, having given up the chance to live as a free woman in France, he gave Hemings privileged treatment for her entire life. Her children were all freed, and after Jefferson's death Hemings lived as a free woman in Charlottesville. According to Annette Gordon-Reed, Jefferson and Hemings had a relationship based more on mutual decisions and agreements—perhaps even affection—than on force or violence. Jefferson's inability to openly acknowledge this relationship, and the children born of it, is one of the great tragedies of his life. That it has taken us over a century and a half to acknowledge the possibility that our third president had a relationship with a mixed-race woman represents one of the tragedies in the American story. But the fact that a Jefferson–Hemings relationship is now openly accepted by so many is also one of the great triumphs of our time. Surely this change in American attitudes would have made William Short very happy, indeed.[169]

5. A Lasting Influence
The "Sons" Appropriate the *Notes*

"I wish to put [the *Notes*] into the hands of the young men at the college," Thomas Jefferson wrote in 1785. He had developed his own philosophies on morality, political theory, and natural law while studying at the College of William and Mary, so when Jefferson composed the book that encapsulated his views on all the vitally important issues Virginians faced, his instinct was to share his work with the future leaders who were studying there. He believed that *Notes on the State of Virginia* would "set our young students into a useful train of thought," his "two great objects" being "the emancipation of their slaves, and the settlement of their constitution on a firmer and more permanent basis." As he told several close friends, "it is to them I look, to the rising generation, and not to the one now in power for these great reformations." In 1789 the appreciative president of the college, Bishop James Madison, wrote his grateful thanks upon receipt of more than thirty copies: "[Y]our Notes judiciously distributed among our young Men here, will tend to excite the spirit of philosophical observation amongst us."[1]

Sending thirty-seven copies of his *Notes* to the College of William and Mary was perhaps Jefferson's boldest antislavery strategy. His other antislavery actions—cosponsoring a bill during his first session as a member of the General Assembly in 1769, writing condemnations of the slave trade and slavery in several revolutionary documents, attempting to prohibit slavery in new territories in the Northwest Ordinance of 1784, drafting an antislavery constitution and an emancipation and colonization amendment for Virginia, urging Congress to end the slave trade in 1806—relied on the support of other lawmakers already in power.[2] Targeting students with his *Notes* was a way of attempting to shift public opinion, of developing a generation of leaders more committed to living out their enlightened principles than his own generation was proving to be. In this chapter, I will argue that Jefferson's educational strategy was successful among young men who were students in the last decade of the eighteenth century and the first decade of the nineteenth, although—tragically—not successful enough to tip the balance of power within Virginia. Despite the prominent voices that invoked Jefferson's name and his antislavery ideals over the years, voices such as those of St. George Tucker and his cousin George Tucker, many of whom had been persuaded that slavery was antithetical to Virginia's revolutionary values when they were young men, tended to accommodate themselves to the peculiar institution as time went on. They came to feel it was simply too difficult a problem to solve; colonization was too expensive; living in equality with free black people was unthinkable. And the self-interested powerful minority—the slaveholding elites who concentrated wealth and votes in the eastern region of the state—would never voluntarily surrender their human property.

Ironically, Jefferson's antislavery principles became more important *outside* his beloved home state than they were within it, as men like Edward Coles took responsibility for shaping Jefferson's legacy into a useable antislavery nationalism. It was in this form that Jefferson's attempt to shape public opinion trickled down to the antebellum era's Republican Party. But those Virginians who had been persuaded against slavery while at William and Mary in the years directly after Jefferson had sent the college his *Notes* watched as his most dire prophecy from that book came true: "I tremble for my country when I reflect that God is just: that his justice cannot sleep forever. . . . The Almighty has no attribute which can take side with us in such a contest."[3]

In 1864 the Union general Winfield Scott, known to his troops as "Old Fuss and Feathers" because of his love for ostentatious uniforms and for punctuality, published his autobiography. Scott (1786–1866) was born into an upper-class Virginian family, a family of slaveholders, but he had also long been an opponent of slavery. In his *Memoirs*, Scott wrote about the origins of those convictions: "In boyhood, at William and Mary College, and in common with most, if not all, my companions, I became deeply impressed with the views given by Mr. Jefferson, in his 'Notes on Virginia,' and by Judge Tucker, in the Appendix to his edition of Blackstone's Commentaries, in favor of a gradual emancipation of slaves." He had not read further on the topic since leaving college, Scott recalled, "but my early impressions are fresh and unchanged." So strong was the emancipationist impulse Scott received from Jefferson and "Judge Tucker," referring to William and Mary professor and judge St. George Tucker, that Scott declared "if I had had the honor of a seat in the Virginia Legislature in the winter of 1831-'2, when a bill was brought forward to carry out those views"—referring to Thomas Jefferson Randolph's ill-fated gradual emancipation measure—"I should certainly have given it my hearty support."[4]

Scott attended William and Mary in 1805, one year after St. George Tucker resigned his position as Chair of Law. Tucker (1752–1827) had taken over the position from George Wythe in 1790, and he soon assumed Wythe's mantle as both a brilliant law professor and one of Virginia's leading intellectual opponents of slavery. Although Jefferson had viewed Wythe's retirement as a huge blow at the time, telling fellow alumnus William Short that Wythe's leaving meant "it is over with the college," Tucker's appointment not long afterward ensured that antislavery perspectives would continue to be circulated at the college and, thus, that Jefferson's *Notes on the State of Virginia* would remain one of the most influential sources for antislavery thought among rising generations of Virginian leaders. This was due to the fact that students continued to read the copies of the *Notes* that Jefferson sent to the college library for that explicit purpose, not to mention that Tucker himself was heavily influenced by Jefferson's work.[5]

Tucker's life, like Jefferson's, was defined primarily by his involvement with the ideals of the American Revolution. Tucker arrived as a nineteen-year-old immigrant from the British colony of Bermuda in 1771, just in time for the early days of debate following the Boston Massacre. In 1772 Tucker began studying law under Wythe, as had Jefferson a decade earlier (William Short would begin his studies with Wythe eight years later, in 1780). But when war broke out, Tucker abandoned his legal practice; he smuggled goods from the Caribbean and served in the militia, fighting alongside Lafayette during the Yorktown Campaign.[6] Tucker biographer Phillip Hamilton asserts that the young immigrant risked his life in the conflict because of his "staunch commitment to the Revolution's liberal principles," including the notion that "all Men are by nature equally free and Independent," as the Virginia Declaration of Rights puts it.[7] Like those of many other patriots, Tucker's finances suffered during the war years, and he had to resume his legal practice despite having married a wealthy widow and acquiring her plantations and slaves. The widow, incidentally, was Frances Bland Randolph—the very same lady described by Short in his remarkable 1798 letter to Jefferson as the perfect example of a woman who was both dark-skinned and beautiful. (Short had not seen Mrs. Tucker since he moved to France in 1785, but she apparently made quite an impression on him.[8])

Tucker was appointed to the college's board of visitors in 1782 and became a judge sitting on Virginia's General Court in 1788. When Wythe left the college in 1790, Tucker was an easy choice to replace him.[9] And like his former mentor, Tucker did not hesitate to instruct his students in the revolutionary principles of natural rights and to raise the troubling question of whether Americans were consistent in the application of those rights: "Whilst America hath been the land of promise to Europeans, and their descendants, it hath been the vale of death to millions of the wretched sons of Africa." Was there, therefore, "due consistency between our avowed principles and our practice" regarding "those unfortunate people"? As Tucker pointed out to his students, Jefferson's declaration that all men are created equal is "indeed, no more than a recognition of the first principles of the law of nature." White Americans should therefore regard those of African descent as "our fellow men," not as subordinate creatures, and should be consistent in advocating political liberty for the new United States as well as emancipation for enslaved people.[10]

Tucker's increasing outspokenness on the issue of slavery coincided with major shifts in his adopted state and in his personal life: in 1788, Tucker's wife, Frances, died at age thirty-six. Not long afterward, Tucker realized that his stepsons' inheritances, the land and property they had expected to acquire from their deceased father, John Randolph of Matoax,[11] would all be seized in payment of long-standing British debts. Without land and slaves to depend on, Tucker told his young stepsons all that remained for them was their own ingenuity and hard work.

The Randolph/Tucker family was not the only one experiencing such a transition from the old lifestyle of the landed gentry: falling land values, decreasing respect among lower classes for elites, and rising immigration to western Virginia all were remaking the face of the state. Virginia's social, economic, and political orders were changing, and in response Tucker sold off his large properties and focused on creating a career for himself as a lawyer, a judge, and a professor. And around the time that Tucker divested himself of his plantations and began living a simpler life in Williamsburg, he began using his platform as a professor to question the incongruence of slavery in a republic.[12]

Although part of Tucker's willingness to question slavery may have derived from his change in lifestyle—from that of a plantation owner dependent on slave labor to that of a professional in the city—his questions were given added urgency by the beginnings of a slave uprising in the French colony of Saint-Domingue (today's Haiti). The island had been in turmoil since 1789, but that turmoil was largely restricted to political agitation among white and free black planters, the latter group working for political equality in the midst of the French Revolution's liberality, with the aid of the Société des Amis des Noirs. In August 1791 a slave insurrection began, transforming a conflict about the equality of freedmen into a complex war in which African-born rebels and free people of mixed race sometimes fought among themselves as well as together against European troops from several different countries. The conflict continued until just after Haiti declared independence in 1804, and it embodied American slaveholders' worst nightmares: Slavery was outlawed (although unfree labor continued), and almost no white people were left alive.[13]

In the early days of the Haitian Revolution, news was scarce and reports contradictory.[14] But any rumor of a slave uprising in the Atlantic world was cause for concern among American slaveholders, who knew those rumors would eventually reach their own enslaved workers. As one Virginian newspaper writer put it: "Slaves have understanding enough to know, when so much noise is made by a part of the community about their emancipation, that the time perhaps may come when they shall be free—and that the time being spun out longer than they have patience to wait for, will be the cause of much bloodshed, by insurrections or other means equally as unlawful and unnatural!"[15] The Haitian Revolution was particularly brutal on all sides; tales of white families slaughtered in gruesome ways—some of these tales exaggerated, others not—terrified Virginians. It did not take long for the rumors to take shape on Virginians' doorsteps: by May 1792 hundreds of slaves in Northampton County were said to be collecting weapons and planning a revolt. Although no actual evidence of weapons or coordinated planning was found, several slaves were whipped and three sold to Cuba as a warning. Across the state white men organized themselves into patrols, and free black people began to be looked at with increasing suspicion, since slaveholders tended to feel that this class provoked jealousy and discontent among the enslaved. In May 1793 French refugees from Saint-Domingue began arriving in Norfolk, bringing with them their slaves in addition to tales of atrocities, and over the next few years nervous white Virginians believed that the presence of these refugees and their dangerous property inspired formerly docile Virginia slaves to organize their own revolts.[16]

Virginia legislators responded not by debating emancipation strategies but instead by passing laws to restrict manumission and limit the options of free black people. One statute from this period specifically prohibited slaves from the West Indies from living in Virginia, whether as slaves or as freedmen. Other bills made it permissible for freed slaves to be seized and re-enslaved to satisfy their deceased masters' debts; banned migration of any free people of color into the state; and required that free black Virginians register with local authorities. Legislation of the early 1790s served to reinforce the line between white and black Virginians and to impose penalties on white people who attempted to aid slaves in unsuccessful freedom suits or who attended any illegal meetings of slaves.[17]

As a judge and Virginia's premier law professor, St. George Tucker studiously observed all these legal developments. Yet he still believed that his fellow Virginians could be receptive to discussions of emancipation—and that he could devise a plan so mild, so uncontroversial, so carefully tailored that it could bypass any possible objections that legislators would have. Tucker began the process in 1795 by collecting the most up-to-date evidence on emancipation in America, inquiring of someone who had already experienced the transition from slave state to free: Jeremy Belknap, a Congregationalist minister in Boston. An outspoken emancipationist with a somewhat open mind about black people's capabilities, Belknap also had an extensive network of acquaintances to whom he forwarded Tucker's questions about emancipation. Vice President John Adams, the free black artisan Prince Hall, and James Sullivan, the attorney general of Massachusetts, were among the respondents. For the most part, these men agreed that the experience of slavery impeded newly freed black people's ability to succeed. This was, they surmised, because slavery corrupted slaves' morals. Moral corruption negatively affected behavior after emancipation, which in turn served to reinforce white stereotypes about black delinquency. Belknap summarized these concerns in his reply to Tucker, adding that, because of the failure of freed slaves to achieve full equality in white society, perhaps they would have been better off remaining as slaves—even though Belknap still believed that the promises of the Declaration of Independence applied to everyone, at least in theory.[18]

Undaunted, Tucker in 1796 published his *Dissertation on Slavery: With a Proposal for the Gradual Abolition of It in the State of Virginia*. Tucker based *Dissertation on Slavery* partly on his lectures at the college and partly on his own conclusions after receiving the information compiled by Belknap, and he drew from such widespread sources as the British abolitionist Granville Sharp and the Marquis de Chastellux. But Tucker's *Dissertation* is primarily in dialogue with *Notes on the State of Virginia*, sometimes referred to as an authoritative source and other times specifically rebutted. Tucker thereby utilized the *Notes* as both foundation and foil for his own far more extensive and complex commentary on race, slavery, and emancipation in Virginia.

Jefferson and Tucker each began discussing Virginian slavery by focusing on the ways in which Virginia's laws were flawed when held up to the state's newly enlightened principles. In *Notes*, Jefferson interrupted his own summary of how he revised Virginia's legal code in the late 1770s in order to explain his (and Wythe's) liberal reasoning for an emancipation and colonization amendment. After describing the plan, Jefferson offered a primarily race-based justification for it. At first glance, Tucker's approach is even more liberal: he devoted the entire first half of his 106-page *Dissertation* to a broad discussion of the ways in which Virginians' treatment of slaves and free people of color contradicted their stated adherence to Enlightenment principles. By way of example, he offered extensive summaries of all Virginia laws dealing with enslaved persons or free people of color from 1620 (when he thought the first slaves were brought to Virginia[19]) through 1796, marking each instance in which a black person was treated more harshly by the law than was a white person. The only instance in which a law was "more favorable to a Negroe than a white person," Tucker pointed out with a decided note of irony, occurred in cases of interracial marriage. At such times, the *white* spouse was the one who would be sent to prison (along with the offending clergyman, of course). Tucker repeatedly commented on the role of racism, which he referred to as "prejudice," in violating the "laws of nature" in Virginia. Nature's obvious principles were "set aside in favor of institutions, the pure result of prejudice, usurpation, and tyranny"; mercy was abandoned merely because the "complexion" of the "wretched culprit" was different "from that of his judges."[20]

However, Tucker's distress regarding institutional racism did not translate into a call for political equality for all people or even a "general and simultaneous emancipation." Instead, Tucker drew from Jefferson's comments on racial inequality to illustrate the impossibility of a multiracial republic. And then he systematically undercut Jefferson's preferred solution—reparation for slavery in the form of emancipation, followed by education and sponsored colonization. Quoting the *Notes*, Tucker agreed with Jefferson that learned attributes of "arrogance and assumption of superiority" rendered white people unfit for equality with their former slaves and that engrained habits of obedience and submission rendered formerly enslaved people unfit for freedom.[21] Jefferson's answer to this conundrum, as well as to the threat of extermination through race war, was to free all slaves born after a certain date, allow them to remain with their parents while young, then educate them "at the public expence" in whatever skill each individual child showed aptitude for. This education would qualify the freed generation for colonization and subsequent self-government in whatever part of the world "the circumstances of the time should render most proper." The state should pay to equip the emigrants with tools, supplies, animals, and whatever else they needed to become "a free and independent people." It would be expensive, but Jefferson implied that justice (as well as self-interest) required such recompense for the sins of slavery. Jefferson's plan would also take time. The first group of colonists would not leave until at least twenty-one years after the passage of the law, and presumably freed slaves would from then on be sent to their colony in waves until the remaining enslaved parents in Virginia became too old to reproduce. And though his plan would be accomplished in stages, Jefferson still advocated abolishing all slavery for everyone born after a certain date and upon their reaching a mature age, as in Pennsylvania (in 1780 Pennsylvania freed future-born slaves at the age of twenty-eight) or New York (in 1799 New York freed future-born boys at twenty-eight and girls at twenty-five).[22]

Tucker, however, decided that an emancipation bill tied to colonization would not work. In fact, in his *Dissertation* Tucker wondered whether the reason that Jefferson and the other members of the committee to revise Virginia's laws (meaning George Wythe) had not submitted their emancipation amendment to the General Assembly was because they knew that it was not practicable and that there were just too many possible objections to their colonization plan.[23] But Tucker did not fully engage with all the details of Jefferson's plan in his criticism: ignoring Jefferson and Wythe's goal of providing adequate education prior to *gradual* colonization, Tucker declared that colonizing slaves "all at once" was cruel, because it would "devote them to a lingering death by famine, by disease, and other accumulated miseries." It would require finding ships and provisions and a friendly patch of land large enough for 12,000 migrants every year, he estimated, and since the migrants would be uneducated and their morals still corrupted by slavery, their society would immediately collapse without extensive, authoritative oversight from a white government. (Perhaps Tucker believed that voters would refuse to pay for the education Jefferson and Wythe hoped would precede colonization and therefore did not bother to discuss how education would improve colonists' chances of success.) But retaining a freed population in Virginia would be equally impracticable, since "they would soon become . . . the caterpillars of the earth, and the tigers of the human race," simultaneously lazy, unproductive, and dangerous. It would be a repeat of Haiti, Tucker implied; Massachusetts—with its tiny population of black people—may have been able to free all its slaves at once, but any state in which a near majority of the population was enslaved would be destroyed through violence if emancipation was not carried out in the slowest way possible.[24]

Tucker was also troubled by the fact that the law of nature encompassed the right to property, even property in slaves, and this right must also not be infringed. Jefferson had hoped when he wrote the *Notes* in the early 1780s that "[t]he spirit of the master is abating," leading to "a total emancipation . . . with the consent of the masters," but Tucker apparently accepted the reality that no Virginia masters in 1796 would actually consent to make the financial sacrifice of their property that Jefferson and Wythe's plan entailed. Furthermore, Virginians who did *not* own slaves would, as the *Notes* explained, have to contribute toward the emancipated generation's colony through their tax dollars, and Tucker did not feel this was fair or feasible.[25]

Tucker's peculiar solution to these conflicting issues—that of the right to freedom on one hand, the right to property on the other, and slavery's ill effects on masters and slaves rendering future coexistence on equal terms impossible—was to declare that abolition could be achieved "without the *emancipation* of a single slave; without depriving any man of the *property* which he *possesses*." Virginians did not need to concern themselves with the tricky details of colonization; nor did they need to worry about reconciling themselves to living alongside black people as equals. Sweeping aside his own concern for the ways in which Virginia's laws violated natural rights by unequally excluding and harshly punishing people simply because of their color, Tucker advocated creating a legal system in which slaves would be freed from slavery over the course of several generations but then remain suspended in a form of "civil slavery." Slaveholders could surely not object to freeing a slave still to be born, for "no man can in reality be *deprived* of what he doth not possess." Furthermore, by deliberately excluding freed slaves from the basic rights of citizens—by "denying them the most valuable privileges which civil government affords"—Tucker believed Virginians could "render it their [the freed peoples'] inclination and their interest to seek those privileges in some other climate." In other words, the former slaves would be so unhappy that they would colonize themselves, freeing Virginians from the expense and the responsibility of their removal.[26]

Tucker's plan is harsh and contradictory; he speaks eloquently of the need for revolutionary integrity—matching up natural rights principles with actions—throughout the first half of his *Dissertation*, only to dedicate the second half to arguing that the best way for Virginians to free their slaves was to do so over the course of many decades while simultaneously oppressing the freed people of color so harshly as to cause them to wish to leave their friends and families and homes in search of reprieve elsewhere.[27] But if Tucker recognized the contradictions inherent in his plan, he nonetheless believed that Jefferson himself had provided the rationale justifying it:

> If it be true, as Mr. Jefferson seems to suppose, that the Africans are really an inferior race of mankind, will not sound policy advise their exclusion from a society in which they have not yet been admitted to participate in civil rights; and even to guard against such admission, at any future period, since it may eventually depreciate the whole national character? And if prejudices have taken such deep root in our minds, as to render it impossible to eradicate this opinion, ought not so general an error, if it be one, to be respected?

Prejudice might be an "error," one from which Tucker himself did not "pretend to be wholly exempt." Still, he declared that because prejudice was inevitable—"whoever proposes any plan for the abolition of slavery, will find that he must either encounter, or accommodate himself to prejudice"—it was best to work around it by passing whatever ameliorative law the prejudiced culture would accept. He even hoped that by institutionalizing prejudice—racism—for long enough, and thereby rendering people of color harmless in the white imagination, the state might "obliterate those prejudices" and eventually end up with more open-minded white citizens.[28]

Tucker may have disagreed with Jefferson's plan, but he had respect for Jefferson himself, and vice versa. The two men were even related, in the roundabout way common among elite Virginian families: Jefferson's mother was a Randolph, and Jefferson's darling oldest daughter, Martha, was married to Thomas Mann Randolph, whose sister Judith was married to Tucker's stepson Richard Randolph. While Tucker was at work on his *Dissertation* in 1795, he and Jefferson were on friendly terms. (Jefferson genially invited the judge to escape the "heats and drunken noise of Charlottesville" by spending the night at Monticello when Tucker was in the area on business, for example.) Tucker sent his manuscript to Philadelphia to be printed; as soon as he received copies, he sent three to Albemarle County so that Jefferson could have one and pass the others to Monroe and Madison.[29]

Jefferson quickly wrote to thank Tucker for the copy, stating his broad agreement with the "doctrines" Tucker professed. In his typical nonconfrontational manner, Jefferson did not comment specifically on the ways in which Tucker's plan contradicted his own, instead gently noting that "as to the mode of emancipation, I am satisfied that that must be a matter of compromise between the passions[,] the prejudices, and the real difficulties which will each have their weight in that operation." But Jefferson still believed that colonization was a necessity, as indeed he would claim to believe for the rest of his life.[30] He told Tucker that the real question was "[w]hither shall the coloured emigrants go?" Time was of the essence, since "the sooner we put some plan under way, the greater hope there is that it may be permitted to proceed peaceably to it's ultimate effect. But if something is not done, and soon done, we shall be the murderers of our own children." The revolution in Haiti was, to Jefferson as to Tucker, an ominous portent of things inevitably to come: "[T]he revolutionary storm now sweeping the globe will be upon us, and happy if we make timely provision to give it an easy passage over our land." Jefferson was also obviously worried that Tucker's plan would take far too long: "If we had begun sooner, we might probably have been allowed a lengthier operation to clear ourselves, but every day's delay lessens the time we may take for emancipation." Virginia's awful "combustion," Jefferson concluded, "must be near at hand."[31]

Despite their differences over details, Jefferson and Tucker at least agreed that something needed to be done immediately to emancipate and remove the state's slaves, but it seems most of the state legislature felt differently. Tucker genuinely thought he had created something that met all possible objections: "I proposed the most gradual plan," he reported to Jeremy Belknap in Massachusetts, "that could possibly eventually produce the desired effect. I guarded it with every restriction that I supposed timidity or prejudice could insist on; and I endeavoured to lull avarice itself to sleep by demonstrating the slow progress and insencible effects of my proposal." Tucker was therefore dumbfounded when, after he had created the easiest possible way for slaveholders to gradually emancipate their slaves, the House of Delegates refused to discuss or even hear about the *Dissertation* he sent them. The Senate of Virginia was, Tucker heard, more disposed to receive his plan, but since all bills had to originate in the House of Delegates, the plan died. Tucker bemoaned this tragedy: "Nobody, I believe, had read it; nobody could explain its contents. Nobody was prepared to meet the blind fury of the enemies of freedom." Now Tucker wanted his northern friend Belknap to know that he did not cherish even "the smallest hope of advancing a cause so dear to me as the abolition of slavery." Only an actual slave uprising and subsequent "suffering" would "open the oppressor's eyes"—"perhaps."[32]

While the members of the House of Delegates rejected Tucker's plan out of hand, there were some Virginians who felt he had not gone far enough. Robert Pleasants (1723–1801) was a Quaker whose belief in the God-given equality of mankind led him to free his own slaves, fight in the courts for two years in order to secure his deceased father's slaves' freedom, found the Virginia Abolition Society, and frequently correspond with leading citizens of the state, exhorting them to do more on behalf of liberty.[33] In 1797 Pleasants wrote to Tucker, pointing out the numerous ways in which Tucker's plan was corrupted by prejudice. Like William Short, Pleasants firmly believed that enslaved workers constituted a valuable part of Virginia's laboring population and should therefore be freed and encouraged to *remain* in the state, not forced to leave by discriminatory practices. Tucker defended himself against the charge of prejudice: he had included the offending passages against black people in his *Dissertation*, he said, because paying lip service to prejudice was the only way any emancipation bill would conceivably convince the more racist Assembly members.[34]

As for himself, Tucker wrote defensively, "there was in one instance" only "a degree of prejudice in my own breast . . . I mean the prohibition of intermarriages." But this was common, "a prejudice so prevalent in the present generation," Tucker contended, that there was no possibility that the two races would intermarry after a general emancipation occurred. Since the two groups would therefore remain visibly separate, if freed black people "could acquire any share in the administration of the state we should soon behold two parties formed & enlisted by nature under different Banners whose Contests would probably convulse the state." Tucker argued that, if Pleasants would just consider the dismal fate of the *Dissertation*, he would change his mind about what was possible in Virginia. After all, Tucker wrote, "cautious as I had been to meet the prejudices of all opposed to the abolition of Slavery I fell very far short of success. The pamphlet . . . addressed to the speaker in as respectful a letter as I could write was treated with ignominy . . . a motion was twice made to send it and the letter back to its author." Pleasants had asked Tucker to support a more sweeping plan; Tucker agreed to sign it but cautioned the Quaker that "your petition . . . asks for much more than I presumed to do" and would thus probably never succeed.[35]

James Madison was also a target of Pleasants's antislavery lobbying efforts, but he was even more concerned than Tucker about their possible side effects. In 1791 he asked Pleasants to please stop sending emancipation petitions to the legislature. Pressuring the Assembly for such a law would "do harm rather than good"; it would strengthen calls to "withdraw the privilege now allowed to individuals, of giving freedom to slaves," or "clog it with a condition that the persons freed should be removed from the Country." Madison wrote from experience: in 1785, when Jefferson was considering publishing his *Notes*, he and Madison had watched in consternation as the legislature almost passed a bill prohibiting emancipations—an angry reaction to Methodist antislavery petitions.[36] And in 1790 Madison was alarmed when two antislavery petitions—sent by Quakers in New York and by the Pennsylvania Society for Promoting the Abolition of Slavery (including Benjamin Franklin, in his last public act)—arrived in the First Congress, only to provoke an explosive debate. Although the petitions asked for the end of both the slave trade and slavery itself, the responding committee in the US House of Representatives decided that the Constitution expressly restrained the federal government from prohibiting either practice—at least until 1808. However, the committee also declared that the federal government *could* tax and regulate the slave trade to ensure humane treatment aboard slave ships.[37]

The immediate outcry from the South Carolina and Georgia congressmen was, according to Madison, "intemperate beyond all example and even all decorum"; he felt the southerners should have let the matter die quietly, using it as an opportunity to recognize both the powers and the restraints imposed on Congress by the Constitution. Instead, in the weeks of angry debates that followed, men such as Thomas Tudor Tucker of South Carolina—cheered by members from Georgia and even Virginia—staunchly warned that any attempt at a general emancipation, at any time, would be met by a civil war. As Richard Newman puts it: "Georgia and South Carolina laid down a political gauntlet for the rest of the Union: drop antislavery or endanger the new Union." As a result, men who had previously been inclined to support the emancipationist cause fell silent, unwilling to destroy the fragile republic that had so recently, and with so much bloodshed, formed.[38]

Fortunately for Tucker, his emancipation plan did not set off a similar firestorm in Virginia's Assembly seven years later; it produced a whimper rather than a bang. Despite his disappointment over the silence from legislators, Tucker did not entirely give up. He decided that his plan was "utopian," with no chance of implementation, but he republished the *Dissertation* anyway, in another format: as an appendix to the 1803 publication of his widely read edition of *Blackstone's Commentaries*. It was in that format that Winfield Scott and other students at the College of William and Mary for years to come encountered Tucker's emancipation strategy. Tucker's plan may not have been popular in the legislature, or have gone far enough for Robert Pleasants, but his condemnation of slavery as incompatible with republicanism joined the *Notes* as a text that was effective in persuading younger Virginians to translate natural rights philosophy into practice.[39]

One such younger reader was a man named Edward Coles (1786–1868). The son of an established landholding family from Albemarle County, Coles was a member of Winfield Scott's class at William and Mary in

1805—among those of Scott's "companions" who "became deeply impressed with the views given by Mr. Jefferson, in his 'Notes on Virginia,' and by Judge Tucker . . . in favor of a gradual emancipation of slaves." Born in 1786, a year before Jefferson sent his *Notes* to the college, Coles was raised to enjoy "the ease and self-indulgence of being waited on" by slaves, as he recalled in his autobiography many years later. But while he attended lectures with his lifelong friend Scott and other future national figures, such as John Crittenden (governor of Kentucky and senator) and John Tyler (US president), Coles's priorities underwent a drastic change.[40]

Although St. George Tucker had retired from teaching by the time Coles arrived in Williamsburg, he still mentored students, and Coles enjoyed social gatherings at his home. Coles also came under the influence of the college president and professor Bishop James Madison, who taught politics and philosophy—and who had been instrumental in encouraging Jefferson to send copies of his *Notes* to the students at the college.[41] Bishop Madison was an opponent of slavery who in 1791 went so far as to bestow upon the British abolitionist Granville Sharp an honorary doctorate. Bishop Madison informed Sharp that he had earned the doctorate in part because too much "[p]raise cannot be given to the truly noble Exertions, which you have made, and are Continuing to make, in a Concern the most interesting to Humanity. . . . [I]f there be a Cause, which we may presume Heaven itself would particularly favour, it must be that which has for its object the Abolition of the Slave Trade."[42]

Bishop Madison took seriously his duty to foster a spirit of free inquiry and pursuit of the truth at William and Mary: he assigned readings from the Scottish common sense school, radical French philosophers, and revolutionaries such as Thomas Paine (and Thomas Jefferson). Partly as a result, the student body in the first decade of the nineteenth century was overwhelmingly anti-Federalist and pro-Jefferson. Coles's older brother Isaac, a recent graduate, proudly served as Jefferson's private secretary when he became president. The nineteen-year-old Edward Coles embraced Jeffersonian politics and imbibed a healthy dose of revolutionary ardor for creating a better world, and he also began to wrestle with the contradictions inherent in Virginian society.[43]

Coles later recalled that Bishop Madison's moral philosophy course was where "I had my attention first awakened to the state of master & slave." "The terms Slavery & Justice," he wrote at the time in his class notes on Rousseau, "are contradictory and reciprocally exclusive of each other." In another set of notes, Coles remarked that it seemed clear that God created all men equal, with equal natural rights; furthermore, man had only two duties: to God and to his neighbor.[44] Just as many intrepid men and women of faith before Coles had come to realize, slavery becomes harder to justify once all other people are viewed as one's neighbor. During a lecture on the rights of man, Coles asked Bishop Madison outright: "[H]ow can man be made the property of man?" Bishop Madison replied that such an action was wrong and unjustifiable, but since Virginians found themselves in the midst of such a system, and since getting rid of it was so hard, slavery persisted. After further conversation, both in class and informally at Madison's home, Coles came to the conclusion that he could not personally abide a life without integrity—without following up beliefs with actions. If he could "not reconcile Slavery with his principles," then "he ought not to hold slaves." It was that simple.[45]

Although Coles was not alone in his conversion to antislavery thought during his time at the college—other students from the period, including Winfield Scott and Chapman Johnson, spoke out against the institution—his personal conviction of the immorality of slavery prompted him to make sacrifices that very few others would be willing, or able, to make. Just before he was to take his final exams at the college in early 1807, Coles was called to the bedside of his sick father. A few months later the elder Coles died, leaving Edward—who was not the firstborn and therefore had both fewer rights and fewer obligations—a 782-acre plantation and up to twenty slaves. Although young Coles had kept his nascent antislavery views secret from his family, after his father's death he felt compelled to inform the rest of his siblings and his mother that he planned to free his human property. His relatives, Coles recalled in his autobiography, all "disapproved & endeavored to reason me out of the determination." They told him that he would fail in life without slaves; he had no profession, only land, and in Virginia no one could "be an agriculturalist without owning or employing slaves."

It would perhaps have been helpful at this point if William Short and Jefferson's Indian Camp experiment in free tenant labor had become more successful and well-known. Instead, Coles had to concede that his relatives were probably right: the labor of enslaved workers was necessary to a successful plantation in Virginia.[46]

Coles's next instinct was to hire his own slaves as tenant laborers, technically keeping them as slaves for the sake of appearances while he lived and then freeing them formally in his will. This plan might have worked, though Coles's relatives and neighbors strenuously objected, telling him that "I, and my unfortunate Negroes, would be considered and treated as pests of society" if he dared carry it out. But by 1806 one very important legal change had taken place that would preclude such a scheme: the General Assembly finally did what Jefferson and Madison had long feared, restricting individuals' ability to free their slaves by making it illegal for a freed slave to remain in Virginia for more than one year. (Madison gloomily marked the event by writing a note to himself in the margin of his copy of the letter to Pleasants, in which he had warned that emancipation efforts would lead to restrictive anti-emancipation bills, "it so happened.") From now on, any antislavery master would have to consider that a slave freed would actually be a slave exiled, forced to leave friends and family and to travel hundreds of miles to the safety of a receptive free state, most likely with few resources to aid in the relocation process.[47]

The 1806 bill was actually a compromise effort designed to balance Virginia's competing problems of the rights to property, to liberty, and to safety. Although legislators hesitated to take away slaveholders' rights to do what they wished with their own property—to keep or to free enslaved people—legislators also wanted to curb the emancipation impulse.[48] Many Virginians feared that, if owners continued to manumit their human chattel, the state would become a more dangerous place to live. These fears were made more strident after an attempted uprising led by an enslaved blacksmith named Gabriel in the summer of 1800. Scholars disagree regarding Gabriel's precise motivations—whether they were class-based or religious in origin—but it seems likely that he was emboldened by the Haitian Revolution. St. George Tucker's stepson John Randolph attended some of the resulting interrogations and remarked with deep concern that the would-be rebels "exhibited a spirit, which, if it becomes general, must deluge the Southern country in blood. . . . They manifested a sense of their rights, and contempt of danger, a thirst for revenge which portend the most unhappy consequences."[49]

The plan had been audacious: Gabriel and his followers would divide into three groups on a Saturday night in Richmond; one group would set fire to some warehouses, and while the townspeople were distracted by the fire the other two groups would take over the state armory and kidnap Governor James Monroe from his mansion. The exhausted townspeople would then be easily killed; the rebels would consolidate their hold on the capital city and demand the abolition of slavery while holding Monroe hostage. Although it is impossible to know how many slaves were involved in the conspiracy, investigators after the fact determined that there were as many as 200 conspirators in Richmond, and it could have stretched throughout the entire state. Only a torrential downpour of rain on the appointed evening, and warnings from several slaves loyal to their masters, foiled Gabriel's planning.[50]

In the aftermath of Gabriel's Conspiracy, as it has become known, seventy black men were put on trial. After ten executions, with more expected, Governor Monroe wrote to his mentor, President Jefferson, for advice. The situation was "unquestionably the most serious and formidable conspiracy we have ever known of the kind," but Monroe worried about "[w]here to arrest the hand of the Executioner." Should every convict be executed? If not, could a slave who had determined to fight for his freedom ever be trusted again? During this period Virginia had no laws allowing condemned prisoners to be transported out of the state rather than be hanged, but Monroe believed mercy, rather than severity, "is the better policy." Jefferson strongly agreed, confirming to his younger friend that "there has been hanging enough." Moreover, Jefferson sympathized with the would-be rebels, believing they had "rights" of their own and that their object—freedom—was righteous. After all, in his *Notes* Jefferson argued that "[t]he Almighty has no attribute which can take side with us in such a contest" between slaves and masters. He recommended that Monroe stop the executions and that the legislature "pass a law for [the rebels'] exportation, the proper measure on this & all similar occasions."[51]

The legislature did allow the governor to begin pardoning some and transporting others out of the state, but it also began passing yet more restrictive legislation designed to curtail the liberties of free black Virginians and even to restrict their access to education and to weapons for self-defense. Although these laws were often not strictly enforced, as Eva Sheppard Wolf explains, they still "served as a message to both blacks and to whites that in spite of the manumission law of 1782 . . . and in spite of the interest some whites had in helping blacks obtain their liberty . . . Virginia ought to be two societies, with whites above and united against slaves" and against free people of color.[52]

St. George Tucker's younger cousin (and another recent William and Mary graduate) George Tucker (1775–1861) was inspired by the events in Richmond to publish an antislavery pamphlet in 1801. The twenty-six-year-old Tucker had moved to Williamsburg to study law with his prominent relative in 1795, and biographers generally agree that he absorbed St. George's antislavery views at that time—but as we shall see, in several respects the younger Tucker was more impressed by Thomas Jefferson's antislavery strategy than by that set forth in St. George's *Dissertation*.[53] In his *Letter to a Member of the General Assembly of Virginia*, the younger Tucker argued that the "late extraordinary conspiracy" had awakened the state to danger and that the threatening population must be removed. George Tucker was just as steeped in the liberal revolutionary tradition as his antislavery forebears at the College of William and Mary had been: He pointed out that love of freedom was implanted by "the God of nature" in every human; that black people were every year gaining skills, such as learning to read, that rendered them more independent (and therefore dangerous); more important, just as white Virginians had progressively developed their ideology of rights and liberty so, too, were black people beginning to claim freedom not "merely as a good; now they also claim it as a right." The only way to stop this perfectly natural progression would be to work harder at keeping slaves in ignorance of their rights. Virginia therefore faced a choice: either oppose progress by making the laws more harsh (but "when you make one little tyrant more tyrannical, you will make thousands of slaves impatient and vindictive"), or acknowledge the inevitable advancement of liberty and free the slaves. St. George Tucker had advocated a plan that would achieve eventual liberty for all Virginia's slaves—but only after a long period of legal oppression designed to encourage the freed population to leave. In the post–Gabriel Conspiracy climate, maintaining a large, discontented class of former slaves no longer seemed like a safe idea. So young George Tucker reached back to the *Notes* to offer a compromise plan.[54]

He recommended that Virginia should establish a colony either in the West or in newly acquired Indian land in Georgia.[55] The state should encourage already-free black people to settle in that colony first by offering financial assistance, then by levying extra taxes on any who dared remain in Virginia. As Jefferson had detailed in the *Notes*, the colony should be "under the protection" of the Virginia or United States government until it achieved prosperity and a large enough population to become self-governing. But *unlike* the plan outlined in the *Notes*, Tucker did not ask the legislature to pass a general emancipation law; instead he believed poll taxes on enslaved property, especially on young females, would both pay for the colony and encourage owners to export their slaves voluntarily. Like his cousin, the young George Tucker stopped short of asking voters to end slavery in Virginia outright.[56]

Although Tucker was pleased by the fame that his publication garnered for him—"I succeeded and was rewarded with the public approbation. My little pamphlet was reprinted in Baltimore, and I was at once ranged in the class of men of letters"—it seems to have had little influence in Richmond. Instead, the General Assembly came within two votes of banning manumissions altogether. In the post-Gabriel era, many believed with George Tucker that freeing slaves, only to oppress them with harsh restrictions on their rights, would never work; they would only keep reaching for equality. And white Virginians—with some rare exceptions, such as the expatriate William Short in Europe—could not imagine living in equality with people of color. So in 1806 the House of Delegates passed a bill decreeing that freed slaves would from now on have to leave the state within one year of their manumission or else be re-enslaved. The measure was effective in at least one respect: from 1806 on "the number of manumissions in Virginia dropped drastically." But the fundamental societal problems—the terrible contradictions of slavery that every day eroded Virginians' virtuous republican values and the fear that only grew every time whispers were heard of some new slave revolt—remained.[57]

For Edward Coles the change to the manumission laws in 1806 meant only one thing: since his enslaved human property could not live free in Virginia, he would have to leave, taking his slaves with him to a free state in the West in order to grant them true liberty and security. In 1809 Coles put his plantation up for sale, but several circumstances conspired to delay his move. The Virginia economy's woes meant that no offers for his land were forthcoming, and the following year President James Madison offered him the same job Jefferson had given William Short: private secretary. Coles almost turned down the position, convinced that it would prevent him from freeing his slaves, but his friend and neighbor James Monroe convinced him that working at the heart of American political life would provide Coles with the connections necessary to undertake a successful voyage of freedom on the frontier. Coles took the job, and he spent the next several years in the service of the president, meeting national leaders and learning the ins and outs of the political world. Unfortunately, he also learned that his plan to leave Virginia for a free state could affect his chance to attract a wife: his fiancée, Marie Antoinette Hay, broke off their engagement in 1812. The lady's father would soon become an outspoken advocate for slavery, while Miss Hay herself likely objected to the idea of giving up wealth and gentility in Virginia for an uncertain life on the frontier.[58]

The following year, an ill (and heartsick) Coles sought medical treatment in Philadelphia. There, living for the first time in a city free from slavery, he befriended the antislavery Quaker and philanthropist Roberts Vaux.[59] This friendship lasted the rest of Coles's life and likely served to strengthen his determination to find a way to free his slaves. But Coles was not content simply to free his own human property: as a close associate of Jefferson and Madison, he attempted over and over to persuade these men to become as passionate about ending slavery as he was. Dolley and James Madison grew fond of the younger man during their years together in the White House (Mrs. Madison and Coles were cousins), and Coles felt free enough in the relationship to directly confront the president regarding the hypocrisy of having open slave markets in the capital of a nation founded on the principles of equality and liberty.[60] On several occasions, Coles told Madison that he was shocked that "just men, & long sighted politicians should not as well in reference to the acknowledged rights of man, as to the true & permanent interests of their Country, take the necessary steps to put in train its termination."[61]

James Madison genuinely opposed slavery and in later years became president of the American Colonization Society (ACS), but as he explained it to Robert Pleasants, the Virginia Quaker and abolitionist, Madison had early come to believe that outspoken protest of slavery was "likely to do harm rather than good." He observed with alarm the immediate pushback from proslavery forces within Virginia after each attempt by antislavery petitioners to move the legislature toward emancipation. Although in 1785 Madison had urged Jefferson that it would be worth the risk to send his *Notes on the State of Virginia* to the College of William and Mary—the *"freedom of your* [criticisms] on some *particular measures* and *opinions* will displease *their respective abettors,"* but "both the facts and remarks which you have assembled [are] too *valuable* not to be made known, at least to those for whom *you destine* them"—by 1791 Madison had become more cautious. The explosive debates over antislavery petitions in Congress had shown him how volatile the issue was at both the state and national levels. Public sentiment had to shift on its own, Madison came to believe (as Jefferson already did), and if antislavery politicians spoke too loudly on the issue they would only provoke defensive anger. Coles was therefore unsuccessful in persuading his employer to take prominent antislavery action.[62]

In 1814 Coles, while still serving as Madison's secretary, decided to try another approach. He wrote directly to Jefferson, who at age seventy-one was living quietly in retirement at Monticello, having endured one of the most contentious political campaigns in American history and served two terms as president. The subsequent correspondence between Coles and Jefferson centered around the question of whether antislavery reforms should be led by members of the older generation or the younger. While Jefferson encouraged Coles to take up the mantle of leadership, strong in his youthful idealism and with many years ahead to oversee the difficult process, Coles insisted that only someone with Jefferson's gravitas could effectively persuade voters to move against slavery. In the end neither was fully correct.

His opening sentence betrays Coles's hesitation at approaching Jefferson on such a fraught subject: "I never took up my pen with more hesitation or felt more embarrassment than I now do in addressing you on the subject of this letter." "My object," continued the twenty-eight-year-old Coles, "is to entreat and beseech you to exert your knowledge and influence, in devising, and getting into operation, some plan for the gradual emancipation of Slavery" in Virginia. Coles hastened to add that Jefferson did not need to be told that man has no right "to enslave his Brother man" or to be instructed about "the moral and political effects of Slavery on individuals or on Society; because these things are better understood by you than by me." Obviously, Coles was familiar with Jefferson's discussion of these very topics in his *Notes*. But Coles still implored the retired statesman to take advantage of the "love and confidence" of a grateful nation by attempting "to put into complete practice those hallowed principles contained in that renowned Declaration, of which you were the immortal author, and on which we bottomed our right to resist oppression, and establish our freedom and independence." In effect, Coles was asking Jefferson to come out of retirement in order to become an activist for the antislavery cause. This task would be "difficult," but Jefferson—as one of the "revered Fathers of all our political and social blessings"—could accomplish it more easily than could "any succeeding statesmen."[63]

Even if Jefferson's efforts were unsuccessful in the short term, Coles believed they would still have great value for the future. Knowing that Jefferson viewed slavery as an archaic vestige of the Old World, and that in his *Summary View of the Rights of British America*, as well as in the Declaration of Independence and in his own *Notes*, Jefferson placed the responsibility for Virginian slavery squarely on the shoulders of the British government, Coles appealed to the older man's revolutionary principles:

> I hope that the fear of failing, at this time, will have no influence in pre-venting you from employing your pen to eradicate this most degrading feature of British [colonial] policy, which is still permitted to exist, not-withstanding its repugnance as well to the principles of our revolution as to our free Institutions. For however highly prized and influential your opinions may now be, they will be still much more so when you shall have been snatched from us by the course of nature.

If Jefferson died before slavery ended—"If therefore your attempt should now fail to rectify this unfortunate evil—an evil most injuri-ous both to the oppressed and to the oppressor"—his words would still not be in vain. Coles had an eye on Jefferson's legacy, foreseeing that even in death the Sage of Monticello would cast a long shadow over Americans' political debates: "[A]t some future day when your memory will be consecrated by a grateful posterity, what influence, irresistible influence will the opinions and writings of Thomas Jeffer-son have on all questions connected with the rights of man, and of that policy which will be the creed of your disciples." More than any other Founder, Coles suggested, Jefferson's words on this topic mat-tered: "[I]t is a duty . . . that devolves particularly on you" as America's spokesman for "the rights of man, & the liberty & independence of your country." Coles suggested that Jefferson could either compose an-other emancipation plan—"an immediate attempt to put in train a plan to commence this goodly work"—or he could at least write a "Testa-ment" against slavery, so that "the weight of your opinion may be on the side of emancipation when that question shall be agitated." Make sure, Coles seems to be telling Jefferson, that you are found by later generations on the right side of history.[64]

If these appeals to Jefferson's humanity or to his generational legacy failed to move the retired president's heart, Coles perhaps thought that a personal challenge might be enough to goad him into taking up his pen again: "I will only add . . . from the time I was capable of reflecting on the nature of political society, and of the rights appertaining to Man,

I have not only been principled against Slavery, but have had feelings so repugnant to it, as to decide me not to hold them; which decision has forced me to leave my native state, and with it all my relations and friends." And with that dramatic declaration Coles ended his letter, having thrown down every rhetorical gauntlet that he could think of.[65]

Jefferson's response to Coles is typically gracious, simultaneously assuring the younger man of his agreement and approving of his youthful zeal for justice—and also denying his request. Jefferson began by assuring Coles that Coles's letter, rather than offending him, had brought "peculiar pleasure." Coles's sentiments on the issue of slavery did him credit, and Jefferson had shared in them since his own youth. He explained that when the Revolutionary War was still a conflict "on paper only," during his first term as a state legislator, Jefferson asked his older cousin Colonel Richard Bland—"one of the oldest, ablest, and most respected members" of the General Assembly—to sponsor a bill that would have allowed owners to manumit individual slaves. The other delegates "denounced" Bland as an "as an enemy to his country, & [he] was treated with the grossest indecorum."[66] Jefferson learned from this incident that members of the generation immediately preceding his own, "who were in the fulness of age when I came into public life," would reject any attempts to liberalize the slave laws.[67]

In his 1798 letter to Jefferson, William Short had told the older man that he had come to believe no one raised in a slave state could help becoming dreadfully biased against people of African descent, since they had only ever known black people "in the state of degradation inseparable from . . . slavery." Now Jefferson repeated his adoptive son's observation to young Coles but applied it to the generation preceding his own: "[N]ursed and educated in the daily habit of seeing the degraded condition, both bodily & mental, of those unfortunate beings," those who governed during the final years of the colonial era did not realize "that degradation was very much the work of themselves & their fathers"—in other words, white people did not realize that the "degradation" that enslaved people exhibited was not natural but instead the result of slavery's oppression. As the result of this cycle of prejudice, oppression, and degradation, white colonial Virginians did not doubt that enslaved people "were as legitimate subjects of property as their horses

or cattle." Jefferson clearly believed that he and many other members
of the Founding generation were more enlightened than their fathers;
they did not view slaves on the level of horses or cattle but instead
questioned the very foundations of colonial society by calling for abolition. Nonetheless, "it was not easy to carry them [the other members
of Jefferson's generation] the whole length of the principles which they
invoked for themselves."[68]

In the years following his early, failed attempt to provoke change in
the Virginia legislature, Jefferson claimed that his revolutionary duties
often drew his attention elsewhere, "so that from that time till my return
from Europe in 1789 . . . and I may say till I returned to reside at home
in 1809 . . . I had little opportunity of knowing the progress of public
sentiment here [in Virginia] on this subject." This statement obscured
the fact that Jefferson had frequently returned to Monticello for long
periods between 1789 and 1809, a fact that Coles would have known.
But Jefferson nonetheless declared ignorance on the issue of public antislavery sentiment. He had always hoped, Jefferson told Coles, that
"the younger generation, receiving their early impressions after the
flame of liberty had been kindled in every breast, and had become as it
were the vital spirit of every American, that the generous temperament
of youth . . . would have sympathised with oppression wherever found,
and proved their love of liberty beyond their own share of it." This was
true; as we have seen, Jefferson expressed these hopes in the late 1780s
when he sent copies of his *Notes* to the College of William and Mary.[69]

The twenty-year period that Jefferson claimed to have been distracted from Virginian public opinion on slavery was particularly
important due to the fact that, for Jefferson, twenty years was approximately the span of a single generation. He had formulated this theory
while living in Paris, famously telling James Madison that "no society
can make a perpetual constitution, or even a perpetual law. The earth
belongs always to the living generation." He had developed a formula
for determining how long one generation could be said to live, and
from that he posited that "every constitution, then, and every law, naturally expires at the end of 19. years." Poor Madison—who had just
led an extended struggle to ratify America's new Constitution—had
diplomatically replied that such a strict calculation was impracticable,

since "a limitation of the validity of national acts to the computed life of a nation, is in some instances not required by Theory, and in others cannot be accomodated to practice."[70] Jefferson was apparently persuaded, and he later clarified his views: "I am certainly not an advocate for frequent and untried changes in laws and constitutions." Instead, Jefferson held that "moderate imperfections had better be borne with"; however, "laws and institutions must go hand in hand with the progress of the human mind." As humanity became better educated, as the light of reason spread, "manners and opinions" would change, and the laws must reflect those changes.[71] And yet, if a new generation refused to embrace liberal changes—such as ending slavery—it was not the place of a representative from the past to tell them what to do. The new generation must be responsible for making its own laws.

And from Virginia in 1809, twenty years after the liberal revolutionary generation had begun discussing the natural equality of mankind, Jefferson informed Coles that the younger man's "solitary but welcome voice" was the only one from the new generation to approach him regarding emancipation. The "general silence" regarding slavery indicated to Jefferson "an apathy unfavorable to every hope," despite the fact that emancipation "will come." This was inevitable; it would either occur because of "the generous energy of our own minds, or by the bloody process of St Domingo," referring to the Haitian Revolution. By the time that Jefferson wrote this reply to Coles, the entire issue was given an added layer of urgency: British forces had just invaded and burned the capital city of Washington, DC. Jefferson added an ominous note: if, as had occurred thirty-nine years earlier with Dunmore's Proclamation during the Revolutionary War, the British offered "asylum & arms to the oppressed" slaves of America, then emancipation would certainly be hastened.[72]

Coles asked Jefferson to lead a new antislavery charge in Virginia; Jefferson's answer was, quite simply, "no." He felt that he would have to buckle "armor, long unused, on shoulders trembling with age," knowing that all the other members of his own generation, with whom "mutual labors and perils begat mutual confidence and influence," had passed away. But Jefferson did not feel that, in refusing Coles's request, he was failing to lay before the public his own views opposing slavery:

"[M]ine on the subject of the slavery of negroes have long since been in possession of the public, and time has only served to give them stronger root." Jefferson even reiterated for Coles the steps already outlined in the *Notes*: "I have seen no proposition so expedient on the whole, as that of emancipation of those born after a given day, and of their education and expatriation at a proper age." Jefferson still opposed immediate emancipation on the ground that black people, or "men, probably of any colour," who were raised in the infantilism of slavery could not easily transition to freedom. Moreover, gradual emancipation and exportation of enslaved laborers would give the society time to substitute them for a new "species of labor," such as the German immigrants from northern states or from the Rhine region itself, as Jefferson had begun investigating so many years before during his time as minister to France. Finally, Jefferson utilized the same reasoning that he applied in the *Notes* to once again underscore his preference for colonization: The natural order divided races, and "amalgamation with the other colour produces a degradation to which no lover of his country, no lover of excellence in the human character can innocently consent."[73]

At the time Jefferson wrote this missive to Coles, Sally Hemings's youngest son, Eston, was six years old. Beverly, the oldest child, was sixteen; Harriet was fifteen, and Madison was nine. It is possible that Jefferson was parroting his own earlier views on racial separation to maintain a fiction that most members of society, North or South, proslavery or abolitionist, demanded—that is, the fiction that racial mixing was always abhorrent. Even if he had found a form of satisfactory domesticity with the woman who looked so much like his deceased wife, Sally's own half-sister, Jefferson could never under any circumstance admit that fact, and neither could his children after his death. To do so would have aroused every prejudice existing within the society of that day, a prejudice that still exists in some circles even today. Or perhaps Jefferson was completely self-deceived, able to act one way in private—or, at the very least, to turn a blind eye when another male member of his family fathered numerous light-skinned children with Hemings—and then condemn such practices in public. The answer as to Jefferson's inner thoughts on this topic remains hidden, as he seems to have intended it should.[74]

But Jefferson did not wish to keep his opposition to slavery hidden, and despite his refusal to become an active participant in the political battles over the topic he did not rebuff Coles completely. "[T]his enterprise is for the young," he told Coles, for a younger leader could "follow it up, and bear it through to it's consummation." And here Jefferson gave one of his most controversial pieces of advice: "I hope then, my dear Sir, you will reconcile yourself to your country and it's unfortunate condition," remaining in Virginia rather than leaving in order to free his human property. At first glance, it seems that Jefferson was rejecting Coles's humanitarian plan in favor of an apathetic approach, that is, waiting around until some vague point in the future at which public opinion miraculously shifted and only then pursuing emancipation. But Jefferson in fact urged Coles to remain in Virginia to take a leadership role for his own generation: "[C]ome forward in the public councils, become the Missionary of this doctrine truly Christian, insinuate & inculcate it softly but steadily thro' the medium of writing & conversation, associate others in your labors, and when the phalanx is formed, bring on & press the proposition perseveringly until it's accomplishment." He ended by referencing William Wilberforce and his recent success in ending the British slave trade, remarking that this event was proof that "no good measure was ever proposed which, if duly pursued, failed to prevail in the end."[75]

Jefferson's refusal to endorse Coles's bold emancipation strategy grates on modern readers; it is particularly distasteful because Jefferson followed it up by encouraging Coles to take up a paternalistic stance toward his human property, taking responsibility for their food and clothing and refusing to sell them because that would "commit them to those whose usage of them we cannot controul." Such an attitude—combined with the racist belief that free black people could not care for themselves—would become a comforting rationale among proslavery thinkers of the antebellum era. But Jefferson's concern here was not so much that Coles should become the ideal Virginian paternalist master as that he not withdraw his influence from the state. As historians have come to believe, when antislavery Virginians migrated from the state in search of free territory they unintentionally strengthened the peculiar institution's hold on the Old Dominion. Philip Schwartz notes that "[i]f those who migrated had stayed in Virginia, they might have worked against human bondage." The Old Northwest, where men like Coles dreamed of creating a society of free labor, became "a safety valve for slavery. . . . [E]ven intentional antislavery migration may have indirectly upheld slavery in Virginia, at least until the Civil War." Or, as Jefferson put it to Coles, if the younger man left he would "lessen [Virginia's] stock of sound disposition by withdrawing your portion from the mass."[76]

Coles was not convinced. He replied to Jefferson that if Coles thought he could be "in the slightest degree useful" in "bringing about a liberation, or that I could by my example meliorate the condition of these oppressed people," he would certainly remain in Virginia. But Coles believed he lacked the "extensive powers both of mind and influence" that were necessary to "effect so great and difficult an object." An older man such as Jefferson would most certainly possess those qualities, and in addition an established statesman could more easily withstand the "waves of opposition" that would certainly come. His career concluded, Jefferson would not be led astray by ambition in the way a younger man might. Moreover, Coles argued passionately that only a statesman of Jefferson's stature possessed the power "effectually to arouse and enlighten the public sentiment, which in matters of this kind ought not to be expected to lead but to be led." The general public was apathetic and would remain so, weighted down by the "influence of habit and interest." A "mere passive principle of right" had no chance against habit and interest unless someone with a "great weight of character" intervened to persuade the people to do the right thing. And just in case the seventy-one-year-old Jefferson replied again that he was simply too aged to undertake the cause, Coles ended their conversation by reminding him of "Doctor Franklin," who in 1790 had sent the petitions to Congress that provoked several southern representatives to threaten civil war—when he was eighty-four years old and still active as the president of the Pennsylvania Society for Promoting the Abolition of Slavery. Coles overlooked the dangerous controversy that Franklin created, choosing instead to remember that Franklin "was as actively and as usefully employed on as arduous duties after he had past your age as he had ever been at any period of his life." Take that, Mr. Jefferson.[77]

Aside from one short missive Coles sent in his official capacity two months later, informing the former president that the current vice president had died suddenly that morning, there is no more record of correspondence between the idealistic young man and the statesman he had pinned his hopes on. Despite Jefferson's encouragement, Coles was convinced that he would be useless at affecting change in his home state. In a letter to his dear friend Nicholas Biddle, Coles repeated the same doubts and fears he had laid bare for Jefferson: "Oh that I had talents and acquirements to become the champion of humanity! . . . But having only the power to perceive its wrongs, and feel its sufferings, without the capacity of relieving it, all that I can do is to preserve my principles, and save my feelings, by flying from the scene of its oppression."[78]

His determination was strengthened by a tour that Coles took of Europe in 1816 and 1817, having been sent to negotiate on President Madison's behalf with the emperor of Russia. Coles was struck by the unfree labor systems he encountered, and like Jefferson and William Short he concluded that the Americans had much to learn from the Old World's agricultural practices. In Russia Coles saw that the serfs, who could also be called "VASSALS or slaves," were "by law subject to the will and pleasure of their lords and masters"; however, they were also "inseparably connected with the soil . . . and can only be disposed of along with it." Serfs were often treated better than American slaves, he observed, and the fact that they could not be sold away from the lands they worked resulted in more stable family structures and communities, adding to their quality of life. As he traveled through France, Holland, Ireland, and England, Coles befriended Lafayette and other members of the nobility and concluded that American institutions were superior to those of the Old World—with the exception of slavery. The peculiar institution grated ever more on Coles's senses; he saw it as a "blot" that, on America's "otherwise enchanting escutcheon, was the more apparent & the more disfiguring."[79]

Although he was tormented by the fear that life on the frontier would mean he would end up lonely, unmarried, and without any fruitful occupation, after his return from Europe Coles was more determined than ever to do his part to end slavery in America. And as a wealthy bachelor with few debts and no white dependents—so different from Jefferson—Coles was uniquely positioned to turn his principles into actions. In April 1819 the thirty-two-year old Coles and his human property set sail down the Ohio River, en route to the brand-new state of Illinois. Somewhere on that river Coles informed his slaves that they were now free and that, once they reached their new home in Edwardsville, Illinois, he would give every adult 160 acres of his land. James Monroe had been right when he advised his friend that taking the post of private secretary to Madison would one day pay off: Coles utilized his hard-won connections in Washington political society to secure an appointment to the post of Register of the Land Office in Edwardsville, and he set about helping his former slaves succeed in their new lives as independent farmers by buying them supplies, hiring several to work his lands, providing education for the children, and generally watching out for their interests.[80]

Although Coles moved to Illinois under the belief that it was entering the Union as a free state, not long after his arrival he discovered that Illinois was rapidly passing laws to severely restrict black people's civil rights, reflecting the harsh antiblack prejudice still held by most of the state's white inhabitants and their fear that free black people would become competitors for land and jobs. Worse yet, many state legislators supported the legalization of slavery in Illinois. Despite his best efforts to escape, what he had fled from in Virginia had simply followed him to his new home.[81]

In 1821 Coles entered the gubernatorial race at the urging of several antislavery friends, running as the only candidate committed to keeping Illinois free. When opponents attacked his antislavery credentials, questioning his sincerity, Thomas Jefferson came to the rescue—or at least Coles used his connection with Jefferson to lend weight to his own reputation. Jefferson may have refused to become an active participant in the antislavery cause, but Coles did not give up on using the older man's influence to effect change. He published Jefferson's 1814 correspondence with him in the *Illinois Intelligencer*, believing that the beloved retired president's stirring words would demonstrate to voters that not only did the Founding generation support the antislavery cause but that Jefferson himself supported Edward Coles. Jefferson had told Coles to become an antislavery "missionary," after all, to "press the proposition perseveringly until it is accomplished." Although Coles had believed his youth disqualified him from taking a leading role in the antislavery cause—at least in Virginia—in the young state of Illinois Coles proved to be the perfect person to lead the charge.[82]

Elected governor in 1822, Coles successfully worked to block a proslavery attempt to revise the state constitution. To achieve this goal, Coles contributed his entire salary to the cause, bought a newspaper to share the antislavery perspective, and successfully organized antislavery political committees across the state. He suspected that proslavery activists set a fire that destroyed much of his (and several of his freed slaves') property, but he persevered. When his opponents sued him in 1823, accusing him of illegally freeing his slaves without posting the correct bond, Coles fought the charges until he was finally vindicated by the state supreme court in 1826.[83] Most important, Coles and his allies contributed to a growing ideology of antislavery nationalism, a combination of arguments based on the value of free soil and on the conviction that the Founders—Jefferson especially—never intended slavery to continue in the American republic.[84] Coles corresponded with Nicholas Biddle and Roberts Vaux in Philadelphia, purchasing from them pamphlets and essays written to bolster the idea that slavery harmed the economy and the equality of white men and then distributing them across Illinois. When the proslavery side was decisively defeated, Coles was both proud of the accomplishment and disappointed—disappointed because, over the course of this yearslong battle, he had seen firsthand that "antiblack prejudice was an essential motivating factor. . . . [O]nly an antislavery program that promoted the interest of free white men was likely to succeed." Most voters did not oppose slavery for the sake of the slaves, but only because they wished to maintain the economic value and social dignity of free (white) labor.[85]

Edward Coles was not the only younger Virginian who looked to Jefferson to take up the antislavery charge after his retirement from the presidency. Two years after the Coles–Jefferson correspondence yielded no fruit, William Short challenged his adoptive father in the same way.

In 1810 Short had taken up permanent residence in Philadelphia, where he befriended the antislavery Quaker (and Coles's good friend) Roberts Vaux. Perhaps through Vaux, or another mutual acquaintance, Coles and Short also became friends, and after Coles permanently relocated to Philadelphia himself in 1831 the two men moved in the same social and philanthropic circles.[86] Whether on his own initiative or because of conversations with Coles, Short wrote to Jefferson, his adoptive father, in 1816, utilizing a similar argument to persuade the elder statesman to write something new against slavery. First, Short referenced *Notes on the State of Virginia*, which he still valued greatly (also asking Jefferson to please send Short a spare copy, since Short had misplaced his). Then, although acknowledging that Jefferson had earned the right to retire— to "'the softest pillow for the head of old age'"—Short nonetheless argued that Jefferson should consider making statements on important political matters as a "legacy to your successors."[87]

Short gave two possible motivating factors for such actions, public and private. First, Jefferson had a duty to perform: "The idea of having been useful to your country not only during your whole life, but to continue to be so after your death must be a motive worthy of you." Second, Short appealed to Jefferson's personal legacy, noting that, while Short and many others knew that Jefferson opposed the slave trade, "there are some who do not"—people who only saw that Jefferson himself lived in a slave state and owned human property (although this was simply "the unavoidable lot of an inhabitant of such a state," Short added conciliatorily). If Jefferson could therefore "in some public way" urge Congress to do a better job of enforcing its prohibition on the slave trade it would bolster his own reputation and demonstrate to skeptics that Jefferson, even though he owned slaves, did not support slavery.[88]

Jefferson's reply to Short's entreaty is worth quoting in its entirety:

> To your encouragements to take up the political pen, I must turn a deaf ear. My repugnance to that is insuperable, as the thing itself is unnecessary. The present generation will be as able, as that which preceded them to do for themselves what is necessary for their own happiness; and that which shall succeed them will do what they shall leave undone. Constitutions &

laws should change with the changes of times and circumstances. Those made now may as little suit our descendants, as we should be suited by those of our Gothic ancestors. The concerns of each generation are their own care.[89]

And that was the end of it: Jefferson's view on generational authority was unchanged and unyielding. His generation was finished, he claimed, and it was up to the young to chart their own course. This was Jefferson's default position during his retirement years: when supplicants approached him, asking him to publicly support one cause or another, he generally refused. "I want to be quiet," he told another younger Virginian friend. "I feel safe, and happier in leaving every thing to those whose turn it is to take care of them." (Of course, Jefferson's correspondents often published his letters, so his privately stated opinions frequently did indirectly become public knowledge—and he was always aware of that possibility.)[90]

The one project Jefferson did devote his time and energy to, in these last years of his life, was education—specifically building the University of Virginia so that the next generation of young leaders would have an excellent public institution at which to train. But although the university produced many well-educated Virginians, none became so well known for their opposition to slavery as had members of the first generations to read Jefferson's *Notes on the State of Virginia* after he sent it to the College of William and Mary in 1787. Truly, Jefferson had been correct to believe that the young men being trained by George Wythe and his immediate successors were the best hope for the future of the state.

6. The Jeffersonian Legacy in Virginia, 1820–1832

In his retirement years Thomas Jefferson may have decided to avoid all public discussion of slavery, but when his son-in-law entered politics and proposed emancipation, the former president looked on with pride. Thomas Mann Randolph Jr., a teenager at the University of Edinburgh while Jefferson was living in Paris, was actually the first college student to whom Jefferson had sent a copy of his *Notes on the State of Virginia*. After marrying Jefferson's daughter Martha Jefferson, Tom (as he became known among family circles) became more like a son than a son-in-law, living with or near to his father-in-law much of the time and helping to manage Jefferson's estates. Although Tom Randolph's political career was not nearly so illustrious as he would have hoped, its pinnacle came in 1819 when he was elected governor of Virginia. As the state—and indeed the nation—roiled in the turmoil caused by the Missouri Crisis, he represented the Jeffersonian legacy by condemning those who accommodated themselves to slavery and by proposing a gradual emancipation and colonization plan to the General Assembly.

After Jefferson's death in 1826, his surviving family members struggled to make ends meet. The most wrenching aspect of their new poverty, according to Martha, was how it ended their ability to keep their enslaved workers' families together.[1] Jefferson's eldest—and favorite—grandson, Thomas Jefferson Randolph (known as Jeff), attempted to find ways to free the family's human property; when that failed he worked to keep the Jefferson slaves living near one another in the vicinity of Monticello. Like Edward Coles, Jeff became disillusioned enough with slavery in his home state that he tried, on several occasions, to move away. Unlike Coles, Jeff was too encumbered by debts and dependents to ever make this plan work. When the state legislature finally, for the first and last time, debated slavery openly during the session of 1831–1832, Jeff and Coles were both there. Coles urged Jeff to take up his grandfather's mantle and speak on behalf of freedom, and Jeff did so. Invoking Jefferson proved to be a powerful tool: Jeff boldly contended that Virginia should free her slaves because Thomas Jefferson had always wished for this to occur. Citing Jefferson's *Notes*, letter to Coles of 1814, and vision of a more democratic society, Jeff laid out a powerful set of arguments in favor of abolition and in opposition to the rising opinion that slavery could ever be a positive good for the state. Thomas Jefferson may have retired in 1808 and died in 1826, but for many years after he stopped speaking publicly on the issue, his family members were still actively engaged in antislavery politics. In this way, they honored both his moral stance on slavery and his strong belief that each generation had to find its own set of leaders; and although in the end the antislavery side lost the battle for Virginia, in the Jefferson–Randolph clan it always found supporters.

Even before Martha Jefferson married Thomas Mann Randolph Jr., the Randolphs and the Jeffersons were connected by blood and friendship. In his youth Thomas Jefferson grew up with Thomas Mann Randolph Sr., so when Tom went to the University of Edinburgh while Jefferson was living in Paris, the older man took it upon himself to look out for the son of his longtime friend. Jefferson wrote several letters of advice regarding Randolph Jr.'s character development, education, and future career options. The younger Randolph was a talented scientist and early expressed a desire to go into politics, which Jefferson encouraged: "Your country . . . has much for you to do," for though the worst American laws were better than those of any other nation, there was still room for improvement. "It will remain therefore to those now coming on the stage of public affairs," like young Tom, "to perfect what has been so well begun by those going off it."[2]

Jefferson recommended that Tom follow in William Short's footsteps, living for a few months in a French village to learn the language, traveling through France and Italy, then returning to Virginia to study law with George Wythe for a year, after which "you will be ready to enter on the public stage, with superior advantages."[3] But instead, Randolph Sr. called him home before he could graduate. Tom and Martha became engaged almost immediately after meeting again in Virginia in 1789; they married a month later, aged twenty-one and seventeen, respectively. Because of a breach with the elder Randolph (Tom's father), a widower who remarried and then all but disinherited his namesake in the early 1790s, the newlyweds became increasingly attached to Jefferson and Monticello. By 1797 a visiting French friend noted the close relationship between Tom and his father-in-law, remarking that the younger man was "more [Jefferson's] son than his son-in-law." He began living at Monticello much of the time, supervising Jefferson's properties while Jefferson was away.[4]

Both Tom and Martha showed early signs of discomfort with their home state's reliance on slavery. Martha, educated at an exclusive Paris convent school, wrote to her father in 1787: "I wish with all my soul that the poor negroes were all freed. It greives my heart when I think that these our fellow creatures should be treated so teribly as they are by many of our country men." Since he was already in Europe when Jefferson's *Notes* was first printed by Stockdale in London, the nineteen-year-old Tom had the honor of being the first college student to receive a copy, and although his hasty marriage prevented him from studying law with Wythe, in his youth Tom Randolph exhibited a similar distaste for the peculiar institution as did other Wythe students.[5] While setting himself up as a farmer in Virginia, Tom expressed his desire to "confine my views to a small tract, just sufficient to supply me with provisions," so that he would not have to purchase any more slaves. When his father Thomas Sr. pressured him to purchase Edgehill, a larger estate, Tom reported to Jefferson that "[m]y desire to gratify my Father would induce me to attempt it if there was a prospect of my making myself whole, without employing slaves in the cultivation of the lands." In the end, the "small tract" idea proved unfeasible, and young Tom Randolph did have to purchase more slaves, in addition to those he and Martha were given by their parents at their marriage.[6]

Tom Randolph gained a reputation as a kind master who often spoke about trying to make his workers' lives easier, but like even the best-intentioned masters he could not prevent his human property from suffering due to his own indebtedness. In 1818 he revealed some of his thoughts on what he called the South's "hideous monster" of slavery to his own future son-in-law, Nicholas P. Trist. Tom Randolph had just heard of the suicide of a neighbor's slave; this young man was admired throughout the neighborhood for his hard work and integrity, but when the master brought in a new, overzealous overseer, disaster struck. The overseer, who could not "understand the value of character in a slave, and concluded that fear would be safer security for good conduct," whipped the young worker for "some trifling misdemeanor," which humiliated the "brave" and "manly" slave so badly that he hanged himself. Shaking his head at the overseer's actions, Tom Randolph concluded that "Power seldom reasons well," and one of the injustices of slavery was that even "the greatest Dastard" could have power to make stupid decisions that then affected brave men.[7]

More gifted as a botanist than a farm manager, eventually Tom's life became bogged down in the Virginia planters' typical cycle of crop failures, crushing debts, and falling land values. After a few years of happy marriage, mental health issues began to deeply affect Tom's relationship with his wife and with Jefferson, and he struggled for the rest of his life with insecurity and a fear that he was "essentially & widely different from all" the other members of the family, feeling like a "silly bird . . . in the company of the Swans."[8]

Despite his personal trials and increasingly desperate financial situation, Tom Randolph was twice elected to Congress during the Jefferson administration (1801–1809), and he served as a colonel in the Virginia Militia during the War of 1812.[9] Elected governor of Virginia in 1819, Randolph was concerned in February 1820 to hear rumors of a slave insurrection in Petersburg, Virginia.[10] Even more significant, Randolph's governorship coincided with one of the most tense periods of the antebellum years: the Missouri Crisis, from 1819 to 1821. The crisis began when New York congressman James Tallmadge Jr. proposed to allow Missouri to enter the union only on the condition that it be a free state. Virginia's official response was that Congress had no constitutional right to impose such a condition, since all other states made their own decisions over slavery within their borders. Congressmen from Northern states argued that slavery was incompatible with republican values; Southerners disagreed, pointing out that the Constitution contained a fugitive slave provision and the Three-Fifths Clause, indicating that the Founders were at least willing to compromise over the existence of slavery. In the end, Congress compromised by admitting Maine as a free state and Missouri as a slave state, thereby maintaining the balance of national power. But now a "a geographical line, coinciding with a marked principle, moral and political," divided the nation in half, and this division would become "deeper and deeper" over the ensuing years.[11]

Jefferson's own perspective on the issue was something of a personal compromise: whereas he had previously supported banning slavery in all new states (as original author of what became the Northwest Ordinance of 1784), he had now come to believe that diffusing the evil across many states would make it easier for owners to free their slaves. Moreover, he rejected Congress's ability to decide "the condition of the different descriptions of men composing a state," for "this certainly is the exclusive right of every state." The difference between the situation in the early 1780s and in 1820 may have been that Jefferson always supported people's rights to choose their own laws in their own lands; whereas in the case of what became the Northwest Ordinance Jefferson was suggesting legislation for mainly unsettled lands, in the case of Missouri the territory was already inhabited by slaveholders. In fact, Jefferson's primary concern was that, as he put it to his old friend John Adams, "the Missouri question is a breaker on which we lose the Missouri country by revolt, and what more, God only knows." To others, Jefferson prophesied that drawing a line across the country to separate slave from free states would mean civil war, which surely meant the end of the Union—and with it the death of "self-government and happiness."[12]

Governor Thomas Mann Randolph Jr. watched the Missouri Crisis with equal gloom, but he focused on another alarming development that the situation exposed in his fellow Southerners: a "new morality which tolerates perpetuity of Slavery." Randolph believed, when reading accounts of the congressional debates over the matter, that he was witnessing a fundamental shift in the ideology of Southern republicanism, a "new doctrine of the Civil benefits supposed to be derived from that system" of slavery. Every "prudent and liberal mind" should be alarmed, Randolph wrote, at the fact that so many congressmen were now embracing the notion that an "injustice," no matter how severe, should be tolerated so long as it was "for the benefit of a society." Randolph had heard a report that South Carolinian Charles Pinckney compared emancipation to giving back American lands to the Native Americans, declaring that "it would be equally absurd to think of restoring the Blacks to liberty, at any time, or in any manner." Randolph scoffed at this "unsound" analogy, which was "ungratefull to all humane and liberal feelings." Adopting Jeffersonian language, Randolph told Trist, his own future son-in-law, that "[a]ll the Nations of the Earth have a share in the unemployed part of the surface of the Earth, and of course have a right to require something like a fair distribution. But all men have a right to liberty, and if forced to yield it in exchange for life at one time may legitimately resume it, whenever an opportunity offers." In other words, a slave who lost his liberty due to captivity in a war—who exchanged his freedom in return for his life—did not permanently lose his right to liberty. As Jefferson had decided while a student at William and Mary so many years before, Randolph subscribed to the post-Lockean belief that "if we have no right to the life of a captive, we have no right to his labor."[13]

Like his father-in-law, Randolph also did not expect that slaves should endure their oppression without complaint; they had a natural right to rebel, to reclaim their liberty, and had to be "kept in a state of barbarous ignorance" of their natural rights in order to prevent such an uprising. Even with such oppressive measures in place, it would be "impossible that the slave system should continue" for long, since slaves reproduced at higher rates than the free white population; eventually it would all end in a "great, long, and obstinate struggle." This would not happen in his day, Randolph predicted, but he feared on behalf of his descendants. Moreover, like Jefferson, Randolph believed the Missouri Crisis would likely result in "a disolution of the union, and a Civil War in consequence."[14]

As governor of Virginia, Randolph attempted to avert at least the first of these future disasters—a massive and prolonged slave uprising—by trying to persuade the General Assembly, during an address he gave to the House of Delegates in December 1820, to enact a moderate emancipation-and-colonization bill. A relatively forward-thinking governor, Randolph began his address by raising several of the other issues Jefferson had also been concerned with as a state legislator, including providing better access to education for Virginian children and reforming the penal code. Randolph argued that prisoners should be given jail time rather than harsh physical punishments; recalling the overzealous overseer who whipped an undeserving slave, Randolph held that "[i]ngenuity is very little likely to be excited, skill acquired, or industrious habits established, by violent means, always attributed to tyranny, which is too often produced, in fact, by the exercise of such authority."[15]

Randolph then turned his attention to what he described as the major obstacle to Virginia's prosperity: slavery, or what he described as "[t]he deplorable error of our ancestors in copying a civil institution from savage Africa." Blaming King George for American slavery carried little resonance by 1820, so Randolph found a more racially satisfying target for his audience to picture. As the governor, he framed his critique of slavery in terms of Virginia's economic and intellectual failings compared to other states. Enslaved laborers were deficient in moral motives and in intellectual abilities (although Randolph made sure to mention that he was unsure whether that was the result of slavery itself or of "nature"). Randolph noted that every year his state's production was hindered by massive amounts of waste—and this wastefulness on the part of slaves was deliberate and logical due to their own "reason and self interest." Why should an enslaved person expend more than minimal effort when no reward would be forthcoming and when working slowly was an effective form of individual resistance? When it came to industrialization, the enslaved population could not be relied upon for "the dextrous management of complicated machinery," and thus Virginia had been "outstripped in those important pursuits of civilized man, by states, to which nature has been far less bountiful" in terms of natural resources. "It is painful to calculate," he concluded, "what *might* have been under other circumstances, the amount of the general wealth in Virginia."[16]

Randolph next presented his strategy for reducing the evil of slavery in Virginia, and the Jeffersonian principles underlying most of his ideas are obvious. In the 1780s Jefferson could still imagine a future point at which Virginians would agree to emancipate an entire generation at once, spend state funds to educate them, and then colonize them to whatever location would be best at the time; in 1820 Randolph did not even try to convince the legislators to sanction a general emancipation or to educate black people, but he did try to convince them to use tax dollars to purchase and emancipate teenage slaves. He also believed, as Jefferson had concluded, that the perfect location for a colony had appeared: Haiti, now an independent republic already displaying "[f]aculties for self government" and a willingness to accept immigrants. The island nation was close enough to make the trip relatively inexpensive, and it was far enough away that few immigrants would be tempted to return. As an added bonus, "an advantageous commerce with the Island, in the exchange of our corn, meal and flour, for their coffee and sugar . . . might be the reward of our generosity in a few years." Though acknowledging that this project would depend on individual masters agreeing to have the government purchase their slaves, and would therefore move excruciatingly slowly, Randolph concluded that "[i]t would be a measure not only of magnanimity, but of sound policy, to consecrate the whole revenue now derived to our Treasury from [taxes on] slaves" toward emancipation.[17]

The legislature's response to Randolph's speech was not overwhelmingly positive, to put it mildly. Joseph Cabell, a mutual friend of Randolph and Jefferson, reported to the older man that Randolph's friends in the legislature "regretted greatly the introduction of some topics into his message," namely, "the parts respecting slavery & religion." (Randolph was outspoken about his skepticism toward traditional Christianity, and on this occasion he had managed to offend many listeners with his comments.) Randolph's irascible personality prevented him from forming the political coalitions necessary to pursue real political change; another Jefferson ally described him as "a high minded, independent & honorable man; but greatly deficient in good sense and discretion."[18] Jefferson himself was proud of his son-in-law, who "had the courage to propose to our legislature a plan of general emancipation & deportation of our slaves." Although Jefferson had no expectations that the legislature would act on Randolph's ideas, he hoped that the speech would "force a serious attention to this object by our citizens, which the [near vicinity] of St Domingo brings within the scope of possibility." To the US minister to France, Albert Gallatin, Jefferson was less optimistic: the governor's plan would not actually work, even if it had political support, "for while it proposes to devote to that object one third of the revenue of the State, it would not reach one tenth of the annual increase" of enslaved people due to high reproduction rates. Jefferson still held to his original plan (emancipate, educate, expatriate), plus Haiti: "My proposition would be that the holders should give up all born after a certain day, past, present, or to come, that these should be placed under the guardianship of the State, and sent at a proper age to S. Domingo." Like Randolph, Jefferson viewed Haiti's location as one of its best advantages; "taxation aided by charitable contributions" from Europeans and the "Eastern states," both of whom Jefferson held partly responsible for slavery's existence due to their role in the slave trade, would provide sufficient funds. This was wishful thinking by the seventy-seven-year-old Jefferson, as he perhaps knew; he added as an afterthought that "the proceeds of the land office, if appropriated, would be quite sufficient."[19]

In any event, Randolph's plan came to nothing, and he did not make any further attempts—public or private—to end slavery. In 1824, finding himself bankrupt, his marriage to Martha Jefferson in shambles, and his relationships with his eleven surviving children strained, Randolph left the family for several years, despite Jefferson's pleas for reconciliation. He returned only to die at Monticello in 1828, and his death necessitated the sale of his family's enslaved property to pay off his debts. The dire prospect of having to sell their slaves at an auction was deeply disturbing to the entire Randolph clan, who found ways in the end to at least keep as many families together as they could. After watching enslaved families face the possibility of permanent separation, Martha wrote to her daughter Ellen, safely married and living in Boston: "The discomfort of slavery I have borne all my life, but it's sorrows in all their bitterness I had never before conceived. . . . [N]othing can prosper under such a system of injustice."[20]

Edward Coles's success in leading the antislavery fight in Illinois changed his perspective on the possibilities for Virginia's future. By the late 1820s he had begun to hope that public opinion in Virginia was swinging toward emancipation and colonization, and the election of men like John Rutherfoord, his antislavery brother-in-law, to the House of Delegates in 1826 was especially encouraging. Coles and Rutherfoord were at this point both supporters of the American Colonization Society, a national coalition founded by a Virginian in 1816. As a coalition, the ACS acknowledged that its members had a variety of goals. Some, like Coles and William Short, became members because they genuinely opposed slavery and believed that a national organization that promoted colonization in practical ways might have a measurable effect in helping enslaved people to freedom. Other ACS members only wished to rid the country of free black people; supporting voluntary colonization to Liberia was a supposedly benevolent attempt to make America more white and to civilize and spread Christianity to Africa. In general, however, members of the ACS repeated a refrain that was dear to Coles's heart: Slavery was incompatible with America's founding principles, and the ACS itself—supported by prominent Founders such as James Madison and James Monroe—was therefore a "legacy of the founding generation" that showed real signs of support among Virginians during the antebellum period.[21]

Coles was optimistic for Virginia's future, in part because of the anecdotal evidence reaching him regarding an increasing openness throughout the state to emancipation and colonization, and in part because throughout the 1820s support was growing for a constitutional convention. Jefferson had first argued that such a convention was necessary in the 1770s, believing that Virginia's constitution was deeply flawed because it had been put in place merely during a regular legislative session—not in a specially called convention—and because it resulted in unequal representation. This was due in part to the fact that much of the voting power was concentrated in the hands of the eastern Tidewater elites simply because their slaves counted as part of the population. The slaveholding east therefore had more delegates in the General Assembly than the western regions, which had larger proportions of free white people. As we have seen, Jefferson believed his *Notes* would be controversial partly because of its attack on slavery and partly because of its criticism of the state constitution; he told his friends that he hoped his *Notes* would convince young men to oppose slavery *and* to seek a constitutional convention.[22]

Now, three years after Jefferson's death in 1826, it seemed to Coles that Jefferson's wishes might finally be coming true. In 1829, largely due to the lobbying of westerners who were underrepresented in the Assembly, a constitutional convention was called in Virginia. To Coles, the convention represented not only an opportunity for a more equitable division of power among the state's white voters but also a chance to "promote emancipation by advancing his antislavery nationalism among the ambitious representatives of Virginia's western residents." Slavery was much less widespread in the western region of the state, and Coles recognized similar circumstances as those that he had successfully exploited in Illinois: when non-slaveholding white men competed against elites who relied on slavery to grant them disproportionate political power, a "free soil" ideology could become highly persuasive. Coles identified slavery itself as the root of western Virginians' political discontents, and he journeyed to Richmond for the convention in the hope that he could convince the more democratic westerners to join with him in supporting emancipation and colonization.[23]

Two weeks after the convention debates began, Coles resurrected Thomas Jefferson to once again speak out publicly against slavery by publishing his 1814 letter (in which the retired Jefferson had refused to publicly speak out again against slavery but had also reiterated his abhorrence for the institution). In an editorial note, Coles expressed his hope that the correspondence would "enlighten the minds of those members of the Convention who have not sufficiently reflected on the evils" of slavery. Jefferson had recommended general emancipation linked with colonization, and now Coles did the same, believing that, since so many prominent Virginians were now colonizationists, Jefferson's idea would find wide-ranging support. And if these slaveholding colonizationist elites were not persuaded, the westerners at least might be swayed, since the primary debate at the heart of the convention was over how representation in the Assembly was determined. If it was calculated based purely on white population, it would be equitable; if it were to remain (as the Tidewater class wished) based on white population *and* the amount of taxes paid by each county, then power would remain unfairly concentrated in the wealthier (because of their enslaved labor force) east. Emancipation was in the westerners' interests.[24]

In the end, Coles miscalculated; nascent support for the ACS aside, many easterners not only refused to compromise with the western reformers, sensing an attack on their property rights (and therefore their wealth and social status), but also began laying the groundwork for a robust proslavery argument. The western reformers, for their part, willingly espoused free soil ideas, but as Eva Wolf puts it, they "held back from attacking slavery directly since they wanted slaveholders to agree to their demands." Although members of the Founding generation such as James Monroe sided with the reformers, speaking out against slavery and for gradual emancipation and colonization, members of a new generation of conservatives responded angrily, rejecting the revolutionary generation's notions of equality. The thirty-nine-year-old Benjamin Watkins Leigh, for instance, argued that "*Liberty* is only a *mean*: the *end* is happiness," meaning the Assembly should focus on safeguarding the property of whites (slaveholders especially) rather than spouting an unrealistic "dose of French rights of man." Under the compromise constitution of 1830, between one-third and one-half of all white male Virginians still could not vote, and the slave population still counted toward representation—virtually guaranteeing that eastern elites would never vote to end slavery.[25] Coles printed one more essay in Jefferson's name—arguing that "the plan suggested by Mr. Jefferson more than 40 years ago" of gradual emancipation and colonization would still work in 1820—before giving up and retreating to Illinois.[26]

As had occurred with the Haitian Revolution and Gabriel's Conspiracy, it took an armed uprising from slaves to prompt white Virginians to publicly discuss emancipation once more. On a hot summer night in August 1831, a Virginian slave and religious mystic named Nat Turner began a three-day revolt in which a group of up to sixty slaves killed approximately sixty white people, including women and infants. In response, the white community in Southampton and the surrounding areas killed or captured all the rebels and continued hunting and executing other suspected rebels or co-conspirators for some time.[27] The uprising was a watershed moment for Virginia and for the rest of the nation; states that imported large numbers of slaves from Virginia closed their markets, fearing that they would import dangerous rebels, and white Virginians worried that they—and their insurgent population—were becoming even more isolated.[28] For the first and last time in Virginia, slavery was openly and publicly debated in all forums, from local courthouse steps to the Assembly itself. Horrified and angry newspaper editorials, petitions, and memorials appeared all over the state, calling for the legislature to do something about slavery—or at least about free black people, who were once again blamed for somehow causing the uprising. And once again, Thomas Jefferson's condemnation of slavery and his emancipation-tied-to-colonization strategy, first expressed in his *Notes*, were appropriated by one of his "sons" in an effort to legitimize a new antislavery effort. This time, the Jeffersonian heir was Thomas Jefferson Randolph, Thomas Mann Randolph's son and Jefferson's eldest and favorite grandson.[29]

Thomas Jefferson Randolph, or "Jeff" as the family called him, was born in 1792. By the time he was old enough for formal education, his grandfather had little confidence in the College of William and Mary, and Jefferson paid for Jeff to be sent to the University of Pennsylvania instead in 1808. While studying in the North, which was heavily Federalist in its political loyalties, the young man had to accustom himself to hearing criticism of Jefferson, who was the head of the Democratic–Republican Party. Jeff became furious and "took fire when he heard any illiberal remarks on his Grandfather" but was, fortunately, prevented from entering into impulsive duels. His concerned grandfather, still President Jefferson at the time, penned a now-famous letter in which he recalled the firm impressions of virtue made on him in his own youth by George Wythe, Governor Fauquier, and professor William Small. Jefferson advised the hot-tempered young Jeff to follow their footsteps by "never entering into dispute or argument with another." Jefferson warned that "arguing," "becoming rude," or (heaven forbid) "shooting one another" never actually brought about positive change. Jeff would unfortunately have to get used to having political partisans attack him "because of the relation in which you stand with me and [because they] hate me as a chief in the antagonist party." Resolute politeness and occasional "humor," even in the face of ignorance and insult, were the means by which Jefferson had succeeded in his long political career, and he now urged his namesake to follow his own example by remaining calm at all costs.[30]

From the White House the president supervised Jeff's studies in Philadelphia and hoped he would become a surgeon, but in the end the young man preferred farming to intellectual pursuits. This propensity actually turned out to be a boon for the entire Jefferson–Randolph clan, and in his early twenties Jeff took over management of his father's and his grandfather's affairs. Both men were deeply in debt, Randolph so much so that young Jeff assumed legal responsibility for not only his father's debts but also his assets. Unfortunately, Thomas Jefferson's financial downfall ultimately occurred, indirectly, because of young Jeff's marriage: his bride's father, Wilson Cary Nicholas, asked Jefferson to serve as guarantor for a loan in 1818, and Jefferson could hardly say no to someone who was now a relative as well as an old friend. The following year, the credit markets crashed and the bank called in part of the loan; Nicholas suddenly died a few months later, and the extra $20,000 of resulting debt "gave the finishing blow" to the Jefferson family's financial fortunes. When Jefferson died in 1826, with debts totaling more than a million dollars in today's money, young Jeff inherited all his problems as well, and though it took him the rest of his life, he eventually repaid all his father's and grandfather's creditors. Perhaps because of these great burdens, as well as the responsibility for caring for his large extended family and twelve children of his own, Jeff became an intensely serious man, stubborn and proud.[31]

Like his father and grandfather, as well as his mother and sisters, Jeff was reliant on slavery but hated it and what it had done to Virginia. Slavery was a particular torment in the final years of Jefferson's life, when the aged Sage of Monticello believed his beloved home would be lost and his extended "family"—white and black, slave and free—torn apart because of his debts. Jeff spent months before his grandfather's death traveling in northern states, trying to raise money to pay the debts through a lottery scheme. When Jefferson died, the lottery plan fell through, and as executor Jeff had to oversee the sale of almost all his grandfather's slaves in order to begin satisfying creditors (Jefferson had freed several loyal household servants, and all of Sally Hemings's children, either informally or in his will). For a brief time, it seemed possible to avoid the creditors and free all the remaining enslaved people: in discussions with family friend John H. Cocke, Jeff realized that the Polish abolitionist Thaddeus Kosciuszko had, in 1798, left Jefferson money in his will for the express purpose of buying, educating, and liberating Virginian slaves—even Jefferson's own slaves. The story of Kosciuszko's will is complex, as it went through several versions in different nations and was not finally settled until the US Supreme Court in 1852 decided that an 1816 version nullified the 1798 will. But after Jefferson's death in 1826, Jeff and Cocke—not knowing that Kosciuszko had written other wills—attempted to gain access to the funds. Jeff wished "as many of [the Jefferson slaves] as choose to accept their liberty on the condition of being sent to the Colony at Liberia, to be purchased, & provision for their instruction there, made from this fund." Emancipation, expatriation, and education—all the elements of Jefferson's plan from *Notes on the State of Virginia* seemed, for a brief while, to be possible for the enslaved workers of Monticello. Unfortunately, nothing came of this effort.[32]

When selling their human property became absolutely necessary, the Jefferson–Randolph family tried to find owners that the enslaved people themselves approved of, as well as selling some slaves as cheaply as possible so that they could be purchased by their own (already free) relatives. Jeff also refused to sell any of the enslaved workers to distant Georgia, although they would have fetched higher prices there. The tragedy of slavery meant that all the care the Jefferson–Randolph family showed toward their human property was not enough to keep every single family together, and neither were the heartbreaking sales enough to rescue the white residents of Monticello from poverty. Even after selling most of Jefferson's property and watching in distress as their slaves were auctioned off, Martha Jefferson Randolph and most of her children and grandchildren remained in desperate financial straits.[33]

After his grandfather's death, Jeff became the de facto head of the family, and his grateful mother felt he had truly become "what your dear grandfather called you, a 'god send.'"[34] For several years he led the family in considering emigrating elsewhere, although "to the west or to the east . . . it is hard to say." Finding a free state was an important consideration; after witnessing the sale of the Jefferson slaves, one granddaughter wrote "it is better to submit to any personal inconveniences however numerous and annoying they may be" in another location "than to live in a state of society where such things as these are of daily occurrence."[35] Although the family's letters often evince more frustration with the system of slavery itself than actual empathy for the enslaved workers, they generally recognized that slavery corrupted society, hindered efficient agricultural production, and caused (different forms of) suffering for all concerned. Jeff himself earned his mother-in-law's anger on more than one occasion for, as she put it, "indulging" in feelings of compassion toward enslaved people at the expense of his own family's financial well-being.[36]

In 1829 Jeff ran for a seat in the Virginia Assembly and lost—something that came as a great relief to his family members, who wanted him to remain concentrated on the family's dire financial situation rather than become entangled in state politics.[37] His biographer argues that Jeff's loss most likely occurred because he supported the more democratic western reformers' constitution instead of siding with the eastern elites he would have been representing.[38] Although Jeff lost his chance to participate in the heated debates over reforming the constitution, he won election in time for Nat Turner's Rebellion and its drastic fallout. For Jeff's wife, Jane Randolph, the stories of "unpitying & horrible slaughter" emerging from Southampton were more frightening than "my worst fears & most torturing imagination." Almost ill with terror, expecting that she and her family could easily meet the same fate, Jane urged her husband to move the family to a free state as soon as possible. They considered Ohio, and Jane was confident that Jeff could thrive there due to his "peculiar talent for managing & acquiring influence over the poorer class of whites," among whom she expected they would live and whom they could presumably employ on their farm. The other ladies in the family were less frantic about an uprising but subscribed to their patriarch's prediction that a full-scale race war was inevitable at some distant point. Jeff's sister Mary hoped that "the people of this state are opening their eyes to the truth. I wish it may be so & that they may continue to keep their eyes open after the excitement of the present moment is over & until they have taken measures to remove the evil."[39]

Mary Randolph was not alone in her opinions, and in December 1831 and January 1832 around forty petitions arrived in the Virginia House, urging Jeff and the other delegates to do something drastic in response to Turner's slave rebellion. Signed by more than 2,000 Virginians, most called for the deportation of free black people, but some also urged the Assembly to pass some sort of gradual emancipation-and-colonization bill. Only two petitions specifically stated that all slaves born after a certain date should be emancipated and that the state should provide a colony to which these freed slaves (and any willing free black people) could emigrate. One petition specifically mentioned Jefferson and endorsed his plan, which had by this point been in public circulation for almost fifty years in the *Notes*, but this petition gained only seventeen signatories, and one of those signers changed his mind and removed his name after the fact.[40]

The vague wording of many of these petitions reflects the conflicting motives that Virginians felt regarding the subject: rather than wishing to end an evil institution for the sake of the enslaved people, most white Virginians—such as Jane Randolph—were acting out of fear that *they* would be the next ones to face armed rebels in the middle of the night. The petitions also reflected geographically based concerns: Virginians from the eastern Tidewater counties who relied heavily on enslaved labor were more concerned with removing free black people to (supposedly) strengthen slavery, whereas those from western counties wished to remove both slavery and black Virginians (who, once freed, could compete for land and jobs).[41] Into this fray stepped Thomas Jefferson Randolph, feeling all the weight of his grandfather's legacy. He was encouraged by Edward Coles, who once again was filled with hope on behalf of his abandoned home state: "To avert all the innumerable & incalculable evils resulting from a continuance of the present state of things," Coles wrote to Jeff at the end of 1831, "for God's sake step forward & put a stop to this downward course." Ironically, Coles now repeated to Jeff precisely the same controversial advice that Jefferson had given him in 1814: "[H]old out inducements to the Whites to remain." No matter how good their intentions, white people who emigrated from Virginia were "increas[ing] more rapidly the relative number of the Blacks," which in turn was making emancipation more difficult and armed rebellion more likely. To stop the westward migration and prevent catastrophe, as well as to end the "unnatural" relationship between master and slave, so contrary to "the spirit of the age," Jeff should lead the Assembly's response by introducing a gradual emancipation-and-colonization bill.[42]

Coles felt that Jeff was uniquely qualified for this task because he had "inherited the feelings & principles of your illustrious Grand Father" and because of his age (thirty-nine). No one else "of the young generation could be more suitable to lead or could bring more moral & political weight of character to aid the good work" than could Thomas Jefferson's grandson. Again paraphrasing Jefferson's own 1814 advice to him, Coles urged Jeff to fight the good fight "regardless of the scoffs & frowns of the perverse & short sighted," knowing that the reward would be "the happy consolation of doing a great good to your fellow man & to your Country."[43]

Cognizant of the opposition any such bill would face, Coles proposed a plan based partly on recognizing all black people's right to be free and partly on respect for property rights and the worries of Virginians regarding the economic value of their human property. Taxes had to be kept relatively low and slave values had to be kept high in order for owners to support any emancipation bill. Coles therefore recommended emancipating all slaves born after a certain date (as Jefferson would have wished), but Coles believed that, rather than having the state pay to educate and colonize the freed generation, they should have to work long enough to repay their owners for emancipation and to earn passage on a ship headed to Africa (until age twenty-one, plus two years). Furthermore, the state should levy a "small" tax on all black persons (enslaved and free), the proceeds going toward their transportation costs. If the legislature refused to consider this gradual plan, Coles suggested that Jeff try to hold a referendum so that the people of the state could vote directly on a matter that affected them all. Coles had achieved antislavery success in Illinois with the referendum that defeated a (proslavery) constitutional convention, and he trusted the voters of Virginia would prove similarly reasonable.[44]

On 10 January 1832, proslavery delegates in the House of Delegates moved that the committee charged with reviewing petitions be allowed to ignore the ones proposing emancipation. Jeff saw his chance and introduced a counter-resolution asking that the committee instead discuss submitting to "the vote of qualified voters" in Virginia a plan for all slaves born after 4 July 1840 to become "the property of the commonwealth" at ages eighteen (females) and twenty-one (males). They would then be rented out until they earned enough money to pay the state for "removal, beyond the limits of the United States." The floodgates had been thrown open: Jeff's proposal had too much support to be ignored, and a full-fledged debate over emancipation commenced.[45]

Following eight days of heated attacks and counterattacks, Jeff felt he had to rise again in order to defend himself and his plan, though like his grandfather he struggled with speaking in public and would have preferred "to have been a silent spectator of the debate passing before me." Jeff partly felt compelled to speak up because his fellow delegates misunderstood his initial proposal as being that of "Mr. Jefferson" himself. Now, Jeff assured his colleagues that Mr. Jefferson's only plan was already published; Jeff's plan was inspired by his grandfather, not authored by him.[46] But that did not mean, as some delegates implied, that Thomas Jefferson would not have approved of Jeff's ideas. When one man asserted that Jefferson never outlined concrete antislavery steps, but rather had a vague "vision of his philanthropic mind" during his youth, Jeff pulled out Jefferson's 1814 reply to Edward Coles once again. This letter, of course, details precisely not only Jefferson's antislavery philosophy but also the steps Jefferson desired the younger man to take in order to achieve concrete results: "[Y]our solitary, but welcome voice is the first which has brought this sound to my ear, and I have considered the silence which prevails on this subject, as indicating an apathy unfavorable to every hope. Yet the hour of emancipation in advancing in the march of time." Emancipation was inevitable, and Edward Coles should lead the charge toward freedom in Virginia, Jefferson had said: "[C]ome forward in the public councils, become the missionary of this doctrine truly Christian . . . press the proposition perseveringly until its accomplishment." Not only did Jefferson encourage Coles to lead an abolition charge in 1814, but Jeff reminded the delegates that Jefferson had written similar sentiments throughout his life. Indeed, if abolition was merely a dream for Jefferson, as some of the proslavery delegates had argued, it was one that "lasted a long time"—as Jeff put it, in "1770, 1814, 1824, he still deemed abolition indispensible."[47]

Perhaps most important, Jeff eloquently argued that the revolution in which they now found themselves—a revolution of slaves, temporarily halted by the Southampton militia—was just as important as the American Revolution and that the legislators had just as much of a responsibility to inform and consult with the voters on the topic: "[T]he people are the best judges of their own interest." If his grandfather were alive, Jeff informed the Assembly, he would be pleased to see that the same body that had attacked Richard Bland so viciously in 1769 when he and Jefferson first attempted to ameliorate slavery was now able to debate abolition openly, without (many) insults. Times had changed; a majority of the delegates now supported some kind of emancipation plan; and the people deserved to be consulted on the issue. The Assembly should put an emancipation proposal to a popular vote: nothing less than the future of the entire state was at stake.[48]

Jeff's final words in this debate were about race and religion. Like his grandfather, Jeff doubted that black people and white people could live as equals in Virginian society. No matter whether a black man was "a Newton or a Descartes, a Tell or a Washington, he is chained down by adamantine fetters; he cannot rear himself from the earth without elevating his whole race with him, to the utter destruction of all above him." This difference of race was "the melancholy difference between modern and ancient slavery," as Jefferson had also argued in the *Notes*; ancient Greece and Rome had slaves of the same skin color (or so Jefferson thought), and these societies could therefore free slaves without dealing with racial amalgamation. But Africans and Europeans were too different and could not "exist on the same soil in an equality of condition"—and by the 1830s even Virginia's equality-loving Quakers had apparently accepted this as fact.[49] However, Jeff absolutely refused to move from this line of racial thought to consider the nascent "positive good" arguments that some other delegates were propagating. When Willoughby Newton from the Tidewater county of Westmoreland "appealed to the Christian religion in justification of slavery," for instance, Jeff angrily—and sarcastically—asked him "upon what part of those pure doctrines does he rely"? "[Is it] that which teaches charity, justice, and good will to all, or is it that which teaches 'that ye do unto others as ye would they should do unto you?'" Although known for their religious skepticism, members of the Jefferson–Randolph family were not opposed to invoking Christian principles to combat slavery, and they absolutely rejected arguments that slavery could be, in any way, a positive good.[50]

Jeff was pleased with his speech in the House of Delegates; he reported to his beloved wife, Jane, who was still terrified that a slave uprising would occur in her home county, that he had been asked to sit for a portrait as one of the "distinguished orators on the abolition question." He joked that when he posed he was doing his best to portray the "stern & deep feeling which I certainly felt in replying to my opponents" in the debate. The "Friends of abolition have gained all that they asked" in the Assembly, Randolph told his wife—"a decision to bring these things to the public mind" and to offer the possibility of "future action" on emancipation. But Randolph was being too sanguine; although he was far from the only member of the House to support some form of emancipation plan, the delegates were simply too disparate in their goals to form any kind of consensus—except that they all wanted white Virginians to be safe. After two weeks of debate, the Assembly approved merely a resolution stating that the "condition of the colored population" presented "great evils"; that the free black population should be removed; and that "it is inexpedient for the present, to make any legislative enactments for the abolition of slavery." Nonetheless, Jeff was encouraged: "[A] revolution has commenced which can not go back ward. [S]ilence was the strongest bulwark to slavery[;] public opinion has broken this silence and it is open to discussion."[51]

His participation in the slavery debate was the high point of Jeff's political career, and it made his mother (Jefferson's daughter) proud. As Martha described it: "My dear Jefferson came forward last winter very boldly in the cause" of ending slavery, and although "[m]y father's political enemies make every thing a party matter in which he has ever been concerned, and visit upon Jefferson 'the sins of his Grandfather' [for] he was assailed with sneers & ridicule by some, and . . . [suffered] abuse in every shape which avarice & malice could suggest," she still hoped that "the cause of justice and Mercy will finally prevail, and that the fears of the people will at least counteract their avarice if their sence of justice can not do it." Jeff was reelected once, in 1832, after a fierce fight in which he ran under the slogan "The 'avowed & unflinching advocate of abolition.'" But when it became apparent that nothing in the state would change, and that Jeff's views had rendered him quite unpopular in his home county, the family once again determined to leave. For a time, Jeff planned a move to Missouri, a slave state— because of his "tenderness for his negroes," according to his mother. Jeff could not afford to free his slaves all at once, as Coles had almost two decades prior; if he freed them in Virginia, they would be seized as collateral for his debts, but if they came with him to Missouri, then "being surrounded with free states they will in time disappear by degrees and without danger or violence as they [move toward] the north." But these plans, too, did not come to fruition. The Randolphs remained living near Jefferson's beloved Monticello, now falling into disrepair, until after the Civil War, when their enslaved workers finally became free.[52]

In 1818, thirteen years after Winfield Scott and Edward Coles both developed an opposition to slavery at the College of William and Mary, another young Virginian began his illustrious academic career there. His name was Thomas Roderick Dew (1802–1846); he graduated with a master's degree, spent several years in Europe, and then returned to the college to teach law. In 1832 Dew published his most influential work, titled *Review of the Debate in the Virginia Legislature of 1831–1832*. It met with wide acclaim throughout the South, and Dew was rewarded with the presidency of the college. There he partnered with Nathaniel Beverly Tucker (1784–1851), St. George Tucker's son, to create a home for the next generation of Virginian leaders—a generation that would utterly reject George Wythe, Thomas Jefferson, and St. George Tucker's beliefs regarding the existence of a universal natural right to liberty, their abhorrence of slavery, and their view that Virginia must become free if it were to prosper. Instead, under Dew and Tucker's leadership the College of William and Mary became a center for states' rights and for paternalism, as Tucker taught his students that the relations between slaves and masters were natural and mutually beneficial, with rights and responsibilities on both sides. Northerners simply could not understand the family structure of the South, the younger Tucker claimed; they did not comprehend the paternal affection felt by masters toward their enslaved families nor the benefits that black people accrued from the patient attentions of the white master race.[53]

No longer were the antislavery philosophies contained in Jefferson's *Notes* foundational in the college curriculum. Instead, students read the works of authors such as Dew and his *Review of the Debate*, in which Dew singled out Jeff Randolph's plan for ridicule as impracticable, as infringing upon property rights, and as economically unsound. Moreover, Dew deconstructed those sections of Jefferson's *Notes* that opposed slavery; "as Mr. Jefferson has given the sanction of his great name to this charge," he claimed, it deserved "respectful deference." Jefferson had argued that slavery corrupted Virginian society; it taught children to be tyrants. But Dew brought the weight of his experience to bear against Jefferson's argument; he had seen that masters were not always cruel—they were often kind!—and therefore children could learn virtuous behavior from watching their parents interact with slaves. Slaveholders in general, Dew argued, were generous and hospitable people. Offering several more anecdotes as proof, Dew turned to Jefferson's contention that a slave could never cultivate the amor patriae (love of one's country, or patriotism) necessary for good citizenship and therefore should be freed and given a country of his own. But Dew's observations had convinced him that slaves did not *need* love of country, since they actually loved their masters: "Every one acquainted with southern slaves, knows that the slave rejoices" in the master's success and happiness. Having thus offered his own personal perspective as proof, Dew dismissed Jefferson's philosophies and turned to argue other points, such as ways in which southern slavery actually rendered its white inhabitants more equal than whites living in non-slaveholding states.[54]

During the ensuing years, many Virginians followed Dew's example and turned inward, measuring their virtue by their own scales and determining that slavery must be correct, and a positive good, since they *felt* it to be so. Those who harbored philosophical objections but did not have the means or the will to leave, like Jeff Randolph, accommodated themselves to slavery as best they could, comforting themselves that their human property was better off in their own care than they would be anywhere else. But from the outside looking in, Jefferson's granddaughter Ellen Wayles Randolph Coolidge—who married a northerner and lived most of her life in Boston—recognized the shift in her home state. It made her "blush" to see "the justifying *on principle* of slavery . . . a perversion of judgement and an obliquity of moral feeling which makes me shudder." Jefferson would never have agreed, she wrote: "In my day, when our Grandfather's opinions had weight in the community, we deeply deplored the unprincipled avarice of our British lawgivers which had laden us with the guilty burden of domestic slavery." But now "our 'peculiar institutions' are things to be proud of." The "old landmarks" of principle have been "swept away by the overwhelming tide of a corruption, both private & political, so merciless as to confound all distinctions of right & wrong. . . . I cannot tell you into what discredit the race of America has fallen abroad, nor how universal is the abhorrence felt for the doctrines believed to be American."[55]

Someone who cultivated America's reputation as carefully as did Thomas Jefferson certainly would have agreed with Ellen. As a member of a transatlantic Republic of Letters, Jefferson subscribed to revolutionary, liberal principles that he believed would one day circle the globe, bringing the light of liberty with them. Fortunately, he was right and Dew was wrong. Although Jefferson's *Notes* did not accomplish all that he hoped at the College of William and Mary, they did provide the bulwark of a principled antislavery argument for three generations of Virginians. And eventually, through the work of men like Edward Coles, they were transformed into an American antislavery nationalism that helped lead the country both into and out of the Civil War, toward a diverse future that even Jefferson himself could not have dreamed of.

Epilogue

But Jefferson is alive, and therefore dangerous. By his best examples and his worst, he still eats at American consciences. Among the founders of this democracy, Washington was its father and Madison was its mind, but Jefferson was its conscience. That he could not live up to his own high principles . . . is not the same as saying that he betrayed those principles, or that the principles themselves embodied some hidden evil. Failure, or hypocrisy, always attends high ideals. The imperfection of the morally ambitious is not surprising; it is only the most rudimentary information about how the moral life is actually lived.

—Sean Wilentz, "The Details of Greatness" (2004)

We need your voice, Edward Coles and William Short told Jefferson in the final years of his life. You are the spokesman for liberty in America; your opinion on the issue of slavery matters. Posterity will be guided, in some measure, by your words on this issue. When Jefferson refused to speak out on what was by that point one of the most divisive issues facing the nation, he claimed to be doing so because of his fundamental belief that each generation should choose for themselves what laws they would follow: the living should guide themselves rather than be constricted by the beliefs of the dead. But Jefferson refused to say anything new while also firmly believing that his statement on slavery had already been loudly and clearly made, and was still available in bookstores around the country, in the form of his *Notes on the State of Virginia*. Moreover, every time someone wrote to ask him another question on the issue, and he responded, he did so in the knowledge that his letter could be published in a newspaper—as indeed many of them were. These letters became valuable additions to Jefferson's antislavery record. Edward Coles, for example, wielded Jefferson's 1814 reply to him as a very effective weapon in the Illinois debate over slavery in the constitution and again later—to less effect—in Virginia in 1829. In 1832 Thomas Jefferson Randolph read the Coles letter into the record of the House of Delegates as proof that Jefferson's antislavery convictions had not changed over the years and that he endorsed actual emancipation and colonization plans rather than mere vague platitudes.

Today Jefferson is frequently understood as being far too silent on the issue of slavery and far too loud on the issue of race. This is not a new critique: just three years after Jefferson's death in 1826, a free black writer named David Walker published a powerful and influential pamphlet titled *Walker's Appeal in Four Articles; Together with a Preamble, to the Coloured Citizens of the World, but in Particular and Very Expressly to Those of the United States of America* (1829). Born the son of a slave in North Carolina, Walker had grown up free and eventually settled in Boston, but he deeply resented the evils of slavery and the repression faced by free black people in a racist society. His *Appeal* is a revolutionary call to arms on behalf of black people, particularly slaves: "[H]ad I not rather die, or be put to death, than to be a slave to any tyrant, who takes not only my own, but my wife and children's lives by the inches?" Walker specifically rejected the colonization movement, arguing that black Americans had more right to the land than did white people, since they had enriched the soil with "our blood and tears."[1]

For Walker, Jefferson's *Notes* was an instrument of oppression—a manifesto for racism, and therefore a justification for slavery. "Has Mr. Jefferson declared to the world, that we are inferior to the whites, both in the endowments of our bodies and of minds? It is indeed surprising, that a man of such great learning, combined with such excellent natural parts, should speak so of a set of men in chains," Walker wrote. It was as if Jefferson placed "one wild deer in an iron cage, where it will be secured, and [held] another by the side of the same, then let it go, and expect[ed] the one in the cage to run as fast as the one at liberty." Walker encouraged all black men to buy a copy of the *Notes* for their own sons to read so that the "charges of Mr. Jefferson" could be "refuted by the blacks *themselves*." This was necessary because "Mr. Jefferson was one of the great characters as ever lived among the whites," and his words concerning black people "have sunk deep into the hearts of millions of the whites." Therefore "unless we try to refute Mr. Jefferson's arguments respecting us, we will only establish them." And the only way to refute Mr. Jefferson's remarks, Walker argued, was to rise up in armed revolt:

[T]he blacks, once you get them started, they glory in death. The whites have had us under them for more than three centuries, murdering, and treating us like brutes; and, as Mr. Jefferson wisely said, they have never *found us out*—they do not know, indeed, that there is an unconquerable disposition in the breasts of the blacks, which, when it is fully awakened and put in motion, will be subdued, only with the destruction of the animal existence. Get the blacks started, and if you do not have a gang of tigers and lions to deal with, I am a deceiver of the blacks and of the whites.[2]

The most damaging thing that Jefferson wrote, according to Walker, was his appeal to "lover[s] of natural history" who should wish to "keep those in the department of MAN as *distinct* as nature has formed them" by prohibiting interracial marriage. "This very verse," Walker declared forty-five years after the *Notes* was first printed, "having emanated from Mr. Jefferson, a much greater philosopher the world [was] never afforded, has in truth injured us more, and has been as great a barrier to our emancipation as any thing that has ever been advanced against us."[3]

Charles Thomson, the secretary of the Congress and American Philosophical Society member who provided Jefferson with a lengthy commentary on the *Notes* manuscript, had warned Jefferson about this eventuality. In 1784 he told Jefferson that "though I am much pleased with the dysertation on the difference between the Whites & blacks & am inclined to think the latter a race lower in the scale of being yet for that very reason & *because such an opinion might seem to justify slavery* I should be inclined to leave it out." Jefferson's response, as we have seen, was to revise his *Notes*, removing some sections and adding several paragraphs that served to strengthen his condemnation of slavery and to soften his declarations on race:

Whether further observation will or will not verify the conjecture, that nature has been less bountiful to them in the endowments of the head, I believe that in those of the heart she will have been found to have done them justice. . . . The opinion, that they are inferior in the faculties of reason and imagination, must be hazarded with great diffidence. . . . I advance it therefore as a suspicion only, that the blacks, whether originally a distinct race, or made distinct by time and circumstances, are inferior to the whites.

None of these changes were sufficient, as David Walker pointed out. Jefferson may have made his opposition to slavery more clear, but his equivocations on racial inferiority served to fatally weaken his *Notes* and his moral credibility—for his generation and for all those who followed.[4]

Jefferson was not exceptional in his prejudice. His views on racial difference were not new or remarkable for his time, and he believed himself to be summarizing the best scientific treatises in his discussion of the topic rather than creating a new racial discourse for America. Yet because of Jefferson's brilliance with the pen, and because of his status as America's best spokesman for liberty, his words on race held the power to codify what was at that time still vague. He pronounced that black people were likely inferior in many respects, listing examples such as the ability to love, to grieve, to think deeply and abstractly—all of the most powerful aspects of being human, in other words—and in doing so he unwittingly contributed to an insidious current of racism that would eventually become a major excuse in the South for delaying or denying emancipation. It became possible to believe that all men were created equal and deserved liberty and simultaneously to believe that white men and women would be unbearably injured by having to share their country with free black men and women.

One of the greatest ironies of Jefferson's life and legacy is that, despite his repeated pronouncements on racial difference and the necessity of colonization, repeated up until the very end of his life, privately Jefferson was surrounded by attractive, intelligent, hardworking African-descended people and people of mixed race, particularly the Granger and Hemings families who occupied the skilled positions of the household. As John Boles puts it, Jefferson deliberately insulated himself from all the "common instances of slave resistance and thus from the inhumanity of the institution," consequently making his personal experience with slavery quite benign. Perhaps Jefferson even became, toward the end of his life, more comfortable with the contradictions of slavery and liberty coexisting in Virginia. As he waited for his philosophical "sons" like Coles and the Randolph men to move the state toward emancipation, he lived peacefully in the midst of a self-made paradox, surrounded by relatives who were slave and free, black and white.[5]

Jefferson insisted on lenient treatment for the enslaved workers on all his plantations, in particular for those who directly served the Jefferson and Randolph families at Monticello. These enslaved people, primarily members of the large Hemings clan, were often literate, received larger clothing allowances and nicer dwellings, and were given higher levels of responsibility and authority. The mixed-race Hemings family members were often quite light-skinned, leading some scholars to speculate that Jefferson favored them because their "white blood" rendered them somehow more capable. However, this theory becomes less credible when one considers that the enslaved worker George Granger, who did *not* seem to be of mixed race, was entrusted with the position of overseer at Monticello from 1791 until 1799, when he died. Indeed, it is possible that, after Jefferson's retirement to Monticello in 1809, his close proximity to so many obviously responsible and intelligent slaves caused him to soften some of his harsh views of black (and mixed-race) people's capabilities.[6]

The enslaved person whom Jefferson seems to have known most intimately, of course, was Sally Hemings. Although very little detailed evidence survives regarding Hemings, several witnesses described her as beautiful; she had long, straight dark hair, with very light skin, and perhaps resembled her half-sister, Jefferson's long-deceased wife, Martha Wayles Jefferson.[7] We also know that Hemings spoke French and that she was a skilled seamstress who, after returning from France with Jefferson and his daughters in 1789, was probably tasked with caring for Jefferson's clothing and his private rooms. Her four surviving children were born between 1798 and 1808, and each one of them was freed, formally or informally, by Jefferson.[8]

Belying every instance in which he had declared that white and black people should live separately, that freed slaves should be "removed beyond the chance of mixture," when it came to Hemings's children Jefferson had no problem allowing them to leave Monticello and live successful lives as free people in America. In the cases of Beverley and Harriet, their skin tones were so light that they chose to "pass" into

white society, changing details about their backgrounds in order to ob-
scure their slave ancestry.[9] Jefferson's granddaughter Ellen Wayles Randolph Coolidge later wrote: "It was [Jefferson's] principle . . . *to allow
such of his slaves as were sufficiently white to pass for white men*, to withdraw quietly from the plantation; it was called running away, but they
were never reclaimed. I remember four instances of this, three young
men and one girl, who walked away and staid away—their whereabouts
was perfectly known but they were left to themselves—for they were
white enough to pass for white."[10] Although Ellen Coolidge married
and moved to Boston as a young woman, and became one of the most
outspoken of the Jefferson grandchildren in her opposition to slavery,
she did not accept—or at least she did not wish others to accept—that
her beloved grandfather could have had children with his slave. She
was particularly disgusted by rumors that Jefferson had heartlessly sold
off his enslaved children for profit. In response to these tales, Coolidge
told her husband that all of Sally's living children—some of whom were
rumored to bear a resemblance to Jefferson—were fathered by Jefferson's nephew, Samuel Carr.[11]

During the Civil War, the extended Jefferson–Randolph–Hemings
family was torn apart, as were so many other American families. Jeff
Randolph, still living near Monticello, supported the Confederacy,
though he retained his staunch opposition to slavery and called himself
an abolitionist until his death.[12] His brother, George Wythe Randolph,
served briefly as the Confederate secretary of war. Those members of
the family who were living in the North tended to fight for the Union,
including Ellen Coolidge's son Sydney, who was killed while fighting
for Jefferson's beloved Union in the Battle of Chickamauga. From the
Hemings family—including both those who were living as white people and those who retained their identities as African Americans—four
brave young men fought for the right to freedom and full membership
in the community of citizens. Madison Hemings's son Thomas Eston
perished in a Confederate prison.[13] As David Walker had predicted,
when black men fought bravely they did win newfound respect from
many white people, and by war's end colonization was no longer considered a feasible—or desirable—option.

The war finally brought an end to the institution that Jefferson had long believed would tear the country apart and bring divine judgment on slaveholders. And in part because of the courageous actions taken by men like the Jefferson–Hemings grandsons, African Americans were granted citizenship with the ratification of the Fourteenth Amendment in 1868. Almost exactly a hundred years later, writing from a jail cell in Birmingham, Alabama, Martin Luther King Jr. reminded his readers that Thomas Jefferson had been an "extremist" of the very best kind. In an age of almost universal slavery he had dared to write:

We hold these truths to be self-evident, that all men are created equal.[14]

To modern audiences it may seem that Jefferson failed to live up to the standard he immortalized in the Declaration of Independence. He never publicly argued that black men and women were as intelligent, or as beautiful, as were whites—but he did argue consistently that "whatever be their degree of talent it is no measure of their rights. [Just b]ecause Sir Isaac Newton was superior to others in understanding, he was not therefore lord of the person or property of others."[15] Jefferson never publicly claimed that white and black people could live in peace and equality together—but his physical and intellectual descendants proved that such a thing was possible. Just as Jefferson had hoped, later generations of Americans embraced liberty even more than many in his own generation could. As moral standards improved over time, public opinion advanced. And laws changed. The "ball of liberty," which Jefferson helped "first put . . . into motion," continues its "roll round the globe."[16]

Notes

1. John T. Brown of Petersburg, speech given in the Assembly on 18 Jan. 1832, in Erik S. Root, ed., *Sons of the Fathers: The Virginia Slavery Debates of 1831–1832* (Lanham, MD: Lexington Books, 2010), 175.

2. Thomas Jefferson (hereafter "TJ"), *Notes on the State of Virginia* (London: Stockdale, 1787); Speech of Thomas J. Randolph, 20 Jan. 1832, in *Sons of the Fathers*, 215–224, quote at 215.

3. Speech of Thomas J. Randolph, 20 Jan. 1832, in *Sons of the Fathers*, 222. For evidence of Jefferson's continued opposition to slavery at the end of his life, see Thomas Jefferson to William Short, 18 Jan. 1826, from the Thomas Jefferson and William Short Correspondence, transcribed and edited by Gerard W. Gawalt, Manuscript Division, Library of Congress, www.loc.gov/resource /mtj1.055_0829_0830.

4. TJ to Chastellux, 7 June 1785. Unless otherwise noted, all Jefferson correspondence and papers may be found in *The Papers of Thomas Jefferson Digital Edition*, ed. Barbara B. Oberg and J. Jefferson Looney, http://rotunda.upress .virginia.edu/founders/TSJN. Unless otherwise noted, all original documents are presented as they were written, including spelling errors (e.g., "its" and "it's" are often confused) and errors in punctuation. For the books, see TJ to George Wythe, with Enclosure, 16 Sep. 1787; Coolie Verner, *Mr. Jefferson Distributes His Notes: A Preliminary Checklist of the First Edition* (New York: New York Public Library, 1952), 17.

5. TJ to James Madison, 8 Feb. 1786. Jefferson himself misleadingly dated the first publication "1782" when, in fact, it was continually being revised until 1784, published in 1785 in French, and not (officially) published in English until 1787. The spy in question was Charles Williamos; see TJ to Williamos, 7 July 1785; Philip Mazzei to TJ, 26 Oct. 1785; TJ to Abigail Adams, 20 Nov. 1785. By 1800, the *Notes* had been released in French, excerpted in German, and printed in as many as ten English editions, each slightly different from the one preceding it.

6. Douglas L. Wilson, "The Evolution of Jefferson's *Notes on the State of Virginia*," *Virginia Magazine of History and Biography* 112, no. 2 (2004): 98–133. One essay that does analyze Jefferson's antislavery intentions for the *Notes* but that does not deal with his revision process is William Merkel, "Jefferson in

Paris: Rewriting the Problems of Slavery, Slaveholding, Family, and Codependency," in Mark Holowchak, *Thomas Jefferson and Philosophy: Essays on the Philosophical Cast of Jefferson's Writings* (Lanham, MD: Lexington Books, 2014), 91–134. Another work that acknowledges Wilson's dissection of the manuscript, but does not discuss the revision, is Peter Thompson, "'I Have Known': Thomas Jefferson, Experience, and *Notes on the State of Virginia*," in *A Companion to Thomas Jefferson*, ed. Francis D. Cogliano (Malden, MA, and Oxford, UK: Wiley-Blackwell, 2012), 60–74.

7. Dustin A. Gish and Daniel P. Klinghard recently addressed this deficit in their political analysis of the *Notes* and its publication history; they argue that Jefferson timed its publication to influence the Constitutional Convention. I agree with Gish and Klinghard that Jefferson was far more intentional in his composition and distribution of the *Notes* than other scholars have realized, but I primarily focus on Jefferson's sections dealing with race and slavery and argue in particular that his controversial opposition to slavery—and desire to positively influence Virginian debates on that topic—were key elements in Jefferson's publication process. See Gish and Klinghard, "Republican Constitutionalism in Thomas Jefferson's *Notes on the State of Virginia*," *Journal of Politics* 74, no. 1 (Jan. 2012): 35–51; and *Thomas Jefferson and the Science of Republican Government: A Political Biography of Notes on the State of Virginia* (Cambridge, UK: Cambridge University Press, 2017). The only other book (to date) that focuses solely on the *Notes* is a study of Jefferson's deliberate structuring of the text: see David Tucker, *Enlightened Republicanism: A Study of Jefferson's Notes on the State of Virginia* (Lanham, MD: Lexington Books, 2008).

8. Malone did not discuss the issue of slavery until the final volume of his multivolume biography, published in 1981; see Dumas Malone, *Jefferson and His Time*, 6 vols. (Boston: Little, Brown and Company, 1948–1981); Marie Goebel Kimball, *Jefferson: War and Peace, 1776 to 1784* (New York: Coward-McCann, 1947); see also Adrienne Koch, *Jefferson and Madison: The Great Collaboration* (New York: Alfred A. Knopf, 1950). Another sympathetic biography is Merrill D. Peterson, *Thomas Jefferson and the New Nation: A Biography* (New York: Oxford University Press, 1975); see also Peterson, "Thomas Jefferson's *Notes on the State of Virginia*," in *Studies in Eighteenth-Century Culture*, vol. 7 (Madison: University of Wisconsin Press, 1978), 49–62. By far the most nuanced and thorough treatment of Jefferson and slavery in a biography is John. B. Boles, *Jefferson: Architect of American Liberty* (New York: Basic Books, 2017).

9. Winthrop D. Jordan, *White Over Black: American Attitudes Toward the Negro, 1550–1812* (Chapel Hill: Published for the Institute of Early American

History and Culture at Williamsburg, VA, by the University of North Carolina Press, 1968), 427.

10. John Chester Miller's *The Wolf by the Ears: Thomas Jefferson and Slavery* (New York: Free Press, 1977) summarizes much of the revisionist work of the 1960s and 1970s, albeit in a somewhat contradictory way that still emphasizes Jefferson's lifelong hatred of slavery.

11. William Cohen, "Thomas Jefferson and the Problem of Slavery," *Journal of American History* 56, no. 3 (1969): 503–526.

12. Fredrika Teute Schmidt and Barbara Ripel Wilhelm, "Early Proslavery Petitions in Virginia," *William and Mary Quarterly* 30, no. 1 (1973), esp. 133; Robert McColley, *Slavery and Jeffersonian Virginia* (Urbana: University of Illinois Press, 1964).

13. Francis Cogliano, *Thomas Jefferson: Reputation and Legacy* (Edinburgh: Edinburgh University Press, 2006).

14. Wilson, "Jefferson and the Character Issue," *Atlantic Monthly* 270, no. 5 (1992): 57–74; Paul Finkelman, "Jefferson and Slavery: 'Treason Against the Hopes of the World,'" in *Jeffersonian Legacies*, ed. Peter Onuf (Charlottesville: University of Virginia Press, 1993), 210.

15. Cogliano, *Thomas Jefferson*, 216.

16. In 1972 William Freehling argued that revisionists had gone too far and offered a new way of viewing the actions—and silences—of the revolutionary generation by demonstrating that their main concern was the survival of the republic and that they did what they could to eventually doom slavery (although he reversed himself on this issue several years later). See William W. Freehling, "The Founding Fathers and Slavery," *American Historical Review* 77 (1972), 81–93. See also Edmund S. Morgan, *American Slavery, American Freedom: The Ordeal of Colonial Virginia* (New York: Norton, 1975), and Joseph J. Ellis, *American Sphinx: The Character of Thomas Jefferson* (New York: Alfred A. Knopf, 1997).

17. Cogliano, *Thomas Jefferson*, 224. Cogliano further posits that "we can make sense of Jefferson's views on slavery by grounding them in Enlightenment thought," adding that contextualizing is not the equivalent of excusing, for "we can place Jefferson's engagement with slavery in its appropriate context without divesting ourselves of ethical judgments."

18. Peter S. Onuf, *Jefferson's Empire: The Language of American Nationhood* (Charlottesville: University Press of Virginia, 2001); Ari Helo and Onuf, "Jefferson, Morality, and the Problem of Slavery," *William and Mary Quarterly* 60, no. 3 (2003): 583–641; Ari Helo, *Thomas Jefferson's Ethics and the Politics of Human Progress: The Morality of a Slaveholder* (New York: Cambridge University

Press, 2013); William Merkel, "Jefferson in Paris"; Merkel, "Jefferson's Failed Anti-Slavery Proviso of 1784 and the Nascence of Free Soil Constitutionalism," *Seton Hall Law Review* 38 (2008): 555–603; Boles, *Jefferson*; see also Mark D. McGarvie, "'In Perfect Accordance with His Character': Thomas Jefferson, Slavery, and the Law," *Indiana Magazine of History* 95, no. 2 (1999): 142–177. Another scholar who contributes to this line of reasoning, albeit regarding all the Founders and not just Jefferson, is Matthew Mason, "A Missed Opportunity? The Founding, Postcolonial Realities, and the Abolition of Slavery," *Slavery & Abolition* 35, no. 2 (2014): 199–213. Mason's work stands in opposition to that of Paul Finkelman, who argues that Jefferson must be tested not according to whether he "was better than the worst of his contemporaries, but whether he was the leader of the best." See Paul Finkelman, "Thomas Jefferson and Antislavery: The Myth Goes On," *Virginia Magazine of History and Biography* 102 no. 2 (1994), quote at 199.

19. Helo and Onuf, "Jefferson, Morality, and the Problem of Slavery," 585.

20. Helo and Onuf, 586.

21. Helo and Onuf, 603.

22. See Malone, *Jefferson the Virginian*, 121–122; Miller, *Wolf By the Ears*, 5–6; David Thomas Konig cautions us not to interpret this sentiment too broadly, however; Jefferson was arguing that, since no positive law applied to his client, "the situation reverted to the law of nature," in which all men were born free. The argument was antislavery but within the confines of the law at the time. See David Thomas Konig, "Jefferson and the Law," *A Companion to Thomas Jefferson*, ed. Francis D. Cogliano (Malden, MA, and Oxford, UK: Wiley-Blackwell, 2012), 355. For more on Jefferson and amelioration, see Christa Dierksheide, *Amelioration and Empire* (Charlottesville: University of Virginia Press, 2014).

23. TJ, "Revised Report of the Committee, 22 March 1784," in *Papers*, ed. Boyd, 6:607. For the Northwest Ordinance as an example of an antislavery action on Jefferson's part, see Merkel, "Jefferson's Failed Anti-Slavery Proviso."

24. Thomas Jefferson, *Autobiography of Thomas Jefferson, 1743–1790: Together with a Summary of the Chief Events in Jefferson's Life*, ed. Paul Leicester Ford (Philadelphia: University of Pennsylvania Press, 2005), 77. Jefferson wrote *another* draft constitution for Virginia (1783) during the time that he was editing the *Notes;* in this constitution he proposed banning both the trade and slavery itself after the year 1800. See "Jefferson's Draft of a Constitution for Virginia [May–June 1783]."

25. Thomas Jefferson, "Jefferson's Second Draft," in *The Papers of Thomas Jefferson*, ed. Julian P. Boyd, vol. 1, 1950 (Princeton, NJ: Princeton University Press), 353.

26. TJ to Wythe, 13 Aug. 1786.

27. After several antislavery petitions caused a major stir in Congress in 1790, emancipation became a much more difficult topic to debate at the national level as well. See Richard S. Newman, "Prelude to the Gag Rule: Southern Reaction to Antislavery Petitions in the First Federal Congress," *Journal of the Early Republic* 16, no. 4 (1996): 571–599, quote at 574. For more on this incident, see Boles, *Jefferson*, 216.

28. See Samuel Shephard, *The Statutes at Large of Virginia for October Session 1792, to December Session of 1806* . . . , 3 vols. (Richmond, VA, 1835–1836), 1:128, which reads "all slaves so emancipated, shall be liable to be taken by execution, to satisfy any debt contracted by the person emancipating them before such emancipation is made." See also T. H. Breen, *Tobacco Culture: The Mentality of the Great Tidewater Planters on the Eve of the Revolution* (Princeton, NJ: Princeton University Press, 2001); and Herbert Sloan, *Principle and Interest: Thomas Jefferson and the Problem of Debt* (Charlottesville: University of Virginia Press, 2001). For Jefferson's plan to emancipate his slaves, see TJ to Edward Bancroft, 26 Jan. 1788.

29. Onuf, *Jefferson's Empire*, 160. Onuf and Helo develop this thesis further by arguing that Jefferson believed a stunted moral sense prohibited former slaves from immediate participation in the American republic; see Onuf and Helo, "Jefferson, Morality, and the Problem of Slavery."

31. Only one full-length study has been published about Short (hereafter "WS"), and it has significant flaws in its documentation: see George Shackelford, *Jefferson's Adoptive Son: The Life of William Short, 1759–1848* (Lexington: University Press of Kentucky, 1993). However, his book is based on Shackelford's 1955 dissertation, which is much more thorough and extensively footnoted ("William Short: Jefferson's Adopted Son, 1758–1849" [PhD diss., University of Virginia, 1955]). Shackelford also published a few articles that focused on different aspects of Short's life: George Shackelford, "William Short: Diplomat in Revolutionary France, 1785–1793," *Proceedings of the American Philosophical Society* 102, no. 6 (1958): 596–612, and "To Practice Law: Aspects of the Era of Good Feelings Reflected in the Short-Ridgely Correspondences, 1816–1821," *Maryland Historical Magazine* 64, no. 4 (1969): 342–395. Other notable articles include: Marie Kimball, "William Short, Jefferson's Only 'Son,'" *North American Review* 223 (1926): 471–486; Blanche Allendena Garfield, "William Short and His Diplomatic Career from 1789–1792," Master's thesis, West Virginia University, 1931; Myrna Bryce, "The Diplomatic Career of William Short," *Journal of Modern History* 15 (1943): 97–119; Yvon Bizardel and Howard C. Rice, "Poor in Love Mr. Short," *William and Mary Quarterly*, 3rd ser., vol. 21, no. 4 (1964): 516–533; Lucille McWane Watson, "William Short America's First

Career Diplomat: Jefferson's 'Adopted Son' Took Paris by Storm," *William and Mary Alumni Gazette* vol. 50, no. 1 (1982). A recent fictional book includes an intriguing look at Short and his possible romance with Jefferson's daughter Martha: Stephanie Dray and Laura Croghan Kamoie, *America's First Daughter* (Waterville, ME: Thorndike Press, 2016).

32. St. George Tucker, *Dissertation on Slavery: With a Proposal for the Gradual Abolition of It* (Philadelphia: Printed for Mathew Carey, 1796).

33. John Thomas Cassidy, "The Issue of Freedom in Illinois under Governor Coles," *Journal of Illinois State Historical Society* 57 (Autumn 1964): 284–288; Ralph L. Ketcham, "The Dictates of Conscience: Edward Coles and Slavery," *Virginia Quarterly Review* 26 (Winter 1966): 46–62; Donald S. Spencer, "Edward Coles: Virginia Gentleman in Frontier Politics," *Journal of Illinois State Historical Society* 61 (1968): 150–151; Elizabeth Langhorne, "Edward Coles, Thomas Jefferson, and the Rights of Man," *Virginia Cavalcade* 23 (1973): 30–37; Robert M. Sutton, "Edward Coles and the Constitutional Crisis in Illinois, 1822–1824," *Illinois Historical Journal* 82 (Spring 1989): 33; David Ress, *Governor Edward Coles and the Vote to Forbid Slavery in Illinois, 1823–1824* (Jefferson, NC: McFarland, 2006); Kurt E. Leichtle and Bruce G. Carveth, *Crusade Against Slavery: Edward Coles, Pioneer of Freedom* (Carbondale: Southern Illinois University Press, 2011); Suzanne Cooper Guasco, *Confronting Slavery: Edward Coles and the Rise of Antislavery Politics in Nineteenth-Century America* (DeKalb: Northern Illinois University Press, 2013). Coles has also been mentioned in several books on other topics, most notably Annette Gordon-Reed, *The Hemingses of Monticello: An American Family* (New York: W. W. Norton & Company, 2008), 538; he also appears in Louis P. Masur, *1831, Year of Eclipse* (New York: Hill and Wang, 2001), 58–61; Don Fehrenbacher, *The Slaveholding Republic: An Account of the United States Government's Relations to Slavery* (New York: Oxford University Press, 2001), 67; and William Freehling, *The Road to Disunion: Secessionists at Bay, 1776–1854* (New York: Oxford University Press, 1990), 140–141.

34. The only full-length biography of Randolph to date is William Harris Gaines, *Thomas Mann Randolph: Jefferson's Son-in-Law* (Baton Rouge: Louisiana State University Press, 1966). For more on Randolph's relationships with the Jeffersons, see Cynthia Kierner, *Martha Jefferson Randolph, Daughter of Monticello: Her Life and Times* (Chapel Hill: University of North Carolina Press, 2012).

35. Joseph Clarke Robert, *The Road from Monticello: A Study of the Virginia Slavery Debate of 1832*, Historical Papers of the Trinity College Historical Society, ser. 24 (Durham, NC: Duke University Press, 1941); William G. Shade,

Democratizing the Old Dominion: Virginia and the Second Party System, 1824–1861 (Charlottesville: University of Virginia Press, 1996); Allison Goodyear Freehling, *Drift Toward Dissolution: The Virginia Slavery Debate of 1831–1832* (Baton Rouge: Louisiana State University Press, 1982); Root, ed., *Sons of the Fathers*.

36. There is one biography of T. J. Randolph: see Joseph Carroll Vance, "Thomas Jefferson Randolph" (PhD diss., University of Virginia, 1957). See also Joseph Randolph Coolidge, *Thomas Jefferson Randolph* (Boston: Beals & Greene, 1875); Jerome A. Hurwitz, "Thomas Jefferson Randolph, Democratic Leader," M.A. thesis, University of Richmond, 1938; George Green Shackelford, ed., *Collected Papers to Commemorate Fifty Years of the Monticello Association of the Descendants of Thomas Jefferson* (Princeton, NJ: Princeton University Press, 1965).

37. T. J. Randolph to Nicholas P. Trist, 4 April 1832, *Family Letters Project* of Monticello, http://tjrs.monticello.org.

38. TJ to Charles Clay, 27 Jan. 1790.

CHAPTER ONE. ANTISLAVERY AT WILLIAM AND MARY

1. Richard Price to Thomas Jefferson (hereafter "TJ"), 2 July 1785. Unless otherwise noted, all Jefferson correspondence and papers may be found in *The Papers of Thomas Jefferson Digital Edition*, ed. Barbara B. Oberg and J. Jefferson Looney, http://rotunda.upress.virginia.edu/founders/TSJN.

2. TJ to Price, 7 Aug. 1785. Several months later, in answer to a Frenchman's queries about the United States, Jefferson made a similar assessment of the state of slavery. See TJ, "Answers to Démeunier's First Queries," 24 Jan. 1786.

3. Price to TJ, 24 Oct. 1785.

4. See, for example, Dumas Malone, *Jefferson and His Time*, vol. 1, *Jefferson the Virginian* (Boston: Little, Brown and Company, 1948); Marie Goebel Kimball, *Jefferson: The Road to Glory, 1743–1776* (New York: Coward-McCann, Inc., 1943); Merrill D. Peterson, *Thomas Jefferson and the New Nation: A Biography* (New York: Oxford University Press, 1970); Gary Wills, *Inventing America: Jefferson's Declaration of Independence* (New York: Doubleday & Co., Inc., 1978); John B. Boles, *Jefferson: Architect of American Liberty* (New York: Basic Books, 2017), ch. 1. The most thorough examination of antislavery thought at William and Mary is Terry L. Meyers, "Thinking About Slavery at the College of William and Mary," *William and Mary Bill of Rights Journal* 21, no. 4 (2013), 1215–1257. The Reconstruction-era William and Mary president (and historian), Lyon G. Tyler, presented Professors St. George Tucker and George

Wythe as antislavery voices whose views would have prevailed if it were not for William Lloyd Garrison's "abuse and incendiarism which in some measure changed the course of sentiment in Virginia" and directly led to Thomas R. Dew and Nathaniel Beverley Tucker's proslavery advocacy at the college. See Lyon G. Tyler, "Early Courses and Professors at William and Mary College," *William and Mary Quarterly* 14, no. 2 (1905): 71–83, quote at 83. For more recent praise of Wythe and Tucker, see Robert M. Cover, *Justice Accused: Antislavery and the Judicial Process* (New Haven, CT: Yale University Press, 1975), 50–55; Wythe and Tucker are also cited as counterparts to proslavery college president Thomas Roderick Dew in Alfred L. Brophy, "Considering William and Mary's History with Slavery: The Case of Thomas Roderick Dew," *William and Mary Bill of Rights Journal* 16 (2008): 1091–1139; and Paul Finkelman praises these two men at the expense of Jefferson in works such as "Thomas Jefferson and Antislavery: The Myth Goes On," *Virginia Magazine of History and Biography* 102, no. 2 (1994), 212.

5. Slavery has existed on every inhabited continent in the world for much of human history, and slavery continues, in varying forms, to the present day. The final country to technically abolish slavery (though the practice continues nonetheless) was Mauritania in 1981. Despite prohibitions on hereditary chattel slavery (in which one person legally owns the life and labor of another person and that person's descendants), the current number of unfree laborers worldwide is estimated to be above thirty million. See for example the research published at www.globalslaveryindex.org/findings.

6. For one excellent discussion of Native engagements with slavery, see Christina Snyder, *Slavery in Indian Country: The Changing Face of Captivity in Early America* (Cambridge, MA: Harvard University Press, 2010).

7. Peter Kolchin, *American Slavery: 1619–1877* (New York: Hill and Wang, 1993), 8.

8. Kolchin, *American Slavery*, 27; Ira Berlin, *Many Thousands Gone: The First Two Centuries of Slavery in North America* (Cambridge, MA, and London: Belknap Press of Harvard University Press, 2009), 54; Gordon S. Wood, *Empire of Liberty: A History of the Early Republic, 1789–1815* (New York: Oxford University Press, 2009), 509.

9. Eva Sheppard Wolf, *Race and Liberty in the New Nation: Emancipation in Virginia from the Revolution to Nat Turner's Rebellion* (Baton Rouge: Louisiana State University Press, 2006), 2.

10. The equivalency of blackness with slavery was not unique to America. For example, in the ninth century, as the Arab slave trade in Africa exploded,

the Arabic word for slave, *'abd*, evolved to mean "black man." See John B. Boles, *Black Southerners, 1619–1869* (Lexington: University of Kentucky Press, 1983), 4. For the classic exploration of the paradox of liberty and slavery in Virginia, see Edmund Morgan, *American Slavery, American Freedom: The Ordeal of Colonial Virginia* (New York and London: W. W. Norton & Company, 1975); and for a convincing complication of Morgan's thesis, see Jan Ellen Lewis, "The Problem of Slavery," in *Devising Liberty: Preserving and Creating Freedom in the New American Republic*, ed. David Konig (Stanford, CA: Stanford University Press, 1995), 265–297. The standard text on the intellectual history of racism in America is Winthrop Jordan, *White Over Black: American Attitudes Toward the Negro, 1550–1812* (Chapel Hill: University of North Carolina Press, 1968); an important response to Jordan is Barbara J. Field, "Ideology and Race in American History," *Region, Race, and Reconstruction: Essays in Honor of C. Vann Woodward*, ed. J. Morgan Kousser and James M. McPherson (New York and Oxford: Oxford University Press, 1982), 143–177.

11. Boles, *Black Southerners*, 14.

12. Wolf, *Race and Liberty*, 3.

13. Wood, *Empire of Liberty*, 517.

14. David Brion Davis, *The Problem of Slavery in the Age of Emancipation* (New York: Alfred A. Knopf, 2014), xv–xvi.

15. Matthew Mason, *Slavery and Politics in the Early American Republic* (Chapel Hill: University of North Carolina Press, 2006), 11. I am not arguing that evangelical belief and antislavery sentiment always coincided; Southern evangelicals eventually used their religion to bolster their proslavery arguments. Nonetheless, Christianity played a vital role in the rise of antislavery movements on both sides of the Atlantic. As Richard Newman puts it, "religion was the primary motivator for generations of abolitionists." Richard S. Newman, *The Transformation of American Abolitionism: Fighting Slavery in the Early Republic* (Chapel Hill: University of North Carolina Press, 2002), 2. For the development of proslavery arguments by southern evangelicals, see, for example, Charles F. Irons, *The Origins of Proslavery Christianity: White and Black Evangelicals in Colonial and Antebellum Virginia* (Chapel Hill: University of North Carolina Press, 2008). For more on the (ongoing) debate among historians regarding the causes of the abolition movement, see Thomas Bender, ed., *The Antislavery Debate: Capitalism and Abolitionism as a Problem in Historical Interpretation* (Berkeley: University of California Press, 1992).

16. Davis notes, however, that not even these two progenitors of Enlightenment advocated abolition; they merely laid a possible foundation for others

to build upon, demonstrating "how remote abolitionism was from even the more liberal minds" of the time (*The Problem of Slavery in Western Culture* [Ithaca, NY: Cornell University Press, 1966], 121). As I will discuss in chapter 2, even later Enlightenment thinkers had no problem simultaneously embracing the concepts of natural equality and of black inferiority.

17. The records of the college for this period were destroyed by fire, and Wythe's enrollment cannot be verified, but most biographies accept this as fact, and William and Mary continues to claim him as an alumnus.

18. J. David Hoeveler, *Creating the American Mind: Intellect and Politics in the Colonial Colleges* (Lanham, MD: Rowman & Littlefield, 2002), 83.

19. Hoeveler, *Creating the American Mind*, 84.

20. Kevin J. Hayes, *The Road to Monticello: The Life and Mind of Thomas Jefferson* (New York: Oxford University Press, 2008), 48.

21. Martin Richard Clagett, "William Small, 1734–1775: Teacher, Mentor, Scientist" (PhD diss., Virginia Commonwealth University, 2003), 152. Alternatively, Kevin Hayes explains the lack of degrees by stating that, whereas in its early days William and Mary had allowed students to graduate with a bachelor's degree in two years, the revised statutes of the 1750s "raised the degree requirements to four years," resulting in more students leaving the college without any degree (*Road to Monticello*, 48). According to Lyon G. Tyler, president of William and Mary from 1888 to 1919, the college's 1727 statutes allowed students to gain bachelor's degrees after four years and a master's after seven. See his account, taken from "Address Before the Phi Beta Kappa Society (Dec. 5, 1904)," in "Early Courses," esp. 72–73.

22. Hoeveler, *Creating the American Mind*, 85, 90.

23. TJ to John Banister Jr., 15 Oct. 1785.

24. Imogene E. Brown, *American Aristides: A Biography of George Wythe* (East Brunswick, NJ: Associated University Presses, Inc., 1981), 23.

25. Virginians today pronounce this name as "FAW-keer."

26. Quoted in Gordon S. Wood, *The American Revolution: A History* (New York: Modern Library, 2001), 102.

27. TJ to Louis Girardin, 15 Jan. 1815.

28. George Wythe Munford, *The Two Parsons* (Richmond, VA, 1884), 416.

29. Benjamin Wilson, "Francis Fauquier (1704?–1768)," oil on canvas, housed in the Foundling Museum, London.

30. TJ to Louis Girardin, 15 Jan. 1815.

31. Clagett, "William Small, 1734–1775," 115–123; for the names and dates of faculty dismissals, see Clagett's Appendix 5, 311. For an analysis of the Great Awakening and the college, see Hoeveler, *Creating the American Mind*, 94; for

another broad discussion of the so-called Two-penny disputes, see Rhys Isaac, *The Transformation of Virginia, 1740–1790* (Chapel Hill: University of North Carolina Press, 1982), ch. 7.

32. Clagett, "William Small," 130.

33. Clagett, 78, 82 (quote), 174–175. For more about William Duncan's common-sense thought and its influence on Jefferson via Small, see Hayes, *Road to Monticello*, 52; William Samuel Howell, "The Declaration of Independence and Eighteenth-Century Logic," *William and Mary Quarterly* 18 (1961): 472; George Alan Davy, "Argumentation and Structure in *Notes on the State of Virginia*," *Eighteenth-Century Studies* 26 (1993): 587.

34. TJ, *The Autobiography of Thomas Jefferson*, ed. Paul Leicester Ford (Philadelphia: University of Pennsylvania Press), 6; see also Clagett, "William Small," 5, 109, 151.

35. Clagett, 164.

36. Malone, *Jefferson and His Time*, 1: 51–52; see also Hayes, *The Road to Monticello*, 50.

37. William and Mary historian Jack Morpurgo sums up this remarkable situation: "That a polymath of such rare quality [Small] should have appeared at William and Mary at just the right moment to teach the outstanding polymath of them all [Jefferson] is one of the happiest coincidences in educational history." J. E. Morpurgo, *Their Majesties Royal Colledge: The College of William and Mary in the Seventeenth and Eighteenth Centuries* (Washington, DC: Hennage Creative Printers, 1976), 138, quoted in Clagett, "William Small," 145. In addition to Jefferson, Small also taught future leaders such as the future governor John Page.

38. TJ to John Harvie, 14 Jan. 1760. This is the earliest surviving letter that Jefferson wrote. For Jefferson's inheritance, see "Will of Peter Jefferson," transcription available at Jefferson Quotes and Family Letters, Monticello.org, https://tjrs.monticello.org/letter/1797.

39. In 1760 Jacob Rowe may have also taught Jefferson for one semester; and in 1761 the board of visitors offered the post of professor of moral philosophy to Richard Graham, despite having previously fired him. He returned to Virginia and took up this post but was, according to another student who was there at the same time as Jefferson, not as good a teacher as Small: "As to the Languages I must depend on myself for all improvement I shall make hereafter in them, As Mr Graham is altogether unqualified to instruct in either." See Clagett, "William Small," 161, 202. Quote at 161 from Walter Jones to Thomas Jones, n.d., Jones Family Papers, Library of Congress.

40. TJ, *Autobiography*, 6.

41. TJ to Messrs. Hugh L. White and others, 6 May 1810.

42. Clagett, "William Small," 133.

43. Malone, *Jefferson and His Time*, vol. 1, quote on 42.

44. Hayes, *Road to Monticello*, 31.

45. TJ, *Autobiography*, 5.

46. Cited by Thomas E. Buckley, S.J., "Placing Thomas Jefferson and Religion in Context, Then and Now," in *Seeing Jefferson Anew: In His Time and Ours*, ed. John B. Boles and Randall Hall (Charlottesville: University of Virginia Press, 2010), 132. Malone notes, however, that Jefferson did not develop his later views on religious tolerance because of Maury, as Maury was deeply concerned with the trend of unqualified Anabaptists teaching potentially heretical views to his parishioners. See Malone, *Jefferson and His Time*, vol. 1, 44, n. 19.

47. TJ, *Autobiography*, 6 ("destinies"); all subsequent quotations from TJ to Louis Girardin, 15 Jan. 1815.

48. TJ, *Autobiography*, 6; TJ to Thomas Jefferson Randolph, 24 Nov. 1808.

49. Thomas Dawson to the Bishop of London, 11 March 1754, quoted in Terry L. Meyers, "Benjamin Franklin, the College of William and Mary, and the Williamsburg Bray School," *Anglican and Episcopal History* 79, no. 4 (2010): 368–393, quote at 389; for William Dawson's use of college resources, see 387. I am indebted to Dr. Meyers, professor of English at William and Mary, not only for his pioneering research into William and Mary's complicated history with slavery but also for his willingness to assist me in my own undertakings.

50. Meyers, "Benjamin Franklin," 393.

51. Meyers, 381.

52. Andrew Levy, *The First Emancipator: The Forgotten Story of Robert Carter, the Founding Father Who Freed His Slaves* (New York: Random House, 2005), 23.

53. Quoted in Shomer S. Zwelling, "Robert Carter's Journey: From Colonial Patriarch to New Nation Mystic," *American Quarterly* 38, no. 4 (1986): 617. For Page on slavery, see T. B. McCord Jr., "John Page of Rosewell: Reason, Religion, and Republican Government from the Perspective of a Virginia Planter, 1743–1808" (PhD diss., American University, 1990), 605, 608, 665.

54. Levy, *First Emancipator*, xii.

55. Zwelling, "Robert Carter's Journey," 625. Later in life, Carter controversially embraced mysticism and the occult, and his temperamental personality and harsh childrearing methods also contributed to his fall from society's good graces.

56. After 1723, in order for an enslaved person to even qualify for

emancipation, he or she had to have performed some "meritorious service" that "aided the white community," such as informing on other slaves who were planning a revolt. The governor *and* his council then had to approve of the emancipation. See Wolf, *Race and Liberty*, 3.

57. Francis Fauquier, "Francis Fauquier's Will," *William and Mary Quarterly* vol. 8, no. 3 (1900), 175, 176.

58. Michael L. Nicholls, "Aspects of the African American Experience in Eighteenth-Century Williamsburg and Norfolk," *Colonial Williamsburg Foundation Library Research Report Series* 330 (Williamsburg, VA: 1991), 18–19; Fauquier, "Francis Fauquier's Will," 175, 176.

59. Clagett, "William Small," 244.

60. The Lunar Circle also included James Watt, an inventor who—with significant input from Small—designed a steam engine that substantially contributed to the Industrial Revolution. See Clagett, "William Small," 256–257.

61. "The Dying Negro" (London, 1773), cited in Meyers, "Thinking About Slavery," 1239. An earlier such poem by Richard Savage appeared in the 1730s; see Davis, *Slavery in Western Culture*, 374.

62. With a few exceptions I use the term "abolitionist" to refer to those who desired immediate emancipation for all slaves and "emancipationist" to refer to those who believed a more gradual approach would also be beneficial.

63. Malone, *Jefferson the Virginian*, 1:174. For the difficulties of dating Jefferson's notebooks, see Douglas L. Wilson, "Thomas Jefferson's Early Notebooks," *William and Mary Quarterly* 42, no. 4 (1985): 434–452.

64. For more on Jefferson's religious beliefs, see Buckley, "Placing Thomas Jefferson and Religion," in *Seeing Jefferson Anew*, 126–151; and Paul Conkin, "The Religious Pilgrimage of Thomas Jefferson," in *Jeffersonian Legacies*, ed. Peter S. Onuf (Charlottesville: University of Virginia Press, 1993), 19–49.

65. Thomas Ahnert, *The Moral Culture of the Scottish Enlightenment, 1690–1805* (New Haven, CT, and London: Yale University Press, 2015), 55.

66. Davis, *The Problem of Slavery in Western Culture*, 375.

67. Francis Hutcheson, *An Essay on the Nature and Conduct of our Passions and Affections*, ed. A. Garrett (Indianapolis: Liberty Fund, 2002), 24.

68. Hutcheson, *A System of Moral Philosophy*, vol. 1 (Glasgow, 1755), 27.

69. Hutcheson, 376.

70. Davis, *Slavery in Western Culture*, 375.

71. Hutcheson, *A System of Moral Philosophy*, 1: 273, 281, 293–303; see also the discussion in Davis, *Slavery in Western Culture*, 377.

72. Davis, *Slavery in Western Culture*, 360.

73. James Beattie, *The Works of James Beattie*, vol. 7 (Philadelphia: Hopkins

and Earle, 1809), 56. William Small arrived at Marischal to complete a four-year degree in 1751, and Beattie graduated in 1753; see Clagett, "William Small," 83; James Harris, ed., *James Beattie: Selected Philosophical Writings* (Exeter, UK: Imprint Academic, 2004), 15. Beattie and fellow Marischal graduate Thomas Reid were among the foremost advocates of the common sense school; Reid and his cousin John Gregory—who was one of William Small's mentors—formed Aberdeen's "Wise Club," or Philosophical Society (1758–1773); see Roger Emerson, "The Contexts of the Scottish Enlightenment," in *The Cambridge Companion to the Scottish Enlightenment*, ed. Alexander Broadie (New York: Cambridge University Press, 2003), 21–22.

74. Daniel Walker Howe, "Why the Scottish Enlightenment Was Useful to the Framers of the American Constitution," *Comparative Studies in Society and History* 31, no. 3 (1989): 579. The disagreement about the relative influence on Jefferson of the Scots versus the radical individualism of Locke and Hobbes—best exemplified by Gary Wills's popular work arguing for Scottish preeminence (*Inventing America*) and the resulting academic backlash on behalf of Locke—is part of a larger debate over whether the Founders' philosophy can best be categorized as "liberal" or "civic republican." This debate can be traced to the 1960s, when Gordon Wood and Bernard Bailyn both wrote works challenging the previous Lockean paradigm and pointing out the influences of classical republican thought, inherited from the Whig tradition of British politics (and, according to J. G. A. Pocock, originally descending from Greek and Italian thinkers). Joyce Appleby became the most prominent critic of the civic republican school, arguing that, although the framers had both civic republican and Lockean thought at their disposal, economic liberalism offered the best way forward; see Joyce Appleby, "The Social Origins of American Revolutionary Ideology," *Journal of American History* 64, no. 4 (1978): 935–958. More recently, scholars have shied away from ascribing strict ideological and chronological divisions to the political philosophies of the Founders. For the antecedent consensus school liberal argument, see Louis Hartz, *The Liberal Tradition in America* (New York: Harcourt, Brace, and Company, 1955); and Daniel J. Boorstin, *The Lost World of Thomas Jefferson* (Chicago: University of Chicago Press, 1993). For the classical republican argument, see Bernard Bailyn, *The Ideological Origins of the American Revolution* (Cambridge, MA: Belknap Press of Harvard University Press, 1967); Gordon S. Wood, *The Creation of the American Republic, 1776–1787* (Chapel Hill: University of North Carolina Press, 1969); and J. G. A. Pocock, *The Machiavellian Moment: Florentine Political Thought and the Atlantic Republican Tradition* (Princeton, NJ: Princeton University Press, 1975). Examples of

critiques of those earlier views, and arguments for a more pluralistic vision of founding political thought, include James Kloppenberg, "The Virtues of Liberalism: Christianity, Republicanism, and Ethics in Early American Political Discourse," *Journal of American History* 74 (June 1987): 9–33; and Daniel Rodgers, "Republicanism: The Career of a Concept," *Journal of American History* 79, no. 1 (1992): 11–38.

75. Samuel Fleischacker, "The Impact on America: Scottish Philosophy and the American Founding," in *The Cambridge Companion to the Scottish Enlightenment*, ed. Alexander Broadie (New York: Cambridge University Press, 2003), 323; Hutcheson, quoted in Fleischacker, 323.

76. Ari Helo and Peter S Onuf, "Jefferson, Morality, and the Problem of Slavery," *William and Mary Quarterly* 60, no. 3 (2003), 589.

77. John Locke, *Two Treatises of Government* (London, 1689); available online at *Liberty Fund*, http://oll.libertyfund.org/titles/locke-the-two-treatises-of-civil-government-hollis-ed.

78. Holly Brewer, "Slavery, Sovereignty, and 'Inheritable Blood': Reconsidering John Locke and the Origins of American Slavery," *American Historical Review* 122, no. 4 (2017): 1038–1078, esp. 1052–1054. The same "just war" rationale applied for Europeans in a variety of situations; for a discussion of the "just war" philosophy at work between Native Americans and French colonists in North America, see Brett Rushforth, *Bonds of Alliance: Indigenous and Atlantic Slaveries in New France* (Chapel Hill: University of North Carolina Press, 2012).

79. TJ to Thomas Law, 13 June 1814.

80. E. Millicent Sowerby, comp., *Catalogue of the Library of Thomas Jefferson*, 5 vols., 2nd ed. (Charlottesville: University of Virginia Press, 1983), 2:11–12.

81. See, for example, Richard D. Brown, "The Idea of an Informed Citizenry in the Early Republic," in Konig, ed., *Devising Liberty*, 141–177.

82. Thomas Hunter, "The Teaching of George Wythe," in *The History of Legal Education in the United States: Commentaries and Primary Sources*, ed. Steve Sheppard (New York: Salem Press, 1999).

83. Historians differ over whether James Monroe studied with Wythe while at William and Mary.

84. The legislative and judicial cases will be discussed below. For the 1795 petition, see "An Act to ameliorate the present condition of slaves, and give freedom to those born after the passing of the act," Library of Virginia, Legislative Petitions microfilm, reel 233, box 294, folder 5. For Wythe freeing his slaves, see Alan Taylor, *Internal Enemy: Slavery and War in Virginia, 1772–1832* (New York and London: W. W. Norton & Co., 2013), 105.

85. T. R. B. Wright, "Judge Spencer Roane," *Virginia Law Register* 2, no. 7 (November 1896): 476.

86. William Munford to John Coalter, 13 June 1790, Brown–Tucker–Coalter Papers, box I, folder 34, Swem Library, College of William and Mary.

87. Richard Randolph to Frances Tucker, 19 May 1786, quoted in Melvin P. Ely, *Israel on the Appomattox: A Southern Experiment in Black Freedom from the 1790s through the Civil War* (New York: A. Knopf, 2004), 23; Richard Randolph Will, quoted in Ely, *Israel*, 450.

88. First and third quotes, TJ to William Duval, 14 June 1806; second quote, TJ to John Sanderson, 31 Aug. 1820; fourth quote, TJ to John Tyler, 25 Nov. 1810. For Wythe's death, see Julian P. Boyd and W. Edwin Hemphill, *The Murder of George Wythe: Two Essays* (Williamsburg, VA: Institute of Early American History and Culture, 1955).

89. First quote, Annette Gordon-Reed, "Logic and Experience: Thomas Jefferson's Life in the Law," in *Slavery and the American South*, ed. Winthrop Jordan et al. (Jackson: University Press of Mississippi, 2003), 10; second quote, David Konig, "Jefferson, Thomas and the Practice of Law," *Encyclopedia Virginia*, Virginia Humanities (7 Dec. 2020), https://encyclopediavirginia.org /entries/jefferson-thomas-and-the-practice-of-law. See also David Konig, *Nature's Advocate: Thomas Jefferson and the Discovery of American Law* (forthcoming); and especially William G. Merkel, "A Founding Father on Trial: Jefferson's Rights Talk and the Problem of Slavery During the Revolutionary Period," *Rutgers Law Review* 64, no. 3 (2012): 595–663.

90. For freedom suits in this period, see Duncan J. Macleod, *Slavery, Race, and the American Revolution* (New York: Cambridge University Press, 1974), 109–126.

91. Merkel, "A Founding Father on Trial," 621. See this article for a thorough and convincing reading of the Howell trial, on which my discussion is based.

92. "Argument in the Case of *Howell v. Netherland*," April 1770, in *The Works of Thomas Jefferson*, 10 vols., ed. Paul Leichester Ford (New York and London: G.P. Putnam's Sons, 1904–1905), I: 376.

93. Merkel, "A Founding Father on Trial," 627.

94. Brunswick County Petition to the Virginia Assembly, 10 Nov. 1785, in Fredrika Teute Schmidt and Barbara Ripel Wilhelm, "Early Proslavery Petitions in Virginia," *William and Mary Quarterly* 30, no. 1 (1973), 144. For the *Somerset* case, see Francis Hargrave, *An Argument in the Case of James Sommersett a Negro, Lately Determined by the Court of King's Bench* . . . (London, 1772), 12–13.

95. See Merkel, "A Founding Father on Trial," 628.

96. See Timothy Sandefur, "Why the Rule against Perpetuities Mattered in *Pleasants v. Pleasants*," *Real Property, Probate and Trust Journal* 40, no. 4 (2006): 667–677.

97. Kevin R. C. Gutzman, *Virginia's American Revolution: From Dominion to Republic, 1776–1840* (Lanham, MD: Lexington Books, 2007), 27 (quotations from the Declaration of Rights), 28 ("did not fall").

98. For a discussion of the *Hudgins* case, see Cover, *Justice Accused*, 50–55. Cover also discusses similar cases, with different outcomes, in states like Massachusetts. After Wythe's death, the *Hudgins* case was appealed; Wythe's racial line of reasoning was affirmed, but the court overturned his natural rights presumption.

99. This would not be the only time Jefferson collaborated with religious organizations to formulate an important bill. According to the early Baptist historian Robert Howell, in 1777 Jefferson and James Madison met with leading Baptists regarding their petition for an act establishing religious freedom, and these conversations influenced Jefferson's draft of such a bill. See Robert B. Howell, *The Early Baptists of Virginia* (Philadelphia: Bible and Publication Society, 1857), 164–165, 167–168. For Jefferson's version, see "A Bill for Establishing Religious Freedom, 18 June 1779," in *The Papers of Thomas Jefferson*, ed. Julian P. Boyd (Princeton, NJ: Princeton University Press, 1950), 2:545–547.

100. Quotations from TJ to Edward Coles, 25 Aug. 1814. See also Malone, *Jefferson the Virginian*, 1:134; Richard K. MacMaster, "Arthur Lee's 'Address on Slavery': An Aspect of Virginia's Struggle to End the Slave Trade, 1765–1774," *Virginia Magazine of History and Biography* 80, no. 2 (Apr. 1972): 149; TJ, *Autobiography of Thomas Jefferson*, ed. Ford, 7. The bill is not reported in the Burgesses' records, but they frequently did not report bills that failed to pass.

101. TJ, *Autobiography*, 7. For amelioration of slavery, see Christa Dierksheide, *Amelioration and Empire* (Charlottesville: University of Virginia Press, 2014).

102. Both motives most likely existed among Virginian elites: George Mason, a known opponent of slavery, wrote in support of a revolutionary ban on slave imports by stating that "we take this opportunity of declaring our most earnest wishes to see an entire stop forever put to such a wicked, cruel, and unnatural trade" (*Virginia Gazette*, 4 Aug. 1776).

103. TJ, *A Summary View of the Rights of British America: Set Forth in Some Resolutions Intended for the Inspection of the Present Delegates of the People of Virginia, Now in Convention* (Williamsburg, VA: Clementina Rind, 1774).

104. TJ, "'Jefferson's Original Rough Draught' of the Declaration of Independence," ed. Boyd, *Papers* 1:426.

105. Peter Onuf agrees with more critical scholars that Jefferson's language was overheated but points out that "Jefferson's rhetoric accurately registered his own complicated sense of the dilemmas that independence would both resolve and precipitate. For Jefferson was not only declaring a state of war between the British and American nations, he was also acknowledging the nationhood of enslaved Africans and the legitimacy of their claims to freedom and independence." See Onuf, "To Declare Them a Free and Equal People," 12. See also Ari Helo, *Thomas Jefferson's Ethics and the Politics of Human Progress: The Morality of a Slaveholder* (New York: Cambridge University Press, 2014), 160.

106. TJ, *Autobiography*, ed. Ford, 33.

107. For the "captive nation" argument, see Onuf and Helo, "Jefferson, Morality, and the Problem of Slavery"; for the equality of all men, see Danielle Allen, *Our Declaration: A Reading of the Declaration of Independence* (New York: W.W. Norton & Co., 2014), 153–155.

108. Both quotations are from Annette Gordon-Reed, "Thomas Jefferson and St. George Tucker: The Makings of Revolutionary Slaveholders," in *Jefferson, Lincoln, and Wilson: The American Dilemma of Race and Democracy*, ed. John Milton Cooper Jr. and Thomas J. Knock (Charlottesville: University of Virginia Press, 2010), 24.

109. TJ, *Autobiography*, 60–61.

110. See editorial note, *Papers*, "Bill to Prevent the Importation of Slaves &c.," 16 June 1777. For these examples of Jefferson's faulty memory, see his *Autobiography*, 6.

111. William Hening, *The Statutes at Large; Being a Collection of All the Laws of Virginia, from the First Session of the Legislature, in the Year 1619*, 13 vols. (Richmond: Samuel Pleasants, 1809–1823), 9:471–472; cited in Wolf, *Race and Liberty*, 25–26. It should be noted, however, that there were exceptions made to the nonimportation clauses.

112. Mason, *Slavery and Politics in the Early American Republic* (Chapel Hill: University of North Carolina Press, 2008), 28; see also Beverly C. Tomek, *Colonization and Its Discontents: Emancipation, Emigration, and Antislavery in Antebellum Pennsylvania* (New York: New York Press, 2012), 22–23.

113. Wolf, *Race and Liberty*, 27. For historians who believe banning the trade was an act of economic self-interest, see, for instance, Duncan MacLeod, *Slavery, Race and the American Revolution* (London and New York: Cambridge University Press, 1975), 38–40; John Chester Miller, *The Wolf by the Ears: Thomas Jefferson and Slavery* (New York: Free Press, 1977), 9; Woody Holton,

Forced Founders: Indians, Debtors, Slaves, and the Making of the American Revolution in Virginia (Chapel Hill: University of North Carolina Press, 1999), 66–72; Taylor, *Internal Enemy*, 37.

114. TJ, *Notes on the State of Virginia*, ed. Shuffelton, 94.

115. Onuf, "Thomas Jefferson and American Democracy," in Boles and Hall, eds., *Seeing Jefferson Anew*, 20.

116. Kevin Gutzman, *Thomas Jefferson, Revolutionary: A Radical's Struggle to Remake America* (New York: St. Martin's Press, 2017).

117. According to Jefferson's calculations, in 1782 there were approximately 296,852 free inhabitants in Virginia and 270,762 slaves. See *Notes on the State of Virginia*, ed. Shuffelton, 94.

118. Tomek, *Colonization*, 7.

119. McDonald, *Confounding Father: Thomas Jefferson's Image in His Own Time* (Charlottesville: University of Virginia Press, 2016), 136.

120. James Sullivan to Dr. Jeremy Belknap, 30 July 1795; Edwards quotation from Jordan, *White Over Black*, 545; both quoted in McDonald, *Confounding Father*, 136.

121. Quoted in Nicholas Guyatt, *Bind Us Apart: How Enlightened Americans Invented Racial Segregation* (New York: Basic Books, 2016), 210. See also Tomek, *Colonization*, 36–37; for a full history of early French, British, and American colonization plans, see Guyatt, *Bind Us Apart*, 197–224. In Massachusetts in 1787, seventy-five free black men also petitioned for state assistance to move to Africa, where they hoped to "be more comfortable" and to spread Christianity; see Matthew Spooner, "'I Know This Scheme is from God': Toward a Reconsideration of the Origins of the American Colonization Society," *Slavery & Abolition* 35, no. 4 (2014): 559–575, quotation at 562.

122. *Notes on the State of Virginia*, ed. Shuffelton, 91.

123. *Notes*, ed. Shuffelton, 91.

124. TJ, *Autobiography*, 66–67.

125. The committee was put together in November 1776, first met in January 1777, and submitted its report to the Assembly in June 1779, after Jefferson had been elected governor. See Peterson, *Thomas Jefferson*, 97–157. Quotation from TJ to George Wythe, 1 Nov. 1778.

126. TJ, *Notes*, 135. There is no manuscript extant for the Report of the Committee of Revisers, which has caused Paul Finkelman and others to doubt that such legislation ever existed. Finkelman suggests that Jefferson made up the amendment when he wrote extensively about it in the *Notes* or that there *was* an emancipation proposal, but it was composed by other, unnamed

"legislators" who "approached Jefferson with draft legislation that would have brought gradual emancipation to Virginia," and then Jefferson "declined to add it to the proposed revisions." See Finkelman, *Slavery and the Founders* (New York: M. E. Sharp, 1996), 120. However, since Jefferson, Wythe, and (to a lesser extent) Edmund Pendleton were the only three people working on revising the laws at this point, exactly who the "legislators" that approached Jefferson could have been is unclear, and Finkelman does not provide any evidence for this claim. Moreover, if Finkelman is correct, it would have been odd for Jefferson to write about the amendment openly in *Notes*, in his letter to the French encyclopedist Jean Nicolas Démeunier in June 1786, and again years later in his autobiography. He not only named Wythe as its coauthor; he indicated also that several other members of the Assembly supported it. One such supporter, James Madison, was actively working to pass Jefferson's bills after he left for France. In a letter to George Washington on 11 Nov. 1785 (*National Archives*, http://founders.archives.gov), Madison first informed Washington that "the Revised Code proposed by Mr Jefferson Mr Pendleton & Mr Wythe" was under consideration by the legislature and then reported that "[t]he pulse of the H. of D. was felt on thursday with regard to a general manumission by a petition presented on that subject. It was rejected without dissent." Although Madison does not mention Jefferson and Wythe's emancipation amendment, his discussion of the Revised Code in conjunction with the legislature's hostility to a general manumission lends credibility to Jefferson's story. Moreover, Madison and Wythe could easily have contradicted Jefferson if he was falsely taking credit for the existence of an antislavery amendment; lying about its existence may even have harmed the reputation of Wythe, a known opponent of slavery and one of the most respected men in Virginia. The only obvious reason to doubt Jefferson's story is the lack of a manuscript version of the amendment. But since we do not have copies of several of the committee's bills, one could argue that we should doubt their existence as well. (See the editorial note under the heading "Revisal of the Laws, 1776–1786," in the *Papers of Thomas Jefferson*, 2:305–324, esp. 308. For another missing bill, see Madison to TJ, 19 June 1786, and editorial note to "A Bill Concerning Public Roads," *Papers* 2:453.) I therefore take the position that there *was* such an amendment and, further, that Jefferson's summary of it in Query XIV of his *Notes* is likely accurate.

127. TJ, *Autobiography*, ed. Ford, 77.

128. Onuf, "Thomas Jefferson and American Democracy," in Boles and Hall, eds., *Seeing Jefferson Anew*, 24. See also Helo, *Thomas Jefferson's Ethics*.

129. TJ to Wythe, 13 Aug. 1786.

130. TJ to Wythe, 13 Aug. 1786.

131. "A Bill for the More General Diffusion of Knowledge," in *Papers*, ed. Oberg and Looney.

132. TJ to James Madison, 20 Dec. 1787.

133. TJ, *Autobiography*, 78; see Hunter, "The Teaching of George Wythe."

134. TJ to James Madison, 26 July 1780.

135. Walker Maury to TJ, 20 April 1784.

136. John Brown to William Preston, 6 July 1780, printed in "Glimpses of Old College Life," *William and Mary Quarterly* ser. 1, vol. 9, no. 2 (Oct. 1900): 79–80.

CHAPTER TWO. WRITING *NOTES ON THE STATE OF VIRGINIA*

1. I am aware of two brief efforts in addition to Jefferson's: John Sullivan of New Hampshire replied to Marbois on 10 Dec. 1780 (printed in Otis G. Hammond, ed., *Letters and Papers of Major-General John Sullivan, Continental Army*, 3 vols. [Concord: New Hampshire Historical Society, 1930–1931], 3:229–239); John Witherspoon of New Jersey began a response that was posthumously published in his *Works*, rev. ed. (Philadelphia: Printed and published by William W. Woodward, 1802), 4:403–412. See Boyd's editorial note in *Papers* 4:167. Virginia congressman Joseph Jones returned to Virginia from Congress in September 1780 and was most likely in Richmond by October, when the General Assembly convened; this is therefore the approximate date by which Jefferson received the queries. Portions of this chapter were previously published as "Jefferson's Changing Audiences: A Reevaluation of *Notes on the State of Virginia*," *Journal of Southern History* 87, no. 2 (May 2021): 171–208.

2. For instance, many scholars erroneously date the *Notes*, relying on its author's preface or on the first London printing date (1787), not realizing that Jefferson first printed his work in 1785, or that a semiauthorized French edition predated the English version.

3. Thomas Jefferson (hereafter "TJ"), *Notes on the State of Virginia* (London: Stockdale, 1787), iv.

4. I am indebted to Douglas L. Wilson for his seminal articles: "The Evolution of Jefferson's *Notes on the State of Virginia*," *Virginia Magazine of History and Biography* 112, no. 2 (2004): 98–133; and "Jefferson Unbound," *Historic Preservation* 53, no. 6 (2001): 48–53. These articles document Wilson's discoveries as he observed archivists at the Massachusetts Historical Society carefully

taking apart the manuscript for the first time. The society has since then made a digital version of the manuscript available for interactive viewing on their website, and that manuscript forms the basis for my analysis in this chapter.

5. TJ to Tench Coxe, 1 June 1795.

6. The theory of New World degeneracy was first posited by George Louis Leclerc, Comte de Buffon, in the 1761 volume of his encyclopedic *Histoire Naturelle, générale et particulière, avec la description du Cabinet du Roy* (1749–1788, 36 vols.). Philosophers from Cornelius de Pauw to the Abbé Raynal also espoused versions of this theory, even adding to it by positing that Europeans who migrated to the Americas would quickly degenerate as well. See Lee Alan Dugatkin, *Mr. Jefferson and the Giant Moose: Natural History in Early America* (Chicago: Chicago University Press, 2009).

7. "Marbois' Queries concerning Virginia [before 30 Nov. 1780]," manuscript written by Joseph Jones, in *The Papers of Thomas Jefferson*, ed. Julian P. Boyd (Princeton, NJ: Princeton University Press, 1951), 4:166–167.

8. TJ, *Autobiography of Thomas Jefferson, 1743–1790: Together with a Summary of the Chief Events in Jefferson's Life*, ed. Paul Leicester Ford (Philadelphia: University of Pennsylvania Press, 2005), 94.

9. TJ to D'Anmours, 30 Nov. 1780. When Jefferson referred to his "country," he frequently meant Virginia.

10. Lafayette to Washington, 8 Sep. 1781, in

11. TJ to Abner Nash, 16 Jan. 1781. See chapter 4, "War Governor," in Merrill D. Peterson, *Thomas Jefferson and the New Nation: A Biography* (New York: Oxford University Press, 1970), esp. 189, 192, 207.

12. TJ, "Diary of Arnold's Invasion and Notes on Subsequent Events in 1781: Versions of 1796[?], 1805, and 1816," in *Papers*, ed. Boyd, 4:258–266; see also Peterson, *Thomas Jefferson and the New Nation*, 206–209.

13. TJ to Marbois, 4 March 1781; for TJ's intention to retire, see John Page to TJ, 22 Sep. and 20 Oct. 1780, and TJ to Timothy Matlack, 18 April 1781.

14. See Boyd's editorial note, *Papers* (1952), 6:78–79.

15. TJ to William Gordon, 16 July 1788.

16. TJ to William Gordon, 16 July 1788.

17. For Jefferson's money troubles in 1782, see TJ to Benjamin Harrison, 7 Aug. 1782.

18. Lord Dunmore, cited in Alan Taylor, *The Internal Enemy: Slavery and War in Virginia, 1772–1832* (New York and London: W. W. Norton & Co., 2013), 23; Taylor's discussion of the Dunmore Proclamation continues on 23–27.

19. TJ to William Gordon, 16 July 1788; Lucia Stanton, *"Those Who Labor*

for My Happiness": Slavery at Thomas Jefferson's Monticello (Charlottesville: University of Virginia Press, 2012), 132.

20. The preceding discussion is drawn from Taylor, *The Internal Enemy*, 27–30; see also Cassandra Pybus, *Epic Journeys of Freedom: Runaway Slaves of the American Revolution and Their Global Quest for Liberty* (Boston: Beacon Press, 2007).

21. TJ, *Notes on the State of Virginia*, ed. William Peden (Chapel Hill: University of North Carolina Press, 1955), 162.

22. TJ to Isaac Zane, 24 Dec. 1781.

23. Peterson, *Thomas Jefferson and the New Nation*, 236, 237. For the accusations against TJ, see John Beckley to TJ, 12 June 1781; Archibald Cary to TJ, 19 June 1781; TJ to George Nicholas, 28 July 1781; George Nicholas to TJ, 31 July 1781. Patrick Henry was thought by Jefferson's friends to be behind both of Nicholas's actions; see Edmund Randolph, "Essay on the Revolutionary History of Virginia," *Virginia Magazine of History and Biography* 44, no. 1 (1936), 321. For a defense of Jefferson's gubernatorial performance, see John B. Boles, *Jefferson: Architect of American Liberty* (New York: Basic Books, 2017), 90–103.

24. TJ to Lafayette, 4 Aug. 1781. See also TJ's accounting entry for 30 June 1781: "Pd Dr. Brown 2. visits," in *Jefferson's Memorandum Books: Accounts, with Legal Records and Miscellany, 1767–1826*, ed. James A. Bear Jr. and Lucia C. Stanton, 2 vols. (Princeton, NJ: Princeton University Press, 1997), 1:511.

25. Jefferson first met Lafayette, whom General Washington had sent to Virginia at the head of a small army to aid the beleaguered state, on 19 April 1781.

26. TJ to Thomas McKean, 4 Aug. 1781.

27. TJ to Lafayette, 4 Aug. 1781.

28. TJ to Giovanni Fabbroni, 23 May 1785. TJ gave a similar account in a letter to his future son-in-law Thomas Mann Randolph: "In the year 1781. while confined to my room by a fall from my horse, I wrote some Notes in answer to the enquiries of M. de Marbois . . . they were hasty and indigested: yet as some of these touch slightly on some objects of [Virginia's] natural history, I will take the liberty of asking the [Edinburgh Natural History Society] to accept a copy of them" (TJ to Thomas Mann Randolph, 6 July 1787).

29. TJ to Marbois, 24 March 1782.

30. "Resolution of Thanks to Jefferson by the Virginia General Assembly, 12–19 December 1781," in *The Papers of Thomas Jefferson*, ed. Julian P. Boyd (Princeton, NJ: Princeton University Press, 1952), 6:135–137. See also Peterson, *Thomas Jefferson and the New Nation*, 237–239.

31. TJ to Abigail Adams, 25 Sep. 1785.

32. See editorial note for "Resolution of Thanks," in *Papers*, ed. Boyd, 6:135–137.

33. See John Tyler to TJ, 16 May 1782. Jefferson's personal life was another reason he needed to decline this election; his wife lay gravely ill after the birth of their daughter Lucy on 8 May, while his widowed sister Martha Carr and her six children had recently come to live at Monticello.

34. TJ to James Monroe, 20 May 1782.

35. TJ to Chastellux, 16 Jan. 1784. See Wilson, "Evolution of Jefferson's *Notes*," 118.

36. TJ to Marbois, 20 Dec. 1781.

37. Many of his memoranda and papers had been sent across the mountains to Augusta County for safekeeping, and he had to make do with a limited supply at Monticello. See TJ to Madison, 24 March 1782. The information he had hoped to find in Richmond that December was not all available either. For instance, he wanted to ask Isaac Zane, a merchant and fellow member of the General Assembly, for "much information" regarding the "quries mathematical, meteorological, geographical, physiological &c. &c." that "a gentleman of science" had posed, but Zane was sick and did not attend the December session. TJ to Isaac Zane, 24 Dec. 1781.

38. Marbois to TJ, 22 April 1782. This translation of Marbois's French letter was undertaken by Lucia Stanton and Derry E. Voysey and is cited by Wilson in footnote 6 of his "Evolution of Jefferson's *Notes*."

39. "About," *American Philosophical Society*,www.amphilsoc.org/about; Bette W. Oliver, *Jacques Pierre Brissot in America and France, 1788–1793: In Search of Better Worlds* (Lanham, MD: Rowman & Littlefield, 2016), 6.

40. TJ to Thomson, 20 Dec. 1781.

41. Thomson to TJ, 9 March 1782.

42. Peterson, *Thomas Jefferson and the New Nation*, 249.

43. Mary Goodwin, "The College of William and Mary," Colonial Williamsburg Foundation Library Research Report Series 210 (1990), http://research.history.org/DigitalLibrary/View/index.cfm?doc=ResearchReports%5CRR0210. xml#p32. Interestingly, Jefferson received a similar honorary doctorate from his alma mater that December (Goodwin, "The College of William and Mary"). The college may have been especially pleased to honor Chastellux in this way, since during the Revolution it was he who helped George Wythe regain the use of the buildings after they had been transformed into a military hospital. See Wythe to TJ, 31 Dec. 1781.

44. Marquis de Chastellux, *Travels in North America in the Years 1780, 1781*

and 1782, trans. and ed. Howard C. Rice, Jr., 2 vols. (Chapel Hill: University of North Carolina Press, 1963), 2:392, cited in Kevin J. Hayes, *The Road to Monticello: The Life and Mind of Thomas Jefferson* (New York: Oxford University Press, 2008), 249.

45. Although Lucy Elizabeth was the fifth daughter to be born, only two of her older siblings were alive at the time; the Jeffersons had lost Jane (1774–1775), an unnamed son (1777), and another Lucy Elizabeth (1780–1781) before the second Lucy Elizabeth's birth in May 1782. Only two of Thomas and Martha's children survived into adulthood.

46. François Jean De Beauvoir, Marquis de Chastellux, *Travels in North America in the Years 1780, 1781, and 1782*, trans. and ed. Howard C. Rice, Jr., 2 vols. (Chapel Hill: University of North Carolina Press, 1963), cited in Peterson, *Thomas Jefferson and the New Nation*, 245. For TJ's description of the Natural Bridge, see *Notes*, ed. Frank Shuffelton (New York: Penguin Group, 1999), 26.

47. In his account of his travels, Chastellux also claimed that deforestation was responsible for sea breezes being felt further inland than previously; Jefferson may have discussed this with Chastellux in 1782, because on a "fair copy" manuscript page (written before Oct. 1783) he also stated that these breezes "formerly did not penetrate far above Williamsburg. They are now frequent at Richmond, and every now and then reach the mountains. . . . As the lands become cleared, it is probable they will extend still further westward." See Chastellux, *Travels*, 2:395–396, cited by Keith Thomson, *Jefferson's Shadow: The Story of His Science* (New Haven, CT: Yale University Press, 2012), 191; TJ, *Notes*, ed. Shuffelton, 83–84.

48. TJ to Walker, 25 Sep. 1783.

49. See Wilson, "Evolution of Jefferson's *Notes*," 113.

50. Chastellux to TJ, 10 June and 30 June 1782.

51. Lucy would pass away in 1784.

52. Peterson, *Thomas Jefferson and the New Nation*, 246.

53. Kimball, *Jefferson: War and Peace*, 307.

54. James Madison, *The Debates on the Adoption of the Federal Constitution in the Convention Held at Philadelphia in 1787*, vol. 5 (Philadelphia, 1836), cited in Kimball, *Jefferson: War and Peace*, 307.

55. TJ to Chastellux, 26 Nov. 1782.

56. See Wilson, "Evolution of Jefferson's *Notes*," 132, n. 43.

57. Unlike a "fair copy draft," a preliminary "composition draft" can be identified by its frequent changes on the sentence level: it is written as the author composes, and it therefore evidences the author's evolving thought process. Jefferson's "fair copy" manuscript can be dated to the summer of 1783

for several reasons, such as the inclusion of an anecdote sent to Jefferson on 29 November 1782, and the fact that Jefferson used paper with the same watermark for the first twenty-two pages of the manuscript and for a letter sent to Madison in June. For more on this, see Wilson, "Evolution of Jefferson's *Notes*," 111.

58. These figures are drawn from the chart of page numbers and additions complied by Wilson and explained on pages 126–128 of his article "Evolution of Jefferson's *Notes*."

59. Wilson, "Jefferson Unbound," *Historic Preservation* 53, no. 6 (2001): 51.

60. See, for instance, TJ to Dr. Thomas Walker, 25 Sep. 1783; Bear and Stanton, eds., *Jefferson's Memorandum Books*, 1: 536. Wilson discusses some of this correspondence in "Evolution of Jefferson's *Notes*," 111, 113; Walker's notes are retained among Jefferson's "loose papers" of research in the Massachusetts Historical Society's collection of *Notes*-related documents. Jefferson also sought Archibald Cary's expertise about animal sizes; see Cary to TJ, 12 Oct. 1783. For his departure date, see TJ to Francis Eppes, 10 Nov. 1783.

61. TJ to Charles Thomson, 4 May 1784; see also Hayes, *Road to Monticello*, 264–265.

62. TJ to Chastellux, 16 Jan. 1784. Jefferson may have given Chastellux a handwritten copy at that time or just shown him Jefferson's own copy—their correspondence does not make this clear.

63. TJ to Thomson, 21 May 1784.

64. TJ to Madison, 25 May 1784.

65. See TJ to Zane, 8 Nov. 1783; TJ to Zane, 17 March 1784; Zane to TJ, 2 July 1784. For the temperature readings, see TJ, *Notes*, ed. Shuffelton, 25. William Short transmitted Zane's information to Paris; see Madison to TJ, 3 July 1784.

66. For his brilliance see TJ to George Washington, 6 April 1784; for effusiveness, see G. K. van Hogendorp to TJ, ca. 6 April 1784.

67. Published in *Brieven en Gedenkschriften van Gijsbert Karel van Hogendorp* (The Hague: Nijhoff, 1866–1903), 1:346–347. See translation in editorial note to G. K. van Hogendorp to TJ, ca. 6 April 1784.

68. TJ to G. K. van Hogendorp, 13 Oct. 1785.

69. On 26 March Dr. Thomas Bond died; since Thomson refers to him in the past tense—"the late Doct Bond"—in his commentary, we know that Thomson must have written after that date. See Wilson, "The Evolution of Jefferson's *Notes*," 132, n. 59.

70. Though Jefferson did not name the committee members, their identities were becoming common knowledge. For example, in 1786 Jean-Nicholas

Démeunier wrote an article on America for the massive ongoing work, *Ency-clopedie methodique*, in which he actually overstated Jefferson's leadership role in making the passing of this antislavery legislation possible, and Jefferson had to correct him. See TJ to Jean Nicolas Démeunier, 26 June 1786.

71. These quotations and the ones following that refer to Jefferson's manu-script can be viewed in their original state on the website of the Massachusetts Historical Society.

72. TJ, *Autobiography*, ed. Ford, 77. For my discussion of this bill, see chap-ter 1 in this book.

73. The historian who first set forth this argument is Paul Finkelman in *Slavery and the Founders: Race and Liberty in the Age of Jefferson* (New York: M. E. Sharpe, 1996), 120, and "Jefferson and Slavery: 'Treason Against the Hopes of the World,'" in *Jeffersonian Legacies*, ed. Peter S. Onuf (Charlottesville: Uni-versity of Virginia Press, 1993), 196. For my full response, see chapter 1.

74. Arthur Scherr, "Thomas Jefferson, White Immigration, and Black Emancipation," *Southern Studies: An Interdisciplinary Journal of the South*, 23 no. 1 (2016): 1–26. See also Robert Pleasants to TJ, 1 June 1796. On that date Pleasants sent Jefferson a plan he had crafted for educating black children, apparently including the children of slaves. Pleasants believed education for enslaved children was both a duty and a practical step toward readying that population for the freedom that "at this enlightened day is generally acknowl-edged to be their right." Jefferson replied on 27 August that he not only sup-ported Pleasants's plan but that he had himself written a "Bill for the More General Diffusion of Knowledge" in 1778 that would provide free public edu-cation for all children—presumably including free black children—and with "very small alterations" could also provide the same to the children of slaves who were "destined to be free." If Pleasants would organize petitions that sup-ported Jefferson's bill, then Jefferson felt sure there already existed enough public support for the bill to succeed in the Assembly. Pleasants subsequently searched for Jefferson's bill but could not find it either in print or in the records of any other legislators. He then discovered the legislature had just passed a different bill that provided for the education of free children; however, as he told Jefferson on 8 February 1797, prejudice would likely ensure that only *white* free children benefited from the measure. In the end, the 1796 bill did little to improve the education levels of either white or black Virginians since it failed to incorporate Jefferson's provision that the state—not localities—oversee the effort.

75. TJ, *Notes*, ed. Shuffelton, 144–145.

76. See chapter 1; Beverly C. Tomek, *Colonization and Its Discontents: Emancipation, Emigration, and Antislavery in Antebellum Pennsylvania* (New York: New York Press, 2012), 36–37.

77. See Nicholas Guyatt, *Bind Us Apart: How Enlightened Americans Invented Racial Segregation* (New York: Basic Books, 2016).

78. Peter S. Onuf, *Jefferson's Empire: The Language of American Nationhood* (Charlottesville: University Press of Virginia, 2001), 148, 149 (last quotation only).

79. TJ, *Notes*, ed. Shuffelton, 145.

80. TJ, *Notes*, ed. Shuffelton, 145.

81. TJ, *Notes*, ed. Shuffelton, 150, 151 (last quotation).

82. "Commentary about Jefferson's draft of Notes on the State of Virginia, by Charles Thomson, late March or April 1784," in Coolidge Collection of Thomas Jefferson Manuscripts, www.masshist.org. Emphasis added.

83. In *Race and Liberty*, Wolf puts the number of free black people in Virginia in 1781 at around 5,500 (45, n.7); for the number of white slaveholding families, see 6, n.6.

84. The first part of Lee's address was printed in Rind's *Virginia Gazette* on 19 March 1767. Although there are no extant copies, the handwritten manuscript is at the College of William and Mary and was reprinted by Richard K. MacMaster, "Arthur Lee's 'Address on Slavery': An Aspect of Virginia's Struggle to End the Slave Trade, 1765–1774," *Virginia Magazine of History and Biography* 80, no. 2 (April, 1972), 153–157.

85. Arthur Lee, *An Essay in Vindication of the Continental Colonies of America* . . . (London, 1764), 42, 31.

86. Anonymous author, *Virginia Gazette* (Williamsburg, VA: Purdie & Dixon), 2 Dec. 1773, quoted in Wolf, *Race and Liberty*, 17.

87. This newspaper exchange is described fully in Wolf, *Race and Liberty*, 17–21, referring to debate in the Richmond *Virginia Gazette, or Weekly Advertiser* (changed in February 1782 to *The Virginia Gazette, and the Weekly Advertiser*), printed variously by Dixon, Nicolson, and Prentis. For more on the complicated history of the several *Virginia Gazette* iterations over the years, see http://www.vagazette.com/about/va-history-front-htmlstory.html #dorm.

88. "A Friend to Liberty," *The Virginia Gazette, and the Weekly Advertiser*, 25 May 1782; *"Am I Not a Man and a Brother": The Antislavery Crusade of Revolutionary America, 1688–1788*, ed. Roger Bruns (New York: Chelsea House, 1977).

89. TJ, *Autobiography*, ed. Ford, 7.

90. Warner Mifflin, *Defence of Warner Mifflin against Aspersions* . . .

(Philadelphia: Sansom, 1796), cited in Wolf, *Race and Liberty*, 34. See also Quakers' petition, 29 May 1782, Legislative Petitions, House of Delegates, Archives Division, Library of Virginia. For the manumission law, see William Hening, *The Statutes at Large; Being a Collection of all the Laws of Virginia from the First Session of the Legislature, in the 1619*, 13 vols. (Richmond, VA: Samuel Pleasants, 1809–23), 2:39–41. Wolf argues that by 1800 "manumission coexisted with slavery and even worked to support rather than to weaken slavery's stability"; and by 1806 the window for unrestricted manumission closed. Wolf's argument challenges the more optimistic accounts of scholars such as Gary Nash and Ira Berlin. See Wolf, *Race and Liberty*, 39; for manumitters' religious commitments, see 55, 59. For the harsh reactions toward individuals who did choose to emancipate their slaves, including violence and legal action, see Taylor, *Internal Enemy*, 38.

91. See John C. Calhoun, "Slavery a Positive Good" (speech before the United States Senate, 6 Feb. 1837), available online at http://teachingamericanhistory .org/library/document/slavery-a-positive-good. Wolf notes that historians have generally believed Americans in the Revolutionary era thought about race "in terms of environmentalism" (17) and that the "positive good" theses of slavery did not develop until the antebellum period; however, these newspaper accounts clearly indicate that "defenders of slavery dehumanized Africans" (17), expressed "coherent proslavery defenses" (18), and argued that slavery benefitted their republic (20). In addition, South Carolina's Rawlin Lowndes made similar "positive good" arguments during the constitutional ratification debates; see M. E. Bradford, "Preserving the Birthright: The Intention of South Carolina in Adopting the U.S. Constitution," *South Carolina Historical Magazine*, 89, no. 2 (1988): 90–101, esp. 94.

92. *The Virginia Gazette, and the Weekly Advertiser*, 31 Aug. 1782.

93. *The Virginia Gazette, and the Weekly Advertiser*, 14 Sep. 1782. See Wolf, *Race and Liberty*, 21.

94. For TJ's longtime commitment to collecting as many newspapers as he could, see Hayes, *Road to Monticello*, 202. Jefferson first subscribed to this particular newspaper in June 1780; see *Jefferson's Memorandum Books*, 498. For his fortnight in Richmond, see TJ to Madison, 7 May 1783.

95. Andrew S. Curran, *The Anatomy of Blackness: Science and Slavery in an Age of Enlightenment* (Baltimore, MD: Johns Hopkins University Press, 2011), 1. The first argument that "blackness" resided not in the skin but in bodily fluids occurred in 1741 (Curran, 2).

96. The *Encyclopédie ou Dictionnaire raisonné des sciences, des arts et des métiers, par une Société de Gens de lettres* (17 vols.), published in Paris

under the direction of Diderot and d'Alembert between 1751 and 1772, must not be confused with its successor, the *Encyclopédie méthodique par ordre des matières* (Methodical encyclopedia by order of subject matter) that was published (in varying amounts of volumes) from 1782 to 1832 by Charles Joseph Panckoucke. Jefferson used the Diderot version to write his *Notes*. While living in Paris, Jefferson subscribed to the follow-up, the *Encyclopédie méthodique*. He also bought his own edition of the Diderot *Encyclopédie* to replace the one owned by the Virginia government, as well as contributing to the *Encyclopédie méthodique* himself as an adviser (see, for example, his "Answers to Démeunier's First Queries," 24 Jan. 1786, and the editorial note in *Papers*, 10:11–20). The University of Chicago is digitizing the Diderot *Encyclopédie*: https://encyclopedie.uchicago.edu. I am very grateful to Endrina Tay of the Jefferson Library for her expertise on this topic.

97. TJ to D'Anmours, 30 Nov. 1780.

98. *The Virginia Gazette*, 9 Dec. 1780, cited in editorial note to *Papers*, "From Amable and Alexander Lory," 16 Dec. 1780. See also Robert Darnton, *The Business of Enlightenment: A Publishing History of the Encyclopédie, 1775–1800* (Cambridge, MA: Harvard University Press, 2009), 318; Sidney L. Jackson, "The *Encyclopédie Methodique*: A Jefferson Addendum," *Virginia Magazine of History and Biography* 73, no. 3 (1965): 303–311.

99. See editorial note for Reverend James Madison to TJ, 22 Jan. 1784.

100. Bruce Dain, *A Hideous Monster of the Mind: American Race Theory in the Early Republic* (Cambridge, MA: Harvard University Press, 2002), 7.

101. Dain, *A Hideous Monster*, 6 (quotation), 32. For one version of the argument that Jefferson caused a "turn" in racial thought, reversing the "rising status of Africans in the west," see Robert P. Forbes, "Secular Damnation: Thomas Jefferson and the Imperative of Race," 4, paper given at "Jeffersonian Democracy: From Theory to Practice" Conference, Princeton University, 17–19 May 2012, on file in Special Collections at the Thomas Jefferson Foundation; available online at http://www.academia.edu/1597821/Thomas_Jefferson_and_the_Imperative_of_Race.

102. James H. Sweet, "The Iberian Roots of American Racist Thought," *William and Mary Quarterly*, 3rd ser., vol. 54, no. 1 (Jan. 1997): 144, 149, 146, 151.

103. For more on the history of race and the senses, see Mark Smith, *How Race Is Made: Slavery, Segregation, and the Senses* (Chapel Hill: University of North Carolina Press, 2008).

104. Eleventh-century Toledo historian Sā'id al-Andalusi cited in Sweet, "The Iberian Roots of American Racist Thought," 146.

105. Sweet, "The Iberian Roots of American Racist Thought," 148. Sweet

notes that an even earlier Jewish version of the Ham narrative, from the fifth century Babylonian Talmud, did not make an explicit connection to Africans, but it did suggest "future racial imagery."

106. Curran, *Anatomy of Blackness*, 220, 221.

107. Curran, 221.

108. Curran, 182, 184. Several scholars have argued that Jefferson was more prejudiced than his peers, creating a virulent form of racism by refusing to move away from an obsession with color and black inferiority when other Enlightenment philosophers did. For example, Robert P. Forbes argues that Jefferson was uniquely unfair to Phyllis Wheatley, refusing to revise his opinion of black people's inferiority after reading her poetry when even Voltaire was willing to "backtrack from his own assertions of black inferiority" because of Wheatley's work. However, while I agree with Forbes that Jefferson treats Wheatley unfairly due to his own racism, it is less clear that Voltaire ever changed his own mind about black inferiority. He was willing to admit that Wheatley composed the poetry attributed to her, but that does not indicate a wholesale revision of his earlier views; in a similar manner, Jefferson was willing to concede that Ignatius Sancho could possibly have written works attributed to him, but that did not convince Jefferson to change his mind about the entire race. See Forbes, "Secular Damnation," 13, citing Edward Derbyshire Seeber, *Anti-Slavery Opinion in France during the Second Half of the Eighteenth Century* (Baltimore: Johns Hopkins Press, 1937), 57.

109. Curran, *Anatomy of Blackness*, 14, citing Voltaire, *Essai sur les moeurs et l'esprit des nations* (1756). Voltaire's most famous antislavery sentiment is expressed in his novel *Candide* (1759).

110. Louis de Jaucourt, "Esclavage," *Encyclopédie ou Dictionnaire raisonné des sciences, des arts et des métiers*, vol. 5 (Paris, 1755), 934–939. Most of Jaucourt's fellow authors tended toward "neutral" discussion of slavery (Curran, *Anatomy of Blackness*, 184). Interestingly, Curran points out that the *Encyclopédie* failed to discuss the "specific European know-how and equipment— such as leg irons, stowage plans, or ship conversion—that made the Middle Passage possible." Although articles about colonial agriculture mentioned African slaves at work, "corresponding articles such as Diderot's meticulous and lengthy treatment of the production of cotton gloss over the slave labor at the core of the manufacturing process" (Curran, *Anatomy of Blackness*, 184).

111. Jaucourt, cited in Curran, *Anatomy of Blackness*, 185; Diderot, cited in Curran, 186.

112. Curran, 180, 191; for the various positions of Enlightenment scholars on poly/monogenesis and slavery, see Curran, table 4.1 and 4.2, 191–192.

113. See, for instance, Query VI ("Productions Mineral, Vegetable, and Animal"). For members of the APS, see J. G. Rosengarten, "The Early French Members of the American Philosophical Society," *Proceedings of the American Philosophical Society* 46, no. 185 (1907): 87–93, esp. 87.

114. Raynal, *Histoire des deux Indes*, 4 vols. (Amsterdam, 1770), 4:121, cited in Curran, *Anatomy of Blackness*, 192 ("mistreated"), 193 ("more effeminate"), 194 ("a different species"); 198–199.

115. Cornelius de Pauw, *Recherches philosophiques sur les Américains* (1st ed. 1768), 1:179; cited in Curran, *Anatomy of Blackness*, 127; see also Curran, 193–198.

116. Guyatt, *Bind Us Apart*, 22.

117. De Pauw, cited in Curran, 127; TJ, *Notes*, ed. Peden, 138 (first and second quotations), 143.

118. As Michael P. Zuckert puts it: "The structure of Jefferson's thought is this: because of natural rights and natural equality, there must be emancipation; because of racial inequality and the legacy of slavery, there must be colonization." In the minds of some readers of the *Notes*, then and now, Jefferson's racial comments undermine his commitment to emancipation, but Zuckert argues that Jefferson "was seduced into" these comments "by his attraction to the natural history of his day." I would add that his personal prejudices also contributed. Zuckert, "Response," in Thomas S. Engeman, ed., *Thomas Jefferson and the Politics of Nature* (Notre Dame, IN: University of Notre Dame Press, 2000), 201.

119. See my discussion of this issue in chapter 1; see also Allen, *Our Declaration*, 153–155.

120. TJ to Henri Gregoire Washington, 25 Feb. 1809; polygraph copy in Library of Congress.

121. This deleted sentence can still be seen in TJ, *Notes*, manuscript, 85–86.

122. TJ, *Notes*, manuscript, tab on 86. In the aftermath of Gabriel's planned slave uprising in 1800, Jefferson would express similar sentiments regarding the accused rebels, suggesting that they were justified and did not deserve the death penalty.

123. TJ, *Notes*, manuscript, tab on 87.

124. TJ, *Notes*, ed. Peden, 138.

125. TJ, *Notes*, manuscript 98. It is interesting to note that, while governor, Jefferson applied similar logic to the case of an enslaved man named Billy who was accused of treason for joining the British forces during the Revolutionary War and condemned to hang. Two dissenting judges in the case appealed to Jefferson, arguing that a slave was not a citizen, had no reason for loyalty to the state, and therefore could not commit treason. Jefferson apparently agreed,

suspending the sentence, and the legislature pardoned Billy a few days later. See the entry for "Billy," by Phillip J. Schwartz, in John T. Kneebone et al., eds., *Dictionary of Virginia Biography, Volume 1: Aaroe-Blanchfield* (Richmond: Library of Virginia, 1998), 490–491.

126. TJ, *Notes*, manuscript 98. The great Enlightenment economist Adam Smith pessimistically pointed to the same cultural issue in a lecture he gave in February 1763: "[T]he love of domination and authority and the pleasure men take in having every thing done by their express orders, rather than to condescend to bargain and treat with those whom they look upon as their inferiors and are inclined to use in a haughty way; this love of domination and tyrannizing, I say, will make it impossible for the slaves in a free country ever to recover their liberty" (*Lectures on Jurisprudence*, R. L. Meek, D. D. Raphael, and P. G. Stein, eds. [Oxford: Clarendon Press, 1978], 186).

127. TJ, *Notes*, manuscript 98.

128. TJ, *Notes*, manuscript 98; *Virginia Gazette and Weekly Advertiser*, 31 Aug. 1782 ("the state of slavery") and 25 May 1782 ("divine retribution").

129. See, for instance, TJ to John Adams, 22 Jan. 1821, in *The Adams-Jefferson Letters*, ed. Lester J. Cappon (Chapel Hill: University of North Carolina Press, 1959), 2:570. By 1821 Jefferson's fears had been exemplified by the actions of former slaves in Haiti.

130. TJ to Thomson, 21 June 1785.

CHAPTER THREE. AUTHORS IN PARIS:
PRINTING THE *NOTES*

1. Quotation from Thomas Jefferson (hereafter "TJ") to C.W.F. Dumas, 2 Feb. 1786. For modesty among authors, see Manushag N. Powell, *Performing Authorship in Eighteenth-Century English Periodicals* (Lewisburg, PA: Bucknell University Press, 2012). Even some early recipients of the first, privately printed, edition of *Notes* were confused as to the authorship; see Joddrel to TJ, 28 Feb. 1787. Portions of this chapter were previously published: see Cara J. Rogers [Stevens], "The French Experiment: Thomas Jefferson and William Short Debate Slavery, 1785–1826," *American Political Thought* 10, no. 3 (2021): 327–362, https://doi.org/10.1086/715006.

2. TJ to Madison, 11 May 1785.

3. TJ to John Trumbull, 1 June 1789. It is interesting to note that Jefferson's only son with wife Martha tragically died as an infant in 1777, just as eighteen-year-old Short was becoming better acquainted with the Jefferson family.

4. Only one full-length study has been published about Short (hereafter

"WS"), and it has significant flaws in its documentation: George Shackelford's *Jefferson's Adoptive Son: The Life of William Short, 1759–1848* (Lexington: University Press of Kentucky, 1993). However, that book is based on Shackelford's 1955 dissertation, which is much more thorough and extensively footnoted ("William Short: Jefferson's Adopted Son, 1758–1849" [PhD diss., University of Virginia, 1955]). Shackelford also published a few articles that focused on different aspects of Short's life: "William Short: Diplomat in Revolutionary France, 1785–1793," *Proceedings of the American Philosophical Society* 102, no. 6 (1958): 596–612; and "To Practice Law: Aspects of the Era of Good Feelings Reflected in the Short-Ridgely Correspondences, 1816–1821," *Maryland Historical Magazine* 64, no. 4 (1969): 342–395. Other notable articles include: Marie Kimball, "William Short, Jefferson's Only 'Son,'" *North American Review* 223 (1926): 471–486; Blanche Allendena Garfield, "William Short and His Diplomatic Career from 1789–1792" (master's thesis, West Virginia University, 1931); Myrna Boyce, "The Diplomatic Career of William Short," *Journal of Modern History* 15 (1943): 97–119; Yvon Bizardel and Howard C. Rice, "Poor in Love Mr. Short," *William and Mary Quarterly* ser. 3, vol. 21, no. 4 (1964): 516–533; Lucille McWane Watson, "William Short, America's First Career Diplomat: Jefferson's 'Adopted Son' Took Paris by Storm," *William and Mary Alumni Gazette* 50, no. 1 (July/August 1982): 23–25. A recent fictional book includes an intriguing look at Short and his possible romance with Jefferson's daughter Martha: Stephanie Dray and Laura Croghan Kamoie, *America's First Daughter* (Waterville, ME: Thorndike Press, 2016).

5. Fredrika Teute Schmidt and Barbara Ripel Wilhelm, "Early Proslavery Petitions in Virginia," *William and Mary Quarterly*, ser. 3, vol. 30, no. 1 (1973): 133–146.

6. TJ to Price, 7 Aug. 1785.

7. TJ stood a striking (for the time) six-feet two-and-a-half inches tall, according to his grandson Thomas Jefferson Randolph, and had red hair; he was approximately six inches taller than the average American male of his period. See "Jefferson's Height," Monticello.org, www.monticello.org/site/research-and-collections/jeffersons-height.

8. Report of the Board of Commissioners for the University of Virginia to the Virginia General Assembly, [4 Aug.] 1818, Special Collections Department, University of Virginia Library.

9. Shackelford, "To Practice Law," 342.

10. For a brief introduction to the patronage culture of Virginia in the eighteenth century, see Fred Anderson, "George Washington's Mentors," in *Sons of*

the Father: George Washington and His Protégés, ed. Robert M. S. McDonald (Charlottesville: University of Virginia Press, 2013), 21–30.

11. Short's mother, Elizabeth Skipwith Short, had died in 1771; see Shackelford, "William Short," 20.

12. Jack Lynch, "'His Integrity Inflexible, and His Justice Exact': George Wythe Teaches America the Law," *Colonial Williamsburg Journal* (Spring 2010), www.history.org/Foundation/journal/ Spring10/educ.cfm; Shackelford, "William Short," 27; Bishop Madison to TJ [1773?] and editorial note for the same. For Madison as an antislavery force at William and Mary, see Terry L. Meyers, "Thinking About Slavery at the College of William and Mary," *William and Mary Bill of Rights Journal* 21, no. 4 (2013): 1238–1239. Madison was not yet a bishop when he began his long tenure at William and Mary, but I refer to him by that title in this chapter for the sake of clarity.

13. See TJ's Memorandum Book entry for July 1781, in "Memorandum Books, 1781," *Founders Online*, National Archives, https://founders.archives .gov/documents/Jefferson/02-01-02-0015.

14. Shackelford, "William Short," 48, 42. For Short passing the bar, see "Jefferson's Certification of William Short as an Attorney," 30 Sep. 1781.

15. Shackelford, "William Short," 52; "James Monroe," Monticello.com; for "partie quarreé," see TJ to Louis Girardin, 15 Jan. 1815, referring to the relationship between TJ, Wythe, Small, and Fauquier; for the length of TJ's hope, see, for instance, TJ to James Monroe, 11 May 1785.

16. Few records remain regarding this legal battle, but see, for example, TJ to WS, 27 Nov. 1782 and 18 March 1784. Unfortunately, Martha's estate would prove to be a greater burden than blessing to Jefferson and their descendants, because Jefferson became liable for his father-in-law's debts, which increased drastically due to the Revolution. See Herbert Sloan, *Principle and Interest: Thomas Jefferson and the Problem of Debt* (Charlottesville: University of Virginia Press, 2001), esp. ch. 1.

17. Peter's father Dabney Carr, who had been Jefferson's best friend, died in 1773, and his widow—Jefferson's sister—had moved to Monticello with her children shortly thereafter. Short continued in this role until leaving to join Jefferson in Europe in 1784, at which time Jefferson turned to James Madison, stating "I have nobody [left] but you to whose direction I could consign [Peter Carr] with unlimited confidence." See TJ to Martha J. Carr and WS, 19 Dec. 1783; TJ to WS, 1 March 1784; TJ to Madison, 8 May 1784.

18. WS to William Nelson, 17 Sep. 1789, Short Papers, Library of Congress (LOC); cited in Shackelford, "William Short," 61 n.27.

19. Cited in Shackelford, "William Short," 66; WS to Peyton Short, 3 Oct. 1783, Price Collection, College of William and Mary.

20. TJ to WS, 29 Dec. 1783. The Nottaways were a small tribe with only female members left alive, according to the *Notes*, and Short was apparently not able to find much information.

21. See WS to TJ, circa 10 March 1784; TJ to James Madison, 20 Feb. 1784; Shackelford, "William Short," 63.

22. WS to TJ, 14 May 1784.

23. WS to TJ, 28 July 1784; see also *Minutes of the Executive Council*, entries for 1 and 8 July 1784, cited in Shackelford, "William Short," 73.

24. Shackelford, "William Short," 76.

25. WS to TJ, 28 July 1784.

26. John B. Boles, *Jefferson: Architect of American Liberty* (New York: Basic Books, 2017), 120.

27. TJ, *Notes on the State of Virginia*, ed. Frank Shuffelton (New York: Penguin Books, 1999), 124, 128.

28. For more about the paper used in the manuscript, see Douglas Wilson, "The Evolution of Jefferson's *Notes on the State of Virginia*," *Virginia Magazine of History and Biography* 112, no. 2 (2004): 99–133.

29. "Jefferson's Draft of a Constitution for Virginia [May–June 1783]," in *Papers*, ed. Oberg and Looney, http://rotunda.upress.virginia.edu/founders. See also "Pennsylvania—An Act for the Gradual Abolition of Slavery, 1780," *Avalon Project*, Yale Law School, http://avalon.law.yale.edu/18th_century /pennst01.asp; and "AN ACT for the gradual abolition of slavery," *New York State Archives*, http://iarchives.nysed.gov/.

30. See TJ to Madison, 7 June 1783.

31. TJ to John Adams, 25 May 1785.

32. Paul Finkelman, *Slavery and the Founders: Race and Liberty in the Age of Jefferson* (New York: M. E. Sharpe, 1996), 257.

33. TJ to Edward Coles, 25 Aug. 1814.

34. William G. Merkel, "Jefferson's Failed Anti-Slavery Proviso of 1784 and the Nascence of Free Soil Constitutionalism," *Seton Hall Law Review* 38 (2008), 569, quote at 561. See also Peter Onuf, *Statehood and Union: History of the Northwest Ordinance* (Bloomington: Indiana University Press, 1987).

35. Jefferson wrote two drafts of this proposal for Congress: the *Report of the Committee* [on Government of the Western Territory] on 1 March and a revised version on 22 March 1784.

36. TJ, "Revised Report of the Committee, 22 March 1784," in *Papers*, ed. Boyd, 6:607.

37. TJ, "Jefferson's Observations on Démeunier's Manuscript," 22 June 1786. The delegate from New Jersey was not seated for the vote, and Merkel also notes that "even the single vote of a further Virginia or North Carolina delegate would have tipped either of those states in favor of enactment" (see Merkel, "Jefferson's Failed Anti-Slavery Proviso," 581).

38. Merkel, 562.

39. TJ to WS, 16 April 1784.

40. Shackelford, "William Short," 91–92. The commission as a whole was also allowed by Congress to have another secretary, Colonel David Humphreys, in order to keep up with the mountains of paperwork.

41. TJ to Madison, 7 May 1783.

42. TJ to WS, 16 April 1784; TJ to John Trumbull, 21 May 1789.

43. WS to TJ, 8 May 1784.

44. Shackelford, "William Short," 60.

45. WS to Peyton Short, 27 Sep. 1784, William and Peyton Short Papers, MSS 65Sh9, box 1, folder one, College of William and Mary, Williamsburg, Virginia. For Short's personal slave, see Nicholas Guyatt, *Bind Us Apart: How Enlightened Americans Invented Racial Segregation* (New York: Basic Books, 2016), 312.

46. WS to TJ, 8 May 1784; WS to TJ, 28 July 1784.

47. Shackelford, "William Short," 90.

48. For the "Belle," see Bizardel and Rice, "Poor in Love Mr. Short," 516–533; Bowdoin to WS, 11 April and 15 June 1785, Short Papers, LOC. For "good boy," see TJ to WS, 2 April 1785.

49. Shackelford, "William Short," 102–105. The best thing about this living situation must surely have been the flushing toilet.

50. Crèvecoeur to TJ, 15 July 1784.

51. Gordon Wood, *The Americanization of Benjamin Franklin* (New York: Penguin Press, 2004), 272.

52. For more on the Duchess and Short, see Kimball, "William Short." For the first manuscript reference to "Rosalie" [Alexandrine-Charlotte de Rohan-Chabot], duchesse de La Rochefoucauld d'Enville, see the Short–La Rochefoucauld Correspondence at the American Philosophical Society.

53. Quoted in Barker, 162.

54. WS to Nelson, 25 Oct. 1786.

55. For an introduction to the culture of the salons in this era, see Dena Goodman, *The Republic of Letters: A Cultural History of the French Enlightenment* (Ithaca: Cornell University Press, 1994).

56. Shackelford, "William Short," 124; Daniel P. Resnick, "The Société des

Amis des Noirs and the Abolition of Slavery," *French Historical Studies* 7, no. 4 (1972): 558–569.

57. Brissot to TJ, 8 March 1787.

58. "Circular to the States," 8 June 1783, in John C. Fitzpatrick, ed., *The Writings of George Washington from the Original Manuscript Sources, 1745–1799* (Washington, DC, 1938), 26: 483–495 (quotation at 26: 485).

59. TJ, *Notes*, cited in Keith Stewart Thomson, *Jefferson's Shadow: The Story of His Science* (New Haven, CT: Yale University Press, 2012), 114. Thomson remarks that, by the time Jefferson printed the *Notes* in Paris, Buffon had in fact done an about-face on several of his claims, although not those respecting animal sizes. Jefferson would have been aware of these changes, but he chose not to edit his criticism of Buffon in the *Notes*, either in 1785 or in the 1787 English (Stockdale) edition, apart from adding one footnote. Thomson speculates this is because Jefferson still needed to combat all the other, unrepentant Buffon-influenced scientists (Thomson, *Jefferson's Shadow*, 115–117).

60. William Carmichael to TJ, 15 Oct. 1787. For a thorough study of early French attitudes toward America, see chapter 1 of Bette Oliver, *Jacques Pierre Brissot in America and France, 1788–1793: In Search of Better Worlds* (Lanham, MD: Rowman & Littlefield, 2016).

61. Mrs. Abigail Adams to Mrs. Elizabeth Cranch, 7 May 1785, cited in Shackelford, "William Short," 112. Her teenage daughter Nabby wrote in her diary that "Mr. S. grows very sociable and pleasant. He appears a well-bred man, without the least formality, or affectation of any kind. He converses with ease, and says many good things." See Mrs. Abigail Adams Smith, *Journal and Correspondence of Miss Adams, Daughter of John Adams, Second President of the United States: Written in France and England, in 1785* (New York: Wiley and Putnam, 1841), 45.

62. David Franks to W. S., 8 June 1787, Short Papers, LOC.

63. TJ to Madison, 11 May 1785.

64. See footnote 1.

65. Gillian Paku puts it this way: "Early print publication might not befit the aristocracy, partly because a gentlemanly skill in composition might then seem to have tawdry implications of trade and partly because printed texts moved in social circles beyond the coterie of one's peers. . . . The class-based stigma of publication persisted, or was still recognized as a trope, in the 1820s when Sir Walter Scott, also known as 'The Great Unknown,' claimed to be unsure of the decorum of publishing novels under his own name because he was a Clerk of Sessions." Paku, "Anonymity in the Eighteenth Century,"

Oxford Handbooks Online, www.oxfordhandbooks.com/view/10.1093/oxford
hb/9780199935338.001.0001/oxfordhb-9780199935338-e-37.

66. Mably (1709–1785) was characterized as a forerunner of the utopian
socialist movement by most modern scholars until Johnson Kent Wright, in
*A Classical Republican in Eighteenth-Century France: The Political Thought of
Mably* (Stanford, CA: Stanford University Press, 1997), argued that, although
he was a socialist, he was also a realist and therefore he should be reposi-
tioned within the classical republican stream. For an introduction to Phillip
Mazzei, see Margherita Marchione, *Philip Mazzei, Jefferson's "Zealous Whig"*
(New York: American Institute of Italian Studies, 1975). Although Florentine
by birth, Mazzei became a naturalized citizen of Virginia and lived next to
Monticello for several years before returning to Europe in 1785.

67. Phillip Mazzei, *Recherches Historiques et Politiques sur les États-Unis de
l'Amérique Septentrionale* (Paris: Chez Froullé, 1788); WS to William Nelson,
25 Oct. 1785, Short Papers, LOC.

68. Oliver, *Jacques Pierre Brissot in America and France*, 11.

69. See my discussion of their friendship in chapter 2.

70. See Howard C. Rice, Introduction to François Jean Chastellux, *Travels
in North America in the Years 1780, 1781, and 1782: A Rev. Translation with
Introd. and Notes by Howard C. Rice, Jr.* (Published for the Institute of Early
American History and Culture at Williamsburg, VA, by the University of
North Carolina Press, 1963), quote at 27.

71. TJ to Chastellux, 2 Sep. 1785.

72. François Jean Chastellux, trans. George Grieve, *Travels in North America in the Years 1780, 1781, and 1782*, 2 vols. (Dublin: Printed for Colles, Moncrieffe, White, H. Whitestone, Byrne, Cash, Marchbank, Henry, and Moore,
1787), 2:194.

73. Chastellux, *Travels in North America*, 196 ("in general"), 197 ("young
men"), 198 ("species"), 199–200.

74. Short's disappointment with Chastellux will be further discussed in
chapter 4.

75. Bishop Madison to TJ, ca. 28 March 1787.

76. See chapter 2 for TJ's concerted efforts to secure a copy for the Vir-
ginian government in 1781; for more on the *Encyclopédie* and Jefferson, see
George B. Watts, "Thomas Jefferson, the 'Encylopédie' and the 'Encyclopédie
Méthodique,'" *French Review* 38, no. 3 (1965): 318–325.

77. See Rochefoucauld to TJ, 4 Jan. 1786; Démeunier to TJ, 6 Jan. 1786 and
21 Jan. 1786, TJ to Démeunier, 24 Jan. 1786.

78. See, for example, TJ to George Washington, 14 Nov. 1786; TJ to van Hogendorp, 25 Aug. 1786.

79. WS to Nelson, 25 Oct. 1786.

80. TJ to Thomson, 21 May 1784. In November, TJ told another enthusiastic supporter of the project, the young Dutchman G. K. van Hogendorp: "Those notes of mine on the state of Virginia which you saw when in America, I am about to print a few copies of here [in Paris]. I shall take the liberty of sending you one according to my promise." Indeed, Hogendorp was among the first to receive a private copy. TJ to Hogendorp, 20 Nov. 1784.

81. Thomson to TJ, 6 March 1785.

82. The date of receipt, 2 May 1785, is known from a notation Jefferson made in his "Summary Journal of Letters." See editorial note for Thomson to TJ, 6 March 1785.

83. TJ to Madison, 11 May 1785.

84. TJ to Wythe, 13 Aug. 1786; Wythe to TJ, 10 Jan. 1786; Coolie Verner, *Mr. Jefferson Distributes His Notes: A Preliminary Checklist of the First Edition* (New York: New York Public Library, 1952).

85. TJ to Benjamin Franklin, cited in Verner, "Mr. Jefferson Distributes His Notes," 163. Each of the copies of the *Notes* had the same message, or one very similar, with a few personalized details.

86. Two recent books set forth strong cases for Jefferson's careful planning, construction of a cohesive argument, and revision of a work that is much more important to understanding his political thought than was previously believed by his biographers: David Tucker, *Enlightened Republicanism: A Study of Jefferson's Notes on the State of Virginia* (Lanham, MD: Rowman & Littlefield, 2008); and Dustin Gish and Daniel Klinghard, *Thomas Jefferson and the Science of Republican Government: A Political Biography of Notes on the State of Virginia* (New York: Cambridge University Press, 2017).

87. John Adams to TJ, 22 May 1785.

88. TJ to James Monroe, 17 June 1785.

89. TJ to Charles Thomson, 21 June 1785.

90. TJ to Chastellux, 7 June 1785.

91. In *Slavery and the Founders*, Paul Finkelman contends that Jefferson "opposed the circulation of his *Notes on Virginia* in part because his comments on slavery might 'produce an irritation.' We might well join David Brion Davis in asking 'how he expected to encourage the cause of emancipation without producing irritation?' This is exactly the problem. Ultimately, Jefferson was more concerned with avoiding 'irritation' than promoting emancipation." See Finkelman, *Slavery and the Founders*, 131, citing David Brion Davis, *The*

Problem of Slavery in the Age of Revolution, 1770–1823 (New York and Oxford, UK: Oxford University Press, 1999), 177.

92. Quotation cited in Eva Sheppard Wolf, *Race and Liberty in the New Nation: Emancipation in Virginia from the Revolution to Nat Turner's Rebellion* (Baton Rouge: Louisiana State University Press, 2006), 28; see also 29–31.

93. Mifflin, cited in Wolf, *Race and Liberty*, 33.

94. Wolf adds that in 1806 "legislators hoped that by making emancipation difficult and inconvenient, by forcing owners to choose on their slaves' behalf between banishment and bondage, they would discourage manumission" (*Race and Liberty*, 122).

95. See Schmidt and Wilhelm, "Early Proslavery Petitions in Virginia," 135; Jordan, *White Over Black: American Attitudes Toward the Negro, 1550–1812* (Chapel Hill: University of North Carolina Press, 1968), 304.

96. For the most thorough view of this issue, see Donald G. Mathews, *Slavery and Methodism: A Chapter in American Morality, 1780–1845* (Princeton, NJ: Princeton University Press, 1965).

97. John Wigger, *American Saint: Francis Asbury and the Methodists* (New York: Oxford University Press, 2009), 116; 142–148.

98. Wigger, *American Saint*, 123.

99. Wolf, *Race and Liberty*, 58.

100. Wigger, *American Saint*, 467 n.33; 151. In *Discipline*, a conference publication released by Asbury and Coke in 1785, the Methodists declared that it is "contrary to the Golden Law of God on which hang all the Law and the Prophets, and the unalienable Rights of Mankind, as well as every Principle of the Revolution, to hold in the deepest Debasement, in a more abject Slavery than is perhaps to be found in any Part of the World except America, so many Souls that are all capable of the Image of God." Cited in Wigger, *American Saint*, 148–149.

101. Wolf, *Race and Liberty*, 53. Wolf states: "For the majority of white manumitters at the turn of the century liberating slaves served as a way to reward one or two favored individuals for their good service rather than as a way to enact deeply held convictions that slavery was wrong. . . . In total, fewer than a quarter of all deeds of manumissions written from 1794 to 1806 included antislavery statements" (63).

102. Petition from Brunswick County, 10 Nov. 1785, with 266 signatures; see Schmidt and Wilhelm, "Early Proslavery Petitions in Virginia," 144.

103. Petitions from Amelia County, 10 Nov. 1785, with twenty-two signatures; also submitted by Mecklenberg and Pittsylvania Counties, with 223 signatures and fifty-four signatures, respectively. See Schmidt and Wilhelm, 140.

104. Madison to TJ, 22 Jan. 1786.

105. See also Madison to George Washington, 11 Nov. 1785, *National Archives*, http://founders.archives.gov. In this letter, Madison first informs Washington that "the Revised Code proposed by Mr Jefferson Mr Pendleton & Mr Wythe" was under consideration by the legislature, then reports that "[t]he pulse of the H. of D. was felt on thursday with regard to a general manumission by a petition presented on that subject. It was rejected without dissent." Although Madison does not mention Jefferson and Wythe's emancipation amendment to Bill no. 51, his discussion of the Revised Code in conjunction with the legislature's hostility to a general manumission lends credibility to Jefferson's later recounting.

106. For Laurens's membership in the APS, see Gilbert Chinard, "Jefferson and the American Philosophical Society," American Philosophical Society, *Procs.*, 37 (1943), 264.

107. Gregory D. Massey, "The Limits of Antislavery Thought in the Revolutionary Lower South: John Laurens and Henry Laurens," *Journal of Southern History* 63, no. 3 (1997): 495–530, esp. 496.

108. Price to TJ, 2 July 1785.

109. TJ to Price, 7 Aug. 1785.

110. TJ to Price, 7 Aug. 1785. Several months later, in answer to another Frenchman's queries about the United States, Jefferson made a similar assessment of the state of slavery. See TJ, "Answers to Démeunier's First Queries," 24 Jan. 1786.

111. TJ to Price, 7 Aug. 1785.

112. Price to TJ, 24 Oct. 1785.

113. WS to Unknown, 25 July 1785, Short Papers, LOC.

114. Charles Thomson to TJ, 2 Nov. 1785 (received by TJ on 30 Dec. 1785, according to Jefferson's "Summary Journal of Letters," cited in editorial note).

115. Madison to TJ, 15 Nov. 1785. Italicized words were originally written in code.

116. James Monroe to TJ, 19 Jan. 1786.

117. Abigail Adams, 7 May 1785, in C. F. Adams, ed., *Letters of Mrs. Adams* (Boston: 1848), 240.

118. TJ to Williamos, 7 July 1785; Philip Mazzei to TJ, 26 Oct. 1785.

119. TJ to James Madison, 8 Feb. 1786; Morellet to TJ, [ca. Dec. 1785]. Translation my own. For the date of this letter, see the editorial note in *The Papers of Thomas Jefferson Digital Edition*, ed. James P. McClure and J. Jefferson Looney (Charlottesville: University of Virginia Press, Rotunda, 2008–2017), http://rotunda.upress.virginia.edu.ezproxy.rice.edu/founders/TSJN -01–09–02–0127.

120. For an account of the changes, see Gordon S. Barker, "Unraveling the Strange History of Jefferson's 'Observations Sur La Virginie,'" *Virginia Magazine of History and Biography* 112, no. 2 (2004): 134–177. Barker, unlike Jefferson, thinks that the rearrangements and alterations to wording improved the text, which he believes Jefferson constructed in an illogical manner. Jefferson did have some input into Morellet's translation and stylistic decisions, but they seem to have had some trouble in their communication, and Jefferson did not keep Morellet's changes in the English edition; this to me indicates that Jefferson preferred his own version to Morellet's. For communication confusion, see Morellet to TJ, [11? Jan. 1787?]. For an alternative view of the coherence of the *Notes*, see Tucker, *Enlightened Republicanism*. See also Dorothy Medlin, "Thomas Jefferson, André Morellet, and the French Version of *Notes on the State of Virginia*," *William and Mary Quarterly* 35 (1978): 85–99; and Gish and Klinghard, *Thomas Jefferson*, 255ff.

121. TJ to Madison, 8 Feb. 1786. The alternative account of the *Observations* publication is that Jefferson was being less than honest to Madison and other correspondents at the time and many years later when he recalled the incident in his autobiography; and that his distress at the French publication was a smoke screen to cover his willing participation. Gish and Klinghard believe Williamos was a convenient scapegoat, since he was dead, for Jefferson's own decision to publish in French. I have chosen to accept Jefferson's version for two primary reasons: First, Jefferson did not keep Morellet's changes to the style and substance of his text when he published in English, indicating that his displeasure with the changes was genuine; and second, Jefferson would have had to craft an elaborate set of lies that William Short, for one, would have recognized as such. Why go to so much trouble? Jefferson quite obviously used language that overly denigrated his work on several occasions, which was expected of authors at that time, but to craft a detailed ruse regarding the French publication of his work seems excessive.

122. See TJ to David Rittenhouse, 25 Jan. 1786; TJ to C.W.F. Dumas, 2 Feb. 1786.

123. Thomas Jefferson, "Autobiography," in *Thomas Jefferson: Writings*, ed. Merrill D. Peterson (New York: Random House, 1984), 3.

124. TJ to Abbé Morellet, 11 Aug. 1786.

125. TJ to Edward Bancroft, 26 Feb. 1786. For more on the history of the map, see Dumas Malone, Introduction to *The Fry and Jefferson Map of Virginia and Maryland: Facsimiles of the 1754 and 1794 Printings* (Charlottesville: University Press of Virginia, 1966), 8. See also Coolie Verner, "The Maps and Plates Appearing with the Several Editions of Mr. Jefferson's 'Notes on the State of Virginia,'" *Virginia Magazine of History and Biography* 59 (Jan. 1951): 21–33. For a fascinating discussion of TJ's role in the publication of another

rare and highly valuable map around the same time, see the editorial note to TJ to William Stephens Smith, [10] Aug. 1786.

126. Coolie Verner, *A Further Checklist of the Separate Editions of Jefferson's Notes on the State of Virginia* (Charlottesville: Bibliographical Society of the University of Virginia, 1950), 7; see also TJ to Short, 28 March 1786. There exists some confusion over when, exactly, the French (Barrois) edition was released. Verner asserts that this edition was published in 1786 and included a map. We know that Jefferson had London engraver Samuel Neele make the map for him, but this was not complete until December 1786, and it was full of more than 200 errors that TJ and Short had to correct over the ensuing months. The corrections were implemented in Paris by another engraver, M. de lay Haye, and the Parisian printer, Barrois, then paid TJ for the use of the corrected engraving. The same corrected engraving served as the basis for Stockdale's 1787 edition, though with a few differences (Verner, 8). I assume, therefore, that either the Barrois edition, *Observations*, was dated 1786 but not released until 1787, after the map was corrected; or that the map was added to some copies of the Barrois edition that had already been printed in 1786; or that Jefferson drew a simplified version of the map for the Barrois edition that was replaced by the Neele map after the engraving was finally complete. It should also be noted that, according to Verner, Jefferson included copies of the Neele map in some of the privately printed copies of 1785 when he distributed them in later years (6). For the Neele map, see TJ to W.S. Smith, 10 Aug. 1786; Neele to TJ, 21 Dec. 1786; TJ to W.S. Smith, 15 Jan. 1787.

127. TJ to W.S. Smith, 15 Jan. 1787; TJ to Short, 24 Sep. 1785. For Short's involvement with the *Notes*, see, for example, TJ to Short, 28 March 1786; from April 1786 until March 1787 the two men had no need to correspond with one another due to limited travel. For "right hand man," see William Smith to Short, 30 Sep. 1786, Short Papers, LOC. For the dislocation and Short's work as Jefferson's amanuensis, see TJ to Smith, 23 Sep. 1786.

128. Stockdale to TJ, 20 Nov. 1786; TJ finally answered his question on 1 Feb. 1787. It is unclear whether the Frenchmen had with them the "mutilated" Barrois French edition of 1786 or Jefferson's private version of 1785, since the Barrois edition was not printed until winter 1786 at the earliest. Jefferson may have misjudged the trustworthiness of another one of his private copy recipients. Nonetheless, the important fact is that a copy had left France and made its way to a prominent publisher in England within months of Jefferson's first agreeing to print it.

129. Fulwar Skipwith to Short, 12 May 1786, Short Papers, LOC.

130. Fulwar Skipwith to Short, 6 June 1786, Short Papers, LOC.

131. Fulwar Skipwith to Short, 17 Sep. 1786, included in letter of 5 Sep. 1786; Short to Skipwith, 14 Dec. 1786, Short Papers, LOC.

132. See also TJ to William Carmichael, 26 Dec. 1786.

133. Wythe to TJ, 13 Dec. 1786.

134. TJ to Wythe, 13 Aug. 1786.

135. TJ to Richard Price, 7 Aug. 1785; TJ's "Summary Journal of Letters," cited by the editors in footnote to Wythe to TJ, 13 Dec. 1786.

136. TJ to William Smith, 15 Jan. 1787; Short to TJ, 12 and 26 March 1787. For the plate's legibility, see Stockdale to TJ, 10 July 1787.

137. Stockdale to Short, 15 May 1787 (in the Jefferson *Papers*).

138. TJ to Stockdale, 27 Feb. 1787.

139. TJ to Barrois, 22 June 1787; TJ to Stockdale, 1 July 1787.

140. See, for instance, Thomas Mann Randolph Jr. to TJ, 14 April 1787.

141. TJ to Stockdale, 20 Feb. 1787 and 17 July 1787; Stockdale to TJ, 3 Aug. 1787; TJ to Stockdale, 14 Aug. 1787. The unauthorized publication of the *Notes* in America was not necessarily malicious; well-meaning friends like Francis Hopkinson simply ignored or forgot about Jefferson's handwritten note, entered in every one of the private copies he distributed to friends in 1785 and asking the recipient not to allow the book to be published. On 14 April 1786, a seemingly oblivious Hopkinson wrote that he was publishing an extract about animal sizes, hoping it "would not displease you."

142. Joel Barlow to TJ, 15 June 1787.

143. TJ to Stockdale, 17 July 1788. The "bad edition" was printed in 1788 by Prichard and Hall in Philadelphia; it was based on a "pirated copy of the Stockdale edition." Verner notes that a "skeleton map was prepared to accompany this edition but no [existing] copies are known which include this map." See Verner, *A Further Checklist*, 9.

144. Stockdale to TJ, 15 Aug. 1788.

145. Verner, *A Further Checklist*, 6.

146. TJ to George Wythe, with Enclosure, 16 Sep. 1787; Verner, *Mr. Jefferson Distributes His Notes*, 17; quotation from Richmond bookseller cited on 16.

147. For more on Madison, who was not yet a bishop at the time of this correspondence, see Charles Crowe, "Bishop James Madison and the Republic of Virtue," *Journal of Southern History* 30, no. 1 (1964): 58–70; and Jeffery R. Shy, "Early Astronomy in America: The Role of the College of William and Mary," *Journal of Astronomical History and Heritage* 5 (June 2002): 41–64.

148. Bishop Madison to TJ, 27 March 1786. The two copies were in the possession of James Madison (not the bishop) and James Monroe.

149. Bishop Madison to TJ, 28 Dec. 1786.

150. Bishop Madison to TJ, 10 Feb. 1789.

151. *Mercure de France*, 2 June 1787.

152. Barker, "Unraveling the Strange History of Jefferson's 'Observations Sur La Virginie,'" 134–177; see especially 140–143. Although I do not agree with all of Barker's conclusions, I am grateful for his translation and analysis of the *Mercure*'s review.

153. Resnick, "Société des Amis des Noirs," 558–559.

154. See Brissot to TJ, 10 Feb. 1788.

155. Resnick, "Société des Amis des Noirs," 560.

156. Resnick, 562; Resnick adds that "Five to six weeks was not an uncommon interval between meetings, and none was held in August, October, November, or December of 1788; September or October of 1789; January, February, April, or May of 1790. The resume of meetings (Bibl. De l'Institut de France, MS. 857) does not extend beyond June 1790." Resnick further points out that "Clarkson's complaint about the French meetings is registered in his *History of the Slave Trade*, pp. 381–404." He concludes that the networks of abolitionists in England and America were more effective in the long term in large part due to their religious nature; these significantly Quaker and Evangelical groups could more easily spread their messages among their memberships and proved highly motivated, even in the face of opposition.

157. Resnick, "Société des Amis des Noirs," 563; François Furstenberg, "Atlantic Slavery, Atlantic Freedom: George Washington, Slavery, and Transatlantic Abolitionist Networks," *William and Mary Quarterly* 68, no. 2 (1 April 2011): 247–286; see 268–269. Brissot's pamphlet was titled "An Oration, Upon the Necessity of Establishing at Paris, a Society to Co-operate with those of America and London, Towards the Abolition of the Trade and Slavery of the Negroes."

158. Brissot to TJ, 10 Feb. 1788.

159. See Brissot to TJ, 26 Dec. 1786 (wine); 10 Nov. 1786.

160. TJ to Brissot, 11 Feb. 1788.

161. Brissot to TJ, 11 Feb. 1788.

162. Furstenberg, "Atlantic Slavery, Atlantic Freedom," 263.

163. Verner, *A Further Checklist*.

164. Francis Kinloch to TJ, 26 April 1789.

165. Anonymous, written in the margin next to one of TJ's antislavery passages, in a 1785 edition of *Notes* in the University of Virginia library; cited in the introduction to *Notes on the State of Virginia*, ed. Frank Shuffelton, 29.

166. David Ramsay to TJ, 3 May 1786 (it should be noted that Ramsay did not object because he felt that black and white people were *already* equal. He

continued by saying: "I flatter myself that in a few centuries the negroes will lose their black color. I think now they are less black in Jersey than Carolina, their [lips] less thick, their noses less flat. The state of society has an influence not less than climate"); Samuel Stanhope Smith, *An Essay on the Causes of the Variety of Complexion and Figure in the Human Species* . . . (Edinburgh, 1788); Bruce Dain, *A Hideous Monster of the Mind: American Race Theory in the Early Republic* (Cambridge, MA: Harvard University Press, 2002), 43.

 167. Samuel Stanhope Smith, *The Lectures, Corrected and Improved* . . . *on the Subjects of Moral and Political Philosophy* (2 vols., Trenton: D. Fenton, 1812), 2:176–178. For an excellent discussion of Smith, Jefferson, and race, see Guyatt, *Bind Us Apart*, 61–63 and 131–132; see also Guyatt, "Samuel Stanhope Smith," *Princeton and Slavery*, https://slavery. princeton.edu/stories/samuel -stanhope-smith#ref-15; and Mark A. Noll, *Princeton and the Republic, 1768– 1822: The Search for a Christian Enlightenment in the Era of Samuel Stanhope Smith* (Princeton, NJ: Princeton University Press, 1989). For Smith's belief that slaves' features became more "white" if they were house slaves, see Smith, *An Essay*, 92–93.

 168. Dain, *Hideous Monster of the Mind*, 43, 48 (quote).

 169. Benjamin Banneker to TJ, 19 Aug. 1791; *Notes*, ed. Shuffelton, 149. See editorial note to Banneker to TJ, 19 Aug. 1791; see also Silvio A. Bedini, *The Life of Benjamin Banneker* (New York: Macmillan, 1972), 108–109; Jordan, *White over Black*, 429–439, 445–448, 455; Boles, *Jefferson*, 228–230.

 170. TJ to Banneker, 30 Aug. 1791; TJ to Condorcet, 30 Aug. 1791.

 171. Thomas Branagan, *A Preliminary Essay, on the Oppression of the Exiled Sons of Africa* (J. W. Scott: 1804), 233–234. For the correspondence being printed, see Bedini, *Banneker*, 158, 163, 166–8, 183–188. For more on Branagan, who changed his tone on black equality drastically by 1805, see Guyatt, *Bind Us Apart*, 81–83; and the editorial note to Branagan's letter to TJ of 28 April 1815, in *Founders Online*, https://founders.archives.gov/documents/Jefferson /03-08-02-0358.

 172. William Loughton Smith, *The Pretensions of Thomas Jefferson to the Presidency Examined* . . . (Philadelphia[?], 1796), 9–13, quotes at 10 and 13; Thomas Green Fessenden, *Democracy Unveiled, or, Tyranny Stripped of the Garb of Patriotism*, 2 vols. (New York, 1805), 2: 52. See also William Henry Desaussure, *Address to the Citizens of South Carolina, on the Approaching Election of President and Vice-President of the United States* (Charleston, 1800), 16; and Bedini, *Banneker*, 280–281. For examples of other Federalist attacks on Jefferson using various aspects of the *Notes*, see William Linn, *Serious Considerations on the Election of a President Addressed to the Citizens of the United*

States (New York, 1800), 13; Clement Clarke Moore, *Observations upon Certain Passages in Mr. Jefferson's Notes on Virginia, Which Appear to Have a Tendency to Subvert Religion, and Establish a False Philosophy* (New York, 1804).

173. TJ to Henri Gregoire, 25 Feb. 1809, *The Thomas Jefferson Papers* at the Library of Congress, available at www.loc.gov/item/mtjbib019810/.

CHAPTER FOUR. ALTERNATIVES TO SLAVERY, 1785–1798

1. William Short (hereafter "WS") to Thomas Jefferson (hereafter "TJ"), 27 Feb. 1798. Portions of this chapter were previously published: see Cara J. Rogers [Stevens], "The French Experiment: Thomas Jefferson and William Short Debate Slavery, 1785–1826," *American Political Thought* 10, no. 3 (2021): 327–362, https://doi.org/10.1086/715006.

2. For Lafayette's relationship with Washington, see Stuart Leibiger, "George Washington and Lafayette: Father and Son of the Revolution," in Robert M. S. McDonald, ed., *Sons of the Father: George Washington and His Protégés* (Charlottesville: University of Virginia Press, 2013): 210–231.

3. Marquis de Lafayette to George Washington, 5 Feb. 1783, *The Writings of George Washington from the Original Manuscript Sources, 1745–1799*, ed. John Clement Fitzpatrick, 39 vols. (Washington, DC: Government Printing Office, 1931–1944), 26: 300.

4. William Gordon to George Washington, 30 Aug. 1784, *The Papers of George Washington, Confederation Series*, 6 vols., eds. W. W. Abbot and Dorothy Twohig (Charlottesville: University of Virginia Press, 1992–1997), 2:64.

5. Nicholas Guyatt, *Bind Us Apart: How Enlightened Americans Invented Racial Segregation* (New York: Basic Books, 2016), 5–6.

6. Alan Taylor, *The Internal Enemy: Slavery and War in Virginia, 1772–1832* (New York: W. W. Norton & Company, 2014). Thomas Jefferson and George Washington both lost slaves to the British (and freedom) during the Revolution. For more on this topic, including the remarkable life of Washington's former slave Harry, see Cassandra Pybus, *Epic Journeys of Freedom: Runaway Slaves of the American Revolution and Their Global Quest for Liberty* (Boston: Beacon Press, 2007); and Alexander X. Byrd, *Captives and Voyagers: Black Migrants Across the Eighteenth-Century British Atlantic World* (Baton Rouge: Louisiana State University Press, 2008).

7. TJ, *Notes on the State of Virginia*, ed. Frank Shuffelton (New York: Penguin Books, 1999), 145.

8. Willie Rose, *Rehearsal for Reconstruction: The Port Royal Experiment* (Athens: University of Georgia Press, 1999), 123. For further studies on the

transition between slavery and freedom, see also Julie Saville, *The Work of Reconstruction: From Slave to Wage Laborer in South Carolina, 1860–1870* (New York: Cambridge University Press, 1996); and Leslie Schwalm, *A Hard Fight for We: Women's Transition from Slavery to Freedom in South Carolina* (Urbana and Chicago: University of Illinois Press, 1997).

9. The Marquis de Lafayette to George Washington, 6 Feb. 1786, in *The Papers of George Washington*, 3:121, 544. Many years later the English antislavery activist Frances Wright, who called herself the "adopted daughter" of the Marquis de Lafayette, attempted to follow in his footsteps by setting up a similar farm in Tennessee. She purchased land and slaves, offering freedom to those who earned back their purchase price, plus interest, in an attempt to prove that slave owners could be financially compensated for emancipating their own slaves. The experiment was marred, however, partly because of a poor location, partly because Ms. Wright became ill and had to leave after a year, and partly because it became associated with sexual scandal. Wright nonetheless kept her word to free the slaves, paying for their transportation to Haiti and then ending the experiment. See James Madison to Lafayette, [?] Nov. 1826, cited in "Lafayette the Abolitionist," *Lafayette: Citizen of Two Worlds,* Cornell University, http://rmc.library.cornell.edu/Lafayette/exhibition/english/abolitionist/index.html; see also Gail Bederman, "Revisiting Nashoba: Slavery, Utopia, and Frances Wright in America, 1818–1826," *American Literary History* 17, no. 3 (2005): 438–459.

10. Laurent A. Dubois, *A Colony of Citizens: Revolution and Slave Emancipation in the French Caribbean, 1787–1804* (Chapel Hill: University of North Carolina Press Books, 2012), 69–70; "Lafayette the Abolitionist."

11. "La Belle Gabrielle," *Lafayette and Slavery*, Skillman Library Exhibition, Lafayette College, http://academicmuseum.Lafayette.edu/special/specialexhibits/slaveryexhibit/onlineexhibit/page1.htm. France abolished slavery (for the second and final time) in 1848.

12. James Madison to TJ, 22 Jan. 1786. Madison was sending reports on the issue to both Jefferson and Washington; see Madison to Washington, 11 Nov. 1785.

13. Washington to Lafayette, 10 May 1786.

14. Lafayette to Washington, 24 May 1786.

15. See Bancroft to TJ, 16 Sep. 1788. For more on Bancroft, see Thomas Schaeper, *Edward Bancroft: Scientist, Author, Spy* (New Haven, CT: Yale University Press, 2011). For more on the timing of this conversation, see the editorial note to "Jefferson's Notes from Condorcet on Slavery," *Papers*, 14:498.

16. Bancroft to TJ, 16 Sep. 1788.

17. Eleventh-century Toledo historian Sā'id al-Andalusi, cited in James H.

Sweet, "The Iberian Roots of American Racist Thought," *William and Mary Quarterly*, ser. 3, vol. 54, no. 1 (Jan. 1997): 146.

18. TJ, *Notes on the State of Virginia*, ed. Shuffelton, "the blacks," 150–151; sleep, 146; Sancho, 148.

19. Bancroft to TJ, 16 Sep. 1788. For Guiana see Schaeper, *Edward Bancroft*, 3–4.

20. TJ to Bancroft, 26 Jan. 1789. Since it was extremely hard for willing owners to secure the necessary legal permission to free slaves before 1782, the experiments discussed in this letter were probably early, informal attempts to give a measure of liberty to individuals who were still officially in bondage.

21. Frederick Douglass, *My Bondage and My Freedom* (New York: Miller, Orton & Mulligan, 1855), 189–191.

22. TJ, *Notes on the State of Virginia*, ed. Shuffelton, 150.

23. TJ to Bancroft, 26 Jan. 1789. Recent scholarship on slavery has demonstrated that many instances of slaves stealing from their masters can be conceptualized as a form of resistance. See, for instance, Eugene Genovese, *Roll, Jordan, Roll: The World the Slaves Made* (New York: Pantheon Books, 1976). Whereas Genovese believes that these smaller acts of resistance prevented slaves from forming a collective identity and therefore a broader resistance, Walter Johnson more recently argued that the slave trade itself indirectly led to the development of a common antislavery ideology among enslaved people. See Walter Johnson, *Soul by Soul: Life Inside the Antebellum Slave Market* (Cambridge, MA: Harvard University Press, 1999).

24. For Joseph Mayo, see James Currie to TJ, 5 Aug. 1785.

25. See chapter 1.

26. TJ to Bancroft, 26 Jan. 1789.

27. See my discussion of this emancipation amendment in chapter 1.

28. TJ named Wythe as his coauthor in a letter to the French encyclopedist Jean Nicolas Démeunier in June 1786.

29. TJ, *Notes on the State of Virginia*, ed. Shuffelton, 144, 145.

30. TJ, *Notes on the State of Virginia*, ed. Shuffelton, 145. One of Wythe's students, Benjamin Watkins Leigh, later declared that "Mr. Wythe, to the day of his death, was for *simple abolition*, considering the objection to color as founded in prejudice." Wythe raised a mixed-race boy as if he were his own son (and although some historians have asserted that Michael Brown *was* Wythe's natural son, there is no evidence for that claim), educated him in Greek and Latin, left a large part of his estate to him, and put him under Thomas Jefferson's protection in his will—but, tragically, both Brown and Wythe were poisoned by Wythe's jealous grandnephew in 1806. See Melvin

Patrick Ely, *Israel on the Appomattox: A Southern Experiment in Black Freedom from the 1790s Through the Civil War* (New York: Vintage, 2005), 24. Ely cites Appomattox [a pseudonym for Benjamin Watkins Leigh], "To the People of Virginia," 1832; see Ely, 24, fn.28.

31. For Jefferson's conception of slavery as an Old World problem, see Christa Dierksheide, *Amelioration and Empire: Progress and Slavery in the Plantation Americas* (Charlottesville: University of Virginia Press, 2014), 28.

32. Metayage remained in use in France through the nineteenth century; see, for example, Henry Higgs, "'Metayage' in Western France," *Economic Journal* 4, no. 13 (1894): 1–13. It was also utilized, not very successfully, as a postemancipation system in colonies such as Tobago; see Angelo Bissessarsingh, "The Metayers of Tobago," *Trindad and Tobago Guardian*, 24 June 2012, http://www.guardian.co.tt/news/2012-06-24/metayers-tobago.

33. Benezet to Fothergill, 1773, cited in Guyatt, *Bind Us Apart*, 222; "perfect the alchemy" quote is from Guyatt, 222.

34. TJ to James Madison, 28 Oct. 1785.

35. TJ to James Madison, 28 Oct. 1785.

36. George G. Shackelford, "William Short: Jefferson's Adopted Son, 1758–1849" (PhD diss., University of Virginia, 1955), 364.

37. See Kevin Gutzman, *Thomas Jefferson, Revolutionary: A Radical's Struggle to Remake America* (New York: St. Martin's Press, 2017), 4.

38. TJ to Bishop James Madison, 28 Oct. 1785.

39. For French opinions of Monticello's workforce, see, for instance, François Jean Chastellux, trans. George Grieve, *Travels in North America in the Years 1780, 1781, and 1782*, 2 vols. (Dublin: Printed for Colles, Moncrieffe, White, H. Whitestone, Byrne, Cash, Marchbank, Henry, and Moore, 1787), 2: 196. The Italian author Count Luigi Castiglioni had similarly complimentary things to say about Jefferson after his visit to Monticello; see *Viaggio negli Stati Uniti dell'America Settentrionale fatto negli anni 1785, 1786, e 1787 . . .* , 2 vols. (Milan: Stamperia di Giuseppe Marelli, 1790). For more on Castiglioni, see Howard R. Marraro, "Count Luigi Castiglioni. An Early Italian Traveller to Virginia (1785–1786)," *Virginia Magazine of History and Biography* 58, no. 4 (1950): 473–491. I am indebted to William Merkel for his insights into Jefferson's letter to Bishop Madison; see William Merkel, "Jefferson in Paris: Rewriting the Problems of Slavery, Slaveholding, Family, and Codependency," in *Thomas Jefferson and Philosophy: Essays on the Philosophical Cast of Jefferson's Writings*, ed. Mark Holowchak (Lanham, MD: Lexington Books, 2014), 91–134, esp. 100–101.

40. See chapter 3. For more on Jefferson's travels, see George G. Shackelford,

Thomas Jefferson's Travels in Europe, 1784–1789 (Baltimore: Johns Hopkins University Press, 1998).

41. Cited in Higgs, "'Metayage' in Western France," 2, fn. 4.

42. TJ to Lafayette, 11 April 1787. For more on working conditions among the peasantry in France, see Daniel Roche, *France in the Enlightenment*, trans. Arthur Goldhammer (Cambridge, MA: Harvard University Press, 2001), esp. 117.

43. TJ to Lafayette, 11 April 1787. The problem Jefferson outlines here is the same one that rendered metayage minimally successful in Tobago in the mid-nineteenth century: "Under such a system of cultivation there can be no farming; the labourer cultivates his field so long as it remains in heart; it is not his interest to manure it; for as soon as it ceases to produce what will remunerate him for his labour he moves off to a fresh field; there is an entire absence of implemental husbandry; and, owing in a great measure to the bad faith in which, on both sides, the contract is too often carried out, what [is] done is imperfectly done, and from many causes yields little return. I have known canes so planted to remain on the land two years without being cropped." Henry Iles Woodcock, *A History of Tobago* (Ayrshire, UK: Smith & Grant, 1867), 190.

44. TJ to Lafayette, 11 April 1787. Although typically not an outwardly effusive man (at least to those outside his immediate family circle), Jefferson ended this letter by making an endearing confession, telling Lafayette that "according to the ideas of our country we do not permit ourselves to speak even truths when they may have the air of flattery. I content myself therefore with saying once for all that I love you, your wife and children. Tell them so and Adieu."

45. *Papers of Thomas Jefferson*, 11: 419.

46. For Eppes and Lewis, see TJ to Alexander McCaul, 19 April 1786: "My whole estate is left in the hands of Mr. Lewis of Albemarle and Mr. Eppes of Chesterfeild to apply it's whole profits to the paiment of my debts." For Jefferson's debts, see Herbert E. Sloan, *Principle and Interest: Thomas Jefferson and the Problem of Debt* (Charlottesville: University Press of Virginia, 2001).

47. Francis Eppes to TJ, 2 May 1787 (letter no longer extant).

48. TJ to Nicholas Lewis, 29 July 1787. Lucia Stanton notes that, at one point, Jefferson sold 10,000 acres of inherited land, but because of Revolutionary War inflation the sale netted him only enough money to purchase "a great coat." See Lucia C. Stanton, "Jefferson's People: Slavery at Monticello," in *The Cambridge Companion to Thomas Jefferson*, ed. Frank Shuffelton (Cambridge, UK: Cambridge University Press, 2009), 85–86, quote at 86.

49. TJ to Francis Eppes, 30 July 1787.

50. TJ to Nicholas Lewis, 29 July 1787.

51. TJ to WS, 9 April 1788.

52. TJ, "Memorandums on a tour from Paris to Amsterdam, Strasburg and back to Paris," *Papers of Thomas Jefferson*, ed. Julian P. Boyd (Princeton, NJ: Princeton University Press, 1956) 13: 8.

53. TJ, *Notes on the State of Virginia*, ed. Shuffelton, 94.

54. TJ, *Notes*, 90.

55. TJ, *Notes*, 91.

56. TJ, *Notes*, 92.

57. TJ, *Notes*, 94.

58. For Germans as successful American farmers, see James T. Lemon, *The Best Poor Man's Country: A Geographical Study of Early Southeastern Pennsylvania* (Baltimore: Johns Hopkins University Press, 1972).

59. While Jefferson was away, Martha and Maria (Polly) Jefferson were installed in a convent, but Short visited frequently and wrote to his mentor with updates about Jefferson's "little family" often (see, for instance, WS to TJ, 17 March 1788). These attentions have, in part, sparked modern speculation that Short was secretly in love with Jefferson's oldest daughter, Martha. See Cynthia A. Kierner, *Martha Jefferson Randolph, Daughter of Monticello: Her Life and Times* (Chapel Hill: University of North Carolina Press, 2012), esp. 69–71; Stephanie Dray and Laura Kamoie, *America's First Daughter: A Novel* (New York: William Morrow Paperbacks, 2016).

60. TJ to Thomas Shippen, 29 Sep. 1788. For more on Shippen and Rutledge, see Shackelford, "William Short," 138.

61. He wrote to his friend William Nelson in Virginia: "I promise myself great pleasure in walking over a ground of which I have read with so much interest when I was young & when my mind received with ardor all its impressions." WS to Nelson, 5 Sep. 1788, in Short Papers, Library of Congress (hereafter "LOC"). Quoted in Shackelford, "William Short," 149.

62. See Shackelford, "William Short," 145–146; Shippen to WS, letters from Lille, Ghent, and Rotterdam, 11, 15, and 22 May 1788, in Short Papers, LOC.

63. George Fenwick Jones, "The Black Hessians: Negroes Recruited by the Hessians in South Carolina and Other Colonies," *South Carolina Historical Magazine* 83, no. 4 (1982): 287–302; dissection story at 302.

64. WS to Shippen, 11 July 1788, in Short Papers, LOC.

65. See TJ's "Memorandums to William Short" [before 17 Sep. 1788], *Papers*, 27:767. Many of Jefferson's instructions to Short, and Short's letters to TJ, also have to do with wine and investigating whether it would be possible to

cultivate grapes in their home state. Sure enough, it should be noted that today the area around Charlottesville is indeed a wine-producing region.

66. For Jefferson's time in Laye, see "Notes of a Tour into the Southern Parts of France, &c.," *Papers*, 11:419. For Short's observations, see WS to TJ, 2 Oct. 1788.

67. WS to TJ, 2 Oct. 1788.

68. WS to TJ, 28 Oct. 1788. Luigi Castiglioni, *Viaggio negli Stati Uniti dell'America Settentrionale fatto negli anni 1785, 1786 e 1787* (1790). For examples of their correspondence, see the letters of 1788 and 1789 in the Short–La Rochefoucauld Correspondence, BSh63, American Philosophical Society. See also Marraro, "Count Luigi Castiglioni."

69. WS to TJ, 28 Oct. 1788. For Count Barziza, see William Howard Adams, "The Virginians and the Veneto," *Virginia Quarterly Review* 63, no. 4 (1987): 646–660.

70. WS to TJ, 19 Nov. 1788.

71. WS to TJ, 23 Dec. 1788.

72. TJ to Anne Willing Bingham, 11 May 1788.

73. TJ to Adams, 30 Aug. 1787; TJ to Thomas Paine, 13 Sep. 1789. See also TJ to John Jay, 19 Sep. 1789.

74. W. S. to Dr. [James] Currie of Richmond, Paris, 6 Aug. 1787, Short Papers, LOC. Jefferson was even more liberal in many of his wishes than were his friends among the French nobility, but he was tempered by the painful experience of observing the failed Dutch Revolution in 1787. As Ziesche puts it: "In [Jefferson's] view, the Dutch Patriots had tried to implement too many reforms too quickly and thereby driven "moderate Aristocrats" back into the fold of the reigning Stadtholder and brought about "a schism" in their movement." Philipp Ziesche, "Cosmopolitan Patriots in the Age of Revolution: Americans in Paris, 1788–1800" (PhD diss., Yale University, 2006), ProQuest (3214336), 45, fn.59, quoting TJ to John Jay, 6 Aug. 1787.

75. See, for instance, TJ to Comte Diodati, 3 Aug. 1789.

76. For instance, Short developed a plan to feed the starving masses in Paris, which was experiencing period food shortages, by encouraging the importation of American salted beef. Although this cheap and plentiful supply would have greatly aided the city, his proposals were buried amid the chaos of the revolutionary government's attempts to deal with daily crises. Short also suspected that some in power deliberately chose to ignore his plan, desiring to keep the people on the verge of starvation so as to stoke their enthusiasm for change. See WS to Necker, 8 Oct. 1789; WS to Lafayette, 25 Oct. 1789; WS to James Madison, 17 Nov. 1789.

77. WS to TJ, 31 Aug. 1792. Reflecting on Lafayette just after Jefferson's death, Short referred to one of Jefferson's statements—"'an honest speculative politician is the most obstinate animal on earth'"—and then applied it to Lafayette: "Our good & worthy Lafayette is a living proof which I have always considered as confirming this maxim—for notwithstanding all that he has suffered, & all his dear bought experience he has not changed one of the opinions with which he began the French revolution—& he would at this moment be willing to begin [again despite] all that he has suffered—and this because of all the politicians alive he is the most honest & at the same time the most visionary." See WS to John Hartwell Cocke, 12 Aug. 1826, Cocke Papers, box 48, University of Virginia.

78. The estimated travel time is cited in Shackelford, "William Short," 165.

79. TJ to WS, 24 March 1789.

80. TJ to John Trumbull, 1 June 1789.

81. Short met Rosalie in 1785; in July 1786 his friend William Smith wrote him a letter that implies Short was involved in a clandestine relationship, but the lady's identity is obscured—it could be a reference to Rosalie or perhaps to Martha Jefferson. Short was also paying court to a young lady living on the outskirts of Paris in Saint-Germain, where he lodged for several months to immerse himself in French after arriving in the country in 1785. Short's biographer, George G. Shackelford, dates the Short–Rosalie affair to 1785–1786, but all sources agree that by May 1791 the two were almost certainly lovers: see "William Short," 333; Marie Goebel Kimball, "William Short, Jefferson's Only 'Son,'" *North American Review* 223 no. 832 (1926): 471–486, see esp. 473; Yvon Bizardel and Howard C. Rice, "Poor in Love Mr. Short," *William and Mary Quarterly* 21, no. 4 (1964): 516–533, esp. 531. For the Smith correspondence, see William Smith to WS, 18 July 1786, and WS to Smith, 5 Aug. 1786, in Short Papers, LOC.

82. The two young lovers seem to have worked to keep the nature of their relationship secret from the duke, although several of Short's friends knew about it. Rosalie was tormented by guilt, but she also encouraged Short's pursuit of her in secret. For their fear of discovery by the duke, see, for example, Rosalie to WS, 7 May 1791 and 11 Oct. 1791, Short–La Rouchefoucauld Collection, American Philosophical Society (hereafter "APS").

83. Annette Gordon-Reed, *The Hemingses of Monticello: An American Family* (New York: W. W. Norton & Company, 2008), 264. No records of a child born in that year exist, however; either Hemings's first child was not born until 1795, or any child born in 1790 died shortly afterward. The identity of this child is unknown, and there has been controversy regarding whether the child

312   Notes to Pages 163–164

lived, whether Jefferson was indeed the father, and whether Thomas Wood-
lived, whether Jefferson was indeed the father, and whether Thomas Wood-
son was that child. Extensive ink has been spilled in this debate. In addition
to Gordon-Reed's groundbreaking work *Thomas Jefferson and Sally Hemings:
An American Controversy* (Charlottesville: University of Virginia Press, 1998),
the two most comprehensive studies of the controversy itself are: Thomas Jefferson Foundation, "Report of the Research Committee on Thomas Jefferson
and Sally Hemings," published January 2000, available (with appendices) in
PDF format: https://www.monticello.org/site/plantation-and-slavery/report
-research-committee-thomas-jefferson-and-sally-hemings; and Robert F.
Turner, ed., *The Jefferson-Hemings Controversy: Report of the Scholars Commission* (Durham, NC: Carolina Academic Press, 2011).

84. For Short's absences, see Gordon-Reed, *The Hemingses of Monticello*,
274. The significant letter is WS to TJ, 27 Feb. 1789, and it is discussed at length
below. Sally Hemings's daughter Harriet was born in 1795; Hemings had a total
of six children (not including the possible 1790 pregnancy), one of whom died
in infancy.

85. Lafayette and Rosalie's mother-in-law, the Duchesse d'Enville, even sent
glowing letters to Washington and Jefferson, praising Short's character. See
Ziesche, "Cosmopolitan Patriots," 142. He first asked for the promotion in WS
to TJ, 25 Nov. 1789; Jefferson received this letter in late March 1790. Jefferson's
reply didn't arrive in Paris until June 1790. See WS to TJ, 14 June 1790.

86. WS to TJ, 14 June 1790. The Latin quotation is what the poet Horace
used to refer to his friend Virgil in *Odes* I, 3, 8; see George E. Duckworth,
"Supplementary Paper: Animae Dimidium Meae: Two Poets of Rome," *Transactions and Proceedings of the American Philological Association* 87 (1956):
281–316, 282. Jefferson's reply is equally heartfelt: "Had you been here, there
should have been no silence or reserve, and I long for the moment when I can
unbosom to you all that past on that occasion [when the diplomatic posts were
decided]. But to have trusted such communications to writing and across the
Atlantic would have been an indiscretion which nothing could have excused"
(TJ to WS, 16 Oct. 1792).

87. It is important to note that Jefferson's early enthusiasm for the French
Revolution *did* dwindle as time passed and the extent of the Revolution's excesses became more widely known. See Brian Steele, *Thomas Jefferson and
American Nationhood* (Cambridge, UK: Cambridge University Press, 2012),
95; Robert M. S. McDonald, "Thomas Jefferson and Historical Self-Construction: The Earth Belongs to the Living?" *Historian* 61, no. 2 (1999): 289–310,
esp. 295; R. R. Palmer, "The Dubious Democrat: Thomas Jefferson in Bourbon
France," *Political Science Quarterly* 72, no. 3 (1957): 388–404.

88. See the discussion of "Jefferson versus Hamilton" in Boles, *Jefferson*, ch. 15, esp. 227; for Hamilton's perspective, see Ron Chernow, *Alexander Hamilton* (New York: Penguin Press, 2004).

89. TJ to WS, 3 Jan. 1793. Short, who was acting as America's fiscal agent in the Netherlands, believed that he acted as any reasonable person would have, and he asked Jefferson to publish *all* his correspondence with Hamilton so that everyone, including the president, would be able to see the facts of the matter for themselves. Short concluded in his letter of 5 April 1793 that "I do not suppose Mr. Hamilton has done this to injure me; but to save his favorite and that of the President, against whom he thought perhaps there would be still more malevolence than against me" (referring, I believe, to Gouverneur Morris, then minister in Paris). See TJ to WS, 23 March 1793; WS to TJ, 5 April 1793; WS to TJ, 22 May 1794. I am indebted to Ziesche for his excellent discussion of Jefferson, Short, Hamilton, and the "Adam and Eve" letter in "Cosmopolitan Patriots," 98–102. For more on the Hamilton–Short affair, see Shackelford, "William Short," ch. 14. It is also important to note that, when Jefferson wrote his now-infamous "Adam and Eve" letter of 3 January 1793, he was in the middle of months of tense correspondence with a younger man he knew intimately and felt free to admonish in strong terms. This perhaps helps to explain why Jefferson's tone in this particular letter is so extreme ("Were there but an Adam and an Eve left in every country, and left free, it would be better than as it now is"). One of Jefferson's most prominent critics in recent years used this letter to argue that Jefferson would have admired the genocidal dictator Pol Pot. See Conner Cruise O'Brian, *The Long Affair: Thomas Jefferson and the French Revolution, 1785–1800* (Chicago: University of Chicago Press, 1998), 150.

90. Shackelford, "William Short," 327; TJ to WS, 28 Jan. 1792.

91. See the chapter on Short's Spanish mission in Shackelford, "William Short," ch. 13. For Short's commission as a treaty negotiator with Spain, see TJ to WS, 18 March 1782.

92. For rank issues, see WS and William Carmichael to TJ, 19 Feb. 1793. At first, Carmichael and Short were joint treaty commissioners. After Jefferson resigned, Short was appointed sole commissioner plenipotentiary to Spain and later was also appointed sole minister resident. See George Washington and Edmund Randolph, "Short's Commission as Commissioner Plenipotentiary to Spain," 11 July 1794, and George Washington and Edmund Randolph, "Short's Commission as Minister Resident at Madrid," 28 May 1794, both in Short Papers, LOC. See also WS to Secretary of State [Randolph], 12 Aug. 1794, Short Papers, LOC. For the failed marriage proposal, see Shackelford,

"William Short," 391. Rosalie seems to have refused Short at first because she was afraid to leave her distraught grandmother, who was also her mother-in-law, so soon after the duke's murder. Short did what he could to ensure their physical safety and skillfully transferred Rosalie's property and about $60,000 of her funds to his own name in order to save it from confiscation by the revolutionary government. He also continued to hope for marriage at some future point, and their letters during this period of separation are romantic and heart-wrenching.

93. See discussion in Shackelford, "William Short," 442ff.

94. See, for example, WS to TJ, 7 Oct. 1793, 7 Nov. 1793, 22 May 1794.

95. WS to TJ, 7 Oct. 1793.

96. See Daniel P. Resnick, "The Societe des Amis des Noirs and the Abolition of Slavery," *French Historical Studies* 7, no. 4 (Autumn 1972), 558–569; David Brion Davis, *The Problem of Slavery in the Age of Revolution, 1770–1823*, 2nd ed. (New York: Oxford University Press, 1999), 95–100; David Geggus, "Racial Equality, Slavery, and Colonial Secession during the Constituent Assembly," *American Historical Review* 94, no. 5 (1989): 1290–1308; Robin Blackburn, *The Overthrow of Colonial Slavery* (London: Verso, 1988), 169–177.

97. For Jefferson's refusal to join the Société, see TJ to Brissot de Warville, 11 Feb. 1788.

98. Jeffrey D. Waller, "Breaching the Citadel of Slavery: Condorcet, the Abbé Grégoire, and the Assault on Racial Hierarchy in the Colonial Disputes [1788–1791]" (master's thesis, Georgia Southern University, 2017), 6.

99. Not all members of this group were the children of white masters; some were slaves who were rewarded with freedom for their exemplary service or who had purchased their own freedom. See Jeremy D. Popkin, *A Concise History of the Haitian Revolution* (Malden, MA: Wiley-Blackwell, 2011), 23. For more on this topic, see Laurent Dubois, *A Colony of Citizens: Revolution and Slave Emancipation in the French Caribbean, 1787–1804* (Chapel Hill: University of North Carolina Press, 2004). For the disputes between the planter class and *philosophes* in the metropole, see David Allen Harvey, *The French Enlightenment and Its Others: The Mandarin, the Savage, and the Invention of the Human Sciences* (New York: Palgrave Macmillan, 2012), 173–179.

100. Popkin, *Concise History of the Haitian Revolution*, 24.

101. Condorcet, *Réflexions sur l'esclavage des nègres. Par M. Schwartz, Pasteur du Saint-Evangile à Bienne* (Neufchatel: Société Typographique, 1781), reprinted in Paris by Frouillé in 1788. For Condorcet, see David Williams, *Condorcet and Modernity* (Cambridge, UK: Cambridge University Press,

2004). For the dialogue between Condorcet and Malouet, see Waller, "Breaching the Citadel of Slavery," ch. 2.

102. According to the editors of the Jefferson *Papers*, TJ bought two copies on 2 Aug. 1788. See editorial note to "Jefferson's Notes from Condorcet on Slavery," *Papers*, 14: 498.

103. See, for instance, TJ to Condorcet, 30 Aug. 1791, regarding Benjamin Banneker. Condorcet became a victim of the Terror. He was arrested on 24 March 1794; he was found dead in his cell the next day, from either poison or the effects of his long and desperate attempt to escape the radicals who were hunting him. Shackelford, "William Short," 121–122, fn.57.

104. Condorcet, *Réflexions*, 16; cited in Waller, "Breaching the Citadel of Slavery," 20–21.

105. Chastellux, trans. George Grieve, *Travels in North America*; Jacques-Pierre Brissot de Warville, "Testament politique de l'angleterre" (Paris, 1778); WS to Nelson, 25 Oct. 1786, Short Papers, LOC. For a much more flattering view of Chastellux's *Travels*, see Jack Kelly, "Revolutionary Tourist: Chastellux in America," *Journal of the American Revolution*, online, 4 March 2016, https://allthingsliberty.com/2016/03/revolutionary-tourist-chastellux-in-america. See also my discussion of Chastellux's *Travels*, and its reception in France, in chapter 3. It should be noted that Short's admiration for Condorcet ended when the Frenchman abandoned his patron, the Duke de la Rochefoucauld, to join a new faction during the Revolution; the Duke's family—and probably also Short—blamed Condorcet for the Duke's subsequent murder.

106. For letters of introduction, see Shackelford, "William Short," 369, fn.33. For more on Brissot and Washington, see François Furstenberg, "Atlantic Slavery, Atlantic Freedom: George Washington, Slavery, and Transatlantic Abolitionist Networks," *William and Mary Quarterly* 68, no. 2 (2011): 247–286.

107. Chastellux was born in 1734; Brissot was born in 1754.

108. Chastellux, *Travels*, 2:198.

109. Chastellux, 2:198, 200.

110. *Loving v. Virginia*, 388 U.S. 1 (1967); Ferdinando Fairfax, "Plan for Liberating the Negroes Within the United States," *American Museum*, Dec. 1790, 285–287, cited in Guyatt, *Bind Us Apart*, 217.

111. J. P. Brissot de Warville, *New Travels in the United States of America, 1788*, ed. Durand Echeverria, trans. Mara Soceanu Vamos and Echeverria (Cambridge, MA: Harvard University Press, 1964), 168.

112. Brissot de Warville, *New Travels*, 168.

113. Brissot de Warville, 170, 183.

114. Brissot de Warville: Jefferson reference, 171; physician, 172. Brissot even gently criticized George Washington, with whom he had spent two days at Mount Vernon. Washington's slaves were treated very humanely, he wrote, and Washington's commitment to emancipation rendered him "a soul so elevated, so pure, and so disinterested." However, when Washington told Brissot that Virginia was not ready for emancipation—that "it was dangerous to strike too vigorously at a prejudice which had begun to diminish"—and that "[a]lmost all the Virginians . . . believe that the liberty of the Blacks cannot soon become general," Brissot flatly told him that the Virginians were wrong. Although Washington believed Virginia was not ready for an emancipation society like the Société in France, since such a society might "give dangerous ideas to their slaves," Brissot replied that "sooner or later the negroes [will] obtain their liberty every where" and it was in Virginians' best interests to be ready (173, 174). Brissot was also careful to mention that the "virtuous Maddison" stood bravely against the proslavery voices in the federal Congress of 1787 when they reacted to antislavery petitions from Pennsylvania (179).

115. For Brissot on colonization, see Thomas Clarkson, *An Essay on the Impolicy of the African Slave Trade. In Two Parts. By the Rev. T. Clarkson, M.A. To Which Is Added, an Oration, Upon the Necessity of Establishing at Paris, a Society to Promote the Abolition of the Trade and Slavery of the Negroes. By J. P. Brissot De Warville* (Philadelphia, 1788). See Furstenberg, "Atlantic Slavery, Atlantic Freedom"; Resnick, "The Society des Amis des Noirs," 562; Davis, *The Problem of Slavery in the Age of Revolution*, 95. For "generate profits," see Guyatt, *Bind Us Apart*, 212–213.

116. Brissot de Warville, *New Travels*, 183–184.

117. For more on "enlightened" liberals' inability to imagine integration, see Guyatt, *Bind Us Apart*, esp. 224.

118. Brissot de Warville, *New Travels*, 185.

119. Janet Polasky, *Revolutions without Borders: The Call to Liberty in the Atlantic World* (New Haven, CT: Yale University Press, 2015), 89.

120. WS to TJ, 25 Dec. 1789. Short did not discuss Clarkson's visit in this letter, although it prefigured this controversy over the pamphlet.

121. This is a complex shift in strategies that had several motivating factors, partly outlined in Marcel Dorigny, "Mirabeau and the Société des Amis des Noirs: Which Way to Abolish Slavery?" in *The Abolitions of Slavery: From L. F. Sonthonax to Victor Schoelcher, 1793, 1794, 1848*, ed. Marcel Dorginy (UNESCO/Berghahn Books, 2003), 121–132.

122. David Brion Davis, *The Problem of Slavery in the Age of Revolution, 1770–1823* (Ithaca: Cornell University Press, 1975), 143. See also C. L . R. James,

The Black Jacobins: Toussaint L'Ouverture and the San Domingo Revolution,
2nd ed. (New York: Random House, 1963); David P. Geggus, "Racial Equality,
Slavery, and Colonial Secession during the Constituent Assembly," *American
Historical Review* 94, no. 5 (1989): 1290–1308; Dubois, *A Colony of Citizens*;
John D. Garrigus, *Before Haiti: Race and Citizenship in French Saint-Domingue*
(New York: Palgrave Macmillan, 2006); David P. Geggus, *Haitian Revolution-
ary Studies* (Bloomington: Indiana University Press, 2002); Jeremy Popkin,
You Are All Free: The Haitian Revolution and the Abolition of Slavery (New
York: Cambridge University Press, 2010).

123. He did not reply (having not received Short's letter) until 6 April 1790.
By then, Short had written several more letters, and Jefferson did not respond
to each individual issue raised, probably because it would have taken too long.

124. As Nicholas Guyatt recounts it, Short "told his family to treat his only
slave, Stephen, as a free man: he was to come and go as he pleased, choose his
employer, and work for wages" (*Bind Us Apart*, 312). It is unclear what happened to Stephen or why Short did not simply emancipate him—perhaps he
anticipated legal challenges from his father's creditors. For the terms of the
will, see Shackelford, "William Short," 20ff.

125. See Shackelford, "William Short," 493ff; for the sale of the slaves, see
502. When Short later found out that the family slaves had been resold, away
from a friend to strangers, he was wracked with guilt: "I cannot describe to
you the pain this circumstance has caused me," he told Jefferson, since he felt
partly responsible and knew the slaves were separated from their families and
perhaps being mistreated. He attempted to find the slaves and buy them back,
then free the ones who seemed ready and put the children into apprenticeships to prepare them for freedom; the remainder he planned to free in his
will. See WS to TJ, 6 Aug. 1800.

126. Shackelford, "William Short," 496.

127. TJ to WS, 18 March 1792. For the history of Indian Camp, see the "History" page of the Morven website, maintained by the University of Virginia
Foundation—the current owner of the Indian Camp property, which is now
called "Morven," at http://www.uvafoundation.com/history-and-gardens.
Jefferson also mentioned an "Indian Camp" that his wife inherited; this is discussed on the website of the University of Tennessee Archeological program at
http://web.utk.edu/~bheath2/IndianCampA.html; see also TJ to Anne Eppes
Harris, 26 April 1773.

128. TJ to WS, 24 April 1792.

129. TJ to WS, 16 Oct. 1792.

130. Yet another misunderstanding seems to have occurred during Short's

trip back to America; see Jefferson's attempt to reassure Short of his affection in TJ to WS, 12 June 1807.

131. WS to TJ, 30 Nov. 1792.

132. TJ to WS, 11 July 1793.

133. WS to TJ, 7 Oct. 1793.

134. WS to TJ, 7 Oct. 1793.

135. WS to TJ, 7 Oct. 1793.

136. WS to Rosalie, 30 March 1794, Short–La Rochefoucauld Correspondence, APS.

137. "If you insist on remaining with your grandmother—and I admit that her age and your devotion to her would demand it—I shall never again leave you but shall ask permission of my government to remain in Paris. . . . Paris is the only place outside of my own country that I care to live." WS to Rosalie, 23 July 1794, Short–La Rochefoucauld Correspondence, APS. For Short blaming himself, see Shackelford, "William Short," 464–465.

138. WS to TJ, 7 Nov. 1793.

139. TJ to WS, 23. 1793. Jefferson did attempt to purchase plots of developed land in cities, but in 1793 no such plots were affordable in Philadelphia, where he looked. In 1797 he updated Short, telling him he could now find such plots, but hesitated to buy them because "they are so liable to a loss of the capital by fire, that tho proposed by you I have not renewed endeavors to purchase them" (TJ to WS, 12 March 1797).

140. TJ to WS, 25 May 1795.

141. WS to TJ, 2 Sep. 1795. Short remained hesitant regarding the precise location of the property, however, and did not want Jefferson to buy any adjacent lands until he could return and see for himself.

142. WS to TJ, 30 Sep. 1795. Interestingly, in this letter Short tells Jefferson of a recent encounter with an Italian explorer who had just returned from a voyage that took him up the Pacific Coast of America: "You have no doubt heard of Malaspina the Spanish circumnavigator. He is now preparing the account of his late voyage—it will be some time I fear before it will be printed and published. He is a great admirer of your principles and writings—your notes on Virginia are he tells me his *vade mecum* [essential guidebook]."

143. WS to David Humphreys, 1 Aug. 1794, Short Papers, LOC, cited in Shackelford, "William Short," 465. See also WS to Rosalie, 30 Sep. 1794, Short–La Rochefoucauld Correspondence, APS; cited in Shackelford, 466.

144. TJ to WS, 12 March 1797.

145. Shackelford, "William Short," 476.

146. See WS to Rosalie, 29 July 1795, Short–La Rochefoucauld Corres-

pondence, APS. Unfortunately, James Monroe had been America's minister to France since 1794, and Short and Rosalie felt he was cruel in refusing to help them send mail back and forth while Rosalie was under suspicion from the French revolutionary government; Short seems never to have fully forgiven his former friend for this and other offenses. See Rosalie to WS, 14 Dec. 1794, Short–La Rochefoucauld Correspondence, APS.

147. Jefferson referred to her grandmother the Duchess d'Enville's friendship as "one of the most precious of my acquisitions" (TJ to WS, 30 June 1797).

148. WS to TJ, 30 March 1797.

149. WS to TJ, 27 Dec. 1797, *Papers* 29: 597.

150. Annette Gordon-Reed notably drew attention to this remarkable letter in her prize-winning book *The Hemingses of Monticello*, 536–539.

151. WS to TJ, 27 Feb. 1798.

152. Brissot was guillotined in October 1793; Condorcet died in prison in 1794.

153. WS to TJ, 27 Feb. 1798.

154. C. B. Wadstrom, *An Essay on Colonization, Particularly Applied to the Western Coast of Africa . . . Also Brief Descriptions of the Colonies . . . in Africa, Including Those of Sierra Leona and Bulama* (London: Darton and Harvey, 1794).

155. TJ, *Notes on the State of Virginia*, ed. Shuffelton, 146.

156. See editorial note to WS to TJ, 27 Feb. 1798, in *Papers of Thomas Jefferson*, 30: 154.

157. WS to TJ, 21 Feb. 1798.

158. WS to TJ, 27 Feb. 1798.

159. WS to TJ, 27 Feb. 1798.

160. For Mrs. Tucker, see Gordon-Reed, *Hemingses of Monticello*, 537.

161. Sally Hemings's mother, Elizabeth "Betty" Hemings, is widely believed to have had several children, including Sally, with Martha Wayles Jefferson's father, who owned the Hemings family until his death. See Gordon-Reed, *Hemingses of Monticello*, 27.

162. The quotation is attributed to the enslaved blacksmith Isaac Granger Jefferson in James A. Bear, *Jefferson at Monticello* (Charlottesville: University Press of Virginia, 1967), 4.

163. Gordon-Reed, *Hemingses of Monticello*, 538.

164. WS to TJ, 27 Feb. 1798.

165. WS to TJ, 27 Feb. 1798.

166. See the correspondence between TJ and Stevens Thomson Mason in 1798 and 1799; quotation from TJ to Mason, 27 Oct. 1799. For the plots of

land, see TJ to Mason, 11 Oct. 1798. During the years between his service in the Washington administration and his presidency, Jefferson attempted several agricultural reforms; he implemented crop rotation, invented a new plow, began a business making nails, and implemented several other changes designed to improve the efficiency of both his workers and his land. See Lucia C. Stanton, *"Those Who Labor for My Happiness": Slavery at Thomas Jefferson's Monticello* (Charlottesville: University of Virginia Press, 2012), esp. 11; Boles, *Jefferson*, 259–261.

167. Gordon-Reed, *The Hemingses of Monticello*, 583.

168. TJ to WS, 18 Jan. 1826, from the Thomas Jefferson Papers, transcribed and edited by Gerard W. Gawalt, Manuscript Division, Library of Congress www.loc.gov/resource/mtj1.055_0829_0830.

169. Madison Hemings, quoted in Gordon-Reed, *The Hemingses of Monticello*, 326. See Gordon-Reed, *Thomas Jefferson and Sally Hemings: An American Controversy* (Charlottesville: University of Virginia Press, 1997).

CHAPTER FIVE. A LASTING INFLUENCE: THE "SONS"
APPROPRIATE THE *NOTES*

1. Thomas Jefferson (hereafter "TJ") to Madison, 11 May 1785; TJ to Chastellux, 7 June 1785 ("it is to them"); Bishop Madison to TJ, 10 Feb. 1789.

2. Other notable actions Jefferson took to show his opposition to slavery include authoring an antislavery proviso in the Northwest Ordinance of 1784, writing letters denouncing the practice throughout his life, and providing his legal services pro bono in several freedom suits early in his career.

3. TJ, *Notes on the State of Virginia*, ed. Frank C. Shuffelton (New York: Penguin Books, 1999), 169. Jefferson issued this warning in the context of an inevitable slave uprising, declaring that one day the slaves would outnumber *and* overpower the white population and that God would not side with the white people on that day. I invoke it here in the sense that slavery was the primary cause of the Civil War and that enslaved people (or the formerly enslaved, such as Frederick Douglass) themselves were instrumental in bringing about the "revolution" in Virginia, albeit in a less violent way than Jefferson had predicted.

4. Winfield Scott, *Memoirs of Lieut.-General Scott*, vol. 2 (New York: Sheldon and Co., 1864; reprinted Bedford, MA: Applewood Books., n.d.), 372. For Scott's views on slavery, see Timothy D. Johnson, *Winfield Scott: The Quest for Military Glory* (Lawrence: University Press of Kansas, 1998), 145–146, 214, 222. Johnson argues that Scott's moderate stances—supporting gradual

emancipation and either colonization or slow education and integration, but also supporting the Compromise of 1850 (and thus the Fugitive Slave Act)—offended voters in both the North and South, which contributed to his failure as a political candidate.

5. TJ to William Short (hereafter "WS"), 14 Dec. 1789.

6. Melvin Patrick Ely, "Richard and Judith Randolph, St. George Tucker, George Wythe, Syphax Brown, and Hercules White: Racial Equality and the Snares of Prejudice," in *Revolutionary Founders: Rebels, Radicals, and Reformers in the Making of the Nation*, ed. Alfred F. Young, Gary B. Nash, and Ray Raphael (New York: Vintage Books, 2012), 323–336; see 324 for Yorktown.

7. See discussion of Tucker during the Revolutionary War in Phillip Hamilton, *The Making and Unmaking of a Revolutionary Family: The Tuckers of Virginia, 1752–1830* (Charlottesville: University of Virginia Press, 2008), 30–48, quote at 44. The Declaration of Rights may be viewed on the Library of Congress website at www.loc.gov/resource/rbpe.17802200.

8. It was Mrs. Tucker who inspired Short to ask Jefferson, in the midst of a discussion over race mixing, if he remembered "a Mrs. Randolph afterwards Mrs. Tucker,—There is no country that might not be content to have its women like her" (WS to TJ, 27 Feb. 1798). So far as we know, Mrs. Tucker was not of mixed race.

9. Hamilton, *Making and Unmaking*, 78; W. Edwin Hemphill, "George Wythe, America's First Law Professor" (master's thesis, Emory University, 1933).

10. Tucker, quoted in Robert M. Cover, *Justice Accused: Antislavery and the Judicial Process* (New Haven, CT: Yale University Press, 1975), 37–38. See also Hamilton, *Making and Unmaking*, 80–81; Annette Gordon-Reed, "Thomas Jefferson and St. George Tucker: The Makings of Revolutionary Slaveholders," in *Jefferson, Lincoln, and Wilson: The American Dilemma of Race and Democracy*, ed. John Milton Cooper Jr. and Thomas J. Knock (Charlottesville: University of Virginia Press, 2010), 24.

11. There were so many members of the Randolph family living in Virginia (including Jefferson's own relatives), and so many of them with the same first name, that identifying individuals by their property became common. The Tucker family also had confusingly similar names; St. George Tucker is often confused with his younger cousin George Tucker, and historians sometimes ascribe the elder jurist's *Dissertation* to the younger man. Further confusing matters, George Tucker also became a professor and author and wrote an important antislavery essay.

12. Hamilton, *Making and Unmaking*, 71–72.

13. Laurent Dubois, *Avengers of the New World: The Story of the Haitian Revolution* (Cambridge, MA: Belknap Press, 2005). For the slave revolt's beginning, see 94. For unfree labor after independence, see 239ff. For the mass killings of white people at the end of the revolution, see Philippe R. Girard, "Caribbean Genocide: Racial War in Haiti, 1802–1804," *Patterns of Prejudice* 39, no. 2 (2005): 138–161.

14. See WS to TJ, 8 Nov. 1791.

15. *Virginia Independent Chronicle and General Advertiser*, 2 June 1790, quoted in Eva Sheppard Wolf, *Race and Liberty in the New Nation: Emancipation in Virginia from the Revolution to Nat Turner's Rebellion* (Baton Rouge: Louisiana State University Press, 2006), 115.

16. For the ways in which the Haitian Revolution affected the discourse of both slaveholders and antislavery advocates, see Winthrop D. Jordan, *White Over Black: American Attitudes Toward the Negro, 1550–1812* (Chapel Hill: University of North Carolina Press, 1968), ch. 10; David Brion Davis, *The Problem of Slavery in the Age of Revolution, 1770–1823* (Ithaca and London: Cornell University Press, 1975), esp. ch. 3; Merton L. Dillon, *Slavery Attacked: Southern Slaves and Their Allies, 1619–1865* (Baton Rouge and London: Louisiana State University Press, 1990), ch. 3; Matthew J. Clavin, *Toussaint Louverture and the American Civil War: The Promise and Peril of a Second Haitian Revolution* (Philadelphia: University of Pennsylvania Press, 2010); and Alan Taylor, *The Internal Enemy: Slavery and War in Virginia, 1772–1832* (New York: W. W. Norton & Company, 2014), 89–90. For the ways in which the Haitian Revolution was understood by enslaved people in Virginia, see James Sidbury, "Saint Domingue in Virginia: Ideology, Local Meanings, and Resistance to Slavery, 1790–1800," *Journal of Southern History* 63, no. 3 (1997): 531–552; see esp. 540 for the refugees.

17. Wolf, *Race and Liberty*, 116–118.

18. Several pieces of this remarkable correspondence were published by the Massachusetts Historical Society at the time; they are cited in Nicholas Guyatt, *Bind Us Apart: How Enlightened Americans Invented Racial Segregation* (New York: Basic Books, 2016), 18–21. Tucker also wrote to Congressman Zephaniah Swift of Connecticut and referred to his answers throughout the *Dissertation*, although their correspondence is less well known today. See St. George Tucker, *Dissertation on Slavery: With a Proposal for the Gradual Abolition of It* (Philadelphia: Printed for Mathew Carey, 1796), at footnote "c," 12.

19. Tucker's sources were off by one year; the first slaves arrived at Jamestown in 1619. See Peter Kolchin, *American Slavery: 1619–1877*, rev. ed (New York: Hill and Wang, 2003), 3.

20. Tucker, *Dissertation*, 57 ("more favorable"), 66 (all other quotes).

21. Tucker, 77. In Jefferson's words: "[T]he whole commerce between master and slave is a perpetual exercise of the most boisterous passions, the most unremitting despotism on the one part, and degrading submissions on the other" (*Notes*, ed. Shuffelton, 168).

22. TJ, *Notes*, ed. Shuffelton, 145; Kolchin, *American Slavery*, 78.

23. Tucker, *Dissertation*, 83. As we have seen, the other remaining member of the committee to revise the laws, Edmund Pendleton, was ill at the time they worked on this amendment.

24. Tucker, *Dissertation*, 78–79, 84.

25. TJ, *Notes*, ed. Shuffelton, 169; Tucker, *Dissertation*, 80.

26. Tucker, *Dissertation*, 82 ("without"), 97 ("no man"), 94 ("denying them").

27. Tucker's philosophical defense for this tactic echoes the language of the Virginia Declaration of Rights: freed slaves do have "a right to be admitted to all the privileges of a citizen.—But have not men when they enter into a state of society, a right to admit, or exclude any description of persons, as they think proper?" (Tucker, *Dissertation*, 89).

28. Tucker, 89 ("If it be true"), 94 (prejudice), 96 ("obliterate"). See the excellent discussion of racism in Tucker's thought in Wolf, *Race and Liberty*, 104–107. Wolf rightly notes that Philip Hamilton's study of Tucker does not give racism its due importance in understanding why Tucker came to accommodate himself to slavery. See Wolf, *Race and Liberty*, 107, fn.35. For more on Tucker's plan, see Paul Finkelman, "The Dragon St. George Could Not Slay: Tucker's Plan to End Slavery," *William and Mary Law Review* 47, no. 4 (2006): 1213–1243.

29. TJ to St. George Tucker, 15 Sep. 1795. The Tuckers also visited Monticello after the *Dissertation* was published; see TJ to Tucker, 2 Aug. 1798. For Tucker sending the pamphlet, see Tucker to TJ, 2 Aug. 1797.

30. See, for instance, TJ to Jared Sparks, 4 Feb. 1824. In this letter, written two years before his death, Jefferson adhered to the same plan as he had laid out in the *Notes*, with a few exceptions: rather than calling for the state to educate the freed generation of young slaves, he now recognized the unwillingness of voters to spend money on such a project and instead argued that the freed generation could stay with their mothers while small at the state's expense, then work for the masters until old enough to emigrate. Jefferson also now recommended Haiti as the destination for the freed people, believing that Africa would be an inhospitable and cost-prohibitive option despite the work of the American Colonization Society in Liberia. See the discussion of this issue in Arthur Scherr, "Thomas Jefferson, White Immigration, and Black

Emancipation," *Southern Studies: An Interdisciplinary Journal of the South* 23, no. 1 (2016): 1–26.

31. TJ to St. George Tucker, 28 Aug. 1797.

32. St. George Tucker to Jeremy Belknap, 13 Aug. 1797, *Collections of the Massachusetts Historical Society* (Boston: Massachusetts Historical Society, 1877), 3:427–428.

33. For more on Pleasants, see the editorial note for Robert Pleasants to TJ, 1 June 1796, in the *Papers of Thomas Jefferson.* On that date Pleasants sent Jefferson a plan he had crafted for educating black children, apparently including the children of slaves. Pleasants believed education for slaves was both a duty and a practical step toward readying that population for the freedom that "at this enlightened day is generally acknowledged to be their right." Jefferson replied on 27 August that he not only supported Pleasants's plan but also that he himself had written a "Bill for the More General Diffusion of Knowledge" in 1778 that would provide free public education for all white children and, with "very small alterations," could also provide the same to the children of slaves and free black people. If Pleasants would organize petitions that supported Jefferson's bill, then Jefferson felt sure there already existed enough public support for the bill to succeed in the Assembly. Pleasants subsequently searched for Jefferson's bill but could not find it either in print or in the records of any other legislators. He then discovered that the legislature had just passed a different bill that provided for the education of free children; however, as he told Jefferson, prejudice would likely ensure that only *white* free children benefited from the measure. In the end, the 1796 bill did little to improve the education levels of either white or black Virginians, since it failed to incorporate Jefferson's provision that the state—not localities—oversee the effort. See Pleasants to TJ, 2 Aug. 1787.

34. St. George Tucker to Robert Pleasants, 29 June 1797, Tucker–Coleman Papers, Mss. 40 T79, box 63, Earl Gregg Swem Library, College of William and Mary.

35. Tucker to Pleasants, 29 June 1797, *Tucker–Coleman Papers*, College of William and Mary.

36. James Madison to Robert Pleasants, 30 Oct. 1791, quoted in Drew R. McCoy, *The Last of the Fathers: James Madison and the Republican Legacy* (Cambridge and New York: Cambridge University Press, 1989), 305. For my discussion of the reaction to the 1785 antislavery petitions, see chapter 3.

37. For Franklin and the petitions, see "Benjamin Franklin Petitions Congress," *National Archives*, 1 Feb. 2017, www.archives.gov/legislative/features /franklin. For the congressional response, see the *American State Papers:*

Miscellaneous (Washington, DC, 1832), 1st Cong., 2nd sess., available online at the Library of Congress, http://memory.loc.gov.

38. James Madison to Benjamin Rush, 20 March 1790, *Founders Online*, National Archives, last modified 29 June 2017, http://founders.archives.gov/doc uments/Madison/01-13-02-0079; Madison to Edmund Randolph, 21 March 1790, *The Writings of James Madison: 1790–1802* (New York: G. P. Putnam's Sons, 1906), 8; Thomas T. Tucker, quoted in Joseph Gales, ed., *The Debates and Proceedings in the Congress of the United States* (Washington, DC, 1834), 1st Cong., 2nd sess., 1242–1243; Richard S. Newman, "Prelude to the Gag Rule: Southern Reaction to Antislavery Petitions in the First Federal Congress," *Journal of the Early Republic* 16, no. 4 (1996): 571–599, quote at 574. For more on this incident, see John B. Boles, *Jefferson: Architect of American Liberty* (New York: Basic Books, 2017), 216.

39. St. George Tucker, *Reflections on the Cession of Louisiana to the United States* (Washington, DC, 1803), quoted in Hamilton, *Making and Unmaking*, 151.

40. Scott, *Memoirs of Lieut.-General Scott*, 372; Edward Coles, "Autobiography," April 1844, Edward Coles Collection, Historical Society of Pennsylvania (hereafter "HSP"), quoted in Suzanne Cooper Guasco, *Confronting Slavery: Edward Coles and the Rise of Antislavery Politics in Nineteenth-Century America* (DeKalb: Northern Illinois University Press, 2013), 12. See also Kurt E. Leichtle and Bruce G. Carveth, *Crusade Against Slavery: Edward Coles, Pioneer of Freedom* (Carbondale: Southern Illinois University Press, 2011); David Ress, *Governor Edward Coles and the Vote to Forbid Slavery in Illinois, 1823–1824* (Jefferson, NC: McFarland & Co., 2006); and McCoy, *Last of the Fathers*.

41. Guasco, *Confronting Slavery*, 20–21; see also my discussion of Bishop Madison's involvement with the *Notes* in chapter 3.

42. Bishop James Madison to Granville Sharp, 21 June 1791, quoted in Terry L. Meyers, "Thinking About Slavery at the College of William and Mary," *William and Mary Bill of Rights Journal* 21, no. 4 (2013): 1215–1257, quote at 1254.

43. Guasco, *Confronting Slavery*, 24–26; 18. For more on antislavery thought at the college during this period, see Meyers, "Thinking About Slavery at the College of William and Mary."

44. Edward Coles, "Autobiography," April 1844; "Notes on Rousseau"; and other class notes, Edward Coles Collection, HSP, quoted in Guasco, *Confronting Slavery*, 28, 27. The term "neighbor" in this sense does not just refer to the person living next door but is more encompassing. In the parable of the Good Samaritan, found in the Bible in Luke 10, Jesus taught that a "neighbor" could even be one's ethnic enemy.

45. Coles, "Autobiography," 1844, Edward Coles Collection, HSP, quoted in Guasco, *Confronting Slavery*, 30, 31.

46. Coles, "Autobiography," 1844, Edward Coles Collection, HSP, quoted in Guasco, *Confronting Slavery*, 36. For Chapman Johnson, see Guasco, *Confronting Slavery*, 31–32; for John Coles's death, see 35.

47. Coles, "Autobiography," 1844, Edward Coles Collection, HSP, quoted in Guasco, *Confronting Slavery*, 37; James Madison to Robert Pleasants, 30 Oct. 1791, quoted in McCoy, *Last of the Fathers*, 305. Although northern states were in the process of gradually manumitting all slaves by 1806, not all permitted free black immigration. White Virginians often did not bother to enforce the 1806 law, and by 1860 it is possible that as many as one-third of Virginia's free black inhabitants were there illegally (Wolf, *Race and Liberty*, 135).

48. Wolf, 122. The year 1806 was also when St. George Tucker undid the work of his mentor, George Wythe, by ruling that Wythe's earlier verdict in a case of a mixed-race person seeking freedom was illegal. Whereas Wythe applied the Virginia Bill of Rights in its most expansive sense, emphasizing that all men were born free, Tucker noted that the framers of the Bill of Rights would certainly not have wished to lose their property rights by declaring that the African people who were already enslaved had a right to freedom. Tucker also offered a guide for how judges could apply the sense of sight to determine the race of a person who was seeking freedom: only those with white ancestry could qualify, and those of mixed background could be distinguished by hair texture and other measures. See the discussion in Taylor, *Internal Enemy*, 108–109.

49. John Randolph, quoted in Hamilton, *Making and Unmaking*, 150.

50. For the number of conspirators, see James Sidbury, *Ploughshares into Swords: Race, Rebellion, and Identity in Gabriel's Virginia, 1730–1810* (New York: Cambridge University Press, 1997), 8. For an argument focusing on Gabriel's identification with black and white artisans in Richmond, as well as his appropriation of revolutionary ideology (both American and French), see Douglas R. Egerton, *Gabriel's Rebellion: The Virginia Slave Conspiracies of 1800 and 1802* (Chapel Hill: University of North Carolina Press, 1993). For the view that religion and race played more significant roles, see Sidbury, *Ploughshares into Swords*. For a detailed critique of previous accounts and careful account of the conspiracy's events, see Michael L. Nicholls, *Whispers of Rebellion: Narrating Gabriel's Conspiracy* (Charlottesville: University of Virginia Press, 2013).

51. James Monroe to TJ, 15 Sep. 1800; TJ, *Notes*, ed. Shuffelton, 169; TJ to Monroe, 20 Sep. 1800. See Boles, *Jefferson*, 311–312.

52. Wolf, *Race and Liberty*, 120, quote at 121. For more about the complicated ways in which free black people and whites interacted, often in stark contrast to the restrictive nature of these laws, see Ira Berlin, *Slaves Without Masters: The Free Negro in the Antebellum South* (New York: Random House, 1974); Kirt Von Daacke, *Freedom Has a Face: Race, Identity, and Community in Jefferson's Virginia* (Charlottesville: University of Virginia Press, 2012). Von Daacke's study of the county where Jefferson lived, Albemarle County, documents numerous openly accepted (and consensual) interracial relationships and demonstrates that, when free black people owned property and had good reputations in the community, they "acted and lived in ways that contradicted notions of a strictly enforced color line in which blackness was equated with slavery and only whites could be free" (112).

53. See, for example, Hamilton, *The Making and Unmaking*, 150. For Tucker, see Robert Colin McLean, *George Tucker, Moral Philosopher and Man of Letters* (Chapel Hill: University of North Carolina Press, 1961); Tipton Ray Snavely, *George Tucker as Political Economist* (Charlottesville: University Press of Virginia, 1964); and Christine Coalwell McDonald and Robert M. S. McDonald, "More Loved . . . and More Hated: George Tucker on Thomas Jefferson," in *Thomas Jefferson's Lives: Biographers and the Battle for History*, ed. Robert M. S. McDonald (Charlottesville: University Press of Virginia, 2019), 47–61. In 1825 Jefferson hired Tucker to teach moral philosophy at the University of Virginia. The McDonalds demonstrate that, by this time, the two men were personally and politically divided. Moreover, Willie Lee Rose asserts that George Tucker could be the author of an anonymous 1816 work that criticized, in strong terms, Jefferson's views on race as elaborated in the *Notes*, complete with an oblique reference to the rumored hypocrisy of opposing amalgamation while having a relationship with Sally Hemings. However, it is unclear what evidence exists to support Tucker's authorship of the text. By the end of his life, Tucker was strenuously opposing abolitionists, speaking out regarding ways in which he felt slavery benefited the South, and arguing that slavery would eventually, in many years, end due to demographic shifts (not including intermarriage). See "George Tucker Criticizes Jefferson's Views of Racial Difference," in *A Documentary History of Slavery in North America*, ed. Willie Lee Nichols Rose (Athens: University of Georgia Press, 1999), 76–87.

54. George Tucker, *Letter to a Member of the General Assembly of Virginia, on the Subject of the Late Conspiracy of the Slaves: With a Proposal for Their Colonization* (Baltimore: Bonsal & Niles, 1801), 6 ("late"), 7 ("merely"), 10 ("tyrant"). See the discussion in Taylor, *Internal Enemy*, 98–99.

55. Jefferson believed those lands should one day be part of the American republic and therefore not used as a colony, but Tucker argued here that it would cost less than shipping freed people to Africa or the Caribbean.

56. Tucker, *Letter to a Member of the General Assembly of Virginia*, 16. For the colonization plan, see 17–20, quote at 18. Although scholars typically mention George Tucker as influenced by and reiterating his older cousin's emancipation scheme, he actually rejected several of St. George's ideas in favor of Jefferson's. See, for example, Hamilton, *Making and Unmaking*, 150.

57. Tucker, *The Life of George Tucker: Excerpted from The Life and Philosophy of George Tucker*, ed. James Fieser (Bristol, UK: Thoemmes Contiuum, 2004), 37; Wolf, *Race and Liberty*, 125. The 1806 law was, of course, ineffective as a means of preventing future uprisings. Free black people were not major players in Gabriel's Conspiracy; only one free black man was accused, and he was acquitted. Free black people tended to value their liberty and to side with the master class rather than enslaved people. Moreover, as John Minor from Spotsylvania pointed out to his fellow delegates at the time, taking away the possibility of manumission left slaves despondent, and without hope of emancipation they might seek freedom in violent revolt (see Wolf, 125–126). The 1806 law was only selectively implemented; sometimes locals turned a blind eye to free black people living among them, and freed people could petition to remain in the state. But the statute nonetheless could be invoked during times of racial tension or economic downturns, and it deterred owners (such as Coles) who had antislavery motivations for manumitting slaves. See Philip J. Schwarz, *Migrants against Slavery: Virginians and the Nation* (Charlottesville: University of Virginia Press, 2001), 13.

58. Guasco, *Confronting Slavery*, 38–54.

59. Guasco, 39, 58 (for the Philadelphia friendships).

60. Coles, "Autobiography," 1844, Edward Coles Collection, HSP; Guasco, *Confronting Slavery*, 61; see also McCoy, *Last of the Fathers*, 311–312.

61. Coles, quoted in Guasco, *Confronting Slavery*, 61. For the rest of Madison's life, Coles continued to attempt to convince him to do more to end slavery and particularly to free Madison's own slaves. Coles believed he persuaded Madison to free his enslaved property in his will, only to be disappointed when, after Madison's death, the will did not contain that provision—perhaps because Madison mistakenly thought his wife would complete this task for him. See McCoy, *Last of the Fathers*, 318–322.

62. Madison to Pleasants, 30 Oct. 1791, in Robert A. Rutland and Thomas A. Mason, eds., *The Papers of James Madison, Congressional Series* (Charlottesville: University Press of Virginia, 1983), 14:91–92; Madison to TJ, 15 Nov.

1785. Italicized words were originally written in code. For more on Madison's gradualist antislavery views, which in many respects mirrored Jefferson's own, see McCoy, *Last of the Fathers*, ch. 7.

63. Coles to TJ, 31 July 1814.

64. Coles to TJ, 31 July 1814. See the discussion of this topic in Kevin R. C. Gutzman, *Thomas Jefferson, Revolutionary: A Radical's Struggle to Remake America* (New York: St. Martin's Press, 2017), 164–168.

65. Coles to TJ, 31 July 1814.

66. TJ to Coles, 25 Aug. 1814. As the editorial note to this letter in the *Papers of Thomas Jefferson* explains, Jefferson described this incident more fully in his 1821 autobiography; there is no official record of the Bland bill, but that was typical for bills that did not pass.

67. TJ to Coles, 25 Aug. 1814.

68. Short to TJ, 27 Feb. 1798; TJ to Coles, 25 Aug. 1814.

69. TJ to Coles, 25 Aug. 1814.

70. TJ to James Madison, 6 Sep. 1789; Madison to TJ, 4 Feb. 1790.

71. TJ to Samuel Kercheval, 12 July 1816, Library of Congress, www.loc.gov /resource/ mtj1.049_0255_0262.

72. TJ to Coles, 25 Aug. 1814.

73. TJ to Coles, 25 Aug. 1814. The phrase "armor, long unused, on shoulders trembling with age" is a translation of the Latin phrase Jefferson used; I am relying upon the editors of *The Papers of Thomas Jefferson* for this rendering.

74. For Jefferson's summary of Virginia law on racial mixing, which seems to indicate that any children he had with the mixed-race Sally Hemings were actually legally "white" (though, in spite of this fact, not legally free), see TJ to Francis C. Gray, 4 March 1815, in *Papers*, 8:10–12. Although a few couples of mixed race did live together openly in Albemarle County, the scandal caused by James Callender's newspaper campaign against Jefferson during the election of 1800 clearly demonstrated the kind of humiliating publicity that Jefferson and his white descendants would have wished to avoid. See, for instance, Cynthia Kierner's excellent biography, *Martha Jefferson Randolph, Daughter of Monticello: Her Life and Times* (Chapel Hill: University of North Carolina Press, 2012), 119ff. One marker of change as well as of continuity in racial prejudices can be seen in the public response to the marriage of Prince Harry of the United Kingdom to an American woman of mixed (white and black) race, Meghan Markle. See, for example, Robert Booth and Lisa O'Carroll, "Prince Harry Attacks Press Over 'Wave of Abuse' of Girlfriend Meghan Markle," *The Guardian*, 8 Nov. 2016, www.theguardian.com/uk-news/2016/nov/08 /prince-harry-lambasts-press-over-meghan-markle-coverage. For the ages of

the Hemings children in 1814, see Appendix H of the *Report of the Research Committee on Thomas Jefferson and Sally Hemings*, Thomas Jefferson Foundation (Jan. 2000), available online at www.monticello.org/site/plantation-and -slavery/appendix-h-sally-hemings-and-her-children.

75. TJ to Coles, 25 Aug. 1814. The British bill to abolish the slave trade passed on 25 March 1807 after Wilberforce and a committed team of other abolitionists had been laboring for twenty-one years on the project. It took another twenty-six years for the British to abolish slavery itself in 1833. See Christopher Leslie Brown, *Moral Capital: Foundations of British Abolitionism* (Chapel Hill: Omohundro Institute and University of North Carolina Press, 2006).

76. Schwarz, *Migrants against Slavery*, 15; TJ to Coles, 25 Aug. 1814. Jefferson would perhaps have advised Coles differently if the younger man wished to take his slaves out of the state but keep them in bondage. By the 1800s Jefferson had come to advocate diffusion of slavery as a way of ameliorating the condition of the slaves themselves. Jefferson argued that if slaves were spread out across the continent, rather than concentrated in a few states, they would be able to work alongside free white laborers more frequently; they would likely be on farms rather than plantations; and eventually farmers would see that the value of slave labor did not justify the system's continuation. Many areas, rather than just a few, would then share the expenses of educating, emancipating, and colonizing the enslaved population. For a discussion of Jefferson's thought on diffusion, see Christa Dierksheide, *Amelioration and Empire: Progress and Slavery in the Plantation Americas* (Charlottesville: University of Virginia Press, 2014), 42–47.

77. Coles to TJ, 26 Sep. 1814.

78. Coles to TJ, 23 Nov. 1814; Coles to Nicholas Biddle, 6 April 1815, in the Nicholas Biddle Papers, Library of Congress, quoted in McCoy, *Last of the Fathers*, 313.

79. The quotations and summaries of Coles's views on Russian serfdom are in Guasco, *Confronting Slavery*, 68–69. Guasco provides the following references, without specifying which quotation can be found in each of the three sources: "Memoir of Edward Coles," undated, Illinois State Historical Library; Edward Coles to Brother [John], 4 Oct. 1814, Edward Coles Collection, HSP; and Edward Coles to James Monroe, 14 Dec. 1816, Papers of Edward Coles, 1786–1868, Firestone Library, Princeton University. For a comparison of American slavery and Russian serfdom, see Peter Kolchin, *Unfree Labor: American Slavery and Russian Serfdom* (Cambridge, MA: Belknap Press of Harvard University Press, 1987).

80. For Coles's fears about being unable to find a wife, friends, or a career once he moved to the frontier, see Guasco, *Confronting Slavery*, 67, 77, 81. For Coles's journey to Illinois, freeing his slaves, and becoming land registrar, see 82–88.

81. Guasco, *Confronting Slavery*, 86–87.

82. Guasco, *Confronting Slavery*, 94, 98–100; TJ to Coles, 25 Aug. 1814.

83. Guasco, *Confronting Slavery*, 109.

84. This will be discussed more in the following pages, but see, for example, Coles to Robert C. Winthrop, 5 Aug. 1856, in "Letters of Edward Coles," *William and Mary Quarterly* 7, no. 3 (1927), 166; and Coles to Henry S. Randall, 11 May 1857, 167.

85. Guasco, *Confronting Slavery*, 121–125, quote at 131. See also Eric Foner, *Free Soil, Free Labor, Free Men: The Ideology of the Republican Party before the Civil War*, 2nd ed. (Oxford, UK: Oxford University Press, 1995). For examples of Abraham Lincoln's later embrace of this antislavery nationalism, see his remarks on the Founders (Jefferson in particular) and slavery in the third, fourth, and fifth debates between himself and Stephen A. Douglas in 1858.

86. For their acquaintance by 1816, see William Short's letter to his nephew Greenbury Ridgely, 19 Feb. 1819, printed in George Green Shackelford, "To Practice Law: Aspects of the Era of Good Feelings Reflected in the Short—Ridgely Correspondence, 1816–1821," *Maryland Historical Magazine* 64, no. 4 (1969): 342–395, esp. 379. For their social circles after 1831, including membership in the American Philosophical Society, see Guasco, *Confronting Slavery*, 176.

87. WS to TJ, 18 July 1816.

88. WS to TJ, 18 July 1816.

89. TJ to WS, 10 August 1816.

90. TJ to Joseph C. Cabell, 31 Jan. 1814, quoted in Andrew Burstein, *Jefferson's Secrets: Death and Desire at Monticello* (New York: Basic Books, 2006), 138.

CHAPTER SIX. THE JEFFERSONIAN LEGACY IN VIRGINIA, 1820–1832

1. See, for example, Martha Jefferson Randolph to Ellen Wayles Randolph Coolidge, 2 Aug. 1825, *Family Letters Project* of Monticello, http://tjrs.monticello.org/ (hereafter "FLP").

2. For the Randolph and Jefferson families, see Cynthia Kierner, *Martha Jefferson Randolph, Daughter of Monticello: Her Life and Times* (Chapel Hill: University of North Carolina Press, 2012), 16. For Jefferson's fatherly advice,

see, for instance, Thomas Jefferson (hereafter "TJ") to Thomas Mann Randolph Jr. (hereafter "Randolph"), 25 Nov. 1785 and 27 Aug. 1786; quotation from TJ to Randolph, 6 July 1787. For more on the turbulent marriage of Martha and Randolph, see Kierner's excellent biography *Martha Jefferson Randolph*. The only full-length biography of Randolph to date is William Harris Gaines, *Thomas Mann Randolph: Jefferson's Son-in-Law* (Baton Rouge: Louisiana State University Press, 1966).

3. TJ to Randolph, 6 July 1787.

4. Duke de La Rochefoucauld-Liancourt (cousin to the murdered Duke de La Rochefoucauld, whose story is presented in chapter 4), quoted in Kierner, *Martha Jefferson Randolph*, 97. For the wedding, see Kierner, *Martha Jefferson Randolph*, 76–79; for the breach between Tom Jr. and his father Thomas Mann Randolph Sr., see Gaines, *Thomas Mann Randolph*, 32–39, 106–107; for life at Monticello, see Kierner, *Martha Jefferson Randolph*, 88; Gaines, *Thomas Mann Randolph*, 35–49.

5. Although some scholarly sources state (without citation) that Randolph attended the College of William and Mary as well as the University of Edinburgh, I have been unable to find any evidence that Randolph ever attended the school in Williamsburg. According to Gaines, he sailed to Edinburgh in June 1784, at age fourteen, and prior to that date had a private tutor. See Gaines, *Thomas Mann Randolph*, 12.

6. Martha Jefferson to TJ, 3 May 1787; for Randolph receiving the *Notes*, see TJ to Randolph, 6 July 1787; for the newlywed Randolph's slaves, see Kierner, *Martha Jefferson Randolph*, 87; Randolph to TJ, 5 March 1791 ("my desire to gratify").

7. Randolph to Nicholas P. Trist, 22 Nov. 1818, Papers of the Trist, Randolph, and Burke Families, ac. [accession] #10487, box 1, University of Virginia (hereafter "UVA"). Randolph was forced by financial crises to sell slaves on several occasions; see, for instance, Kierner, *Martha Jefferson Randolph*, 165–166.

8. Randolph to TJ, 29 Oct. 1802. Randolph did successfully implement a horizontal plowing system at Edgehill, which Jefferson praised for its ingenuity; see Gaines, *Thomas Mann Randolph*, 72–75.

9. Gaines, 50, 82, 115. Because of their desperate finances, however, Martha arranged for Randolph to be given a federal job as a tax collector, and he reluctantly resigned his commission for the sake of a paycheck. See Randolph to Joseph C. Cabell, 29 Dec. 1813, Southern Historical Collection, University of North Carolina, Chapel Hill.

10. Journal of the Council of State, Virginia, 27 Feb. 1820, microfilm available at the Library of Virginia.

11. TJ to John Holmes, 22 April 1820; Eva Sheppard Wolf, *Race and Liberty in the New Nation: Emancipation in Virginia from the Revolution to Nat Turner's Rebellion* (Baton Rouge: Louisiana State University Press, 2006), 173; see also Don E. Fehrenbacher, *Constitutions and Constitutionalism in the Slaveholding South* (Athens: University of Georgia Press, 1989), chap. 2.

12. TJ to John Holmes, 22 April 1820 ("the condition"); TJ to John Adams, 22 Jan. 1821; TJ to John Holmes, 22 April 1820. For a discussion of the many personal tragedies that most likely contributed to Jefferson's pessimism in 1819 and 1820, see John B. Boles, *Jefferson: Architect of American Liberty* (New York: Basic Books, 2017), 489–491; and Herbert E. Sloan, *Principle and Interest: Thomas Jefferson and the Problem of Debt* (Charlottesville: University Press of Virginia, 2001), 219–221.

13. Randolph to Nicholas P. Trist, 5 June 1820, Nicholas Philip Trist Papers, 1765–1903, Louis Round Wilson Special Collections Library, University of North Carolina, Chapel Hill (hereafter "NPTP"); TJ, comment on Kames, in E. Millicent Sowerby, comp., *Catalogue of the Library of Thomas Jefferson*, 5 vols. (Charlottesville: University of Virginia Press, 1983), 2:11–12.

14. Randolph to Nicholas P. Trist, 5 June 1820, NPTP.

15. Randolph, Speech to House of Delegates, 4 Dec. 1820, *Journal of the House of Delegates of the Commonwealth of Virginia*, Executive Papers of Governor Thomas Mann Randolph, 1819–1822, ac. #41887, Library of Virginia.

16. Randolph, Speech to House of Delegates, 4 Dec. 1820; see also Eugene D. Genovese, *Roll, Jordan, Roll: The World the Slaves Made* (New York: Vintage, 1976), esp. 285–324.

17. Randolph, Speech to House of Delegates, 4 Dec. 1820. For Jefferson and Randolph's views on Haiti as an appropriate location for emancipated slaves, see Arthur Scherr, "Light at the End of the Road: Thomas Jefferson's Endorsement of Free Haiti in His Final Years," *Journal of Haitian Studies* 15, no. 1/2 (2009): 203–216.

18. Joseph C. Cabell to TJ, 22 Dec. 1820, quoted by Gaines, *Thomas Mann Randolph*, 124; William H. Cabell to Joseph C. Cabell, 20 Dec. 1821, Cabell Family Papers, Small Special Collections Library, ac. #38-111-c, box 2, UVA. For more on Randolph's personality hindering his work as governor, see, for instance, Martha Jefferson Randolph to Nicholas P. Trist, 8 Jan. 1822, FLP.

19. TJ to David Bailie Warden, 26 Dec. 1820, in Paul L. Ford, ed., *Works of Thomas Jefferson* (12 vols.; New York, 1904–1905), 12: 181; TJ to Albert Gallatin, 26 Dec. 1820, in Merrill D. Peterson, ed., *Thomas Jefferson: Writings* (New York, 1984), 1450.

20. For the debts and sale, see Kierner, *Martha Jefferson Randolph*, 188–190;

334 Notes to Pages 234–236

Gaines, *Thomas Mann Randolph*, 155–162. Martha Jefferson Randolph to Ellen Wayles Randolph Coolidge, 2 Aug. 1825, FLP. See also TJ to Randolph, 5 June 1825, Thomas Jefferson Collection, Library of Congress, https://www.loc .gov/item/mtjbib025428/. For Randolph's death, see Gaines, *Thomas Mann Randolph*, 185–186.

21. Suzanne Cooper Guasco, *Confronting Slavery: Edward Coles and the Rise of Antislavery Politics in Nineteenth-Century America* (DeKalb: Northern Illinois University Press, 2013), 140. For the history of the ACS, see P. J. Staudenraus, *The African Colonization Movement, 1816–1865* (New York: Columbia University Press, 1961); Douglas R. Egerton, "'Its Origin Is Not a Little Curious': A New Look at the American Colonization Society," *Journal of the Early Republic* 5, no. 4 (1985): 463–480; Eric Burin, *Slavery and the Peculiar Solution: A History of the American Colonization Society* (Gainesville: University Press of Florida, 2008); Beverly C. Tomek, *Colonization and Its Discontents: Emancipation, Emigration, and Antislavery in Antebellum Pennsylvania* (New York: New York University Press, 2012); and Marie Tyler-McGraw, *An African Republic: Black and White Virginians in the Making of Liberia* (Chapel Hill: University of North Carolina Press, 2007). For ACS members declaring their organization was a founding legacy, see, for instance, these three articles: "Colonization Society," "Colonization Society," "Communication," *African Repository and Colonial Journal* 1 (April 1825), 33; 1 (Nov. 1825), 257; and 1 (March 1825), 5, cited in Guasco, 140, fn. 11.

22. TJ to Madison, 11 May 1785. Jefferson also supported free white male suffrage and equal representation based on the white population, as he affirmed when he supported the 1816 Staunton Convention, which called for a constitutional convention in order to achieve those goals. See Wolf, *Race and Liberty*, 184.

23. Guasco, *Confronting Slavery*, 142–144, quote at 142.

24. "Abolition of Slavery, From the Staunton Spectator. Memorial to the Honorable Convention of Virginia," *Richmond Enquirer*, [?] Oct. 1829, in Edward Coles, Commonplace Book, vol. 7, Edward Coles Collection, HSP. For the convention, see Alison Goodyear Freehling, *Drift Toward Dissolution: The Virginia Slavery Debate of 1831–1832* (Baton Rouge: Louisiana State University Press, 1982), ch. 3; William G. Shade, *Democratizing the Old Dominion: Virginia and the Second Party System, 1824–1861* (Charlottesville: University of Virginia Press, 1996), 59–77; Wolf, *Race and Liberty*, 185–195.

25. Wolf, *Race and Liberty*, 186, 194; Benjamin Watkins Leigh, *Proceedings and Debates of the Virginia State Convention of 1829–1830* . . . (Richmond, VA: Samuel Shepherd for Ritchie & Cook, 1830), 151, 173. Guasco presents a

different perspective on the debate, arguing that both conservatives and reformers admitted that slavery was wrong and that Monroe's major error was in indicating that colonization was a national issue that could be supported by the federal government—something that states' rights Virginians could not tolerate hearing (Guasco, *Confronting Slavery*, 149–150).

26. "For the Enquirer: To James Monroe, President of the Convention, signed Jefferson [Edward Coles]," *Richmond Enquirer*, 7 Nov. 1829, in Coles, Commonplace Book, vol. 7, 81, Edward Coles Collection, HSP.

27. The classic text is Herbert Aptheker, *Nat Turner's Slave Rebellion: Including the 1831 "Confessions"* (New York: Humanities Press, 1966), but see especially Patrick H. Breen, *The Land Shall Be Deluged in Blood: A New History of the Nat Turner Revolt* (Oxford and New York: Oxford University Press, 2016).

28. Hank Trent, *The Secret Life of Bacon Tait, a White Slave Trader Married to a Free Woman of Color* (Baton Rouge: Louisiana State University Press, 2017), 71. This closure lasted only a few years.

29. Surprisingly, there are no modern full-length biographies of Thomas Jefferson Randolph (hereafter "TJR"). He is mentioned in books such as Kierner's and Gaines's on his parents, but the best source on TJR is Joseph Carroll Vance, "Thomas Jefferson Randolph" (PhD diss., University of Virginia, 1957). See also Joseph Randolph Coolidge, *Thomas Jefferson Randolph* (Boston: Beals & Greene, 1875); Jerome A. Hurwitz, "Thomas Jefferson Randolph, Democratic Leader" (MA thesis, University of Richmond, 1938); George Green Shackelford, ed., *Collected Papers to Commemorate Fifty Years of the Monticello Association of the Descendants of Thomas Jefferson* (Princeton, NJ: Princeton University Press, 1965). During the 1831–1832 debates in the legislature, other delegates also invoked Jefferson and his plan, as I will discuss below; the debate was in some ways a referendum on Jefferson himself, but in this chapter I focus on Thomas Jefferson Randolph because of symbolic status as Jefferson's grandson and because of his leading role in the debate.

30. First quotation ("took fire") from Charles Wilson Peale to TJ, 2 May 1815, *The Papers of Thomas Jefferson, Retirement Series*, ed. J. Jefferson Looney, 18 vols. (Princeton, NJ: Princeton University Press, 2005–2018), 8: 457–466; all others from TJ to Thomas J. Randolph, 24 Nov. 1808, *Founders Online*, National Archives, www.founders.archives.gov.

31. For the debt, see "Debt," Lucia Stanton, *Monticello*, www.monticello .org/research-education/thomas-jefferson-encyclopedia/debt/. For Jeff's education and intelligence, see Martha Jefferson Randolph to TJ, 31 Jan. 1801; TJ to M. J. Randolph, 11 July 1808; M. J. Randolph to TJ, 15 July 1808; TJ to M. J. Randolph, 18 Oct. 1808, all from *Founders Online*. For Jeff's personality, see

Joseph Coolidge to Nicholas P. Trist, before 14 May 1828, FLP. For the marriage, see T. J. Randolph to Wilson Cary Nicholas, 4 Feb. 1815, FLP. For the $20,000 debt, see Sloan, *Principle and Interest* 11, 218–220; quotation from M. J. Randolph to Ellen W.R. Coolidge, ca. 22 Oct. 1826, FLP. For Jeff repaying the debt, see Vance, "Thomas Jefferson Randolph," 83. For Jeff's fundraising, see William Short to TJ, 6 May 1826, *Founders Online*. Several of Jeff's sisters remained unmarried dependents, and he also provided for various members of the extended family.

32. John H. Cocke to Ralph Randolph Gurley, 18 Aug. 1826, FLP. For a summary of the will, see Boles, *Jefferson*, 287. Jeff and Cocke's attempt to free the Jefferson slaves does not seem to be discussed in Gary Nash and Graham Hodges, *Friends of Liberty: Thomas Jefferson, Tadeusz Kosciuszko, and Agrippa Hull* (New York: Basic Books, 2009).

33. Gordon-Reed, *The Hemingses of Monticello*, 655–656. For Jeff reuniting members of the Granger family, at high personal cost, see Lucia Stanton and David Brion Davis, *Free Some Day: The African-American Families of Monticello* (Charlottesville: Thomas Jefferson Foundation, 2002).

34. Martha J. Randolph to T. J. Randolph, 2 March 1827, Randolph Family Papers, ac. #1397, box 6, Small Special Collections Library, UVA.

35. Mary J. Randolph to Ellen W.R. Coolidge, 25 Jan. 1827, FLP.

36. Cornelia J. Randolph to Ellen W. R. Coolidge, 11 Sep. 1826, FLP (Louisiana or Vermont); see also Virginia Trist to Ellen W.R. Coolidge, 11 Feb. 1827, Ellen W. R. Coolidge Correspondence, ac. #9090, 9090-c, 38–584, UVA; Cornelia J. Randolph to Ellen W. R. Coolidge, 11 Dec. 1826, FLP; Peggy Nicholas to T. J. Randolph, 17 Jan. 1829, Randolph Family Papers, ac. #1397, UVA.

37. See, for instance, Martha J. Randolph to Ellen W. R. Coolidge, 31 Aug. 1829, FLP.

38. Vance, "Thomas Jefferson Randolph," 179.

39. Jane Randolph to Sarah Nicholas, ca. 1831, Randolph Family Papers, ac. #1397, box 7, UVA; Mary J. Randolph to Ellen W. R. Coolidge, 25 Sep. 1831, FLP.

40. The two petitions are discussed in Wolf, *Race and Liberty*, 199–200; they came from Quakers in the eastern counties of Charles City and Buckingham.

41. Wolf, *Race and Liberty*, 202–203. Other analyses of the 1831–1832 debates can be found in Freehling, *Drift Toward Dissolution*, xi–xii; and Shade, *Democratizing the Old Dominion*, 191–213.

42. Coles to T. J. Randolph, 29 Dec. 1831, printed in "Letters of Edward Coles: Edward Coles to Thomas Jefferson," *William and Mary Quarterly* 7, no. 2 (1927): 97–113, quotes at 106, 107.

43. Coles to T. J. Randolph, 29 Dec. 1831, "Letters of Edward Coles," quotes at 106, 107.

44. Coles to T. J. Randolph, 29 Dec. 1831, "Letters of Edward Coles," 107.

45. Speech of Thomas Jefferson Randolph, quoted in *Sons of the Fathers: The Virginia Slavery Debates of 1831–1832*, ed. Erik S. Root (Lanham, MD: Lexington Books, 2010), 9–10.

46. Speech of Thomas Jefferson Randolph, quoted in *Sons of the Fathers*, 215.

47. TJR, in *Sons of the Fathers*, 222.

48. TJR, in *Sons of the Fathers*, 217.

49. TJR, in *Sons of the Fathers*, 224; Wolf, *Race and Liberty*, 219 ("exist").

50. Speech of Thomas Jefferson Randolph, quoted in *Sons of the Fathers*, 224. Thomas Jefferson began this trend in the *Notes* by arguing that God would side with the slaves in an uprising; he continued it in his letter to Coles by stating that Coles should work on behalf of abolition, a doctrine "most Christian," until it was successful. For the foreshadowing of the "positive good" thesis during these debates, see Wolf, *Race and Liberty*, 222–223.

51. T. J. Randolph to Jane Randolph, 11 Feb. 1832, Randolph Family of Edgehill, MSS 6225, box 1, folder 30, UVA (portrait); T. J. Randolph to Jane Randolph, 29 Jan. 1832, Randolph Family Papers, ac. #1397, box 7, UVA ("friends of abolition"); *Journal of the House of Delegates* (begun Dec. 1831), 110; cited in Wolf, *Race and Abolition*, 230.

52. Martha J. Randolph to Ann C. Morris, 6 Sep. 1832 ("My dear Jefferson"); T. J. Randolph to Nicholas P. Trist, 4 April 1832 (slogan); Martha J. Randolph to Ellen W. C. Randolph, 15 Sep. 1833 ("tenderness," "being surrounded"), FLP. For Jeff's political career declining because of his emancipationist views, see Vance, "Thomas Jefferson Randolph," 179.

53. Stephen S. Mansfield, "Thomas Roderick Dew: Defender of the Southern Faith" (PhD diss., University of Virginia, 1968), esp. 12–24, 117, 196, cited in Alfred L. Brophy, "Considering William and Mary's History with Slavery: The Case of President Thomas Roderick Dew," *William and Mary Bill of Rights Journal* 16, no. 4 (2008): 1091–1139; Dew, *Review of the Debate in the Virginia Legislature of 1831–1832* (Richmond: T. W. White, 1832); Drew Gilpin Faust, ed., *The Ideology of Slavery: Proslavery Thought in the Antebellum South, 1830–1860* (Baton Rouge: Louisiana State University Press, 1981), 21–22. For Nathaniel Beverly Tucker, see Phillip Hamilton, *The Making and Unmaking of a Revolutionary Family: The Tuckers of Virginia, 1752–1830* (Charlottesville: University of Virginia Press, 2008); Terry L. Meyers, "Thinking About Slavery at

the College of William and Mary," *William and Mary Bill of Rights Journal* 21, no. 4 (2013): 1215–1257, esp. 1226.

54. Dew, *Review of the Debate*, as reprinted in Faust, ed., *Ideology of Slavery*, 64–66.

55. Ellen W. R. Coolidge to T. J. Randolph, 24 Feb. 1845, Ellen Wayles Randolph Coolidge Correspondence, ac. #38-584, box 3, UVA. Emphasis in original.

EPILOGUE

1. David Walker, *Walker's Appeal in Four Articles; Together with a Preamble, to the Coloured Citizens of the World, but in Particular and Very Expressly to Those of the United States of America* (Boston: Printed by David Walker, 1830), available online at *Documenting the American South*, University of North Carolina at Chapel Hill, www.docsouth.unc.edu/nc/walker/walker.html, quotes at 17, 16 ("blood and tears").

2. Walker, *Walker's Appeal in Four Articles*, 12–13 ("Has Mr. Jefferson"), 17–18 (buying the *Notes*), 18 ("Mr. Jefferson was"), 32 ("have sunk"), 29 ("the blacks").

3. Thomas Jefferson (hereafter "TJ"), *Notes on the State of Virginia*, ed. Frank C. Shuffelton (New York: Penguin Books, 1999), 151, quoted in Walker, *Appeal*, 31.

4. "Commentary about Jefferson's draft of Notes on the State of Virginia, by Charles Thomson, late March or April 1784," in Coolidge Collection of Thomas Jefferson Manuscripts, www.masshist.org. Emphasis added. TJ, *Notes*, 149, 150, 151.

5. John B. Boles, *Jefferson: Architect of American Liberty* (New York: Basic Books, 2017), 465.

6. See Boles, *Jefferson*, 464–477; for more on slavery at Monticello, see Annette Gordon-Reed, *The Hemingses of Monticello: An American Family* (New York: W. W. Norton & Company, 2008); Lucia C. Stanton, *"Those Who Labor for My Happiness": Slavery at Thomas Jefferson's Monticello* (Charlottesville: University of Virginia Press, 2012).

7. Isaac Jefferson, "Memoirs of a Monticello Slave," in *Jefferson at Monticello*, ed. James A. Bear Jr. (Charlottesville: University Press of Virginia, 1967), 1–24, quote at 4.

8. Madison Hemings, "Life Among the Lowly, No. 1," *Pike County Republican*, 13 March 1873, cited in Annette Gordon-Reed, *Thomas Jefferson and*

Sally Hemings: An American Controversy (Charlottesville: University Press of Virginia, 1997), 49.

9. TJ, *Note*, ed. Shuffelton, 151. For passing into white society, see Gordon-Reed, *The Hemingses of Monticello*, 335.

10. Ellen Wayles Randolph Coolidge to Joseph Coolidge, 24 Oct. 1858, in Family Letters Project, Monticello.org.

11. Ellen Wayles Randolph Coolidge to Joseph Coolidge, 24 Oct. 1858, in the Family Letters Project, Monticello.org. Recent DNA testing has decisively shown that Carr could not have been the father of at least one of Hemings's children (her youngest son, Eston), and therefore Carr was likely not involved with Hemings at all. The DNA testing further indicated that a male of the Jefferson line fathered Eston Hemings; if not Thomas Jefferson himself, the father would have been a close relation (such as Jefferson's brother Randolph), and the liaison would have occurred with Jefferson's knowledge and tacit approval. For more on what the DNA testing does (and does not) prove, see the Jefferson Foundation's Report of the Research Committee on Thomas Jefferson and Sally Hemings, available online at www.monticello.org/site/plantation-and-slavery/ii-assessment-dna-study.

12. See, for example, Thomas Jefferson Randolph to Robert W. Hughes, 25 Sep. 1870, in Randolph Family Papers, ac. #5533-c, box 1, folder 23, Small Special Collections Library, University of Virginia.

13. Brian Steele, "Thomas Jefferson, Coercion, and the Limits of Harmonious Union," *Journal of Southern History* 74, no. 4 (2008): 823–854, esp. 824, fn.3. See also George Green Shackelford, "Randolph, George Wythe," in *American National Biography*, ed. John A. Garraty and Mark C. Carnes, 24 vols. (New York: Oxford University Press, 1999), 18:125–126; George Green Shackelford, *George Wythe Randolph and the Confederate Elite* (Athens: University of Georgia Press, 1988), esp. 44–58, 67.

14. Martin Luther King Jr., "Letter from Birmingham Jail," 16 April 1963, available online at http://kingencyclopedia.stanford.edu/kingweb/popular_requests/frequentdocs/birmingham.pdf. Emphasis added.

15. TJ to Henri Gregoire Washington, 25 February 1809; polygraph copy in the Library of Congress.

16. TJ to Tench Coxe, 1 June 1795.

Bibliography

PERIODICALS

(Years refer to issues read, not periodical run.)
Mercure de France, 1787
Richmond Enquirer, 1829
The Virginia Gazette, or Weekly Advertiser (name changed to *The Virginia Gazette, and the Weekly Advertiser*), 1767, 1773, 1776, 1780–1782
Virginia Independent Chronicle and General Advertiser, 1790

ARCHIVES

American Philosophical Society (APS)
    Short–La Rochefoucauld Correspondence
College of William and Mary, Earl Gregg Swem Library
    Brown–Tucker–Coalter Papers
    Price Collection
    Tucker–Coleman Papers
    William and Peyton Short Papers
Historical Society of Pennsylvania (HSP)
    Edward Coles Collection
Library of Congress (LOC)
    Jones Family Papers
    Nicholas Biddle Papers
    Short Papers
    Thomas Jefferson Papers
Library of Virginia
    Executive Papers of Governor Thomas Mann Randolph, 1819–1822
    Journal of the Council of State (Microfilm)
    Legislative Petitions, House of Delegates, Archives Division
Massachusetts Historical Society
    Coolidge Collection of Thomas Jefferson Manuscripts
Princeton University, Firestone Library
    Papers of Edward Coles, 1786–1868

University of North Carolina, Chapel Hill, Louis Round Wilson Special
  Collections Library
    Nicholas Philip Trist Papers (NPTP)
    Southern Historical Collection
University of Virginia, Small Special Collections Library (UVA)
    Cabell Family Papers
    Cocke Papers
    Ellen W. R. Coolidge Correspondence
    Papers of the Trist, Randolph, and Burke Families
    Randolph Family of Edgehill
    Randolph Family Papers

ONLINE SOURCES

Coolidge Collection of Thomas Jefferson Manuscripts. Massachusetts Historical Society. www.masshist.org.
Family Letters Project of Monticello. http://tjrs.monticello.org (FLP).
Founders Online. National Archives. www.founders.archives.gov.
Notes on the State of Virginia Manuscript. Massachusetts Historical Society. http://www.masshist.org.
Papers of James Madison Digital Edition. University of Virginia Press. www.rotunda.upress.virginia.edu/founders/JSMN.html.
Papers of Thomas Jefferson Digital Edition. University of Virginia Press. www.rotunda.upress.virginia.edu/founders/TSJN.html.
People of the Founding Era. University of Virginia Press. www.pfe.rotunda.upress.virginia.edu.
Thomas Jefferson Collection. Library of Congress. https://www.loc.gov.

PUBLISHED PRIMARY SOURCES

Adams, C. F., ed. *Letters of Mrs. Adams.* 4th ed., rev. Boston, 1848.
Adams, John, Abigail Adams, and Thomas Jefferson. *The Adams-Jefferson Letters: The Complete Correspondence Between Thomas Jefferson and Abigail and John Adams.* Edited by Lester J. Cappon. Chapel Hill: University of North Carolina Press, 1988.
Adams Smith, Abigail, Mrs. *Journal and Correspondence of Miss Adams, Daughter of John Adams, Second President of the United States: Written in France and England, in 1785.* Wiley and Putnam, 1841–1842.
American State Papers: Documents, Legislative and Executive, of the Congress of the United States. 38 vols. Washington, DC: Gales and Seaton, 1832–1861.

Bear Jr., James A., and Lucia C. Stanton, eds. *Jefferson's Memorandum Books: Accounts, with Legal Records and Miscellany, 1767–1826.* 2 vols. Princeton, NJ: Princeton University Press, 1997.

Beattie, James. *James Beattie: Selected Philosophical Writings.* Edited by James Harris. Exeter, UK: Imprint Academic, 2004.

———. *The Works of James Beattie.* Vol. 7. Philadelphia: Hopkins and Earle, 1809.

Blackstone, Sir William. *Commentaries on the Laws of England. In Four Books.* Oxford, UK: Printed at the Clarendon Press, 1770.

Branagan, Thomas. *A Preliminary Essay, on the Oppression of the Exiled Sons of Africa.* J. W. Scott, 1804.

Cappon, Lester J. Editor. *The Adams-Jefferson Letters.* Chapel Hill: University of North Carolina Press, 1959.

Castiglioni, Count Luigi. *Viaggio negli Stati Uniti dell'America Settentrionale fatto negli anni 1785, 1786, e 1787. . . .* 2 vols. Milan: Stamperia di Giuseppe Marelli, 1790.

Clarkson, Thomas. *An Essay on the Impolicy of the African Slave Trade. In Two Parts. By the Rev. T. Clarkson, M.A. To Which Is Added, an Oration, Upon the Necessity of Establishing at Paris, a Society to Promote the Abolition of the Trade and Slavery of the Negroes. By J. P. Brissot De Warville.* Philadelphia, 1788.

Coleman, Mary H., ed. "Randolph and Tucker Letters." *Virginia Magazine of History and Biography* 42, no. 3 (1934): 211–223.

Coles, Edward. "Letters of Edward Coles." *William and Mary Quarterly* 7, no. 3 (1927): 158–173.

———. "Letters of Edward Coles: Edward Coles to Thomas Jefferson." *William and Mary Quarterly* 7, no. 2 (1927): 97–113.

Collections of the Massachusetts Historical Society. Boston: Massachusetts Historical Society, 1877.

Coolidge, Joseph Randolph. *Thomas Jefferson Randolph.* Boston: Beals & Greene, 1875.

De Beauvoir, François Jean, Marquis de Chastellux. *Travels in North America in the Years 1780, 1781 and 1782.* Translated and edited by Howard C. Rice, Jr., 2 vols. Chapel Hill: University of North Carolina Press, 1963.

De Caritat, Marquis de Condorcet. *Réflexions sur l'esclavage des nègres. Par M. Schwartz, Pasteur du Saint-Evangile à Bienne.* Neufchatel: Société Typographique, 1781.

De Pauw, Cornelius. *Recherches philosophiques sur les Américains* 1st ed. Berlin, 1768.

Desaussure, William Henry. *Address to the Citizens of South Carolina, on the Approaching Election of President and Vice-President of the United States.* Charleston, 1800.

Dew, Thomas R. *Review of the Debate in the Virginia Legislature of 1831–1832.* Richmond: T. W. White, 1832.

De Warville, Jacques-Pierre Brissot. "Testament politique de l'angleterre." Paris, 1778.

Douglass, Frederick. *My Bondage and My Freedom.* New York: Miller, Orton & Mulligan, 1855.

Du Motier, Gilbert, Marquis de Lafayette. *Memoirs, Correspondence and Manuscripts of General Lafayette.* New York: Saunders and Otley, 1837.

Encyclopédie méthodique par ordre des matières. Edited by Charles Joseph Panckoucke. Paris: 1782–1832.

Encyclopédie ou Dictionnaire raisonné des sciences, des arts et des métiers. 17 vols. Edited by Denis Diderot and Jean le Rond d'Alembert. Paris: 1751–1772.

Essay on the Interests of Britain, in Regard to America: Or, an Outline of the Terms on Which Peace May Be Restored to the Two Countries, An. London: J. Sewell, 1780.

Fairfax, Ferdinando. "Plan for Liberating the Negroes Within the United States." *American Museum* (December 1790): 285–287.

Fauquier, Francis. "Francis Fauquier's Will," *William and Mary Quarterly* 8, no. 3 (1900): 171–177.

Fessenden, Thomas Green. *Democracy Unveiled, or, Tyranny Stripped of the Garb of Patriotism.* 2 vols. New York, 1805.

Fitzhugh, George. *Sociology for the South: Or, The Failure of Free Society.* Richmond, VA: A. Morris, 1854.

Fitzpatrick, John Clement, ed. *The Writings of George Washington from the Original Manuscript Sources, 1745–1799.* 39 vols. Washington, DC: Government Printing Office, 1931.

Gales, Joseph, ed. *The Debates and Proceedings in the Congress of the United States.* Washington, DC: Government Printing Office, 1834.

"Glimpses of Old College Life," *William and Mary Quarterly*, ser. 1, vol. 9, no. 2 (1900): 213–227.

Hammond, Otis G., ed. *Letters and Papers of Major-General John Sullivan, Continental Army.* 3 vols. Concord: New Hampshire Historical Society, 1930–1931.

Hargrave, Francis. *An Argument in the Case of James Sommersett a Negro, Lately Determined by the Court of King's Bench . . . .* London, 1772.

Hening, William *The Statutes at Large; Being a Collection of all the Laws of Virginia from the First Session of the Legislature, in the 1619,* 13 vols. Richmond, VA: Samuel Pleasants, 1809–1823.

Howell, Robert B. *The Early Baptists of Virginia*. Philadelphia: Bible and Publication Society, 1857.

Hutcheson, Francis. *An Essay on the Nature and Conduct of our Passions and Affections*. Edited by A. Garrett. Indianapolis: Liberty Fund, 2002.

———. *A System of Moral Philosophy*. Vol. 1. Glasgow, 1755.

Jefferson, Thomas. *The Autobiography of Thomas Jefferson, 1743–1790, Together with a Summary of the Chief Events in Jefferson's Life*. Edited by Paul L. Ford. Introduction by Michael Zuckerman. Philadelphia: University of Pennsylvania Press, 2005.

———. *Catalogue of the Library of Thomas Jefferson*. Complied by E. Millicent Sowerby. 5 vols. 2nd ed. Charlottesville: University of Virginia Press, 1983.

———. *The Commonplace Book of Thomas Jefferson, a Repertory of His Ideas on Government*. Introduction and Notes by Gilbert Chinard. Baltimore: Johns Hopkins University Press, 1967.

———. *Jefferson's Memorandum Books: Accounts, with Legal Records and Miscellany, 1767–1826*. Edited by James A. Bear and Lucia C. Stanton. Princeton, NJ: Princeton University Press, 1997.

———. *The Life and Selected Writings of Thomas Jefferson*. Edited by Adrienne Koch. New York: Modern Library, 1944.

———. *Memoir, Correspondence, and Miscellanies, from the Papers of Thomas Jefferson*. Edited by Thomas Jefferson Randolph. 4 vols. Charlottesville, 1829.

———. *Notes on the State of Virginia*. London: Stockdale, 1787.

———. *Notes on the State of Virginia*. Edited by William Peden. Chapel Hill: University of North Carolina Press, 1955.

———. *Notes on the State of Virginia*. Edited by Frank Shuffelton. New York: Penguin Books, 1999.

———. *The Papers of Thomas Jefferson*. Edited by Julian P. Boyd et al. 43 vols. Princeton, NJ: Princeton University Press, 1950–2017.

———. *The Papers of Thomas Jefferson, Retirement Series*. Edited by J. Jefferson Looney. 14 vols. Princeton, NJ: Princeton University Press, 2005–2018.

———. *The Portable Thomas Jefferson*. Edited by Merrill D. Peterson. New York: Viking Press, 1975.

———. *A Summary View of the Rights of British America: Set Forth in Some Resolutions Intended for the Inspection of the Present Delegates of the People of Virginia, Now in Convention*. Williamsburg, VA: Clementina Rind, 1774.

———. *Thomas Jefferson: Writings*. Edited by Merrill D. Peterson. New York: Random House, 1984.

Leclerc, George Louis, Comte de Buffon. *Histoire Naturelle, générale et particulière, avec la description du Cabinet du Roy*. 36 vols. Paris: 1749–1788.

Lee, Arthur. *An Essay in Vindication of the Continental Colonies of America . . . .* London: 1764.

Leigh, Benjamin Watkins. *Proceedings and Debates of the Virginia State Convention of 1829–30 . . . .* Richmond, VA: Samuel Shepherd for Ritchie & Cook, 1830.

Linn, William. *Serious Considerations on the Election of a President Addressed to the Citizens of the United States.* New York, 1800.

Locke, John. *An Essay Concerning Human Understanding.* 27th ed. London: R. Griffin and Company, 1836.

———. *Two Treatises of Government.* London, 1689.

Madison, James. *The Debates on the Adoption of the Federal Constitution in the Convention Held at Philadelphia in 1787.* Vol. 5. Philadelphia, 1836.

———. *The Papers of James Madison, Congressional Series.* Edited by Robert A. Rutland and Thomas A. Mason. Charlottesville: University Press of Virginia, 1983.

Malone, Dumas. Introduction to *The Fry and Jefferson Map of Virginia and Maryland: Facsimiles of the 1754 and 1794 Printings.* Charlottesville: University Press of Virginia, 1966.

Mazzei, Filippo. *Philip Mazzei, Jefferson's "Zealous Whig."* Edited by Margherita Marchione. New York: American Institute of Italian Studies, 1975.

———. *Recherches Historiques et Politiques sur les États-Unis de l'Amérique Septentrionale.* Paris: Chez Froullé, 1788.

Mifflin, Warner. *Defence of Warner Mifflin against Aspersions . . . .* Philadelphia: Sansom, 1796.

Moore, Clement Clarke. *Observations upon Certain Passages in Mr. Jefferson's Notes on Virginia, Which Appear to Have a Tendency to Subvert Religion, and Establish a False Philosophy.* New York, 1804.

Munford, George Wythe. *The Two Parsons.* Richmond, VA, 1884.

Price, Richard. *Letters to and from Richard Price, D.D., F.R.S., 1767–1790.* Cambridge, UK: John Wilson and Son, University Press, 1903.

Randall, Henry S. *The Life of Thomas Jefferson.* New York: Derby & Jackson, 1858.

Rush, Benjamin. *The Autobiography of Benjamin Rush: His "Travels through Life" Together with His Commonplace Book for 1789–1813.* Edited by George W. Corner. Princeton, NJ: Princeton University Press, 1948.

Rush, Benjamin, and Granville Sharp. "The Correspondence of Benjamin Rush and Granville Sharp 1773—1809." Edited by John A. Woods. *Journal of American Studies* 1, no. 1 (1967): 1–38.

Scott, Winfield. *Memoirs of Lieut.-General Scott.* Vol. 2. New York: Sheldon and Co., 1864.

Shephard, Samuel. *The Statutes at Large of Virginia for October Session 1792, to December Session of 1806 . . . .* 3 vols. Richmond, VA, 1835–1836.

Smith, Adam. *Lectures on Jurisprudence.* Edited by R. L. Meek, D. D. Raphael, and P. G. Stein. Oxford, UK: Clarendon Press, 1978.

Smith, Samuel Stanhope. *An Essay on the Causes of the Variety of Complexion and Figure in the Human Species.* Edinburgh: C. Elliott, 1788; 2nd ed. New Brunswick, NJ: J. Simpson, 1818.

———. *The lectures, corrected and improved, which have been delivered for a series of years, in the College of New Jersey: on the subjects of moral and political philosophy.* 2 vols. Trenton, NJ: D. Fenton, 1812.

Smith, William Loughton. *The Pretensions of Thomas Jefferson to the Presidency Examined: and the Charges against John Adams Refuted.* Philadelphia, 1796.

Sullivan, John, and Otis Grant Hammond. *Letters and Papers of Major-General John Sullivan, Continental Army.* Concord: New Hampshire Historical Society, 1930.

Tucker, George. *The History of the United States: From Their Colonization to the End of the Twenty-Sixth Congress, in 1841.* Philadelphia: Lippincott, 1858.

———. *Letter to a Member of the General Assembly of Virginia, on the Subject of the Late Conspiracy of the Slaves: With a Proposal for Their Colonization.* Baltimore: Printed by Bonsal & Niles, 1801.

———. *The Life of George Tucker: Excerpted from The Life and Philosophy of George Tucker.* Edited by James Fieser. Bristol, UK: Thoemmes Continuum, 2004.

Tucker, St. George. *Dissertation on Slavery: With a Proposal for the Gradual Abolition of It.* Philadelphia: Printed for Mathew Carey, 1796.

———. *Reflections on the Cession of Louisiana to the United States.* Washington, DC: 1803.

Tyler, Lyon G. "Early Courses and Professors at William and Mary College." *William and Mary Quarterly* 14, no. 2 (1905): 71–83.

van Hogendorp, G. K. *Brieven en Gedenkschriften van Gijsbert Karel van Hogendorp.* Nijhoff, The Hague, 1866–1903.

Verner, Coolie. "The Maps and Plates Appearing with the Several Editions of Mr. Jefferson's 'Notes on the State of Virginia.'" *Virginia Magazine of History and Biography* 59 (1951): 21–33.

Voorhees, Oscar McMurtrie. *The Phi Beta Kappa Key: The Official Publication of the United Chapters of Phi Beta Kappa.* New York: Press of the Unionist-Gazette Association, 1916.

Wadstrom, C. B. *An Essay on Colonization, Particularly Applied to the Western*

Coast of Africa . . . Also Brief Descriptions of the Colonies . . . in Africa, Including Those of Sierra Leona and Bulama. London: Darton and Harvey, 1794.

Walker, David. *Walker's Appeal in Four Articles; Together with a Preamble, to the Coloured Citizens of the World, but in Particular and Very Expressly to Those of the United States of America.* Boston: Printed by David Walker, 1830.

Washburne, E. B. (Elihu Benjamin), and Chicago Historical Society. *Sketch of Edward Coles, Second Governor of Illinois, and of the Slavery Struggle of 1823–4.* Chicago: Jansen, McClurg & Company, 1882.

Washington, George. *The Papers of George Washington, Confederation Series.* Edited by W. W. Abbot and Dorothy Twohig. 6 vols. Charlottesville: University of Virginia Press, 1992–1997.

Wilson, James. *Speech of Mr. James Wilson, of N. Hampshire: On the Political Influence of Slavery, and the Expediency of Permitting Slavery in the Territories Recently Acquired from Mexico.* Washington, DC: J. & G. S. Gideon, 1849.

Witherspoon, John. *Works.* Rev. ed. Philadelphia: Printed and published by William W. Woodward, 1802.

Woodcock, Henry Iles. *A History of Tobago.* Ayrshire, UK: Smith & Grant, 1867.

Wright, T. R. B. "Judge Spencer Roane." *Virginia Law Register* 2, no. 7 (November 1896): 473–489.

SECONDARY SOURCES

Adams, William Howard. "The Virginians and the Veneto." *Virginia Quarterly Review* 63, no. 4 (1987): 646–660.

Ahnert, Thomas. *The Moral Culture of the Scottish Enlightenment, 1690–1805.* New Haven, CT, and London: Yale University Press, 2015.

Allen, Danielle S. *Our Declaration: A Reading of the Declaration of Independence in Defense of Equality.* New York: W. W. Norton, 2014.

"Am I Not a Man and a Brother": The Antislavery Crusade of Revolutionary America, 1688–1788. Edited by Roger Bruns. New York: Chelsea House, 1977.

Anderson, Fred. "George Washington's Mentors." In *Sons of the Father: George Washington and His Protégés,* edited by Robert M. S. McDonald, 21–30. Charlottesville: University of Virginia Press, 2013.

Appleby, Joyce. "Republicanism and Ideology." *American Quarterly* 37, no. 4 (1985): 461–473.

———. "The Social Origins of American Revolutionary Ideology." *Journal of American History* 64, no. 4 (1978): 935–958.

Aptheker, Herbert. *Nat Turner's Slave Rebellion: Including the 1831 "Confessions."* New York: Humanities Press, 1966.

Bailyn, Bernard. *The Ideological Origins of the American Revolution.* Cambridge, MA: Harvard University Press, 1967.

———. *Pamphlets of the American Revolution, 1750–1776.* Cambridge, MA: Harvard University Press, 1967.

———. *To Begin the World Anew: The Genius and Ambiguities of the American Founders.* New York: Knopf, 2003.

Banning, Lance. *The Jeffersonian Persuasion: Evolution of a Party Ideology.* Ithaca: Cornell University Press, 1980.

Barker, Gordon S. "Unraveling the Strange History of Jefferson's 'Observations Sur La Virginie.'" *Virginia Magazine of History and Biography* 112, no. 2 (2004): 134–177.

Bear, James A. *Jefferson at Monticello.* Charlottesville: University Press of Virginia, 1967.

Bederman, Gail. "Revisiting Nashoba: Slavery, Utopia, and Frances Wright in America, 1818–1826." *American Literary History* 17, no. 3 (2005): 438–459.

Bedini, Silvio A. *The Life of Benjamin Banneker.* New York: Macmillan, 1972.

Bender, Thomas, ed. *The Antislavery Debate: Capitalism and Abolitionism as a Problem in Historical Interpretation.* Berkeley: University of California Press, 1992.

Berlin, Ira. *Many Thousands Gone: The First Two Centuries of Slavery in North America.* Cambridge, MA: Harvard University Press, 2009.

———. *Slaves Without Masters: The Free Negro in the Antebellum South.* New York: Random House, 1974.

Bernasconi, Robert, and Tommy L. Lott, eds. *The Idea of Race.* Indianapolis: Hackett Publishing, 2000.

Bernstein, Richard B. *Thomas Jefferson.* New York: Oxford University Press, 2003.

Bevans, Charles I., ed. *Treaties and Other International Agreements of the United States of America, 1776–1949.* Washington, DC: Government Printing Office, 1968.

Bizardel, Yvon, and Howard C. Rice. "Poor in Love Mr. Short." *William and Mary Quarterly* 21, no. 4 (1964): 516–533.

Blackburn, Robin. *The Overthrow of Colonial Slavery.* London: Verso, 1988.

Boles, John B. *Black Southerners, 1619–1869.* Lexington: University Press of Kentucky, 1984.

————. *Jefferson: Architect of American Liberty*. New York: Basic Books, 2017.

Boles, John B., and Randal L. Hall, eds. *Seeing Jefferson Anew in His Time and Ours*. Charlottesville: University of Virginia Press, 2010.

Boorstin, Daniel J. *The Lost World of Thomas Jefferson*. Chicago: University of Chicago Press, 1993.

Boyce, Myrna. "The Diplomatic Career of William Short." *Journal of Modern History* 15, no. 2 (1943): 97–119.

Boyd, Julian P., and W. Edwin Hemphill. *The Murder of George Wythe: Two Essays*. Williamsburg, VA: Institute of Early American History and Culture, 1955.

Bradford, M. E. "Preserving the Birthright: The Intention of South Carolina in Adopting the U.S. Constitution." *South Carolina Historical Magazine*, 89, no. 2 (1988): 90–101.

Braidwood, Stephen J. *Black Poor and White Philanthropists: London's Blacks and the Foundation of the Sierra Leone Settlement, 1786–1791*. Liverpool, UK: Liverpool University Press, 1994.

Breen, Patrick H. *The Land Shall Be Deluged in Blood: A New History of the Nat Turner Revolt*. New York: Oxford University Press, 2016.

Breen, T. H. *Tobacco Culture: The Mentality of the Great Tidewater Planters on the Eve of Revolution*. Princeton, NJ: Princeton University Press, 2001.

Brewer, Holly. "Slavery, Sovereignty, and 'Inheritable Blood': Reconsidering John Locke and the Origins of American Slavery." *American Historical Review* 122, no. 4 (2017): 1038–1078.

Broadie, Alexander, ed. *The Cambridge Companion to the Scottish Enlightenment*. New York: Cambridge University Press, 2003.

Brodie, Fawn M. *Thomas Jefferson: An Intimate History*. New York: W. W. Norton & Company, 1974.

Brophy, Alfred L. "Considering William and Mary's History with Slavery: The Case of President Thomas Roderick Dew." *William and Mary Bill of Rights Journal* 16, no. 4 (2008): 1091–1139.

Brown, Christopher Leslie. *Moral Capital: Foundations of British Abolitionism*. Chapel Hill: Omohundro Institute and University of North Carolina Press, 2006.

Brown, Gordon S. *Toussaint's Clause: The Founding Fathers and the Haitian Revolution*. Jackson: University Press of Mississippi, 2005.

Brown, Imogene E. *American Aristides: A Biography of George Wythe*. Rutherford, NJ: Fairleigh Dickinson University Press, 1981.

Buckley, Thomas. "Placing Thomas Jefferson and Religion in Context, Then and Now." In *Seeing Jefferson Anew in His Time and Ours*, edited by Randal

L. Hall and John B. Boles, 126–151. Charlottesville: University of Virginia Press, 2010.

———. "The Political Theology of Thomas Jefferson." In *The Virginia Statute for Religious Freedom: Its Evolution and Consequences in American History*, edited by Merrill D. Peterson and Robert C. Vaughan. New York: Cambridge University Press, 2003.

Burin, Eric. *Slavery and the Peculiar Solution: A History of the American Colonization Society*. Gainesville: University Press of Florida, 2008.

Burstein, Andrew. *Jefferson's Secrets: Death and Desire at Monticello*. New York: Basic Books, 2006.

Byrd, Alexander X. *Captives and Voyagers: Black Migrants Across the Eighteenth-Century British Atlantic World*. 2nd ed. Baton Rouge: Louisiana State University Press, 2010.

Carmichael, Peter S. *The Last Generation: Young Virginians in Peace, War, and Reunion*. Chapel Hill: University of North Carolina Press, 2009.

Cassidy, John Thomas. "The Issue of Freedom in Illinois under Governor Coles." *Journal of Illinois State Historical Society* 57 (1964): 284–288.

Chernow, Ron. *Alexander Hamilton*. New York: Penguin Press, 2004.

Chinard, Gilbert. "Jefferson and the American Philosophical Society." *Proceedings of the American Philosophical Society* 87, no. 3 (1943): 263–276.

Clagett, Martin. *Scientific Jefferson: Revealed*. Charlottesville: University of Virginia Press, 2009.

———. "William Small, 1734–1775: Teacher, Mentor, Scientist." PhD diss., Virginia Commonwealth University, 2003. ProQuest (3084227).

Clavin, Matthew J. *Toussaint Louverture and the American Civil War: The Promise and Peril of a Second Haitian Revolution*. Philadelphia: University of Pennsylvania Press, 2010.

Clegg, Claude Andrew. *The Price of Liberty: African Americans and the Making of Liberia*. Chapel Hill: University of North Carolina Press, 2004.

Cleves, Rachel Hope. *The Reign of Terror in America: Visions of Violence from Anti-Jacobinism to Antislavery*. New York: Cambridge University Press, 2012.

Cogliano, Francis D. *A Companion to Thomas Jefferson*. Malden, MA, and Oxford, UK: Wiley-Blackwell, 2012.

———. *Thomas Jefferson: Reputation and Legacy*. Edinburgh: Edinburgh University Press, 2006.

Cohen, William. "Thomas Jefferson and the Problem of Slavery." *Journal of American History* 56, no. 3 (1969): 503–526.

Colbourn, H. Trevor. *The Lamp of Experience; Whig History and the Intellectual*

Origins of the American Revolution. Chapel Hill: Published for the Institute of Early American History and Culture at Williamsburg, VA, by the University of North Carolina Press, 1965.

———. "Thomas Jefferson's Use of the Past." *William and Mary Quarterly* 15, no. 1 (1958): 56–70.

Conkin, Paul K. "The Religious Pilgrimage of Thomas Jefferson." In *Jeffersonian Legacies*, edited by Peter S. Onuf, 19–49. Charlottesville: University of Virginia Press, 1993.

Cooper, John Milton, ed. *Jefferson, Lincoln, and Wilson: The American Dilemma of Race and Democracy*. Charlottesville: University of Virginia Press, 2010.

Cover, Robert M. *Justice Accused: Antislavery and the Judicial Process*. New Haven, CT: Yale University Press, 1975.

Crowe, Charles. "Bishop James Madison and the Republic of Virtue." *Journal of Southern History* 30, no. 1 (1964): 58–70.

Curran, Andrew S. *The Anatomy of Blackness: Science and Slavery in an Age of Enlightenment*. Baltimore: Johns Hopkins University Press, 2011.

Curtis, Christopher Michael. *Jefferson's Freeholders and the Politics of Ownership in the Old Dominion*. New York: Cambridge University Press, 2012.

Daacke, Kirt Von. *Freedom Has a Face: Race, Identity, and Community in Jefferson's Virginia*. Charlottesville: University of Virginia Press, 2012.

Dain, Bruce. *A Hideous Monster of the Mind: American Race Theory in the Early Republic*. Cambridge, MA: Harvard University Press, 2002.

Darnton, Robert. *The Business of Enlightenment: A Publishing History of the Encyclopédie, 1775–1800*. Cambridge, MA: Harvard University Press, 2009.

Davis, David Brion. *The Problem of Slavery in the Age of Emancipation*. New York: Alfred A. Knopf, 2014.

———. *The Problem of Slavery in the Age of Revolution, 1770–1823*. Ithaca: Cornell University Press, 1975.

———. *The Problem of Slavery in Western Culture*. Ithaca, NY: Cornell University Press, 1966.

Davis, Richard Beale. *Intellectual Life in the Colonial South, 1585–1763*. Knoxville: University of Tennessee Press, 1978.

Davy, George Alan. "Argumentation and Unified Structure in *Notes on the State of Virginia*." *Eighteenth-Century Studies* 26, no. 4 (1993): 581–593.

Dierksheide, Christa. *Amelioration and Empire: Progress and Slavery in the Plantation Americas*. Charlottesville: University of Virginia Press, 2014.

Dillon, Merton Lynn. *Slavery Attacked: Southern Slaves and Their Allies, 1619–1865*. Baton Rouge and London: Louisiana State University Press, 1990.

Dorigny, Marcel, ed. *The Abolitions of Slavery: From L. F. Sonthonax to Victor Schoelcher, 1793, 1794, 1848*. Paris: Berghahn Books, 2003.

Dray, Stephanie, and Laura Kamoie. *America's First Daughter: A Novel*. New York: William Morrow Paperbacks, 2016.

Dubois, Laurent. *Avengers of the New World: The Story of the Haitian Revolution*. Cambridge, MA: Belknap Press, 2005.

——. *A Colony of Citizens: Revolution and Slave Emancipation in the French Caribbean, 1787-1804*. Chapel Hill: University of North Carolina Press, 2012.

Duckworth, George E. "Supplementary Paper: Animae Dimidium Meae: Two Poets of Rome." *Transactions and Proceedings of the American Philological Association* 87 (1956): 281-316.

Egerton, Douglas R. *Gabriel's Rebellion: The Virginia Slave Conspiracies of 1800 and 1802*. Chapel Hill: University of North Carolina Press, 1993.

——. "'Its Origin Is Not a Little Curious': A New Look at the American Colonization Society." *Journal of the Early Republic* 5, no. 4 (1985): 463-480.

Ellis, Joseph J. *American Sphinx: The Character of Thomas Jefferson*. New York: Knopf Doubleday Publishing Group, 1998.

——. "Jefferson's Cop-Out." *Civilization* 3, no. 6 (1996): 46-53.

Ely, Melvin Patrick. *Israel on the Appomattox: A Southern Experiment in Black Freedom from the 1790s Through the Civil War*. New York: Vintage, 2005.

Emerson, Roger. "The Contexts of the Scottish Enlightenment." In *The Cambridge Companion to the Scottish Enlightenment*, edited by Alexander Broadie, 9-30. New York: Cambridge University Press, 2003.

Engeman, Thomas S. *Thomas Jefferson and the Politics of Nature*. Loyola Topics in Political Philosophy. Notre Dame, IN: University of Notre Dame Press, 2000.

Fabian, Bernhard. "Jefferson's Notes on Virginia: The Genesis of Query XVII, The Different Religions Received into That State?" *William and Mary Quarterly* 12, no. 1 (1955): 124-138.

Faust, Drew Gilpin, ed. *The Ideology of Slavery: Proslavery Thought in the Antebellum South, 1830-1860*. Baton Rouge: Louisiana State University Press, 1981.

——. *A Sacred Circle: The Dilemma of the Intellectual in the Old South, 1840-1860*. Philadelphia: University of Pennsylvania Press, 1986.

Fehrenbacher, Don Edward. *Constitutions and Constitutionalism in the Slaveholding South*. Athens: University of Georgia Press, 1989.

——. *The Slaveholding Republic: An Account of the United States Government's Relations to Slavery*. New York: Oxford University Press, 2001.

————. *Slavery, Law, and Politics: The Dred Scott Case in Historical Perspective.* New York: Oxford University Press, 1981.

Ferguson, Robert A. "'Mysterious Obligation': Jefferson's Notes on the State of Virginia." *American Literature* 52, no. 3 (1980): 381–406.

Fleischacker, Samuel. "The Impact on America: Scottish Philosophy and the American Founding." In *The Cambridge Companion to the Scottish Enlightenment*, edited by Alexander Broadie, 316–336. New York: Cambridge University Press, 2003.

Finkelman, Paul. "The Dragon St. George Could Not Slay: Tucker's Plan to End Slavery." *William and Mary Law Review* 47, no. 4 (2006): 1213–1243.

————. "Jefferson and Slavery: 'Treason Against the Hopes of the World.'" In *Jeffersonian Legacies*, edited by Peter Onuf, 181–221. Charlottesville: University of Virginia Press, 1993.

————. *Slavery and the Founders: Race and Liberty in the Age of Jefferson.* New York: M. E. Sharpe, 1996.

————. "Thomas Jefferson and Antislavery: The Myth Goes On." *Virginia Magazine of History and Biography* 102, no. 2 (April 1, 1994): 193–228.

Foner, Eric. *Free Soil, Free Labor, Free Men: The Ideology of the Republican Party before the Civil War.* 2nd ed. New York: Oxford University Press, 1995.

————. *The New American History.* Philadelphia: Temple University Press, 1997.

Forbes, Robert Pierce. "'The Cause of This Blackness': The Early American Republic and the Construction of Race." *American Nineteenth Century History* 13, no. 1 (2012): 65–94.

————. *Missouri Compromise and Its Aftermath: Slavery and the Meaning of America: Slavery and the Meaning of America.* Chapel Hill: University of North Carolina Press, 2009.

————. "Secular Damnation: Thomas Jefferson and the Imperative of Race." *Torrington Articles*, May 18, 2012. http://digitalcommons.uconn.edu/torr_articles/3.

Foster, Eugene A., et al. "Jefferson Fathered Slave's Last Child." *Nature* 396, no. 6706 (November 1998): 27–28.

Freehling, Alison Goodyear. *Drift Toward Dissolution: The Virginia Slavery Debate of 1831–1832.* Baton Rouge: Louisiana State University Press, 1982.

Freehling, William W. "The Founding Fathers and Slavery." *American Historical Review* 77, no. 1 (1972): 81–93.

————. *The Road to Disunion: Secessionists at Bay, 1776–1854.* New York: Oxford University Press, 1990.

Furet, Francois. *The French Revolution: 1770-1814.* Hoboken, NJ: Wiley-Blackwell, 1996.

Furstenberg, François. "Atlantic Slavery, Atlantic Freedom: George Washington, Slavery, and Transatlantic Abolitionist Networks." *William and Mary Quarterly* 68, no. 2 (2011): 247-286.

Gaines, William Harris. *Thomas Mann Randolph: Jefferson's Son-in-Law.* Baton Rouge: Louisiana State University Press, 1966.

Garfield, Blanche Allendena. "William Short and His Diplomatic Career from 1789-1792." MA thesis, West Virginia University, 1931.

Garraty, John A., and Mark C. Carnes, eds. *American National Biography.* 24 vols. New York: Oxford University Press, 1999.

Garrigus, J. *Before Haiti: Race and Citizenship in French Saint-Domingue.* New York: Palgrave Macmillan, 2006.

Gaustad, Edwin S. *Sworn on the Altar of God: A Religious Biography of Thomas Jefferson.* Grand Rapids, MI: William B. Eerdmans, 1996.

Geggus, David. "Racial Equality, Slavery, and Colonial Secession during the Constituent Assembly." *American Historical Review* 94, no. 5 (1989): 1290-1308.

Genovese, Eugene D. *Roll, Jordan, Roll: The World the Slaves Made.* New York: Vintage, 1976.

———. *Western Civilization Through Slaveholding Eyes: The Social and Historical Thought of Thomas Roderick Dew.* New Orleans: Graduate School of Tulane University, 1986.

Girard, Philippe R. "Caribbean Genocide: Racial War in Haiti, 1802-1804." *Patterns of Prejudice* 39, no. 2 (2005): 138-161.

Gish, Dustin A., and Daniel P. Klinghard. "Redeeming Adam's Curse: The Bible and Enlightenment Science in Thomas Jefferson's *Notes on the State of Virginia.*" *Perspectives on Political Science* 42, no. 2 (April 2013): 103-110.

———. "Republican Constitutionalism in Thomas Jefferson's *Notes on the State of Virginia.*" *Journal of Politics* 74, no. 1 (January 2012): 35-51.

———. *Thomas Jefferson and the Science of Republican Government: A Political Biography of Notes on the State of Virginia.* New York: Cambridge University Press, 2017.

Godson, Susan H. *The College of William & Mary: A History.* Williamsburg, VA: King and Queen Press, Society of the Alumni, College of William and Mary, 1993.

Goodman, Dena. *The Republic of Letters: A Cultural History of the French Enlightenment.* Ithaca: Cornell University Press, 1994.

Gordon-Reed, Annette. *The Hemingses of Monticello: An American Family.* New York: W. W. Norton & Company, 2008.

———. *Thomas Jefferson and Sally Hemings: An American Controversy.* Charlottesville: University of Virginia Press, 1998.

———. "Thomas Jefferson and St. George Tucker: The Makings of Revolutionary Slaveholders." In *Jefferson, Lincoln, and Wilson: The American Dilemma of Race and Democracy,* edited by John Milton Cooper Jr. and Thomas J. Knock. Charlottesville: University of Virginia Press, 2010.

Guasco, Suzanne Cooper. *Confronting Slavery: Edward Coles and the Rise of Antislavery Politics in Nineteenth-Century America.* DeKalb: Northern Illinois University Press, 2013.

Gutzman, Kevin R. C. *Thomas Jefferson—Revolutionary: A Radical's Struggle to Remake America.* New York: St. Martin's Press, 2017.

———. *Virginia's American Revolution: From Dominion to Republic, 1776–1840.* Lanham, MD: Lexington Books, 2007.

Guyatt, Nicholas. *Bind Us Apart: How Enlightened Americans Invented Racial Segregation.* New York: Basic Books, 2016.

Hahn, Steven. *A Nation Under Our Feet: Black Political Struggles in the Rural South, from Slavery to the Great Migration.* Cambridge, MA: Belknap Press of Harvard University Press, 2003.

Hamilton, Phillip. *The Making and Unmaking of a Revolutionary Family: The Tuckers of Virginia, 1752–1830.* Charlottesville: University of Virginia Press, 2008.

———. "Revolutionary Principles and Family Loyalties: Slavery's Transformation in the St. George Tucker Household of Early National Virginia." *William and Mary Quarterly* 55, no. 4 (1998): 531–556.

Hartz, Louis. *The Liberal Tradition in America.* New York: Harcourt, Brace & Company, 1955.

Harvey, David Allen. *The French Enlightenment and Its Others: The Mandarin, the Savage, and the Invention of the Human Sciences.* New York: Palgrave Macmillan, 2012.

Hatzenbuehler, Ronald L. *I Tremble for My Country: Thomas Jefferson and the Virginia Gentry.* Gainesville: University Press of Florida, 2006.

Hayes, Kevin J. *The Road to Monticello: The Life and Mind of Thomas Jefferson.* New York: Oxford University Press, 2008.

Helo, Ari. *Thomas Jefferson's Ethics and the Politics of Human Progress: The Morality of Slaveholder.* New York: Cambridge University Press, 2013.

Helo, Ari, and Peter S. Onuf. "Jefferson, Morality, and the Problem of Slavery." *William and Mary Quarterly* 60, no. 3 (2003): 583–641.

Hemphill, W. Edwin. "George Wythe, America's First Law Professor." Master's thesis, Emory University, 1933.

Higgs, Henry. "'Metayage' in Western France." *Economic Journal* 4, no. 13 (1894): 1–13.

Hoeveler, J. David. *Creating the American Mind: Intellect and Politics in the Colonial Colleges.* Lanham, MD: Rowman & Littlefield, 2002.

Holowchak, M. Andrew. *Dutiful Correspondent: Philosophical Essays on Thomas Jefferson.* Lanham, MD: Rowman & Littlefield, 2012.

———. *Thomas Jefferson and Philosophy: Essays on the Philosophical Cast of Jefferson's Writings.* Lanham, MD: Lexington Books, 2014.

———. *Thomas Jefferson's Philosophy of Education: A Utopian Dream.* London: Routledge, 2014.

Holton, Woody. *Forced Founders: Indians, Debtors, Slaves, and the Making of the American Revolution in Virginia.* Chapel Hill: University of North Carolina Press, 2000.

Horn, James, Jan Ellen Lewis, and Peter S. Onuf. *The Revolution of 1800: Democracy, Race, and the New Republic.* Charlottesville and London: University of Virginia Press, 2002.

Howe, Daniel Walker. "Why the Scottish Enlightenment Was Useful to the Framers of the American Constitution." *Comparative Studies in Society and History* 31, no. 3 (1989): 572–587.

Howell, Wilbur Samuel. "The Declaration of Independence and Eighteenth-Century Logic." *William and Mary Quarterly* 18, no. 4 (1961): 464–484.

Hunter, Thomas. "The Teaching of George Wythe." In *The History of Legal Education in the United States: Commentaries and Primary Sources*, edited by Steve Sheppard, 138–167. New York: Salem Press, 1999.

Hurwitz, Jerome A. "Thomas Jefferson Randolph, Democratic Leader." Master's thesis, University of Richmond, 1938.

Irons, Charles F. *The Origins of Proslavery Christianity: White and Black Evangelicals in Colonial and Antebellum Virginia.* Chapel Hill: University of North Carolina Press, 2008.

Isaac, Rhys. *The Transformation of Virginia, 1740–1790.* Chapel Hill: University of North Carolina Press, 1982.

Israel, Jonathan. *Revolutionary Ideas: An Intellectual History of the French Revolution from The Rights of Man to Robespierre.* Princeton, NJ: Princeton University Press, 2014.

Jackson, Sidney L. "The Encyclopedie Methodique: A Jefferson Addendum." *Virginia Magazine of History and Biography* 73, no. 3 (1965): 303–311.

James, Cyril Lionel Robert. *The Black Jacobins: Toussaint L'Ouverture and the San Domingo Revolution.* 2nd ed. New York: Vintage Books, 1963.

Johnson, Timothy D. *Winfield Scott: The Quest for Military Glory.* Lawrence: University Press of Kansas, 1998.

Johnson, Walter. *Soul by Soul: Life Inside the Antebellum Slave Market.* Cambridge, MA: Harvard University Press, 1999.

Jones, George Fenwick. "The Black Hessians: Negroes Recruited by the Hessians in South Carolina and Other Colonies." *South Carolina Historical Magazine* 83, no. 4 (1982): 287–302.

Jordan, Winthrop D. *White Over Black: American Attitudes Toward the Negro, 1550–1812.* Chapel Hill: Published for the Institute of Early American History and Culture at Williamsburg, VA, by the University of North Carolina Press, 1968.

Jordan, Winthrop D., et al., eds. *Slavery and the American South: Essays and Commentaries.* Jackson: University Press of Mississippi, 2003.

Kastor, Peter J. *The Nation's Crucible: The Louisiana Purchase and the Creation of America.* New Haven, CT: Yale University Press, 2004.

Kelly, Jack. "Revolutionary Tourist: Chastellux in America." *Journal of the American Revolution.* March 4, 2016. https://allthingsliberty.com/2016/03/revolutionary-tourist-chastellux-in-america.

Kennedy, Roger G. *Mr. Jefferson's Lost Cause: Land, Farmers, Slavery, and the Louisiana Purchase.* New York: Oxford University Press, 2003.

Ketcham, Ralph. "The Dictates of Conscience: Edward Coles and Slavery." *Virginia Quarterly Review* 26 (1966): 46–62.

Kierner, Cynthia A. *Martha Jefferson Randolph, Daughter of Monticello: Her Life and Times.* Chapel Hill: University of North Carolina Press, 2012.

Kimball, Marie Goebel. *Jefferson: The Road to Glory, 1743–1776.* New York: Coward-McCann, 1943.

———. *Jefferson: The Scene of Europe, 1784 to 1789.* New York: Coward-McCann, 1950.

———. *Jefferson: War and Peace, 1776 to 1784.* New York: Coward-McCann, 1947.

———. "William Short, Jefferson's Only 'Son.'" *North American Review* 223, no. 832 (1926): 471–486.

Kloppenberg, James T. "The Virtues of Liberalism: Christianity, Republicanism, and Ethics in Early American Political Discourse." *Journal of American History* 74, no. 1 (June 1, 1987): 9–33.

Kneebone, John T., et al., eds. *Dictionary of Virginia Biography, Volume 1: Aaroe-Blanchfield.* Richmond: Library of Virginia, 1998.

Koch, Adrienne. *Jefferson and Madison: The Great Collaboration*. New York: Knopf, 1950.

Kolchin, Peter. *American Slavery: 1619–1877*. Rev. ed. New York: Hill and Wang, 2003.

———. *Unfree Labor: American Slavery and Russian Serfdom*. Cambridge, MA: Belknap Press of Harvard University Press, 1987.

Konig, David, ed. *Devising Liberty: Preserving and Creating Freedom in the New American Republic*. Stanford, CA: Stanford University Press, 1995.

Kousser, J. Morgan, and James M. McPherson. *Region, Race, and Reconstruction: Essays in Honor of C. Vann Woodward*. New York: Oxford University Press, 1982.

LaCroix, Alison L. *The Ideological Origins of American Federalism*. Cambridge, MA: Harvard University Press, 2010.

Langhorne, Elizabeth. "Edward Coles, Thomas Jefferson, and the Rights of Man." *Virginia Cavalcade* 23 (1973): 30–37.

Lefebvre, Georges. *The Coming of the French Revolution*. Edited by Timothy Tackett. Translated by R. R. Palmer. Rev. ed. Princeton, NJ: Princeton University Press, 2015.

Leibiger, Stuart. "George Washington and Lafayette: Father and Son of the Revolution." In *Sons of the Father: George Washington and His Protégés*, edited by Robert M. S. McDonald, 210–231. Charlottesville: University of Virginia Press, 2013.

Leichtle, Kurt E., and Bruce G. Carveth. *Crusade Against Slavery: Edward Coles, Pioneer of Freedom*. Carbondale: Southern Illinois University Press, 2011.

Lemon, James T. *The Best Poor Man's Country: A Geographical Study of Early Southeastern Pennsylvania*. New York: W. W. Norton & Company, 1976.

Levy, Andrew. *The First Emancipator: Slavery, Religion and the Quiet Revolution of Robert Carter: The Forgotten Story of Robert Carter, the Founding Father Who Freed His Slaves*. New York: Random House Trade Paperbacks, 2005.

Levy, Leonard W. *Jefferson & Civil Liberties: The Darker Side*. Cambridge, MA: Belknap Press of Harvard University Press, 1963.

Lewis, Jan Ellen. "The Problem of Slavery." In *Devising Liberty: Preserving and Creating Freedom in the New American Republic*, edited by David Konig, 265–297. Stanford, CA: Stanford University Press, 1995.

Lowance, Mason I. *A House Divided: The Antebellum Slavery Debates in America, 1776–1865*. Princeton, NJ: Princeton University Press, 2003.

Lynch, Jack. "'His Integrity Inflexible, and His Justice Exact': George Wythe

Teaches America the Law." *Colonial Williamsburg Journal* 32, no. 2 (Spring 2010): 37–41.

Lynch, James V. "The Limits of Revolutionary Radicalism: Tom Paine and Slavery." *The Pennsylvania Magazine of History and Biography* 123, no. 3 (1999): 177–199.

MacLeod, Duncan. *Slavery, Race and the American Revolution*. New York: Cambridge University Press, 1975.

MacMaster, Richard K. "Arthur Lee's 'Address on Slavery': An Aspect of Virginia's Struggle to End the Slave Trade, 1765–1774." *Virginia Magazine of History and Biography* 80, no. 2 (April 1, 1972): 141–157.

Maier, Pauline. *American Scripture: Making the Declaration of Independence.* New York: Knopf, 1997.

Malone, Dumas. *Jefferson and His Time.* 6 vols. Boston: Little, Brown and Company, 1948–1982.

Marraro, Howard R. "Count Luigi Castiglioni. An Early Italian Traveller to Virginia (1785–1786)." *Virginia Magazine of History and Biography* 58, no. 4 (1950): 473–491.

Mason, Matthew. "A Missed Opportunity? The Founding, Postcolonial Realities, and the Abolition of Slavery." *Slavery & Abolition* 35, no. 2 (2014): 199–213.

———. *Slavery and Politics in the Early American Republic.* Chapel Hill: University of North Carolina Press, 2006.

Massey, Gregory D. "The Limits of Antislavery Thought in the Revolutionary Lower South: John Laurens and Henry Laurens." *Journal of Southern History* 63, no. 3 (1997): 495–530.

Masur, Louis P. *1831, Year of Eclipse.* New York: Hill and Wang, 2001.

Mathews, Donald G. *Slavery and Methodism: A Chapter in American Morality, 1780–1845.* Princeton, NJ: Princeton University Press, 1965.

Matthews, Richard K. *The Radical Politics of Thomas Jefferson.* Lawrence: University Press of Kansas, 1984.

Matthewson, Tim. *A Proslavery Foreign Policy: Haitian-American Relations During the Early Republic.* Westport, CT: Praeger, 2003.

May, Henry Farnham. *The Enlightenment in America.* New York: Oxford University Press, 1976.

McColley, Robert. *Slavery and Jeffersonian Virginia.* Urbana: University of Illinois Press, 1973.

McCord, Jr., T. B. "John Page of Rosewell: Reason, Religion, and Republican Government from the Perspective of a Virginia Planter, 1743–1808." PhD diss., American University, 1990.

McCoy, Drew R. *The Last of the Fathers: James Madison and the Republican Legacy*. New York: New York University Press, 1989.

McCurry, Stephanie. *Masters of Small Worlds: Yeoman Households, Gender Relations, and the Political Culture of the Antebellum South Carolina Low Country*. New York: Oxford University Press, 1997.

McDonald, Christine Coalwell, and Robert M. S. McDonald. "More Loved... and More Hated: George Tucker on Thomas Jefferson." In *Thomas Jefferson's Lives: Biographers and the Battle for History*, edited by Robert M. S. McDonald, 47–61. Charlottesville: University of Virginia Press, 2019.

McDonald, Robert M. S. *Confounding Father Thomas Jefferson's Image in His Own Time*. Charlottesville: University of Virginia Press, 2016.

———. "Thomas Jefferson and Historical Self-Construction: The Earth Belongs to the Living?" *Historian* 61, no. 2 (1999): 289–310.

———, ed. *Sons of the Father: George Washington and His Protégés*. Charlottesville: University of Virginia Press, 2013.

McGarvie, Mark D. "'In Perfect Accordance with His Character': Thomas Jefferson, Slavery, and the Law." *Indiana Magazine of History* 95, no. 2 (1999): 142–177.

McKivigan, John R, and Mitchell Snay, eds. *Religion and the Antebellum Debate over Slavery*. Athens: University of Georgia Press, 1998.

McLean, Robert Colin. *George Tucker, Moral Philosopher and Man of Letters*. Chapel Hill: University of North Carolina Press, 1961.

Meacham, Jon. *Thomas Jefferson: The Art of Power*. New York: Random House, 2012.

Medlin, Dorothy. "Thomas Jefferson, André Morellet, and the French Version of *Notes on the State of Virginia*." *William and Mary Quarterly* 35, no. 1 (1978): 85–99.

Merkel William G. "A Founding Father on Trial: Jefferson's Rights Talk and the Problem of Slavery During the Revolutionary Period." *Rutgers Law Review* 64, no. 3 (2012): 595–663.

———. "Jefferson in Paris: Rewriting the Problems of Slavery, Slaveholding, Family, and Codependency." In *Thomas Jefferson and Philosophy: Essays on the Philosophical Cast of Jefferson's Writings*, edited by Mark Holowchak, 91–134. Lanham, MD: Lexington Books, 2014.

———. "Jefferson's Failed Anti-Slavery Proviso of 1784 and the Nascence of Free Soil Constitutionalism." *Seton Hall Law Review* 38, no. 2 (2008): 555–603.

———. "Race, Liberty, and Law: Thomas Jefferson and Slavery, 1769–1800." PhD diss., University of Oxford, 2007.

Meyers, Terry L. "Benjamin Franklin, the College of William and Mary, and the Williamsburg Bray School." *Anglican and Episcopal History*. 79, no. 4 (2010): 368–393.

———. "Thinking About Slavery at the College of William and Mary." *William and Mary Bill of Rights Journal* 21, no. 4 (2013): 1215–1257.

Miller, John Chester. *The Wolf by the Ears: Thomas Jefferson and Slavery*. New York: Free Press, 1977.

Monticello Association (Charlottesville, VA), and George Green Shackelford. *Collected Papers to Commemorate Fifty Years of the Monticello Association of the Descendants of Thomas Jefferson*. Princeton, NJ: Princeton University Press, 1965.

Morgan, Edmund S. *American Slavery, American Freedom: The Ordeal of Colonial Virginia*. New York: Norton, 1975.

Morgan, Kenneth. *Slavery and the British Empire: From Africa to America*. New York: Oxford University Press, 2007.

Morpurgo, Jack. *Their Majesties' Royall Colledge: William and Mary in the Seventeenth and Eighteenth Centuries*. Washington, DC: Hennage Creative Printers, 1976.

Nash, Gary B. *Race and Revolution*. Madison, WI: Madison House, 1990.

Nash, Gary B., and Graham Russell Gao Hodges. *Friends of Liberty: Thomas Jefferson, Tadeusz Kosciuszko, and Agrippa Hull*. New York: Basic Books, 2009.

Newman, Richard S. "Prelude to the Gag Rule: Southern Reaction to Antislavery Petitions in the First Federal Congress." *Journal of the Early Republic* 16, no. 4 (1996): 571–599.

———. *The Transformation of American Abolitionism: Fighting Slavery in the Early Republic*. Chapel Hill: University of North Carolina Press, 2006.

Newman, Simon P., and Peter S. Onuf, eds. *Paine and Jefferson in the Age of Revolutions*. Charlottesville: University of Virginia Press, 2013.

Nicholls, Michael L. "Aspects of the African American Experience in Eighteenth-Century Williamsburg and Norfolk." *Colonial Williamsburg Foundation Library Research Report Series* 330. Williamsburg, VA: 1991.

———. *Whispers of Rebellion: Narrating Gabriel's Conspiracy*. Charlottesville: University of Virginia Press, 2013.

Noll, Mark A. *Princeton and the Republic, 1768–1822: The Search for a Christian Enlightenment in the Era of Samuel Stanhope Smith*. Princeton, NJ: Princeton University Press, 1989.

Oast, Jennifer. *Institutional Slavery: Slaveholding Churches, Schools, Colleges, and Businesses in Virginia, 1680–1860*. New York: Cambridge University Press, 2016.

O'Brien, Conor Cruise. *The Long Affair: Thomas Jefferson and the French Revolution, 1785–1800*. Chicago: University of Chicago Press, 1998.

Oliver, Bette W. *Jacques Pierre Brissot in America and France, 1788–1793: In Search of Better Worlds*. Lanham, MD: Rowman & Littlefield, 2016.

Onuf, Peter S. *Jefferson's Empire: The Language of American Nationhood*. Charlottesville: University of Virginia Press, 2001.

———. *The Mind of Thomas Jefferson*. Charlottesville: University of Virginia Press, 2007.

———. *Statehood and Union: A History of the Northwest Ordinance*. Bloomington: Indiana University Press, 1987.

———. "'To Declare Them a Free and Independent People': Race, Slavery, and National Identity in Jefferson's Thought." *Journal of the Early Republic* 18, no. 1 (1998): 1–46.

———. ed. *Jeffersonian Legacies*. Charlottesville: University of Virginia Press, 1993.

Onuf, Peter S., and Nicholas Onuf. *Nations, Markets, and War: Modern History and the American Civil War*. Charlottesville: University of Virginia Press, 2006.

Pace, Robert F. *Halls of Honor: College Men in the Old South*. Baton Rouge: Louisiana State University Press, 2011.

Paku, Gillian. "Anonymity in the Eighteenth Century." *Oxford Handbooks Online*. August 6, 2015. www.oxfordhandbooks.com.

Palmer, R. R. "The Dubious Democrat: Thomas Jefferson in Bourbon France." *Political Science Quarterly* 72, no. 3 (1957): 388–404.

Pasley, Jeffrey L. "Politics and the Misadventures of Thomas Jefferson's Modern Reputation: A Review Essay." *Journal of Southern History* 72, no. 4 (2006): 871–908.

Patterson, Orlando. *Slavery and Social Death: A Comparative Study*. Cambridge, MA: Harvard University Press, 1982.

Peterson, Merrill D. *The Jefferson Image in the American Mind*. New York: Oxford University Press, 1960.

———. *Thomas Jefferson and the New Nation: A Biography*. New York: Oxford University Press, 1970.

———. "Thomas Jefferson's *Notes on the State of Virginia*." In *Studies in Eighteenth-Century Culture*, Vol. 7. Madison: University of Wisconsin Press, 1978.

Pocock, J. G. A. *The Ancient Constitution and the Feudal Law; a Study of English Historical Thought in the Seventeenth Century*. New York: Cambridge University Press, 1957.

———. *The Machiavellian Moment: Florentine Political Thought and the Atlantic Republican Tradition*. Princeton, NJ: Princeton University Press, 1975.

Polasky, Janet. *Revolutions without Borders: The Call to Liberty in the Atlantic World*. New Haven, CT: Yale University Press, 2015.

Popkin, Jeremy D. *A Concise History of the Haitian Revolution*. Malden, MA: Wiley-Blackwell, 2011.

———. *A Short History of the French Revolution*. 6th ed. Boston: Routledge, 2014.

———. *You Are All Free: The Haitian Revolution and the Abolition of Slavery*. New York: Cambridge University Press, 2010.

Post, David G. *In Search of Jefferson's Moose: Notes on the State of Cyberspace*. New York: Oxford University Press, 2008.

Powell, Manushag N. *Performing Authorship in Eighteenth-Century English Periodicals*. Lanham, MD: Rowman & Littlefield, 2012.

Pybus, Cassandra. *Epic Journeys of Freedom: Runaway Slaves of the American Revolution and Their Global Quest for Liberty*. Boston: Beacon Press, 2007.

Quigley, Paul. *Shifting Grounds: Nationalism and the American South, 1848–1865*. New York: Oxford University Press, 2011.

Rebok, Sandra. *Humboldt and Jefferson: A Transatlantic Friendship of the Enlightenment*. Charlottesville: University of Virginia Press, 2014.

Resnick, Daniel P. "The Société Des Amis Des Noirs and the Abolition of Slavery." *French Historical Studies* 7, no. 4 (1972): 558–569.

Ress, David. *Governor Edward Coles and the Vote to Forbid Slavery in Illinois, 1823–1824*. Jefferson, NC: McFarland & Co., 2006.

Richardson, William D. "Thomas Jefferson & Race: The Declaration & Notes on the State of Virginia." *Polity* 16, no. 3 (1984): 447–466.

Robert, Joseph C. *The Road from Monticello: A Study of the Virginia Slavery Debate of 1832*. New York: AMS Press, 1970.

Robson, David. *Educating Republicans: The College in the Era of the American Revolution, 1750–1800*. Westport, CT: Greenwood Press, 1985.

Roche, Daniel. *France in the Enlightenment*. Translated by Arthur Goldhammer. Cambridge, MA: Harvard University Press, 2001.

Rodgers, Daniel T. "Republicanism: The Career of a Concept." *Journal of American History* 79, no. 1 (1992): 11–38.

Rogers [Stevens], Cara. "The French Experiment: Thomas Jefferson and

William Short Debate Slavery, 1785-1826." *American Political Thought* 10, no. 3 (2021): 327-362.

———. "Jefferson's Changing Audiences: A Reevaluation of *Notes on the State of Virginia.*" *Journal of Southern History* 87, no. 2 (May 2021): 171-208.

Root, Erik S. *All Honor to Jefferson? The Virginia Slavery Debates and the Positive Good Thesis.* Lanham, MD: Lexington Books, 2008.

———. *Sons of the Fathers: The Virginia Slavery Debates of 1831-1832.* Lanham, MD: Lexington Books, 2010.

Rose, Willie Lee Nichols. *A Documentary History of Slavery in North America.* Athens: University of Georgia Press, 1999

———. *Rehearsal for Reconstruction: The Port Royal Experiment.* Athens: University of Georgia Press, 1999.

Rosengarten, J. G. "The Early French Members of the American Philosophical Society." *Proceedings of the American Philosophical Society* 46, no. 185 (1907): 87-93.

Rushforth, Brett. *Bonds of Alliance: Indigenous and Atlantic Slaveries in New France.* Chapel Hill: University of North Carolina Press, 2014.

Sadosky, Leonard J., et al., eds. *Old World, New World: America and Europe in the Age of Jefferson.* Charlottesville: University of Virginia Press, 2010.

Sandefur, Timothy. "Why the Rule against Perpetuities Mattered in *Pleasants v. Pleasants.*" *Real Property, Probate and Trust Journal* 40, no. 4 (2006): 667-677.

Sanford, Charles B. *The Religious Life of Thomas Jefferson.* Charlottesville: University of Virginia Press, 1984.

Saville, Julie. *The Work of Reconstruction: From Slave to Wage Laborer in South Carolina 1860-1870.* New York: Cambridge University Press, 1996.

Schaeper, Thomas J. *Edward Bancroft: Scientist, Author, Spy.* New Haven, CT: Yale University Press, 2011.

Scherr, Arthur. "Jefferson's 'Cannibals' Revisited: A Closer Look at His Notorious Phrase." *Journal of Southern History* 77, no. 2 (2011): 251-282.

———. "Light at the End of the Road: Thomas Jefferson's Endorsement of Free Haiti in His Final Years." *Journal of Haitian Studies* 15, no. 1/2 (2009): 203-216.

———. "Thomas Jefferson, White Immigration, and Black Emancipation." *Southern Studies: An Interdisciplinary Journal of the South* 23, no. 1 (2016): 1-26.

Schmidt, Fredrika Teute, and Barbara Ripel Wilhelm. "Early Proslavery Petitions in Virginia." *William and Mary Quarterly*, ser. 3, vol. 30, no. 1 (1973): 133-146.

Schwalm, Leslie Ann. *A Hard Fight for We: Women's Transition from Slavery to Freedom in South Carolina*. Urbana and Chicago: University of Illinois Press, 1997.

Schwarz, Philip J. *Migrants against Slavery: Virginians and the Nation*. Charlottesville: University of Virginia Press, 2001.

Shackelford, George Green. *George Wythe Randolph and the Confederate Elite*. Athens: University of Georgia Press, 1988.

———. *Jefferson's Adoptive Son: The Life of William Short, 1759–1848*. Lexington: University Press of Kentucky, 1993.

———. *Thomas Jefferson's Travels in Europe, 1784–1789*. Baltimore: Johns Hopkins University Press, 1998.

———. "To Practice Law: Aspects of the Era of Good Feelings Reflected in the Short-Ridgely Correspondences, 1816–1821." *Maryland Historical Magazine* 64, no. 4 (1969): 342–395.

———. "William Short: Diplomat in Revolutionary France, 1785–1793." *Proceedings of the American Philosophical Society* 102, no. 6 (1958): 596–612.

———. "William Short: Jefferson's Adopted Son, 1758–1849." PhD diss., University of Virginia, 1955.

Shade, William G. *Democratizing the Old Dominion: Virginia and the Second Party System, 1824–1861*. Charlottesville: University of Virginia Press, 1996.

Shalhope, Robert E. "Toward a Republican Synthesis: The Emergence of an Understanding of Republicanism in American Historiography." *William and Mary Quarterly* 29, no. 1 (1972): 49–80.

Sheppard, Steve. *The History of Legal Education in the United States: Commentaries and Primary Sources*. Pasadena, CA: Salem Press, 1999.

Shuffelton, Frank. *The Cambridge Companion to Thomas Jefferson*. Cambridge, UK, and New York: Cambridge University Press, 2009.

Shy, Jeffery R. "Early Astronomy in America: The Role of the College of William and Mary." *Journal of Astronomical History and Heritage* 5 (2002): 41–64.

Sidbury, James. *Ploughshares into Swords: Race, Rebellion, and Identity in Gabriel's Virginia, 1730–1810*. New York: Cambridge University Press, 1997.

———. "Saint Domingue in Virginia: Ideology, Local Meanings, and Resistance to Slavery, 1790–1800." *Journal of Southern History* 63, no. 3 (1997): 531–552.

Sloan, Herbert E. *Principle and Interest: Thomas Jefferson and the Problem of Debt*. Charlottesville: University of Virginia Press, 2001.

Snavely, Tipton Ray. *George Tucker as Political Economist*. Charlottesville: University of Virginia Press, 1964.

Snyder, Christina. *Slavery in Indian Country: The Changing Face of Captivity in Early America*. Cambridge, MA: Harvard University Press, 2010.

Spalding, Paul S. *Lafayette: Prisoner of State*. Columbia: University of South Carolina Press, 2010.

Spencer, Donald S. "Edward Coles: Virginia Gentleman in Frontier Politics." *Journal of the Illinois State Historical Society (1908–1984)* 61, no. 2 (1968): 150–163.

Spooner, Matthew. "'I Know This Scheme Is from God:' Toward a Reconsideration of the Origins of the American Colonization Society." *Slavery & Abolition* 35, no. 4 (2014): 559–575.

Stanton, Lucia C. "Jefferson's People: Slavery at Monticello." In *The Cambridge Companion to Thomas Jefferson*, edited by Frank Shuffelton, 83–100. Cambridge, UK: Cambridge University Press, 2009.

———. *"Those Who Labor for My Happiness": Slavery at Thomas Jefferson's Monticello*. Charlottesville: University of Virginia Press, 2012.

Stanton, Lucia C., and David Brion Davis. *Free Some Day: The African-American Families of Monticello*. Charlottesville, VA: Thomas Jefferson Foundation, 2002.

Staudenraus, P. J. *The African Colonization Movement, 1816–1865*. New York: Columbia University Press, 1961.

Steele, Brian. "Thomas Jefferson, Coercion, and the Limits of Harmonious Union." *Journal of Southern History* 74, no. 4 (2008): 823–854.

———. *Thomas Jefferson and American Nationhood*. New York: Cambridge University Press, 2012.

———. "Thomas Jefferson's Gender Frontier." *Journal of American History* 95, no. 1 (2008): 17–42.

Sutton, Robert M. "Edward Coles and the Constitutional Crisis in Illinois, 1822–1824." *Illinois Historical Journal* 82, no. 1 (Spring 1989): 33–46.

Sweet, James H. "The Iberian Roots of American Racist Thought." *William and Mary Quarterly* 54, no. 1 (1997): 143–166.

Taylor, Alan. *The Internal Enemy: Slavery and War in Virginia, 1772–1832*. New York: W. W. Norton & Company, 2014.

Thomas Jefferson Foundation. "Report of the Research Committee on Thomas Jefferson and Sally Hemings." Monticello.org, 2000.

Thompson, Peter. "'I Have Known': Thomas Jefferson, Experience, and *Notes on the State of Virginia*." In *A Companion to Thomas Jefferson*, edited by Francis D. Cogliano, 60–75. Malden, MA, and Oxford, UK: Wiley-Blackwell, 2012.

Thomson, Keith Stewart. *Jefferson's Shadow: The Story of His Science*. New Haven, CT: Yale University Press, 2012.

Tomek, Beverly C. *Colonization and Its Discontents: Emancipation, Emigration, and Antislavery in Antebellum Pennsylvania*. New York: New York University Press, 2012.

Trent, Hank. *The Secret Life of Bacon Tait, a White Slave Trader Married to a Free Woman of Color*. Baton Rouge: Louisiana State University Press, 2017.

Tucker, David. *Enlightened Republicanism: A Study of Jefferson's Notes on the State of Virginia*. Lanham, MD: Lexington Books, 2008.

Turner, Robert F. *The Jefferson-Hemings Controversy: Report of the Scholars Commission*. Durham, NC: Carolina Academic Press, 2011.

Tyler-McGraw, Marie. *An African Republic: Black and White Virginians in the Making of Liberia*. Chapel Hill: University of North Carolina Press, 2007.

Vance, Joseph Carroll. "Thomas Jefferson Randolph." PhD diss., University of Virginia, 1957.

Verner, Coolie. *A Further Checklist of the Separate Editions of Jefferson's Notes on the State of Virginia*. Charlottesville: University of Virginia Press, 1950.

———. *Mr. Jefferson Distributes His Notes: A Preliminary Checklist of the First Edition*. New York: New York Public Library, 1952.

Waller, Jeffrey D. "Breaching the Citadel of Slavery: Condorcet, the Abbé Grégoire, and the Assault on Racial Hierarchy in the Colonial Disputes (1788–1791)." Master's thesis, Georgia Southern University, 2017.

Watson, Lucille McWane. "William Short, America's First Career Diplomat: Jefferson's 'Adopted Son' Took Paris by Storm." *William and Mary Alumni Gazette* 50, no. 1 (July/August 1982): 23–25.

Watts, George B. "Thomas Jefferson, the 'Encylopédie' and the 'Encyclopédie Méthodique.'" *French Review* 38, no. 3 (1965): 318–325.

Wayson, Billy L. *Martha Jefferson Randolph: Republican Daughter & Plantation Mistress*. Palmyra, VA: Shortwood Press, 2013.

Weeks, Stephen Beauregard. *Southern Quakers and Slavery: A Study in Institutional History*. Baltimore: Johns Hopkins University Press, 1896.

Wiecek, William M. *The Sources of Antislavery Constitutionalism in America, 1760–1848*. Ithaca: Cornell University Press, 1977.

Wiencek, Henry. *Master of the Mountain: Thomas Jefferson and His Slaves*. New York: Farrar, Straus and Giroux, 2013.

Wigger, John H. *American Saint: Francis Asbury and the Methodists*. New York: Oxford University Press, 2009.

Wilentz, Sean. "The Details of Greatness." *The New Republic* online, March 29, 2004. https://newrepublic.com/article/61007/the-details-greatness.

———. "Life, Liberty, and the Pursuit of Thomas Jefferson." *The New Republic* 216 (1997): 32–40.

Wiley, Bell Irvin. *Slaves No More : Letters from Liberia, 1833–1869*. Lexington: University Press of Kentucky, 1980.

Williams, David. *Condorcet and Modernity*. New York: Cambridge University Press, 2004.

Wills, Garry. *Inventing America: Jefferson's Declaration of Independence*. Garden City, NY: Doubleday, 1978.

———. *Negro President: Jefferson and the Slave Power*. Boston: Houghton Mifflin, 2003.

Wilson, Douglas L. "The Evolution of Jefferson's 'Notes on the State of Virginia.'" *Virginia Magazine of History and Biography* 112, no. 2 (2004): 98–133.

———. "Jefferson Unbound." *Historic Preservation* 53, no. 6 (2001): 48–53.

———. "Thomas Jefferson and the Character Issue." *Atlantic Monthly* 270, no. 5 (1992): 57–74.

———. "Thomas Jefferson's Early Notebooks." *William and Mary Quarterly* 42, no. 4 (1985): 434–452.

———. "Thomas Jefferson's Library and the French Connection." *Eighteenth-Century Studies* 26, no. 4 (1993): 669–685.

———, ed. *Jefferson's Literary Commonplace Book*. The Papers of Thomas Jefferson. 2nd ser. Princeton, NJ: Princeton University Press, 1989.

Wolf, Eva Sheppard. *Race and Liberty in the New Nation: Emancipation in Virginia from the Revolution to Nat Turner's Rebellion*. Baton Rouge: Louisiana State University Press, 2006.

Wood, Gordon S. *The Americanization of Benjamin Franklin*. New York: Penguin Books, 2004.

———. *The American Revolution: A History*. New York: Modern Library, 2001.

———. *The Creation of the American Republic, 1776–1787*. Chapel Hill: Published for the Institute of Early American History and Culture at Williamsburg, VA, by the University of North Carolina Press, 1969.

———. *Empire of Liberty: A History of the Early Republic, 1789–1815*. New York: Oxford University Press, 2009.

———. "Jefferson in His Time." *Wilson Quarterly* 17, no. 2 (1993): 38–51.

Wood, Nicholas P. "John Randolph of Roanoke and the Politics of Slavery in the Early Republic." *Virginia Magazine of History and Biography* (Summer 2012): 106–143.

Woodward, C. Vann. *Origins of the New South, 1877–1913*. Baton Rouge: Louisiana State University Press, 1951.

Wright, Johnson Kent. *A Classical Republican in Eighteenth-Century France: The Political Thought of Mably*. Stanford, CA: Stanford University Press, 1997.

Yarbrough, Jean. "Race and the Moral Foundation of the American Republic: Another Look at the Declaration and the Notes on Virginia." *Journal of Politics* 53, no. 1 (1991): 90–105.

Young, Alfred F., Gary B. Nash, and Ray Raphael, eds. *Revolutionary Founders: Rebels, Radicals, and Reformers in the Making of the Nation.* New York: Vintage Books, 2012.

Ziesche, Philipp. "Cosmopolitan Patriots in the Age of Revolution: Americans in Paris, 1788–1800." PhD diss., Yale University, 2006. ProQuest (3214336).

Zuckert, Michael P. *The Natural Rights Republic: Studies in the Foundation of the American Political Tradition.* Notre Dame, IN: University of Notre Dame Press, 1996.

Zwelling, Shomer S. "Robert Carter's Journey: From Colonial Patriarch to New Nation Mystic." *American Quarterly* 38, no. 4 (1986): 613–636.

Index

Page numbers followed by n refer to notes, with note number.

on impossibility of multi-racial
society, 244
inability to free slaves, 246
Jefferson's influence on, 15
letter from Jefferson, on calm in face
of criticisms, 237–238
management of Randolph and
Jefferson business affairs, 238, 239
political career of, 1, 240, 246
and slavery debate in Virginia
legislature, 1–2, 225–226, 241–245,
247, 249–250
wife's family debt, 238
Randolph, Thomas Mann, Jr. "Tom"
antislavery views of, 227–228, 230
character of, 232
copy of *Notes* sent by Jefferson to, 126,
137, 225, 227
death of, and forced sale of slaves, 233
education, 332n5
effort to farm without slaves, 227
emancipation plan presented to
Virginia legislature, 230–233
financial problems, 228, 233
as governor of Virginia, 225, 228,
229–232
Jefferson's mentoring of, 92, 226
Jefferson's support for, 232
as like a son to Jefferson, 225, 227
marriage to Martha Jefferson, 200,
225, 226–227, 233
mental health problems, 228
and Missouri Crisis, 230
and penal reform, 231
plan for colony for former slaves, 232
political career of, 228
on proslavery sentiment in Virginia,
229–230
reputation as kind master, 227
residence at Monticello, 227
slaves owned by, 227
and War of 1812, 228, 332n9
Randolph, Thomas Mann, Sr., 226–227
Randolph family in Virginia, 226,
321n11
Raynal, Abbé, 61, 81, 102, 107, 129, 278n6

*Review of the Debate in the Virginia
Legislature* (Dew), 246–247
Rochefoucauld, Duke de la, 100, 106,
130, 165
Rochefoucauld, Rosalie, Duchess de la
love affair with Short, 100, 103, 162,
164, 177–178, 311nn81–82, 318–
319n146, 318n137
persecution in French Revolution, 176,
178, 318–319n146
refusal of Short's proposals, 164, 179,
313–314n92
Royal African Company, 41–42

Saint-Domingue
population, by race, 166
slave revolt on, 129, 172, 183, 193–194,
206–207, 232–233
Scott, Winfield, 190–191, 203, 204, 205,
320–321n4
Scottish Enlightenment, 23
Sharp, Granville, 195, 204
Short, Peyton, 94, 99, 172–173
Short, William
aborted legal career of, 90, 93, 94
antislavery views of, 90, 139, 165
background and education, 52, 90,
92, 185
on black capabilities, 171, 179, 180
on Chastellux's *Travels*, 106
close relationship with Jefferson and
family, 93
death of father, 92
on Diderot's *Encyclopédie*, 106
on *Encyclopédie méthodique*'s Virginia
entry, 107
in Europe, after Jefferson's departure,
160–165, 173–174, 178
and father's estate, 99, 172–173
handling of Jefferson's personal legal
matters, 93–94
as Jefferson's "adopted son," 90, 98, 138
Jefferson's advice on marriage to, 162
and Jefferson's daughters, 309n59
and Jefferson's hope for younger
generation, 91